Themes in the Economics of Aging

A National Bureau
of Economic Research
Conference Report

Themes in the Economics
of Aging

Edited by   **David A. Wise**

The University of Chicago Press

Chicago and London

DAVID A. WISE is the John F. Stambaugh Professor of Political
Economy at the John F. Kennedy School of Government, Harvard
University, and the director for health and retirement programs at the
National Bureau of Economic Research.

The University of Chicago Press, Chicago 60637
The University of Chicago Press, Ltd., London
© 2001 by the National Bureau of Economic Research
All rights reserved. Published 2001
Printed in the United States of America
10 09 08 07 06 05 04 03 02 01   1 2 3 4 5
ISBN: 0-226-90284-6 (cloth)

Library of Congress Cataloging-in-Publication Data

Themes in the economics of aging / edited by David A. Wise.
     p.   cm. — (A National Bureau of Economic Research
  conference report)
  Includes bibliographical references and index.
  ISBN 0-226-90284-6 (cloth : alk. paper)
  1. Aging—Economic aspects. 2. Aged—Economic
conditions. I. Wise, David A. II. Series
HQ1061 .T467 2001
305.26—dc21   2001035162

♾ The paper used in this publication meets the minimum
requirements of the American National Standard for Information
Sciences—Permanence of Paper for Printed Library Materials, ANSI
Z39.48-1992.

Contents

Preface

This volume consists of papers presented at a conference held at Carefree, Arizona in May 1999. Most of the research was conducted as part of the Program on the Economics of Aging at the National Bureau of Economic Research. The majority of the work was sponsored by the U.S. Department of Health and Human Services, through National Institute on Aging grants P01-AG05842 and P20-AG12810 to the National Bureau of Economic Research. Any other funding sources are noted in individual papers.

Any opinions expressed in this volume are those of the respective authors and do not necessarily reflect the views of the National Bureau of Economic Research or the sponsoring organizations.

Introduction

David A. Wise

This is the eighth in a series of volumes on the economics of aging. The previous volumes were *The Economics of Aging, Issues in the Economics of Aging, Topics in the Economics of Aging, Studies in the Economics of Aging, Advances in the Economics of Aging, Inquiries in the Economics of Aging,* and *Frontiers in the Economics of Aging.* The papers in this volume discuss important implications of private and (potential) public personal retirement plans, discuss aspects of the health and wealth relationship, consider several aspects of health care in the United States, analyze the retirement effects of social security provisions in the United States and Germany, and consider new evidence on bequests and dissaving at older ages. The papers are summarized in this introduction, which draws heavily on the authors' own summaries.

Personal Retirement Plans

Three papers direct attention to personal retirement plans. The first considers private 401(k) plans and the accumulation of retirement assets. The second paper considers the implications of personal retirement saving plans as part of a possible Social Security reform. The third considers annuitization, which will become increasingly important with the rapid expansion of private personal retirement saving plans.

David A. Wise is the John F. Stambaugh Professor of Political Economy at the John F. Kennedy School of Government, Harvard University, and the director of health and retirement programs at the National Bureau of Economic Research.

Private Personal Accounts: Preretirement Cashouts and 401(k) Assets

About half of U.S. families are now eligible for a 401(k) plan, and the use of these plans is spreading rapidly. In the previous volume of this series, James Poterba, Steven Venti, and I considered the "Implications of Rising Personal Retirement Saving." We concluded that the cohorts that reach age sixty-five between 2024 and 2034 will have 401(k) assets that greatly exceed the personal financial assets of current retirees, and that these assets are likely to exceed their Social Security assets, perhaps by a great deal. In this volume we consider "Preretirement Cashouts and Foregone Retirement Saving: Implications for 401(k) Asset Accumulation." Although many analysts have emphasized the prevalence of cashouts and their presumed effect on the accumulation of retirement assets, we find that the importance of cashouts has been greatly exaggerated and that, in fact, cashouts have only a minor effect on retirement asset accumulation.

The way households support themselves in retirement is changing rapidly. Historically, households in the United States have relied on a combination of Social Security, employer-provided defined benefit pensions, and personal saving to support their retirement years. In the last fifteen years, however, retirement saving programs such as 401(k) plans have become an increasingly common component of household retirement planning. Today, more than 35 million workers participate in 401(k) saving plans, and the annual contribution flow to these plans exceeds $100 billion. The tax-deferred nature of wealth accumulation in 401(k)-type plans, coupled with often generous employer matching contributions that enhance the value of employee contributions, make these plans a powerful vehicle for accumulating retirement wealth.

In Poterba, Venti, and Wise (PVW) (1998a), we showed that even with conservative assumptions about the future growth of 401(k) contributions, the average 401(k) balance for households reaching retirement between 2024 and 2034 would likely exceed average actuarial present value of Social Security benefits.

Although 401(k) plan accumulations are likely to account for a very substantial share of the net worth of future retirees, unlike Social Security benefits, they can be affected by a number of individual decisions. Individuals who work at firms that offer 401(k) plans must decide whether to participate in their employers' plans. Those who do not participate forego the opportunity to accumulate retirement wealth in this tax-deferred form. Conditional on participating, individuals must decide how much of their earnings to contribute to these plans. In particular, participants who leave their jobs can also choose to leave their 401(k) accumulations in their former employers' plans, or to roll over their assets either into an individual retirement arrangement (IRA) or into the 401(k) plan of a new employer. The flexibility afforded by these three options enhances the portability of 401(k) benefits. It reduces the risk, not uncommon in defined benefit pension plans, of forfeiting pension benefits as a result of job change. However, the flexibility associated with the 401(k) withdrawal option raises the possibility that 401(k) participants may draw down their account balances before retirement, and thereby reach retirement without assets in a 401(k) account.

A number of recent studies have noted that conditional on choosing to withdraw assets from the 401(k) system—i.e., conditional on receiving a "lump-sum distribution"—many individuals use their withdrawals in ways that do not preserve retirement saving. In PVW (1998b) we showed, however, that older workers, and those who receive larger lump-sum distributions, are much more likely to preserve the retirement benefits of their lump-sum distributions through IRA rollovers or other forms of saving.

In the current paper, we use data on past 401(k) participation rates by age and income decile, along with information on average 401(k) contribution rates, to project the future 401(k) contribution trajectories of households that are currently headed by individuals between the ages of twenty-nine and thirty-nine. We allow for the possibility of preretirement withdrawal of 401(k) assets when individuals experience employment transitions. By combining data from the Health and Retirement Survey (HRS) on the likelihood of cashing out a 401(k) account conditional on a job change with data from other sources on the probability of job change, it is possible to estimate the prospective preretirement "leakage" from 401(k) accounts. We confirm that for households reaching retirement age between 2024 and 2034, 401(k) balances are likely to be a much more important factor in financial preparation for retirement than they are today. We estimate that average 401(k) balances in 2024 will be between five and ten times the size they are today, and would represent 50 to 200 percent of a retiree's Social Security wealth (depending on investment allocation and based on current Social Security provisions). For persons retiring in 2034 we estimate that 401(k) balances will be 75 to 250 percent of their Social Security wealth. Moreover, we find that preretirement withdrawals have a small effect on the balance in 401(k) accounts. We estimate that these withdrawals typically reduce average 401(k) assets at age sixty-five by about 5 percent. This is largely because most households whose members are eligible for lump-sum distributions when they change jobs choose to keep their accumulated 401(k) assets in the retirement saving system. These households either leave their assets in their previous employers' 401(k) plans, or they roll the assets over to another retirement saving account, such as a new 401(k) or an IRA. Most of those who do withdraw assets have very small accumulated balances. By comparison, the expense ratio charged by the financial institutions administering 401(k) accounts has a larger effect on retirement resources than does the possibility of pre-retirement withdrawal.

We also evaluated the possible variation in average returns due to variation in market returns over many years. To do this we made projections based on random draws of returns from the empirical distribution of historical returns. The results show that the *median* 401(k) balance at retirement, especially when a substantial share of the 401(k) portfolio is invested in equities, is below the *mean*. In the case of a 50–50 bond-stock portfolio, for example, the mean 401(k) and rollover balance is $98,800, while the median value is $94,600. The mean in this case lies between the 50th and 60th percentiles of the distribution. For the all-stock case, the mean is between the 60th and 70th percentiles of the distribution of realized outcomes. The most appropriate single measure is unclear. The results also draw attention to the great differences between the bond and stock distributions. For example, 95 percent of bond returns are below $85,800, but only slightly more than 20 percent of stock returns are below this level.

We plan further work in the future on random asset returns and the growth of 401(k) balances. The results above, however, make clear the wide variation in potential system-wide returns, especially stock market returns.

Public Personal Accounts: Market Outcomes and Risk

In the past several years there has been a great deal of analysis of the implications of Social Security reform, in particular of the incorporation of personal retirement accounts into the Social Security system. Although the vast recent literature on personal Social Security accounts makes virtually no reference to the rapidly expanding and overriding importance of private personal accounts, both public and private accounts have many features in common, including market risk. In "The Personal Security Account 2000 Plan, Market Outcomes, and Risk," Sylvester J. Schieber and John B. Shoven consider the market risk implications of the plan. They conclude that an individual who chooses to invest personal accounts in equities would run only a small risk of accruing benefits lower than those provided by the current Social Security system.

In early 1997, the 1994–96 Advisory Council on Social Security released its final report, which remarkably altered the nature of the debate in the United States about the reform of our national retirement system. It did so by giving legitimacy to recommendations that some element of Social Security reform should include individual accounts held by workers. The majority of the council's members actually advocated such reform. To be sure, there had been other people and groups who previously had advocated these types of Social Security reform in this country—but never before had a group of individuals assembled under an official charter by a presidential administration come close to such a recommendation. Since the council's report was released there have been several serious proposals put forward for reforming Social Security that include some element of individual accounts. There have also been numerous criticisms of this approach to Social Security reform.

In their paper, Schieber and Shoven present a framework for assessing Social Security reform proposals by evaluating a specific reform plan. This plan is one derived from the original Personal Security Account (PSA) developed by the 1994–96 Advisory Council on Social Security (1997). This plan has been dubbed PSA 2000 and its full elaboration is presented in Schieber and Shoven (1999). In part, the PSA 2000 plan was developed to respond to some of the criticisms of the original PSA plan.

The authors' key finding is that the PSA 2000 plan allows risk-averse individuals to retain benefits at least as high as current-law benefits. Those who choose to take the risks inherent in stocks bear some chance of having to live on lower than current-law benefits in retirement. These risks are modest, however, and the poor are significantly protected by the presence of the tier-one benefits.

The authors describe a particular partial privatization plan that relies more heavily on individual accounts than do most other proposals, and evaluate its overall actuarial soundness and the outcomes that individuals would face if it were adopted. The plan passes the actuarial soundness test and would permit individuals to enjoy safe benefits approximately equal to current-law benefits if U.S. government inflation-indexed bonds were offered and invested in. If participants invested their tier-two accounts in common stocks, they would face a small probability of having significantly less in retirement than current-law benefits. However, these risks are reduced by the presence of the flat tier-one benefits. This first tier is relatively more important for low-income households, who would enjoy benefits at least as great as current benefits with a high degree of certainty.

It is not surprising that the PSA 2000 plan performs well with respect to the principles set out by the authors. The first-tier defined benefits feature provides an important safety net against poor investment returns and permits the retention of the basic progressive structure of the current program (Principle 1). A primary feature of the program is the mandatory contribution of 2.5 percent of covered payroll. Although these additional contributions would be partially offset by the actions of individuals, there would be a significant net increase in national saving (Principle 2). The disability and early survivor programs would be retained, and if the proportion of the projected federal government surpluses suggested by President Clinton were allocated to the program, there would be enough money to cover the long-run deficit of the disability program (Principle 3). Under all of the scenarios examined, the PSA 2000 plan would be in balance or surplus after seventy-five years and would offer the prospects of payroll tax reductions (Principle 4). Most retiring couples would be treated as two single individuals, thereby improving the equity between these participant classes (Principle 5). The tier-two contributions and payouts would be directly connected. In fact, the tax element of payroll deductions would be reduced by the 2.5 percent rebate in the form of a 1:1 match of tier-two contributions (Principle 6).

The authors examine the risks borne by individuals and judge them to be tolerable. In particular, the amount of risk one would bear would be a matter of personal choice. Furthermore, the risks are least for low-income households (Principle 7). The PSA 2000 plan has relatively low administrative cost partly because it has relatively large (5 percent) individual accounts (Principle 8). The authors do not advocate in this paper the particulars of the PSA 2000 plan; they do, however, advocate that the riskiness of all serious proposals be evaluated in a manner similar to the procedure they follow in their paper. The authors emphasize that what is "heartening" about the findings is that a plan that relies heavily on individual accounts can still be relatively safe for individual participants.

Annuitization and Retirement Benefits

Mandatory annuitization is an important feature of the current Social Security system and will pose an ever more important question with respect to the increasingly common and likely future accumulation of large private retirement accounts. In "Are the Elderly Really Over-Annuitized? New Evidence on Life Insurance and Bequests," Jeffrey R. Brown focuses on this issue. He does so by considering whether individuals with bequest motives purchase life insurance to offset mandatory annuitization of Social Security benefits. He concludes that the answer is no, and that the evidence is not sufficient to argue against mandatory annuitization of current Social Security benefits.

It is well established in the economics literature that annuities ought to be of substantial value to life-cycle consumers, who face an uncertain dates of death. Buying a life insurance contract is analogous to selling an annuity. It is generally viewed as an appropriate product for working-age individuals who seek to protect their families against the loss of future labor earning. However, it appears to serve little purpose in the portfolio of a retired life-cycle consumer who is concerned only with self-financing retirement out of accumulated wealth. With no labor earnings to insure, an elderly individual should be purchasing annuities in order to provide a certain consumption stream in retirement, not selling annuities through the purchase of life insurance. Even if the individual wishes to leave a portion of wealth to heirs in the form of gifts or bequests, this can be achieved by investing this portion of wealth in ordinary bonds or other nonannuitized assets. In fact, if life insurance premiums are higher than actuarially fair, holding riskless bonds would strictly dominate life insurance as a form of wealth transfer.

Yet elderly households in the United States overwhelmingly hold life insurance, while only a small fraction hold privately purchased annuity contracts. In the Asset and Health Dynamics among the Oldest Old (AHEAD) survey, which consists of households aged seventy and up, privately purchased annuity contracts (excluding private pensions) are held by fewer than 8 percent of couples, while 78 percent of these couples own a life insurance policy on at least one member. According to the Life Insurance Ownership study (Life Insurance Market Research Association [LIMRA] 1993), ownership of individual (nongroup) life insurance policies is actually higher among the age sixty-five and up group than any other age cohort. Although this difference is offset by much lower coverage by group (usually employer-based) policies, the overall incidence of coverage among the elderly is quite high by any measure.

One suggestion is that life insurance is being held by elder households to offset an excessive level of mandated annuitization in the form of Social Security. To the extent that this "annuity offset model" is true, it has at least two important implications. First, it would be indicative of very strong bequest motives, which constitute an issue of perennial controversy in the economics literature. Second, if individuals are over-annuitized due to these strong bequest motives, it would indicate a potential welfare gain from lessening the extent of mandated annuitization.

This paper reexamines the annuity offset model using more recent and better data than have previously been available. The paper presents substantial evidence that the reason the elderly hold life insurance is not to offset mandated annuitization in the form of Social Security in order to leave a bequest. This finding is relevant to the current debate over the future of the Social Security system because it bears upon the question of whether mandatory annuitization is desirable. Were it the case that a substantial fraction of elderly households were over-annuitized by the existing Social Security system due to the existence of strong bequest motives, it would be evidence in favor of allowing choice over the annuitization decision. The results of this paper suggest that households are not over-annuitized by Social Security for bequest reasons. Therefore, Brown concludes, the simple fact that many elderly households own term life insurance is not a sufficient argument against mandatory annuitization of retirement resources. This finding is consistent with the idea that annuities are of substantial value in the retirement portfolios of elderly individuals. As a result, mandatory annuitization may be desirable to overcome adverse selection in the annuity market. However, Brown emphasizes, this conclusion should be tempered by the acknowledgment that individuals may be over-annuitized for reasons other than bequest motives.

Wealth and Health

The relationship between wealth and health has received increasing attention in recent years. A key issue has been the direction of causality:

Does wealth affect health, or does health determine wealth? Two papers in this volume address this relationship, but from different perspectives. The first focuses on the relationship between income and health; the second focuses on the predictors of mortality.

Income and Health

Individuals for whom family income was less than $5,000 in 1980 could expect to live about 25 percent fewer years than people whose family income was greater than $50,000. This finding is explored by Angus Deaton and Christina Paxson in their paper on "Mortality, Education, Income, and Inequality among American Cohorts." A key finding is that greater income reduces the risk of death, even after controlling for education.

The strong relationship between mortality and socioeconomic status (SES) has been a major concern in demography, epidemiology, and public health for many years, and is beginning to attract the attention of economists. The concept of SES is used more widely outside the field of economics than within it and one of the issues that remains to be settled is the extent to which these differences are caused by income or by other factors correlated with income (education being the most obvious). Many writers believe that there is at least some direct protective effect of income, and in a recent body of literature much identified with the work of Richard Wilkinson, it is argued that, while higher income is protective (at least at the individual level), *income inequality* is a health hazard that raises mortality, if not at the individual level at least in the general population or larger subpopulations. Wilkinson postulates that *inequality itself* is a health hazard and that it is less healthy both for rich and for poor to live in a more unequal society. It is hardly necessary to emphasize the importance of such a link, if it indeed exists. The proponents of some changes (e.g., improvement in school quality, or raising the return on Social Security) make a plausible case that such changes will make everyone better off, although some will be more so than others. If such changes increase inequality, as almost certainly they would, the cost of lives lost would have to be offset against the economic benefits.

The authors' main purpose in this paper is not to try to come to judgment based on the review of the evidence, but to offer some new evidence based on income, income inequality, and mortality data for birth cohorts of Americans observed over the two decades from 1975 to 1995. It seems that birth cohort data—as opposed to individual data, state data, or country data—have not previously been used in this context; and unlike other sources, birth cohorts offer both a cross-sectional and a time series dimension to the same data. The model developed in the paper is designed as a framework for empirical application, and provides a way of thinking about the effects of income and income inequality in a context in which, although causality runs from income to health, it is not absolute income that matters for health but income relative to that average of an (unobservable) reference group. Although inequality has no direct effect on health, the fact that reference groups are not observed means that the slope of the observed relationship between health and income varies with the ratio of between- to within-group inequality. The model can be readily extended readily to incorporate a direct effect of inequality by making health depend on the absolute size of income differences within the reference group; but equally plausible specifications give different results so that, according to the theory, income inequality can be either protective or hazardous. Deaton and Paxson give detailed consideration to the aggregation of the relationship between health and income, and to how it can be expected to change as it is examined with different sources of data, such as individual records, averages of states or countries, or averages of birth cohorts. The authors document the strongly protective effects of income and examine how those effects vary at different points in the life cycle. As to inequality, the authors fail to find not only that it increases the risk of mortality, but that there is actually a protective effect, in apparent contradiction with not only the Wilkinson hypothesis but with much of the theory developed in this paper.

Deaton and Paxson also give a good deal of attention to the role of education: whether income is a mask for education, how income and education affect mortality in the cross-section and over time, and whether the treatment of income and education affects our results on the role of inequality. In a cross-section of birth cohorts, income and education are closely correlated so that, in order to disentangle their effects, the authors rely on the time series dimension of the cohort data, supplemented by individual-level data from the National Longitudinal Mortality Study (NLMS). The individual-level data show that both income and education are separately protective against mortality and that only some of the effect of income is removed when we attempt to allow for reverse causality from nearing death to income. In the cohort data, by contrast, income appears to increase the risk of mortality conditional on education, a result that the authors tentatively ascribe to the short-run or business-cycle effects of income on mortality. In concluding, the authors emphasize:

> Our original purpose was to use birth-cohort data to examine the links between mortality and inequality. Controlling for income, we find that higher inequality is associated with lower mortality, a conclusion that comes from negative association of mortality and inequality in the United States in the late 1970s and early 1980s. While it is possible that such a result has some real basis—and there are theoretical mechanisms that could produce it—it is hardly established by these results. In particular, the sign of the effect is implausible, if only because of the expected operation of Jensen's inequality, and the magnitude of the effect is quite sensitive to the way in which other variables are introduced, particularly income and education. Indeed, we suspect that the current priority should not be the investigation of the effects of inequality, but the un-

packing of "socioeconomic status" into its components . . . so as to allow them to respond to income and education in different ways. The results reported here make it clear that this is no easy task; the way in which education and income affect mortality is not the same for men as for women, nor for young adults as for older adults; it is different over long time periods and over the business cycle, and it is different in the cross-section from over time. We find evidence that short-term increases of income may raise the risk of mortality, particularly for young men. In the cohort data, however, the longer-term effects of income, or of income linked to education, are protective. Yet this evidence needs to be reconciled with the individual-level data from the follow-up studies, which show that, especially for men, income plays a role as large as or larger than that of education. Work on these issues has hardly begun (162).

Socioeconomic Status and Death Rates

In contrast to Deaton and Paxson, Michael D. Hurd, Daniel McFadden, and Angela Merrill conclude in their paper on "Predictors of Mortality among the Elderly" that their findings are consistent with the view that the primary cause of the relationship between wealth and health is unobserved individual characteristics that cause both early death on the one hand and lower wealth and less education on the other.

The authors point out that differential mortality by (SES) has been observed over a wide range of data on population, but because of data limitations, the measures of SES have typically been occupation or education. In the Health and Retirement Survey (HRS) and the AHEAD survey there is scope for expanded studies of differential mortality (the mortality gradient), because these panel surveys follow a large number of older persons and obtain extensive data on income, wealth, and health conditions as well as on occupation and education. Furthermore, the fact that the AHEAD population is almost completely retired means that a very strong confounding effect of health on income via work status is eliminated.

The goal of the paper is to study the predictors of mortality in the AHEAD population. The authors focus on the mortality gradient as a function of wealth. They emphasize that this gradient is important because it causes difficulty in understanding life-cycle behavior from cross-sectional variation in wealth: Besides cohort effects that would, by themselves, cause wealth to decline with age in cross-section, the mortality gradient will cause wealth to increase both in cross-section and in panel. As a cohort ages, those with less wealth die, leaving survivors from the upper part of the wealth distribution. Thus, even if no couple or single person dissaved after retirement, the wealth of the cohort would increase with age. This makes it difficult to study life cycle wealth paths based on synthetic cohorts, which will eliminate cohort differences in lifetime resources but not differential mortality. These difficulties carry over to studies of income and consumption in synthetic cohorts.

A second focus of this paper is the determinants and predictive power of the subjective probability of survival. Respondents were asked to give an estimate of their survival chances to a target age, which was approximately twelve years in the future. In the HRS this variable has been shown to be a significant predictor of mortality between waves 1 and 2. A goal of this paper is to determine whether it has similar predictive power over the AHEAD population.

The authors conclude that the mortality gradient, whether a function of wealth, income, or education, apparently decreases with age. The authors say that any explanation at this point would be rather speculative, but the finding is consistent with the view that the primary cause of the gradient is unobserved individual characteristics that cause both bad health (and therefore early death) and lower earnings (and therefore lower wealth and less education). Were the causality to run primarily from economic resources to health and mortality, the authors argue, we should see a persistent difference in mortality outcomes in very old age between those with substantial resources and those with few. The authors say they do not see this, but they also say this should be confirmed by further analysis. If the differential is due to unobserved individual differences, the mortality gradient operating at younger ages will have truncated the distribution, so that in extreme old age the variation in individual characteristics would be greatly reduced. Therefore, classifying people by SES would not produce any substantial differences in mortality.

The subjective survival probability predicts actual mortality as in the HRS, and the authors say this should increase our confidence that it can be used to construct individualized lifetables for models of life cycle saving behavior as proposed by Hurd, McFadden, and Gan (1998). Whether such lifetables will have substantial explanatory power for saving remains to be determined as more waves of AHEAD become available.

Health Care

Three papers consider different aspects of health care in the United States. Medicare spending in real terms has doubled in the past two decades, even though the health of the older population has improved; two papers aim to reconcile this apparent contradiction. A third paper develops a method for understanding the reasons for the wide differences in health care expenditures among firms in the United States.

End-of-Life Spending, Declining Mortality, and Potential Health Care Saving

Lower mortality, and thus better health at a given age, might reduce the cost of medical care; but this potential reduction can be offset by increasing expenditure given health status. In their paper on "Trends in Medicare

Spending Near the End of Life," Jeffrey Geppert and Mark McClellan find that increasing intensity of health care for both survivors and decedents has far outweighed reductions in cost due to decreasing mortality—and thus the continuing rise in health care expenditures.

Recent decades have witnessed dramatic improvements in health at older ages, including reductions in both mortality and morbidity. Although real growth in health care costs has accompanied improvements in health for the past fifty years, improvements in health give hope that avoided medical utilization due to better health may lower health care costs, or at least significantly reduce the rate of growth. This might occur as a result of mortality improvements, because decedents on average have much higher health care costs than survivors, because average spending in the last year of life declines with age, and because people are dying at older ages. Spending in the last year of life accounts for nearly 30 percent of total Medicare program payments, so a reduction in average spending per decedent might significantly influence total Medicare outlays. A similar argument applies to the decline in the prevalence of chronic disability. Elderly patients with chronic disabilities cost more than the nondisabled elderly, so reducing disability prevalence also holds the promise of lowering Medicare cost.

However, the importance of such program savings from the shift of beneficiaries to lower-cost, more healthy states over time also depends on the changes in expenditures, given health status, that occur at the same time. Expenditures per capita are rising, and much evidence suggests that rising intensity of treatment is the principal cause. Changes in expenditures given treatment may be responsible for some of the improvements in health, and in any event changes in health and in expenditures will continue to occur together. Despite these facts, prior studies generally have not considered both factors jointly, to determine whether the savings that result from improving health over time are likely to have a quantitative impact on expenditure growth. In this paper, Geppert and McClellan determine the importance of changes in Medicare cost that resulted from declines in age-specific mortality between 1988 and 1995, and calculate how much Medicare expenditure trends would have differed in the absence of the mortality improvement.

The authors reach several conclusions. First, despite the fact that mortality has continued to fall, the share of Medicare program payments accounted for by persons in the last year of life has remained relatively constant, declining only slightly over the past two decades.

Second, the rate of spending growth was similar for survivors and decedents—actually, slightly larger for the oldest male survivors than for other demographic groups—as a result of relatively greater growth in spending for nonacute services. Thus, spending growth for survivors continues to account for most of the growth in Medicare cost.

Third, for both decedents and survivors, the composition of spending growth has changed in recent years. In the most recent decade, growth in spending for nonacute services has accounted for half of overall spending growth. Thus, spending growth for decedents was not primarily the result of increasing the heroic, intensive measures near the end of life. In addition, although greater coverage of nonacute alternatives might be expected to affect end-of-life costs disproportionately, growth rates for nonacute services were even greater for older survivors than for decedents. Large utilization effects for both acute and nonacute services occurred in both groups.

Fourth, although improvements in mortality have been a factor leading to lower Medicare spending over time, this effect has been swamped by the much larger increases in expenditures given survival status for decedents and survivors alike. Without the survival improvements, the authors' estimates suggest that Medicare spending would have grown only 4 percent more than it did.

Thus, the authors conclude that increasing utilization for both survivors and decedents has been a far more important determinant of Medicare spending over time than have improvements in mortality.

The Concentration of Medical Spending

In "The Concentration of Medical Spending: An Update," David M. Cutler and Ellen Meara conclude that the explanation for rising health care cost in the face of declining disability is the increase in the use of "postacute service," in particularly home health care and skilled nursing home care. That is, Cutler and Meara try to point to the specific factors that have led to rising costs, given age, that Geppert and McClellan also emphasize.

Cutler and Meara point out that during the last two decades, the number of Medicare beneficiaries has increased by 50 percent, and Medicare spending per beneficiary has doubled in real terms. These findings are difficult to understand, however, in light of changes in the health of the elderly. Disability rates are falling among the elderly by about 1.5 percent per year. Since the disabled spend much more than the nondisabled on medical care, it seems that in relative (if not absolute) terms, spending on the elderly should be falling over time. The combination of large increases in per-person spending and the reduction in disability leads to a paradoxical situation, in which policy analysts call simultaneously for reforms to control Medicare cost growth (to bring spending for the elderly in line with that for other age groups) and for Medicare to cover currently uncovered services such as prescription drugs (to promote further health improvements).

The goals of this paper are to document how trends in spending by age have changed among elderly Medicare beneficiaries in the last decade, and to reconcile the decline in disability rates with rapid increases in spending among the elderly. In particular, the authors consider what has happened to age-specific spending since 1987. The authors then attempt to reconcile increased spending with sharply declining disability. In particular, these relate medical spending by age to six factors: demographics, disability, time until death, intensity of treatment, prices, and changes in the nature of care.

Cutler and Meara reach two central conclusions. First, they find that the trend of disproportionate spending growth among the oldest old has continued during the decade between 1985 and 1995. Between 1985 and 1995, spending for the younger elderly (ages sixty-five to sixty-nine) rose by 2 percent annually in real, per-person terms, while spending for the older elderly (ages eighty-five and up) rose by 4 percent. This is similar to the differential increase in spending by age over the 1953–87 period, the authors say.

Second, Cutler and Meara conclude that the reason for the large increase in spending on the oldest elderly in comparison to the younger elderly is the rapid increase in use of postacute services—home health care and skilled nursing care in particular—among the oldest old. People aged eighty-five and older used, on average, $241 in postacute services in 1985 and $1,887 in 1995, a 20 percent annual increase. The younger elderly, in contrast, increased their use of postacute services from $49 to $257, a 15 percent annual increase. Use of acute-care services, in contrast, grew relatively evenly by age, 1.2 percent annually for the younger elderly and 0.7 percent annually for the older elderly.

The increase in the use of postacute service, the authors say, is the explanation for the discrepancy between rising medical spending and falling disability. Lower disability by itself contributes to lower spending than we would otherwise observe; but the increase in use of nontraditional services more than offsets the effects of improved health. The increase in postacute service use is also a major difference between the pre- and post-1987 trends. In earlier work these authors found that rising expenditures on the older population were a result of increased intensity of acute-care services for that age group. In the post-1987 period, intensity changes in acute-care treatments do not account for a substantial discrepancy by age.

The authors suggest that increase in postacute service use may reflect several factors: true increased service use for people who were not receiving care in the past; "gaming" of the Medicare system, whereby providers now use out-of-hospital services instead of in-hospital services; or outright fraud. They are unable to discriminate among these explanations, although they suspect each is important.

The Reasons for Expenditure Differences among Firms

Medical expenditure per employee varies enormously across firms in the United States. In our paper on "The Sources of Cost Difference in Health

Insurance Plans: A Decomposition Analysis," Matthew Eichner, Mark Mc-Clellan, and I develop a method to identify and quantify the importance of the factors contributing to the wide differences across employer-provided health plans. Our results suggest that further efforts to understand the differences should focus on the relatively intensive inpatient care, and must address both the variation in admission for intensive treatment and the variation in cost given treatment.

We are engaged in a long-term project to analyze the determinants of cost differences across firms. In particular, we look forward to an estimation that can predict the effect on medical expenditures of specific changes in medical insurance plan provisions. The project is based on insurance claims records from a large number of employers. The vast amount of information in insurance claims records is both a blessing and a curse. A key advantage of claims data is the detail they provide, but the detail also poses a challenge: how best to summarize and convey the information contained in the millions of claims filed each year under a typical employer-provided plan.

Our goal in this paper is to present a method that allows us conveniently to summarize information contained in the claims data. In particular, we want to describe the sources of cost differences across plans. We consider eight plans that vary in average expenditure for those filing claims, from a low of $1,645 to a high of $2,484. We then propose a method to decompose these differences into their component parts. The goal is to quantify the contribution of each component to total cost differences across firms. We believe that this method allows us to point directly to the sources of cost difference and thus will help us to focus subsequent analysis where it is most likely to make a difference.

We first present a statistically consistent method for decomposing the cost differences across plans into component parts due to demographic characteristics of plan participants, the mix of diagnoses for which participants are treated, and the cost of treatment given particular diagnoses. The goal is to quantify the contribution of each component to the difference between average cost and the cost in a given firm. The demographic mix of plan enrollees accounts for wide differences in cost ($649). Perhaps the most noticeable feature of the results is that, after adjusting for demographic mix, the difference in expenditures accounted for by the treatment costs given diagnosis ($807) is almost as wide as the unadjusted range in expenditures ($838). Differences in cost due to the various mixes of illness that are treated, after adjusting for demographic mix, also accounts for large differences in cost ($626). These components of cost do not move together; for example, demographic mix may decrease expenditure under a particular plan, whereas the diagnosis mix may increase costs.

We also provide an approximate decomposition of the "variation" in expenditures across firms. Although outpatient care accounts for almost 50 percent of expenditures on average, it accounts for only about 20 per-

cent of the variation in expenditures across firms. Inpatient care accounts
for about 34 percent of expenditures on average, but almost 59 percent of
the variation in expenditures. Thus, one can conclude that variations in
high-cost inpatient treatments are a principal cause of the substantial cost
variation across firms. (A "residual" group accounts for about 16 percent
of expenditure and about 20 percent of variation in expenditure across
firms.) The most important component of variation is the diagnosis rate,
which accounts for about 52 percent of variation across firms. Treatment
cost differences, given treatment, account for about 40 percent, with the
remainder accounted for by the interaction between the two.

Our results suggest that efforts to understand the substantial differences
in private insurance expenditures should focus on the relatively intensive
inpatient care, and that further analysis should address the sources of variation in both admissions for intensive treatment (the diagnosis rate) and
the cost given treatment.

Social Security Provisions and Retirement

Two papers consider the relationship between retirement and the provisions of social security plans. The first, based on German data, emphasizes
a method to estimate the effect of plan provisions when it is uncertain
under which of several programs a person could retire. The second paper
directs attention to Social Security retirement incentives in the United
States.

Uncertain Eligibility and Retirement in Germany

Analyses of the retirement incentive effects of public and private pension plan provisions typically have assumed that the eligibility for a particular plan is known. In many countries, however, this is not the case. There
are often several pathways to retirement, with disability and unemployment insurance programs essentially serving as social security early retirement programs. This the case in many European countries, for example.
In his paper on "Incentive Effects of Social Security under an Uncertain
Disability Option," Axel Börsch-Supan considers methods to estimate retirement incentive effects when the pathways available to an individual are
uncertain (to the analyst). He finds that an instrumental variable estimate
that uses expected incentive effects in an option value retirement model
provides reliable estimates. His judgment is confirmed in the discussion of
the paper by Daniel McFadden.

In most industrialized countries, old-age labor force participation declined dramatically during the last decades. Together with population
aging, this puts the pay-as-you-go social security systems of the industrialized countries under a double threat: Retirees receive pensions for more
years while there are fewer workers per retiree to shoulder the financial

burden of the pension system. The decline of old-age labor force participation has turned attention to the incentive effect of social security systems: Is a significant part of the threat homemade because pension systems provide overly strong incentives to retire early? This "pull" view—that labor supply has declined because early retirement provisions pull old workers out of employment—is in contrast to the "push" view—that a secularly declining demand for labor has created unemployment, which pushes older workers into early retirement.

The pull view is prominently advanced in a recent volume edited by Gruber and Wise (1999). The authors from eleven countries argue that the declining old-age labor force is strongly correlated with the incentives created by generous early retirement provisions. Formal econometric analyses (Stock and Wise 1990a for the United States; Meghir and Whitehouse 1997 for the United Kingdom; and Börsch-Supan 1992, 2000 for Germany) find strong incentive effects of public and private pension rules.

Incentive effects of pension rules are usually estimated under the assumption that the institutional environment provides a single pathway for retirement age, or an opinion value of postponing retirement at any prospective retirement age. However, most countries provide competing pathways that include several early-retirement options in addition to normal retirement, typically at age sixty-five. In particular, this is true in Germany, where early retirement due to a "disability" before age sixty has been the most common pathway to retirement.

Social Security Incentives for Retirement in the United States

In their paper on "Social Security Incentives for Retirement," Courtney Coile and Jonathan Gruber direct attention to the incentives for retirement by considering the distribution of Social Security wealth accrual at different ages for participants in the HRS. Although Social Security benefits are intended to be actuarially fair between ages sixty-two and sixty-five, Coile and Gruber show that there is enormous variation in accrual depending on individual circumstances. For example, for about one-third of survey participants, accrual is negative between ages sixty-two and sixty-three, so that for these people there is a penalty on work at age sixty-two.

One of the most striking labor force phenomena of the second half of the twentieth century has been the rapid decline in the labor force participation rate of older men. In 1950, for example, 81 percent of sixty-two-year-old men were in the labor force; by 1995, this figure had fallen to 51 percent.

Much has been written about the proximate causes of this trend, in particular about the role of the Social Security program. A large number of articles have documented pronounced spikes in retirement at ages sixty-two and sixty-five, which correspond to the early and normal retirement ages for Social Security, respectively. Although there are some other explanations for a spike at age sixty-five, such as entitlement to health insurance under the Medicare program or rounding error in surveys, there is little reason for a spike at sixty-two other than the Social Security program. Indeed, this spike at age sixty-two emerged only after the early-retirement eligibility age for men was introduced in 1961.

The presence of these strong patterns in retirement data suggest that Social Security is playing a critical role in determining retirement decisions. In order to model the impact of Social Security reform on retirement behavior, however, it is critical to understand what this role is. The evidence of a spike at age sixty-two, for example, is consistent with at least three alternative hypotheses. The first is that there is an actuarial unfairness built into the system penalizing work past age sixty-two, so that there is a "tax" effect that leads workers to leave the labor force at that age. The second is that workers are liquidity constrained: They would like to retire before age sixty-two, but cannot because they are unable to borrow against their Social Security benefits and have no other sources of retirement support. In this case, there will be a large exit at age sixty-two as benefits first become available. The third is that workers are myopic or information constrained: They either do not understand or do not appreciate the actuarial incentives for additional work past age sixty-two, so they retire as soon as benefits become available.

The Coile-Gruber paper is an investigation of the tax effect along four dimensions. First, the authors assess whether the tax rate Diamond and Gruber (1999) compute (using a synthetic individual with annual earnings at the median of his cohort) is similar to the tax rate of the real median person. We might expect a difference, as the shape of the earnings history is a significant determinant of Social Security incentives—through the dropout years provision—and this is not appropriately reflected with a synthetic earnings history. Second, the authors assess the distribution of retirement incentives across the population. Even if there is no significant disincentive for the typical worker, disincentives for a large subset of workers could still be associated with a spike in the aggregate retirement data. Third, they assess the importance of considering incentives for retirement in the next year versus incentives for retirement over all future years, drawing on the insights of the option value model of Stock and Wise (1990a,b). Finally, they incorporate the role of private pensions, an important determinant of retirement for a large share of workers.

The strategy is to consider a set of real individuals, the older persons surveyed in the HRS. These data allow the authors to compute carefully the retirement incentives from Social Security and pensions, both for the median individual and across all survey participants.

The authors confirm that there is, in fact, a small subsidy to work at ages sixty-two to sixty-four at the median. However, they also show that there is substantial heterogeneity across persons. There is a net tax on work at age sixty-two for about one-third of their sample, which is consistent with a spike in the hazard rate at age sixty-two.

Bequests and Dissaving

Wealth accumulation before retirement and decumulation after retirement have been the subjects of longstanding and intensive study by economists. In their study of "Anticipated and Actual Bequests," Michael D. Hurd and James P. Smith use new data from the HRS to deepen our understanding of the role of bequests in household decisions about these processes.

Important advances have recently been made in documenting the process of wealth accumulation by households. New data have increased our knowledge about the facts surrounding the distribution of household wealth and, to a lesser extent, household saving behavior. However, this improved factual base has not yet been translated into a deeper understanding about the theoretical reasons people save. The candidates remain much the same: life cycle timing, risk aversion, and bequests. Understanding bequest motives has been particularly difficult, in part due to the inherent difficulties in measuring anticipated and actual bequests.

In their paper, Hurd and Smith study the role of inheritances and bequests in shaping household decisions about wealth accumulation. They study bequests by using new methods of measuring anticipated and actual bequests. They examine actual bequests made by deceased individuals and compare them with their previously stated bequest intentions. Using panel data with two measurements of subjective bequest probabilities, they explore the reasons an individual might revise his or her bequest expectations. Among other things, these reasons may include new information on health or economic conditions of household members. Their results are based on wealth, anticipated bequests, and actual bequests from two waves each of the HRS and AHEAD. Because the paper uses two new types of data, considerable attention is directed to validating these new data.

Actual bequests are measured in exit interviews given by proxy respondents for 774 AHEAD respondents who died between waves 1 and 2 of the AHEAD survey. Among other things, these exit interviews provide data about the medical and nonmedical costs associated with the illnesses of the deceased respondents and the value and distribution of the estates. Even though the deceased were quite ill before they died, medical expenses did not cause substantial reduction in their estates. Because the exit interview obtained estate information that is representative of the population, the distribution of these estate values is quite different than one would suppose from estate records, which are obtained for only a wealthy subset of the population.

Anticipated bequests were measured in two waves of HRS and AHEAD by the subjective probability of leaving bequests. The authors study the reasons for between-wave revisions of the subjective bequest probabilities. They find that increases in the subjective probability of surviving, increments in household wealth, and widowing were all associated with increases in bequest probabilities, whereas out-of-pocket medical expenses reduced the likelihood of a bequest. By comparing bequest probabilities with baseline wealth, Hurd and Smith are able to test a main prediction of the life cycle model: that individuals dissave at advanced old age. The authors conclude that respondents anticipate substantial dissaving before they die.

References

Advisory Council on Social Security. 1997. *Report of the 1994–96 Advisory Council on Social Security.* Vol. 1, *Findings and recommendations.* Washington, D.C.: GPO.
Börsch-Supan, A. 1992. Population aging, social security design, and early retirement. *Journal of Institutional and Theoretical Economics* 148:533–67.
———. 2000. Incentive effects of social security on labor force participation: Evidence in Germany and across Europe. *Journal of Public Economics* 78:25–49.
Diamond, P., and J. Gruber. 1999. Social Security and retirement. NBER Working Paper no. 7830. Cambridge, Mass.: National Bureau of Economic Research.
Gruber, J., and D. A. Wise. 1999. *Social Security and Retirement around the World.* Chicago: University of Chicago Press.
Hurd, M. D., D. McFadden, and L. Gan. 1998. Subjective survival curves and life cycle behavior. In *Inquiries in the economics of aging,* ed. D. A. Wise. Chicago: University of Chicago Press.
Life Insurance Market Research Association (LIMRA) International. 1993. Profiles in coverage: The widening gap in U.S. life insurance ownership. Windsor, Conn.: LIMRA.
Meghir, C., and E. Whitehouse. 1997. Labour market transitions and retirement of men in the UK. *Journal of Econometrics* 79:327–54.
Poterba, J. M., S. F. Venti, and D. A. Wise. 1998a. Implications of rising personal retirement saving. In *Frontiers in the economics of aging,* ed. D. A. Wise, 125–67. Chicago: University of Chicago Press.
———. 1998b. Lump sum distributions from retirement saving plans: Receipt and utilization. In *Inquiries in the economics of aging,* ed. D. A. Wise, 85–105. Chicago: University of Chicago Press.
Schieber, J., and J. B. Shoven. 1999. *The real deal: The history and future of Social Security.* New Haven, Conn.: Yale University Press.
Stock, J. H., and D. A. Wise. 1990a. The pension inducement to retire: An option value analysis. In *Issues in the economics of aging,* ed. D. A. Wise, 205–30. Chicago: University of Chicago Press.
———. 1990b. Pensions, the option value of work, and retirement. *Econometrica* 58 (5): 1151–80.

I

Personal Retirement Plans

1

Preretirement Cashouts and Foregone Retirement Saving
Implications for 401(k) Asset Accumulation

James M. Poterba, Steven F. Venti, and David A. Wise

The way households support themselves in retirement is changing rapidly. Historically, households in the United States have relied on a combination of Social Security, employer-provided defined benefit pensions, and personal saving to support their retirement years. In the last fifteen years, however, retirement saving programs such as 401(k) plans have become an increasingly common component of household retirement planning. Today, more than 35 million workers participate in 401(k) saving plans, and the annual contribution flow to these plans exceeds $100 billion. The tax-deferred nature of wealth accumulation in 401(k)-type plans, coupled with often generous employer matching contributions that enhance the value of employee contributions, make these plans a powerful vehicle for accumulating retirement wealth. Mass market books, such as Iwaszko and O'Connell (1999) and Merritt (1997), have extolled the wealth-building power of 401(k) accounts.

In Poterba, Venti, and Wise (hereafter PVW; 1998a), we showed that even with conservative assumptions about the future growth of 401(k) contributions, the average 401(k) balance for households reaching retirement

James M. Poterba is the Mitsui Professor of Economics at the Massachusetts Institute of Technology and director of the public economic research program at the National Bureau of Economic Research. Steven F. Venti is professor of economics at Dartmouth College and a research associate of the National Bureau of Economic Research. David A. Wise is the John F. Stambaugh Professor of Political Economy at the John F. Kennedy School of Government, Harvard University, and director of health and retirement programs at the National Bureau of Economic Research.

We are grateful to Michael Noel for excellent research assistance, to Stan Panis for providing us with tabulations from the Health and Retirement Survey, to Unicon Inc. for providing us a copy of the Current Population Survey Utilities, to David Laibson, Andrew Samwick, and especially John Shoven for helpful discussions, and to the National Institute on Aging and National Science Foundation (Poterba) for research support.

in 2025 will be approximately equal to the average actuarial present value of Social Security benefits. This represents roughly a tenfold increase in the importance of 401(k) accumulations between the late 1990s and 2025.

Although 401(k) plan accumulations are likely to account for a very substantial share of the net worth of future retirees, unlike Social Security benefits, they can be affected by a number of individual decisions. Individuals who work at firms that offer 401(k) plans must decide whether to participate in their employers' plans. Those who do not participate forego the opportunity to accumulate retirement wealth in this tax-deferred form. Conditional on participating, individuals must decide how much of their earnings to contribute to the plan.

When 401(k) participants leave jobs at which they have participated in a 401(k) plan, they can withdraw their accumulated 401(k) assets from the retirement saving system. When such withdrawals occur before the recipient is fifty-nine and one-half years old, they are taxed as ordinary income, as all 401(k) payouts are, and they are also subject to a 10 percent early withdrawal penalty tax. Participants who leave their jobs can also choose to leave their 401(k) accumulations in their former employers' plans, or to roll over their assets either into an individual retirement arrangement (IRA) or into the 401(k) plan of a new employer. The flexibility afforded by these three options enhances the portability of 401(k) benefits. It reduces the risk, not uncommon in defined benefit pension plans, of forfeiting pension benefits as a result of job change. However, the flexibility associated with the 401(k) withdrawal option raises the possibility that 401(k) participants may draw down their account balances before retirement, and thereby reach retirement without assets in a 401(k) account.

A number of recent studies have noted that conditional on choosing to withdraw assets from the 401(k) system, i.e., conditional on receiving a "lump-sum distribution," many individuals use their withdrawals in a way that does not preserve retirement saving. In PVW (1998b) we showed, however, that older workers, and those who receive larger lump-sum distributions, are much more likely to preserve the retirement benefits of their lump-sum distributions through IRA rollovers or other forms of saving. These findings, based on data from the Current Population Survey, are confirmed in Sabelhaus and Weiner's (1999) analysis of tax return information.

Until recently, there was no information on the probability that a worker leaving a job would decide to withdraw assets from the employer's 401(k) plan and therefore receive a lump-sum distribution. Analyzing the behavior of those who received lump-sum distributions therefore provided only a partial account of benefit leakage from 401(k) plans. In an important recent study, however, Hurd, Lillard, and Panis (1998) analyze data on the disposition of defined contribution pension assets when workers change jobs. They analyze information from the Health and Retirement Survey and find that very few participants in these pension plans select the withdrawal option when they leave their jobs.

In this paper we draw together previous research on withdrawals from retirement saving plans to gauge the importance of such withdrawals on the saving balances of future retirees. We expand the algorithm for projecting future 401(k) balances that we developed in PVW (1998a) to allow for job changes during an individual's working life, and the associated risk of 401(k) asset withdrawal. While we abstract from many detailed features of the asset withdrawal process, we allow for age-specific job termination risks, and for balance-specific probabilities of withdrawing assets from a 401(k) account. We also allow for realistic expenses of managing the assets in 401(k) plans.

We find that even though a substantial number of workers change jobs, and *could* withdraw their 401(k) assets, the modest withdrawal rate and the small size of most withdrawals reduce retirement saving only modestly. Our central estimates suggest that the opportunity to take 401(k) withdrawals reduces retirement saving at retirement by approximately 5 percent. Even after allowing for preretirement withdrawals, we find that 401(k) saving will expand rapidly over the next three decades, and that 401(k) assets at retirement are likely to grow, on average, to be roughly as important as current Social Security wealth in contributing to households' retirement financing.

This paper is divided into six sections. Section 1.1 summarizes the recent studies that have explored the importance of lump-sum distributions from 401(k) plans and other retirement saving plans. Section 1.2 describes our algorithm for projecting the 401(k) balances of future cohorts of retirees, and particularly our attempts to allow for preretirement asset withdrawals. We calibrate our model using data from the 1993 Survey of Income and Program Participation and the Health and Retirement Survey. Section 1.3 presents evidence on how actual 401(k) balances for households in the Health and Retirement Survey compare with the balances that our algorithm would have predicted for these households, had we not known their actual plan balance. Section 1.4 reports our projected future account balances and examines the importance of preretirement withdrawals in affecting these balances. Section 1.5 reports preliminary statistics on 401(k) participation from the 1995 Survey of Income and Program Participation, and uses these data to provide some indication of the plausibility of our projected rates of 401(k) expansion. Finally, a brief concluding section suggests several directions for further work.

1.1 What Do We Know about Lump-Sum Distributions and 401(k) "Leakage"?

The growth of retirement saving accounts, in particular 401(k) accounts, during the last two decades has substantially expanded the financial assets of many U.S. households. The expansion of personal retirement saving has raised new questions about the impact of individual financial decisions on preparation for retirement. Poterba and Wise (1999) note that there are several dimensions, including plan participation, contribution level, asset allocation, date of asset withdrawal, and whether to annuitize account payouts, along which individuals can influence their 401(k) retirement accumulations.

One of the most important decisions individuals face is whether to draw down assets in retirement saving accounts before retirement. A number of summary statistics on the prevalence of lump-sum distributions have raised concern about the possibility that households are not preserving their retirement saving. The most recent data on the extent and use of such distributions are from the U.S. Department of Labor (1995). The data are based on the September 1994 "Retiree Pension and Health Benefits Supplement" to the Current Population Survey (CPS). This survey shows that 9.1 million individuals (all over the age of forty) reported that they had received at least one lump-sum distribution from a pension plan or retirement saving account. This is nearly 10 percent of the over-forty population, and it is an even greater share of the labor force in this age range.

The mean lump-sum distribution, measured in 1994 dollars, was $22,309. More than half of these distributions (52.8 percent) were received by workers who were between the ages of thirty and forty-nine at the time of the distribution. The CPS questionnaire included information on lump-sum distributions from a range of different retirement plans. Payouts from defined benefit plans in which the separating employee had accumulated only a small vested pension benefit, from traditional defined contribution pension plans, as well as from 401(k)-like retirement saving programs were included in the CPS survey. Of the 9.1 million lump-sum distributions reported in the survey, 2.7 million were identified as from defined benefit plans, 5.3 million were from defined contribution plans, and 1.1 million distributions were received by individuals who could not identify the type of plan that they were from.

Probably the greatest concern with the substantial number of lump-sum distributions is that many of their recipients report that they did not use their distributions to provide income in retirement. Table 1.1 shows the uses of lump-sum distributions reported in the 1994 CPS supplement. More than one quarter of those who reported a single primary use of their lump-sum distribution (1.82 million of the 6.85 million respondents with a primary use) indicated that their distributions were used to finance consumer durable purchases or to pay other expenses. Only 33.9 percent reported that they rolled over their lump-sum distributions into IRAs or retirement plans with new employers. A substantial additional group, comprising 39.5 percent of the primary-use respondents, indicated that their distributions were used for something that could be construed as saving, but were not targeted for retirement income support. Responses in this category include depositing the lump-sum distribution in a saving account, paying off debts, or using the proceeds for home renovations.

Table 1.1   **Uses of Lump-Sum Pension Plan Distributions Reported in September
                   1994 Current Population Survey Supplement**

Use of Lump-Sum Distribution	Number of Recipients (millions)	Percent of Primary-Use Recipients
Retirement saving	2.32	33.9
Business or home expansion, or repaying debts	1.46	21.3
Other saving or investments	1.25	18.2
Current spending	1.82	26.6
Total identifying primary use	6.85	100.0
Multiple uses	1.53	—
Other uses, or no response	0.73	—
Total	9.10	—

Source: U.S. Department of Labor (1995), table C5.

Previous work on lump-sum distributions, which includes Chang (1996), PVW (1998b), and Yakaboski (1993, 1997) has shown that the use to which a lump-sum distribution is put is a function of household age and the size of the distribution. Thus an asset-weighted version of table 1.1 would show a different allocation of lump-sum distributions than the person-weighted tabulation that is actually reported in the table. Older workers, and those with larger distributed balances, are more likely to choose a rollover option or to report that they saved their distributions. The fraction of lump-sum distribution *dollars* that are withdrawn from the 401(k) system is much smaller than the fraction of *individuals* who receive lump-sum distributions who report that they withdrew funds from their retirement saving. There is also some evidence, reported, for example, in Bassett, Fleming, and Rodriguez (1998) and Chang (1996), that the share of lump-sum distributions that are rolled over into saving vehicles or new retirement saving accounts has increased over time.

The critical difficulty with using data on lump-sum distributions to study asset leakage from the 401(k) system is that individuals who leave jobs with 401(k) plans can choose whether to receive lump-sum distributions. The sample of lump-sum distribution recipients provides no insight on the probability that an individual experiencing a job separation will decide to withdraw funds from the 401(k) system. The individual could also choose to allow the 401(k) balance to remain with the previous employer, or to roll the 401(k) balance into a 401(k) plan with a new employer. Neither of these options would trigger a lump-sum distribution. If most individuals experiencing a job separation choose one of these options, then the probability of 401(k) leakage might be quite small even if most of those taking lump-sum distributions do not roll over their 401(k) assets.

Hurd, Lillard, and Panis (1998) use data on individuals in the Health and Retirement Survey (HRS) who experience a job change between either the first and second survey waves, or between the second and third waves, to estimate the probability of asset withdrawal. Their findings show that only 20.5 percent of the workers leaving defined contribution pension plans (including 401[k] plans), and 16.4 percent of those leaving jobs with defined benefit plans, choose to cash out their accumulations in the form of lump-sum distributions. Moreover, the cashout probability is lower for those with large balances. Only 6.7 percent of the assets held in defined contribution plans by those who experience job termination are withdrawn from the retirement saving system. These statistics suggest that the possibility of withdrawing assets from a 401(k) plan is not likely to have a large impact on the prospective growth of assets in these plans.

Engelhardt (1999) performs a related calculation using data from the HRS. Using data on individual reports of past lump-sum distributions, he "accumulates" the value of these withdrawals under the counterfactual assumption that they had been left in retirement saving accounts. He finds that for the median household that received a lump-sum distribution, the current value of this distribution is between 8 and 11 percent of the value of Social Security wealth and other pension wealth. The range depends on assumptions about the way 401(k) participants invest their assets.

These findings suggest that lump-sum distributions from 401(k)-type plans have probably not had a large effect on the accumulated balances in these retirement saving accounts. However, it is still possible that such distributions will have a larger effect on *future accumulations* in these accounts, since 401(k) plans will be available to more young workers in the future than in the past. Young workers have much higher job turnover rates than older workers. The calculations we present below are designed to provide new insight on the prospective importance of such preretirement payouts.

1.2   An Algorithm for Projecting Future 401(k) Balances

This section describes our approach to forecasting the 401(k) balances at retirement for currently working cohorts. We build on our prior work, reported in PVW (1998a), but expand our previous algorithm to incorporate job change, lump-sum distributions, and potential asset leakage from the 401(k) system into our analysis. We also introduce administrative costs of asset management into our forecasting algorithm.

Our procedure for projecting the 401(k) assets of future retirees relies on a cohort representation of data on 401(k) participation and contribution behavior. The notation C(j) refers to the cohort of age j in 1984. C(27), for example, refers to the cohort aged twenty-seven in 1984. Figure 1.1, which is reproduced from our earlier paper, shows 401(k) eligibility rates for six cohorts that are based on Survey of Income and Program Participation

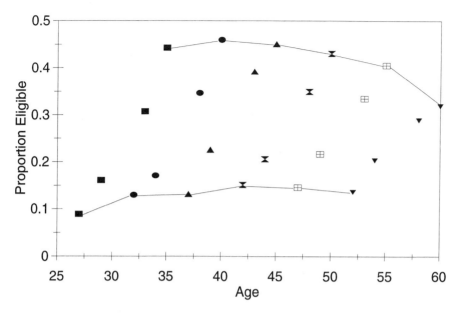

Fig. 1.1   401(k) eligibility by cohort, 1984, 1987, 1991, 1993

(SIPP) data for 1984, 1987, 1991, and 1993. Our analysis focuses on the C(25) and C(15) cohorts, which were aged thirty-four and twenty-four, respectively, in 1993. For the C(25) cohort, age fifty-five occurs in 2014, and age sixty-five in 2024. The C(15) cohort reaches each of these ages ten years later.

To ensure adequate sample sizes, each of the cohort points plotted in figure 1.1 is based on a group of families with household heads born in a five-year interval. The C(27) cohort therefore includes families with heads aged twenty-five to twenty-nine in 1984. The C(27) cohort is identified by the square symbols. The eligibility rate of this cohort averaged less than 10 percent in 1984, but it had risen to almost 45 percent by 1993 when the cohort was thirty-six years old. A similar increase in eligibility is evident for each of the other five cohorts. It is also clear that there is a very large "cohort effect." At any age each successively younger cohort has a higher contribution rate than the cohort five years older. This difference is approximately 20 percentage points. For example, 44 percent of the C(27) cohort was 401(k) eligible when this cohort was thirty-five years old, compared with about 20 percent of the five-year-older C(32) cohort when it was thirty-five.

The information in figure 1.1 illustrates the cross-sectional relationship between age and eligibility at each survey date. The six markers along the top of the figure represent the 1993 cross-sectional relationship between age and eligibility. It shows rising eligibility at young ages, followed by a plateau. Comparable data for earlier years show a less pronounced effect of age on eligibility.

1.2.1 Projecting Future 401(k) Participation Rates

Extrapolation of cohort trends would quickly lead to the implausible projection of eligibility rates of over 100 percent. On the other hand, it is equally clear that when the C(27) cohort reaches age forty its eligibility rate will be greater than the rate of the C(32) cohort at age forty. Thus, instead of extrapolating the cohort data, we parameterize the relationship between age and eligibility, assuming that the apparent cohort effects in the figure are year effects and simply represent the spread of 401(k)'s with time. With reference to figure 1.1, this means that we estimate eligibility by allowing the cross-sectional relationship to shift upward over time. When we allow for both cohort and year effects in regression equations in which 401(k) participation rates are the dependent variables, the cohort effects are typically not statistically significantly different from zero and the time effects exhibit most of the explanatory power.

The difficulty with extrapolating past experience to project future 401(k) balances can be illustrated by reference to the C(27) cohort. If 401(k) plans continue to spread, then the 1993 cross-sectional relationship between eligibility and age will clearly understate the future eligibility of the C(27) cohort. In part this is simply because 401(k)s will undoubtedly continue to expand. In addition, however, the 1993 relationship is determined in part by how the past diffusion of 401(k) plans occurred. If the diffusion of plans has been slower in small firms with younger workers than in large firms, then the cross-sectional relationship would tend to look as it does in the figure. In the 1993 cross-section there is a noticeable reduction in eligibility with age. This is much less apparent in the 1984 cross-section. Thus we can use only formal estimates as a guide to future patterns.

We assume that by 2013, which is twenty years after the 1993 survey on which our data are based, the eligibility rate for fifty-six-year-olds (the C[27] cohort) will be 50 percent higher than the eligibility rate of the cohort that was fifty-six in 1993. This assumption is based on the past growth in eligibility and participation rates reported on IRS Form 5500 and in CPS data. Form 5500 reports[1] show that the number of 401(k) participants increased by 52 percent over the five-year period between 1988 and 1993. Employment grew by 4 percent over this period. Data from the CPS show a 45 percent increase in the participation *rate* in 401(k) plans, which is roughly consistent with the Form 5500 data. The Form 5500 data also

---

1. See U.S. Department of Labor (1997). The Form 5500 reports tabulate contributions to private sector 401(k) plans. They do not include contributions to Section 457 (public sector) or 403(b) (nonprofit) plans, or public employees' contributions to 401(k) plans.

show that aggregate 401(k) contributions increased by 76 percent, or by much more than the increase in participation. Aggregate earnings increased about 25 percent over this period, so if the average fraction of earnings contributed were stable, the growth in earnings and participation would predict a 77 percent increase in aggregate contributions. This is very similar to the observed change.

1.2.2   Cross-Sectional Age Participation Profiles and Participation Projections

Our projections are based on recent 401(k) participation data along with assumptions on the future evolution of both eligibility and participation. We recognize throughout our analysis that there is an important relationship among earnings, eligibility, and participation, and we allow for this by estimating cross-sectional probit equations relating eligibility or participation to age and indicator variables for earnings deciles. We model participation (P_i) for household i as

$$(1) \qquad P_i = \beta_1 AGE_i + \beta_2 (AGE_i)^2 + \sum_{d=1}^{10} \gamma_d D_{di} + \varepsilon_i,$$

where AGE is age and the D_d are indicator variables that identify the household's earnings decile. The most important parameters are the γ_d, which indicate the effect of earnings decile D_d on participation. These coefficients are the basis for our stratification of 401(k) accumulation patterns by household earnings. In PVW (1998a), we report estimation results from models like equation (1) for eligibility, participation given eligibility, and participation, using 1988 and 1993 SIPP data. We do not reproduce those results here.

We use our projection algorithm to explore future 401(k) balances for households headed by individuals in the C(25) cohort, the C(15) cohort, and for a cohort that is exposed to a mandatory 401(k)-type program with universal contributions. The last case resembles some of the proposals that have recently been discussed in the U.S. Social Security reform debate.

To project future 401(k) asset accumulation for the C(25) cohort, we assume that when this cohort is fifty-five years old (in 2014) it will have a 401(k) participation rate 50 percent higher than that of the cohort that was fifty-five in 1994. We further assume that its participation rate at sixty-five will be 5 percent higher than this—that is, 55 percent higher than that of the cohort aged fifty-five in 1994. The projections by earnings decile start from the 1993 401(k) participation rates. Because higher-income households have higher participation rates, the projections yield a widening difference between the participation rates of high- and low-income families as they age. The extent of this dispersion is likely to be one of the most uncertain features of our projections.

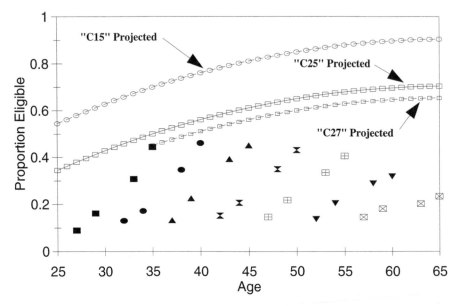

Fig. 1.2   401(k) eligibility by cohort with illustrative projections

Figure 1.2, also drawn from PVW (1998a), illustrates the C(25) projection as well as the C(15) projection. To place the projections further in the context of the historical data, a projection for the C(27) cohort is also shown in the figure.

The members of the C(15) cohort were fifteen years old in 1984. Even though this cohort is only ten years younger than the C(25) cohort, we find it substantially more difficult to make plausible assumptions about their future 401(k) participation rates. We think of the C(15) projections as representing 401(k) accumulation in a setting in which participation is substantially higher than with the C(25) projections, but considerably short of universal coverage. We believe that future 401(k) participation will indeed be higher than the C(25) projections suggest. Our C(15) projections assume that 401(k) participation rates for the median wage earner are 20 percentage points greater than the C(25) rates. Rates for the highest and lowest decile workers in the C(15) cohort are assumed to be slightly less than 20 percent greater than those of comparable workers in the C(25) cohort.[2] This 20 percentage point increase in 401(k) participation for co-

2. We projected participation for all ages of the C(15) cohort by adding a constant term to the participation probit equation so that the C(25) projections for the 5th and 6th income deciles would increase by 20 percentage points. The same constant term was added to the probit equations for all income deciles. The highest deciles do not increase by 20 points because of the upper limit of 100 percent; the lower deciles increase less than 20 points, because of the properties of the probit functional form.

horts ten years apart is modest compared with what we have observed in recent years. In figure 1.1, for example, we find that 401(k) eligibility has risen by 20 percentage points for cohorts only five years apart. Our projections therefore assume future 401(k) eligibility growth at roughly half the recent rate.

Finally, we consider a third scenario for future 401(k) growth, in which everyone contributes a fixed share of their salaries to a 401(k) plan. Universal coverage might arise if 401(k)'s spread even more rapidly in the future than they have in the past, or it might arise as part of a mandatory saving program. Various types of mandatory saving systems have been suggested as one way to address the prospective funding difficulties of the Social Security system.

1.2.3   Earnings Histories

Our projections of future 401(k) balances assume that all households that contribute to a 401(k) plan contribute 9 percent of their earnings. In PVW (1998a), we show that the average contribution rate as a share of earnings is extremely stable across earnings deciles. There is, of course, great variation across households within deciles, but we are interested primarily in forecasting averages. A household's earnings history is therefore a critical determinant of its 401(k) accumulation.

The starting point of our algorithm is a set of "pseudo-earnings histories" of HRS respondents beginning at age twenty-five. In analyzing the HRS earnings histories, we have divided the families in the HRS into deciles according to their 1992 earnings. In principle, the Social Security earnings histories of the HRS respondents can be used to determine average earnings by age within each decile. Venti and Wise (1999) note, however, that there is one important limitation to this method. Historical earnings are reported only up to the Social Security earnings limit, while actual earnings in the top two or three deciles may be substantially higher than Social Security reported earnings. Because of this limitation, we rely on information in the annual March CPS data files, which report earnings well above the Social Security maximum.[3] The ratio of the CPS maximum to the Social Security maximum has ranged from a low of just under 2 in 1981 to a high of more than 20 in 1964. In 1991 the CPS reported earnings up to a maximum of $200,000, while the Social Security maximum was $53,400.

Our procedure for constructing earnings histories for HRS households is as follows. We first identify earnings deciles, as described above, using

---

3. These data were obtained from the CPS Utilities, provided to us by Unicon Inc. We actually construct a "synthetic HRS" sample of persons aged forty-one to fifty-one in each of the ten earnings deciles in 1982. This sample is "aged" through 1992, assigning families to participate and contribute to a 401(k) at rates determined by the estimates from the SIPP and the CPS and recognizing the possibility of job terminations.

the 1992 earnings of each HRS family. Then, using the March CPS data, we calculate earnings deciles by age for the years 1964–91. Using published data on median earnings prior to 1964, we extrapolate this series back to 1956, thereby obtaining earnings histories by decile for the years 1956 to 1991. Finally, we assign each HRS household to a CPS decile according to the household's 1992 earnings decile. The CPS earnings histories begin at age twenty-five and a given household is assumed to have been in the same decile since age twenty-five.[4]

1.2.4   The Projection Algorithm

Given a household's pseudo-earnings history, we construct a "pseudo-401(k) contribution record." Within each earnings decile, each household is randomly assigned to 401(k) participation status, based on the 401(k) participation probabilities discussed above. Then, as the household ages, we vary its 401(k) participation status. In PVW (1998a), we assumed that if a household had a 401(k) account at a given age, it remained a 401(k) participant until retirement. In the present paper, we allow for job separations that lead some 401(k) participants to become nonparticipants.

To illustrate the procedure, we suppress variation across earnings deciles, which we use in our actual projections. We define P_a as the participation rate in 401(k) plans at age a. Suppose that L_a is the probability that an a-year-old person with a 401(k) plan leaves his employer. This event will end a 401(k)-participation spell, although it is possible that another 401(k)-participation spell will begin when the affected individual finds another job.

The difference between the fraction of the population participating in 401(k) accounts at ages a and $a + 1$ reflects two offsetting flows. These are the fraction of the population that enters 401(k) participation at age a, E_a, and the fraction of the population that participated in a 401(k) plan at age a, but left the 401(k) system by age $a + 1$. The fraction of the population that leaves a 401(k) job at age a is $L_a \cdot P_a$. The net change in 401(k) participation at age a is therefore

$$(2) \qquad P_{a+1} - P_a = E_a - L_a \cdot P_a .$$

We know the values of P_{a+1} and P_a, and we can estimate the probability of job-leaving. We can therefore derive the flow of new entrants to the 401(k) system that is necessary to generate observed age-specific participation rates. This is just

$$(3) \qquad E_a = P_{a+1} - P_a(1 - L_a),$$

---

4. This is a significant assumption, since in fact relative household income does vary from year to year. Whether such variation matters substantially for 401(k) accumulations over a lifetime is an issue we hope to consider in the future.

where P_a denotes the probability of 401(k) participation at the beginning of the year when a cohort is age a, and L_a denotes the probability of leaving 401(k) participation during the year when the cohort is age a.

New 401(k) entrants must be drawn from the nonparticipant pool at age a. The probability that an a-year-old nonparticipant will join a 401(k) plan (J_a) is simply the ratio of the fraction of the population that represents new 401(k) entrants, E_a, to the fraction that is currently not participating in 401(k) plans, $1 - P_a(1 - L_a)$. This implies that

$$(4) \qquad J_a = \frac{E_a}{1 - P_a(1 - L_a)} = \frac{P_{a+1} - P_a(1 - L_a)}{1 - P_a(1 - L_a)}.$$

It is possible for someone who joins the 401(k) participant group to be a previous 401(k) participant. This means that the number of current 401(k) participants will, in general, differ from the number of individuals who have ever participated in a 401(k). It also implies that some new entrants to 401(k) participation at age a will have positive 401(k) balances as a result of 401(k) participation on a prior job.

We should note in passing that this algorithm for projecting the evolution of 401(k) participation corrects a previous modeling error. If there is no chance of leaving a 401(k) job, so that $L_a = 0$ as in our previous work, then $J_a = (P_{a+1} - P_a)/(1 - P_a)$, from equation (4). In PVW (1998a), we *incorrectly* set the probability that nonparticipants would become 401(k) participants to $(P_{a+1} - P_a)$. Thus we underestimated the probability of joining a 401(k) plan, which had the effect of understating the fraction of currently young households who would participate in a 401(k) plan before retirement. This underestimated the future importance of 401(k) account balances. We note the size of this error below.

Our projections consider three possible rate-of-return scenarios, corresponding to nominal rates of return of 6.0 percent, 9.3 percent, and 12.7 percent on 401(k) assets. We think of these returns as the returns, on average, on an all-bond portfolio, a 50-50 split between bonds and stocks, and an all-stock portfolio. Ibbotson Associates (1997) reports that the historical average pretax return on corporate bonds has been 6.0 percent per year, while large-capitalization stocks have returned an average of 12.7 percent per year since 1926. These returns are the pretax returns available on a portfolio with no management fees. Because most 401(k) plans are administered by financial intermediaries who charge for their services, we also consider the effect of reducing the feasible return on the bond portfolio by 35 basis points, and the return on the equity portfolio by 70 basis points. Our calculations highlight the importance of such asset management costs in determining 401(k) wealth at retirement.

We also demonstrate the effect of the randomness of stock and bond returns. We do this by drawing annual returns for our bond and stock portfolios from the empirical distributions of returns on corporate bonds, and large company stocks, in Ibbotson Associates (1997). We construct 1,000 projections using this random draw algorithm, and then show the distribution of returns. It is important to emphasize that randomness represents macrovariation, which affects all plan members. We do not account for variation among participants due to differences in asset allocation among our three assets, nor do we give attention to individual variation within earnings deciles due to different 401(k) participation rates. Moreover, of course, we do not account for additional variation that would result from investment in, for example, individual stocks. In future work we will address this individual risk.

We now turn to the problem of modeling the dynamics of 401(k) account balances. When a household leaves a job with a 401(k) plan, one of two things may happen to the accumulated asset balance. In principle, a job-leaver could decide to divide a 401(k) accumulation between these alternatives, but we assume that there are no fractional account balances.

First, the job-leaver may decide to preserve the assets in the retirement system. He or she could leave the assets in the former employer's 401(k) plan, although no further contributions would be made, or roll the assets over into an IRA. In this case, the assets will continue to accumulate until retirement. We use $1 - Q_a$ to denote the probability that 401(k) assets remain in the retirement system at the time of a job transition.

Second, with probability Q_a, a job-leaver can decide to withdraw the assets from the 401(k) system. This would trigger a lump-sum distribution, and would create "leakage" from the stock of retirement assets. We use the notation A_a to define 401(k) plan assets for a household of age a, and B_a to denote the asset balance of job-leavers who cash out their 401(k) assets. We allow Q_a to depend on the size of the 401(k) account balance (A_a) at the time of the job termination, so $Q_a = Q_a(A_a)$.

If r is the rate of return, the equation for the evolution of 401(k) balances is therefore

$$(5) \qquad A_{a+1} = A_a(1 + r) + C_{a+1} \cdot P_{a+1} \cdot I_{a+1} - B_a,$$

where C_{a+1} denotes the 401(k) contribution rate as a fraction of income, and I_{a+1} denotes household income. We can express B_a as the product of three terms:

$$(6) \qquad B_a = A_a \cdot L_a \cdot Q_a(A_a),$$

where A_a is the 401(k) balance at the beginning of the year when a cohort turns age a, L_a is the probability of leaving the 401(k) job during that year, and $Q_a(A_a)$ is the probability of withdrawing the balance conditional on leaving the job. We allow the job-leaving probability to vary with age, and the probability of asset withdrawal conditional on job separation to depend on the accumulated asset balance. We calculate Q_a separately for each household, so it depends on each household's accumulated 401(k) balance. In future work we hope to expand the set of household characteristics that affect each of these probabilities.

1.2.5   Calibrating the Rates of Job Separation and Cashout

Two key parameters that determine the magnitude of 401(k) leakage are the age-specific job-leaving probability, L_a, and the asset balance–specific probability of cashing out a 401(k) plan balance, $Q_a(A_a)$.

There is a substantial literature on both the rate at which jobs end, and the characteristics of individuals and jobs that are associated with job termination. For example, Farber (1997) reports age-specific rates of job losing, and Neumark, Polsky, and Hansen (1999) present recent evidence on both job turnover rates and job tenure distributions from the CPS. None of the existing literature provides precisely the values of L_a that we require. This is because we are interested in job termination rates for employees at firms that offer 401(k) plans. Some previous evidence suggests that job termination rates are lower at firms that offer pension plans, and that termination rates are also declining in the length of the job's tenure. Gustman and Steinmeier (1995) report, for example, that in the 1984 and 1985 SIPP, men aged thirty-one to fifty without a pension had a 19.5 percent annual separation rate. In the same data set, men with either a defined benefit or defined contribution pension plan had a 6.1 percent separation rate.

To provide more recent evidence on mobility rates, we analyzed data from the retrospective section of the HRS. By working backward from the current job, it is possible to assemble information on both pension coverage on previous jobs, and on the respondent's age at the time when the job ended. Table 1.2 reports our findings for separation rates at jobs with defined contribution pension plans. The job mobility rates are much lower than those in most other studies of labor market turnover. For forty-year-old men, for example, the rate is only about 1.2 percent per year. This may be an artifact of the long-term retrospective nature of the HRS questions, or it may be the result of other factors.

Since we are not sure why the HRS-based mobility rates are so low, and

Table 1.2	Probability of Leaving a Job at Various Ages, Conditional on Job Offering a Defined Contribution Pension Plan		
	Age	Men (%)	Women (%)
	30	1.25	1.73
	35	1.47	1.36
	40	1.19	1.18
	45	2.05	1.69
	50	3.51	4.21
	55	5.26	4.26

Source: Authors' tabulations using HRS wave 1.

since very low mobility rates will make the risk of withdrawals from the 401(k) system seem very small, we are reluctant to use the HRS findings without some modification. We have therefore assumed that the job-leaving probability (L_a) for persons aged twenty-five to thirty-four is 6.0 percent. We assume that this probability declines to 4.5 percent for those aged thirty-five to forty-four and to 4.0 percent for those aged forty-five to fifty-four, then rises to 5.0 percent for those aged fifty-five to sixty-four. We believe that an argument can be made for using even lower mobility rates, in which case the impact of potential 401(k) leakage would be even smaller than our findings below suggest.

In calibrating $Q_a(A_a)$, the probability of withdrawing assets from a 401(k) plan as a function of the accumulated asset balance, we rely on the work of Hurd, Lillard, and Panis (1998). They provide the only comprehensive analysis of dispositions from defined contribution plans. Their analysis uses the HRS to calculate the probability of various uses of existing defined contribution plan balances conditional on a job separation. We treat their probabilities of retaining an account through the former employer's 401(k) plan (their probabilities refer to all defined contribution plans), rolling assets over into an IRA or other tax-advantaged saving vehicle, and annuitizing the 401(k) balance, as rollovers. Each of these dispositions has, in a different way, the effect of preserving the 401(k) balance so that the assets can be used to support retirement consumption. A fourth option in their classification scheme, cashing out the 401(k) balance, is the one that we regard as triggering asset leakage from the 401(k) system.

Hurd, Lillard, and Panis (1998) find that the likelihood of cashing out is strongly related to the size of the 401(k) account balance. They provided us with unpublished tabulations that indicate the cashout probabilities for various 401(k) balances, as well as the number of observations in the HRS dataset that were used to estimate each of these balance-specific probabilities. Table 1.3 reports these probabilities and associated summary statistics. We use the data in table 1.3 to assign randomly the balances of job-leavers to cashout or rollover status.

One difficulty that arises in using a set of balance-specific probabilities for asset withdrawal, as we use here, is that the Hurd, Lillard, and Panis (1998) findings relate to balances at a single point in time. We need to apply them to potential 401(k) cashouts over an entire working lifetime. To do this we assume that 401(k) balances at different dates can be converted to balances in 1992 dollars using a 3.2 percent annual inflation rate.

1.3 Validating the Algorithm: Projecting 401(k) Balances for Current Health and Retirement Survey Households

Before projecting the 401(k) assets at retirement for future cohorts of retirees, we tried to evaluate the ability of our algorithm to predict the

Table 1.3   **Probability of Cashing Out a Defined Contribution Plan, Conditional on Opportunity to Withdraw Funds and on Size of Defined Contribution Balance**

401(k) Balance at Time of Separation ($1992)	Number of Sample Observations	Cashout Probability
<2,000	60	60.00
2,000–5,000	44	38.64
5,000–10,000	40	27.50
10,000–15,000	30	13.33
15,000–25,000	52	21.15
25,000–50,000	46	2.17
50,000–100,000	41	4.88
>100,000	34	2.94
All	347	23.92

Source: Tabulations from the HRS by Constantijn Panis.

observed 401(k) balances of current cohorts of retirees and near-retirees. We use our algorithm to predict 401(k) balances for households in the HRS. We did this using a basic version of our algorithm, without any administrative costs for 401(k) asset management and with certain returns. In essence, we ask whether the SIPP cohort data on 401(k) participation, together with the CPS data on contributions, can explain the observed distribution of 401(k) balances in the HRS. While a high correspondence between actual and predicted values in this case does not necessarily demonstrate the validity of our algorithm, it provides at least one way of checking for the plausibility of our findings.

Table 1.4 reports the mean 1992 assets of the HRS respondents, stratified according to earnings decile. (This table is drawn from PVW 1998a.) It provides a point of reference against which to evaluate our projected 401(k) balances. The table reports only mean asset balances because our 401(k) balance projections focus on means. While the median asset holdings for many categories are substantially below the mean holdings, the primary comparison that we make is between 401(k) balances and Social Security wealth. Mean and median Social Security wealth are very similar.

We estimate accrued Social Security wealth at age sixty-five for the HRS respondents, assuming that each respondent were to work until that age. A family's Social Security wealth is the simple sum of the mortality-weighted present value of each member's benefit stream; we do not consider survivorship benefits, which could raise the total value of Social Security wealth by more than one-third. These accrued benefit levels are converted to 1992 dollars using the Social Security Administration's intermediate forecast of the average annual interest rate provided by the board of trustees of the Old-Age, Survivors, and Disability Insurance (OASD) trust fund. For comparability, the projected 401(k) balances discussed below also assume

Table 1.4   **Mean 1992 Assets of Health and Retirement Survey Families (by asset category)**

Earnings Decile	Total Wealth	Total Wealth, Excluding Social Security	Employer Pension Assets	Total Personal Retirement	Nonretirement Financial	401(k) Assets	Social Security Wealth
1st	270,238	208,721	39,162	9,679	44,964	620	61,517
2nd	228,538	154,438	40,002	11,114	27,692	1,025	74,100
3rd	251,170	167,115	34,394	9,857	27,194	2,648	84,055
4th	269,872	176,423	36,749	10,586	29,904	2,192	93,449
5th	301,348	199,755	52,522	20,754	36,609	4,049	101,593
6th	378,252	270,121	75,745	21,483	45,592	6,366	108,131
7th	415,763	301,077	94,361	31,245	46,029	11,322	114,686
8th	479,383	354,268	105,368	40,228	61,423	13,514	125,115
9th	590,440	458,410	133,091	44,373	84,192	19,767	132,030
10th	1,007,740	864,328	219,055	109,441	148,277	48,709	143,412
All	415,833	312,441	82,212	30,465	54,724	10,808	103,392

Source: Authors' tabulations from 1992 HRS wave 1.

Notes: All entries are measured in 1992 dollars. The sample includes all families with head aged fifty-one to sixty-one, at least one member employed, and with matched Social Security records. The Social Security wealth does not include the value of spousal survivorship benefits. It is the sum of benefits based on the husband's and the wife's earnings.

that a person works until age sixty-five. The actual HRS 401(k) balances reported in table 1.4, however, are 1992 balances when the respondents were aged fifty-one to sixty-one. Personal retirement balances could easily double by the time the respondents attain age sixty-five, through the combined effect of asset returns and additional contributions during remaining years of employment.

When the 401(k) program began in 1982, members of the 1992 HRS sample were forty-one to fifty-one years old. We assume that in 1982, these families began to participate in 401(k) plans at rates estimated from the SIPP and to contribute at rates estimated from the CPS. We ask how close simulated balances based on these assumptions are to the actual 1992 balances of the HRS respondents.

We first use the SIPP data to estimate participation profiles by age for the cohorts whose members were fifty-one to fifty-five and fifty-six to sixty in 1992, at the time of the HRS. Then, to estimate contributions, we use family earnings histories, derived as described above. Within each earnings decile, beginning in 1982, we randomly assign families to participation status, based on SIPP estimates of participation by age and earnings decile for each of the two cohorts. We then randomly assign job-change and cash-out status, also as described above. Based on our estimates from the CPS data, we assume a contribution rate of 8 percent in all years between 1982 and 1992. This is somewhat less than the average rate of 8.7 percent— including both employee and employer matching contributions—reported in the 1993 CPS data, and the 9 percent rate that we assume throughout our projections of future 401(k) balances. This is because there is some evidence that 401(k) contribution rates have increased over time, and we are trying to track the 1982–92 experience.

Table 1.5 shows our projected 401(k) balances, as of 1992, for the HRS sample. This table is similar to a table in PVW (1998a), but it is based on an algorithm that allows for job terminations. The table reports results stratified by earnings decile. On average, the simulated values do not differ greatly from the observed balances reported in the HRS. Using the bond rate of return seems to give the closest match. Even the simulated balances by earnings decile are typically not far from the HRS reported balances. These results suggest that with roughly accurate assumptions about contribution and participation behavior, we are able to replicate the actual distribution of 401(k) balances. We do not necessarily view our ability to track the past evolution of 401(k) balances as a strong endorsement for the future success of our algorithm, because our historical success does not provide any evidence that our assumptions for the future are plausible.

1.4 Projections of 401(k) Balances of Future Retirees

We now use our projection algorithm to estimate the balances at age sixty-five of future cohorts. We assume that our estimated earnings profiles

Table 1.5 Means of Simulated 401(k) Balances and 401(k) Plus Rollover Balances

Earnings Decile	Observed HRS 401(k) Balance ($)	Means of Simulated 401(k) Balances ($)			Means of Simulated 401(k) and Rollover Balances ($)		
		Bonds	50-50	S&P 500	Bonds	50-50	S&P 500
1st	620	164	175	185	183	196	208
2nd	1,025	666	710	753	755	809	862
3rd	2,648	1,677	1,794	1,908	1,968	2,110	2,251
4th	2,192	2,665	2,853	3,038	3,133	3,373	3,621
5th	4,049	4,205	4,504	4,797	5,023	5,407	5,781
6th	6,366	6,467	6,929	7,383	7,743	8,341	8,924
7th	11,322	9,407	10,079	10,739	11,316	12,184	13,038
8th	13,514	13,990	14,997	15,987	16,766	18,027	19,289
9th	19,767	20,612	22,106	23,574	24,806	26,716	28,619
10th	48,709	29,677	31,788	33,863	35,944	38,688	41,409
All	10,808	8,953	9,593	10,223	10,764	11,585	12,400

Source: Authors' tabulations and projections from 1992 HRS.

represent the past earnings of the HRS families, and we estimate what they would have accumulated in a 401(k) had they had the participation rates that we project for the C(25) and C(15) cohorts. We also consider what would have happened if there had been universal 401(k) coverage in past years. The projections reported below assume a 35 basis point annual administrative cost on 401(k) investments in bonds, and a 70 basis point cost on stock investments.

Table 1.6 reports the results of our projections for the C(25) cohort, the group that will turn sixty-five in 2024. The first column of the table shows the average value of Social Security wealth for each earnings decile. The remaining columns show our projected 401(k) balances when the C(25) cohort reaches age sixty-five. These values are reported in 1992 dollars, for comparability with the first column. Our projected 401(k) balances are the *pretax* balances in 401(k) accounts. A family with these balances would pay taxes as the 401(k) balance was drawn down, so the after-tax value of the 401(k) accumulation is smaller than what we report. In contrast, no tax will be paid on most Social Security benefits. To place our estimates in perspective, it is helpful to refer to the family wealth data in table 1.4. One statistic that provides a useful point of reference is the mean actual 1992 balance in 401(k) accounts for HRS respondents: $10,808. We can compare the average value of projected 401(k) balances against this magnitude. In addition, we can compare the 401(k) balances to Social Security wealth, under current provisions, and these values are shown in the first column of the table.

Table 1.6 shows two components of 401(k) accumulation, or potential accumulation, for each asset allocation assumption. The first column under each assumption is the sum of the projected 401(k) balance plus the balances in any rollover accounts at age sixty-five. Since we view assets that are kept within the retirement saving system as tantamount to 401(k) assets, we group these two asset categories together. We do not report the split between 401(k) and rollover assets, although in many of our projections, the rollover balance actually exceeded that in the 401(k) account. We suspect that this reflects job mobility rates that are too high, over some age ranges, for our 401(k) participants. We also report the value of "Foregone Saving" for each earnings decile. This is the additional amount that would have been available for retirement support had the assets not been cashed out. It is the value of simulated 401(k) withdrawals accumulated to age sixty-five under various assumptions about the rate of return on 401(k) assets. Engelhardt (1999) presents a similar statistic for actual lump-sum distributions claimed by HRS respondents.

The results in table 1.6 suggest that preretirement withdrawals from 401(k) plans do not have significant effects on 401(k) balances at retirement. For those who will reach retirement in 2024, the C(25) cohort, we project 401(k) assets at retirement ranging from $57,900 to $181,400,

Table 1.6   Projected Mean 401(k) and Rollover Balances at Retirement, and Foregone Saving Due to 401(k) Withdrawals (C[25] cohort with 35 basis point reduction for bonds and 75 basis point reduction for stocks)

Earnings Decile	Social Security Wealth	All-Bond Portfolio		50-50 Bond/Stock Portfolio		All-Stock Portfolio	
		401(k) plus Rollover	Foregone Saving	401(k) plus Rollover	Foregone Saving	401(k) plus Rollover	Foregone Saving
1st	61.5	0.7	0.2	1.4	0.3	2.7	0.6
2nd	74.1	5.1	0.5	9.2	0.9	17.3	1.8
3rd	84.1	11.7	0.9	20.7	1.6	38.8	3.1
4th	93.4	22.1	1.4	38.8	2.5	72.9	4.8
5th	101.6	29.4	1.6	50.7	3.0	93.9	6.1
6th	108.1	40.2	2.0	69.2	3.8	128.0	7.8
7th	114.7	67.4	2.4	116.6	4.8	216.4	10.1
8th	125.1	89.3	3.2	153.5	6.3	283.4	13.2
9th	132.0	123.4	3.7	210.5	7.7	386.7	16.1
10th	143.4	189.4	4.8	317.6	9.5	574.2	19.6
Total	103.4	57.9	2.1	98.8	4.0	181.4	8.3

Source: Authors' tabulations and projections from 1992 HRS.
Note: All entries in thousands of 1992 dollars.

depending on our assumption about how the assets are invested. These levels are large relative to the average Social Security wealth of $103,400 for these households, and they are much larger than the (actual) mean 401(k) balance of $10,800 in 1992, when the HRS respondents were aged fifty-one to sixty-one.

For each projection, the ratio of projected 401(k) to Social Security wealth varies a great deal depending on lifetime earnings. Because the C(25) projections assume the continuation of current low participation rates in the lowest income deciles, families in the 1st and 2nd income deciles accumulate very little in 401(k) assets, no matter what the rate of return. Beginning with the 3rd decile, however, 401(k) assets at retirement would likely be substantial relative to Social Security wealth. For families with incomes in the upper four deciles of the income distribution, the mean 401(k) balance exceeds Social Security wealth provided at least half of the 401(k) assets were allocated to stocks. The after-tax income associated with the 401(k) balance could still fall below the value of Social Security payments for some of these households, since 401(k) distributions are likely to be taxed more heavily than Social Security benefits.

If 401(k) participants invest all of their assets in stocks, and if stocks continue to deliver returns like those in the last seven decades, then 401(k) plus rollover wealth would exceed Social Security wealth (on average) in the five highest income deciles. Since Social Security benefits do not rise substantially with lifetime income above roughly the median of the income distribution, it is not surprising that 401(k) balances, which are based on contributions that were proportional to earnings, become larger than Social Security benefits at higher income levels. We suspect that our C(25) projections underestimate future 401(k) participation by low-income households, but we have yet to find a way to address this difficulty.

As emphasized above, in comparing the projected differences in participation rates by earnings decile, it is important to recognize that actual experience for particular households could well be quite different from our mean projections, even if our average participation rates are realistic. The dispersion of 401(k) accumulations is substantial in every earnings decile.

The second column under each assumed asset allocation heading in table 1.6 reports the value that 401(k) assets that were withdrawn in the form of lump-sum distributions would have attained if they had been allowed to remain within the 401(k) system. The results show that the value of this foregone saving is small relative to the value of 401(k) balances for most earnings deciles. On average, the foregone saving is less than 5 percent of the value of the 401(k) and rollover balance. For households in the bottom deciles of the earnings distribution, the foregone saving is larger relative to the 401(k) accumulation. This is because we have assumed that the probability of cashing out a smaller 401(k) balance is larger than that for a larger balance. Households in the bottom part of the earnings distribution are more likely to have small balances than are households higher up in the earnings distribution.

One way to place the magnitude of such lump-sum distributions in perspective is to note that the impact of a 35 or 70 basis point annual administrative charge on 401(k) accounts is much larger, in terms of assets at retirement, than the impact of lump-sum distributions. The foregone saving, due to preretirement withdrawals, reduces accumulated assets in the all-bond portfolio by 3.5 percent and in the all-stock portfolio by 4.4 percent. If we had not charged 401(k) accounts with any expenses for investment management, the projections would have ranged from $61,200 to $209,200, or between 5 and 13 percent greater than the projections we report. That is, the administration expense reduces accumulated balances in the bond portfolio by 5.4 percent and balances in the stock portfolio by 13.3 percent. Thus, reductions in administrative expenses could do more to increase saving than reduction in preretirement withdrawals.

Table 1.7 presents information similar to that in table 1.6, except that we now focus on the C(15) cohort. Under the C(15) assumptions, the mean 401(k) balances at age sixty-five range from $74,300 to $247,100. These projections imply substantially larger 401(k) assets relative to Social Security wealth for the lower earnings deciles than the earlier C(25) projections. In the C(15) case, even the families in the 3rd decile could accumulate pretax 401(k) assets that could be an important fraction of Social Security wealth. If 401(k) accounts were invested in assets that earned returns as high as those on equities in the last seventy years, then even those in the 4th income decile would accumulate 401(k) assets that were larger, on average, than their Social Security wealth.

Finally, table 1.8 presents additional information like that in tables 1.6 and 1.7, except that we now consider the case of *universal* coverage for 401(k) plans. In modeling universal coverage, we assume that all workers contribute to a 401(k) plan, but that they may withdraw their accumulated 401(k) balances if they change jobs. One could alternatively model the case in which account balances must be held until the individual reaches age sixty-five. By adding together our 401(k) and rollover balance, and the foregone saving entry, we can evaluate the balance that would accumulate in such accounts.

We project that universal 401(k) coverage, even with withdrawals allowed at job change, would result in substantially higher mean 401(k) balances at age sixty-five than either our C(25) or C(15) participation assumptions. The differences are particularly pronounced in the lower part of the income distribution. We project mean 401(k) balances at age sixty-five ranging from $98,100 to $356,300, depending on the asset allocation for 401(k) accounts. Universal coverage could yield mean pretax 401(k) balances that would exceed Social Security wealth in all but the lowest lifetime earnings decile, at least if 401(k) investors earned returns comparable

Table 1.7   Projected Mean 401(k) and Rollover Balances at Retirement, and Foregone Saving Due to 401(k) Withdrawals (C[15] cohort with 35 basis point reduction for bonds and 75 basis point reduction for stocks)

Earnings Decile	Social Security Wealth	All-Bond Portfolio		50-50 Bond/Stock Portfolio		All-Stock Portfolio	
		401(k) plus Rollover	Foregone Saving	401(k) plus Rollover	Foregone Saving	401(k) plus Rollover	Foregone Saving
1st	61.5	2.0	0.4	3.8	0.8	7.5	1.6
2nd	74.1	10.7	1.1	19.4	2.1	37.6	4.2
3rd	84.1	21.8	1.7	39.6	3.0	76.5	6.2
4th	93.4	36.7	2.3	66.3	4.3	128.1	8.8
5th	101.6	47.3	2.5	84.0	5.0	160.1	10.6
6th	108.1	61.7	3.0	109.3	6.0	207.8	12.9
7th	114.7	89.7	3.4	159.5	6.9	304.7	14.9
8th	125.1	112.4	4.2	198.4	8.7	377.0	18.7
9th	132.0	145.6	4.5	255.0	9.6	482.0	20.5
10th	143.4	215.4	5.6	370.7	11.5	689.9	24.2
Total	103.4	74.3	2.9	130.6	5.8	247.1	12.2

Source: Authors' tabulations and projections from 1992 HRS.

Note: All entries in thousands of 1992 dollars.

Table 1.8   Projected Mean 401(k) and Rollover Balances at Retirement, and Foregone Saving Due to 401(k) Withdrawals (assuming universal 401(k) participation with 35 basis point reduction for bonds and 75 basis point reduction for stocks)

Earnings Decile	Social Security Wealth	All-Bond Portfolio 401(k) plus Rollover	All-Bond Portfolio Foregone Saving	50-50 Bond/Stock Portfolio 401(k) plus Rollover	50-50 Bond/Stock Portfolio Foregone Saving	All-Stock Portfolio 401(k) plus Rollover	All-Stock Portfolio Foregone Saving
1st	61.5	11.3	2.5	22.4	4.9	47.3	10.1
2nd	74.1	33.1	3.6	64.7	7.3	134.5	15.6
3rd	84.1	49.9	4.0	96.3	8.1	198.4	17.9
4th	93.4	65.2	4.4	124.5	8.9	254.8	18.9
5th	101.6	80.6	4.6	151.5	9.7	305.7	21.8
6th	108.1	95.9	5.1	178.4	10.6	356.7	24.0
7th	114.7	113.5	4.6	209.3	9.7	415.7	21.9
8th	125.1	133.9	5.4	244.2	11.4	480.8	25.7
9th	132.0	163.6	5.4	295.5	11.6	577.2	25.6
10th	143.4	234.0	6.5	413.3	13.6	792.1	29.1
Total	103.4	98.1	4.6	180.0	9.6	356.3	21.1

Source: Authors' tabulations and projections from 1992 HRS.
Note: All entries in thousands of 1992 dollars.

to those on equities over the last seven decades. In the case of universal coverage, 401(k) assets would almost surely represent an important share of Social Security wealth even in the lowest income deciles.

The results in tables 1.6–1.8 can be used to assess the importance of our earlier modeling error in the definition of J_a. By adding together the "401(k) + Rollover" column and the "Foregone Saving" column, we can estimate the total 401(k) balance at retirement if there were no potential withdrawals. Table 1.9 reports new calculations that are comparable to our previous estimates. In particular, our previous calculations did not allow for administrative costs on 401(k) investments. The results in table 1.9 preserve this assumption, and therefore differ from the results in tables 1.6 and 1.7. Comparing the results in table 1.9 with those in our earlier paper suggests that our modeling error understated the projections by about 20 percent.

All of our projections so far assume that 401(k) investors earn the same return in every year, conditional on their asset allocations. In practice, both stock and bond returns are random, and there is substantial uncertainty surrounding the retirement wealth that will be associated with a given contribution history. To consider this possibility, we replaced our assumption of certain returns with a random returns scenario. We illustrate our findings for the C(25) cohort. In each year of our projection, we draw one value from the post-1926 distribution of actual bond and stock returns reported in Ibbotson Associates (1997). Because returns are now random, the projected value of 401(k) balances at retirement will differ across projections, depending on the random returns that happen to be

Table 1.9   **Projected 401(k) Balances at Retirement as Reported in Poterba, Venti, and Wise (1998a)**

Earnings Decile	Cohort C(25) (age 65 in 2024)			Cohort C(15) (age 65 in 2034)		
	Bonds	50-50	Stocks	Bonds	50-50	Stocks
1st	974	1,839	3,699	2,556	4,927	10,123
2nd	5,759	10,691	21,175	12,605	24,000	48,841
3rd	13,092	24,173	47,843	24,506	46,469	94,560
4th	24,820	45,500	89,863	41,142	77,766	158,417
5th	32,848	59,385	115,971	53,390	99,686	201,061
6th	45,282	81,172	159,549	69,710	129,458	260,355
7th	74,286	134,308	262,478	98,953	184,478	372,183
8th	98,624	177,764	346,543	124,006	229,812	461,382
9th	134,707	240,686	465,290	159,150	292,720	583,877
10th	204,271	357,826	680,483	233,532	420,937	825,739
All	63,466	113,394	219,289	81,955	151,034	301,654

Source: Authors' calculations as described in the text. Results for universal 401(k) participation are the same as those in Poterba, Venti, and Wise (1998a).

drawn in a given projection. We ran 1,000 such projections for the C(25) cohort, and tabulated our findings.

Table 1.10 shows the distribution of the mean 401(k) wealth at retirement, averaged across all earnings deciles. The entries in this table are comparable to the last row of table 1.6. The results are graphed in figure 1.3. The results show that the *median* 401(k) balance at retirement, especially when a substantial share of the 401(k) portfolio is invested in equities, is below the *mean*. In the case of a 50-50 bond-stock portfolio, for example, table 1.6 shows a mean 401(k) and rollover balance of $98,800, while the median value is $94,600. The mean in this case lies between the 50th and 60th percentiles of the distribution. For the all-stock case, the mean is between the 60th and 70th percentiles of the distribution of realized outcomes. The most appropriate single measure is unclear. The results also draw attention to the great differences between the bond and stock distributions. For example, 95 percent of bond returns are below $85,800, but only slightly more than 20 percent of stock returns are below this level.

We plan further work in the future on random asset returns and the growth of 401(k) balances. The results above, however, make clear the wide variation in potential system-wide returns, especially stock market returns.

1.5   An Early Review of Post-1993 401(k) Participation and Contribution Behavior

The projections of future 401(k) growth reported above were based on 1993 data from the Survey of Income and Program Participation. We now have SIPP data for 1996 which permit us to evaluate the plausibility of our 1993-based projections. We have not yet recalibrated the projections to use the 1996 data, because we are waiting for some additional SIPP information on pension coverage and household net worth.

The 1996 SIPP data suggest that, if anything, our projections for 401(k) expansion have been conservative. Figure 1.4 is just like figure 1.1, but with two additions. The 1996 data have been added for each cohort, and data for two younger cohorts—C(22) and C(17)—have been added. The C(27) starting point for our earlier projections is circled. It is clear that eligibility rates have continued to rise. The figure shows age-specific 401(k) eligibility rates for different age cohorts.

Figure 1.5 shows participation rates for these same cohorts, including the 1996 data. The participation-rate increases between 1993 and 1996 were very substantial. Following the dotted lines on the figure can identify differences between the participation rates of successive cohorts at selected ages. For example, the participation rate of persons in the C(27) cohort at age thirty-eight was about 10 percentage points higher than the rate of persons in the C(32) cohort at age thirty-eight. The difference between the

Table 1.10 Distribution of Projected Mean 401(k) and Rollover Balances at Retirement, and Foregone Saving Due to 401(k) Withdrawals (C[25] cohort, 1,000 draws from empirical distribution of returns adjusted for administrative costs; 35 basis points for bonds and 75 basis points for stocks)

Percentile	All-Bond Portfolio		50-50 Bond/Stock Portfolio		All-Stock Portfolio	
	401(k) plus Rollover	Foregone Saving	401(k) plus Rollover	Foregone Saving	401(k) plus Rollover	Foregone Saving
5th	39.9	1.3	50.3	1.8	49.6	1.7
10th	43.3	1.4	57.7	2.1	60.6	2.2
20th	46.4	1.6	68.1	2.5	81.6	3.1
30th	49.7	1.7	76.7	2.9	102.2	4.1
40th	52.1	1.8	83.7	3.3	123.5	5.1
50th	56.1	1.9	94.6	3.7	145.8	6.3
60th	59.1	2.1	103.5	4.2	177.1	7.8
70th	63.1	2.3	115.1	4.7	211.4	9.6
80th	68.8	2.5	127.9	5.4	255.0	12.2
90th	76.6	2.8	149.0	6.5	345.0	16.9
95th	85.8	3.2	178.3	7.8	450.2	27.2

Source: Authors' tabulations and projections from 1992 HRS.

Note: All entries in thousands of 1992 dollars.

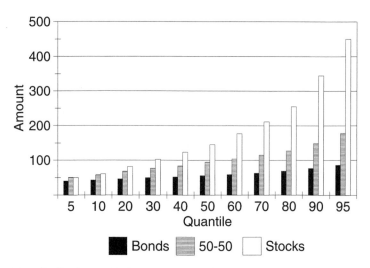

Fig. 1.3   Distribution of 401(k) assets for the C(25) cohort

C(17) and C(22) cohorts at age twenty-eight is 8 percentage points. Recall that our projections assume that 401(k) participation rises by 20 percentage points every ten years. Note that while we refer to the latest data as being from 1996, in fact, these data were collected closer to 2.5 years after the 1993 survey. Thus the *annual* increase in eligibility has been greater than the graphical comparison implies.[5]

Figure 1.5 includes the information in figure 1.2 as well as 1996 data and data for the C(22) cohort. The actual eligibility rate of the C(27) cohort at age thirty-eight is in fact somewhat greater than our projected rate. In addition, the C(22) rate at age thirty-three is well above the projected rate for the C(25) cohort at that age. These comparisons suggest that our projections are conservative, at least over their first few years. One of our future plans is to use the 1996 data, along with new SIPP-based information on asset balances, to recalibrate our benchmark participation and contribution rates for different ages.

1.6   Conclusions and Future Directions

This paper presents new evidence on amount of retirement saving that currently-working households are likely to accumulate in their 401(k) plans. Today's young and middle-aged households have much higher

5. The actual survey dates and the number of "years" after the 1984 wave 4, which was interviewed between September and December 1994, are as follows: 1985 wave 7 *and* 1986 wave 4, January–April 1987 (two years); 1990 wave 4, February–May 1991 (six years); 1991 wave 7 and 1992 wave 4, February–May 1993 (eight years); and 1993 wave 9, October 1995–January 1996 (eleven years).

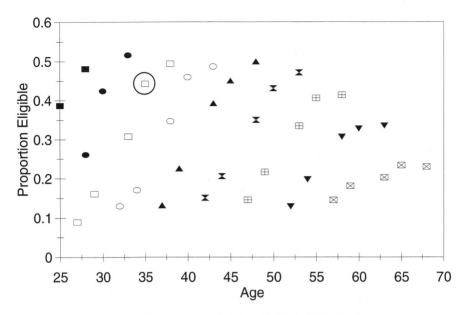

Fig. 1.4   401(k) eligibility by cohort, 1984, 1987, 1991, 1993, 1996

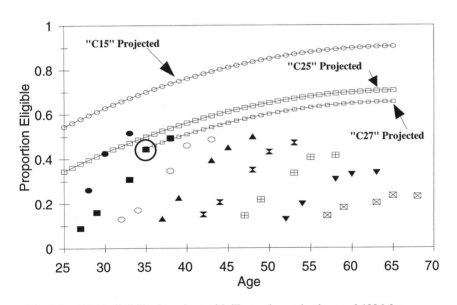

Fig. 1.5   401(k) eligibility by cohort with illustrative projections and 1996 data

401(k) participation rates than current retirees did at similar ages. In addition, the rate of 401(k) participation has risen and seems likely to continue to rise for all age groups. As a result, 401(k) saving is likely to play a much larger part in the financial preparation for retirement of future retirees than it has for current and past retirees.

We present new estimates of the amount of such saving that households reaching age sixty-five in 2024, and in 2034, are likely to accumulate. We improve on previous estimates by recognizing explicitly the possibility of preretirement withdrawals from the 401(k) system through lump-sum distributions, and by allowing for asset management costs associated with 401(k) accounts. We find that lump-sum distributions have a relatively small impact on the amount of saving that households accumulate in 401(k) accounts. The possibility of taking lump-sum distributions appears to reduce retirement accumulations by only about 5 percent relative to what they would be if households were prevented from taking such distributions. This effect is smaller than the effect of allowing for modest administrative expenses for these accounts.

Our calculations assume that participation and contribution behavior would be the same if there were no lump-sum distributions as they are at present. In fact, the very option of withdrawing assets as a lump sum may encourage 401(k) participation by some households. Recognizing the potential effect of 401(k) plan provisions on participation decisions is a topic we reserve for future work.

Projecting the average 401(k) account balance for those who will retire two and three decades into the future is necessarily fraught with great uncertainty. Some sources of uncertainty, such as systematic changes in household attitudes toward saving, or reforms of the Social Security system that alter the basic structure of financial preparation for retirement, are difficult to predict. There are other sources of uncertainty in our projections, however, that can be reduced with further empirical work.

One difficulty with our current algorithm is that it is based on data that are less reliable for younger individuals than for older ones. With respect to lump-sum distributions, the CPS asks only individuals over age forty about their pension benefits and past lump-sum payouts. The HRS, the other premier source of information on pension benefits, is limited because the basic sampling frame was individuals between the ages of fifty-one and sixty-two in 1992. Although the HRS includes retrospective questions that elicit some data on employment transitions before individuals joined the HRS panel, there is naturally some concern about the quality of the resulting data for job separations that occurred long ago. Job transitions that occur early in an individual's career typically do not involve large 401(k) balances, but because there are many years remaining before the individuals receiving these balances would retire, they could grow to represent substantial retirement resources.

A second area in which our algorithm could be improved is in the link between job separation and job tenure. Jobs that have already lasted a long time tend to have lower probabilities of ending than do "younger" jobs. At the moment, our algorithm allows for age-dependent probabilities of job separation, but we have not allowed for an individual's job tenure, or an individual's earnings decile, to affect the probability of a job transition and the associated possibility of a 401(k) withdrawal. The ideal database for our purposes would identify workers who participate in 401(k) plans, and would then permit estimates of job-change probabilities conditional on age, earnings, and the worker's job tenure. The significant expansion of the set of questions about pension coverage in the 1996 SIPP should provide much of the information that is needed for such a detailed calculation.

Finally, our analysis has focused on retirement as an event that occurs at age sixty-five. In practice, some 401(k) participants are likely to leave the labor force before that age, and therefore to begin drawing down their 401(k) account balances earlier than our assumptions imply. Other workers may remain in the labor force after age sixty-five, particularly in future decades when the Social Security retirement age is higher than at present. For these workers, 401(k) assets are likely to be larger than our projections suggest, both because they will have more years for accruing tax-deferred returns and because they will contribute for more years than our calculations suggest. Allowing for a distribution of retirement ages is something we hope to incorporate in future versions of our algorithm.

In addition, although we give some attention to the system-wide risk that is due to randomness in market returns, we do not treat the additional individual risk that is due to 401(k) participation and individual asset allocation decisions.

References

Bassett, W. F., M. J. Fleming, and A. P. Rodriguez. 1998. How workers use 401(k) plans: The participation, contribution, and withdrawal decisions. *National Tax Journal* 51:263–89.

Chang, A. 1996. Tax policy, lump-sum pension distributions, and household saving. *National Tax Journal* 49:235–52.

Engelhardt, G. V. 1999. Pre-retirement lump-sum distributions and retirement income security: Evidence from the health and retirement survey. Dartmouth College. Mimeograph.

Farber, H. S. 1997. The changing face of job loss in the United States, 1981–1995. *Brookings Papers on Economic Activity, Microeconomics:* 55–128. Washington, D.C.: Brookings Institution.

Gustman, A., and T. Steinmeier. 1995. *Pension incentives and job mobility.* Kalamazoo, Mich.: Upjohn Institute.

Hurd, M., L. Lillard, and C. Panis. 1998. An analysis of the choice to cash out, maintain, or annuitize pension rights upon job change or retirement. Working Paper no. DRU-1979-DOL. Santa Monica, Calif.: RAND Corporation.
Ibbotson Associates. 1997. *Stocks, bonds, bills, and inflation 1997 yearbook.* Chicago: Ibbotson Associates.
Iwaszko, K., and B. O'Connell. 1999. *The 401(k) millionaire.* New York: Villard Books.
Merritt, S. 1997. *How to build wealth with your 401(k): Everything you need to know to become more than a millionaire over the course of your working lifetime.* Melbourne, Fla.: Halyard Press.
Neumark, D., D. Polsky, and D. Hansen. 1999. Has job stability declined yet? New evidence from the 1990s? Michigan State University. Mimeograph.
Poterba, J. M., S. F. Venti, and D. A. Wise. 1998a. Implications of rising personal retirement saving. In *Frontiers of the economics of aging,* ed. D. Wise, 125–67. Chicago: University of Chicago Press.
———. 1998b. Lump sum distributions from retirement saving plans: Receipt and utilization. In *Inquiries in the economics of aging,* ed. D. A. Wise, 85–105. Chicago: University of Chicago Press.
Poterba, J. M., and D. A. Wise. 1999. Personal retirement accounts and personal choice. In *Personal saving, Personal choice,* ed. D. A. Wise. Stanford: Hoover Institution Press.
Sabelhaus, J., and D. Weiner. 1999. Disposition of lump sum pension distributions: Evidence from tax returns. *National Tax Journal* 52 (September): 593–613.
Unicon Research Corporation. 1996. CPS Utilities. Santa Monica, Calif.
U.S. Department of Labor. 1995. *New findings from the September 1994 Current Population Survey.* Washington, D.C.: U.S. Department of Labor, Pension and Welfare Benefits Administration.
———. 1997. *Private pension plan bulletin: Abstract of 1993 Form 5500 annual reports.* Washington, D.C.: U.S. Department of Labor, Pension and Welfare Benefits Administration.
Venti, S. F., and D. A. Wise. 1999. Lifetime income, saving choices, and wealth at retirement. In *Wealth, work, and health: Innovations in survey measurement in the Social Sciences,* ed. J. Smith and R. Willis, 87–120. Ann Arbor: University of Michigan Press.
Yakoboski, P. 1993. New evidence on lump sum distributions and rollover activity. *EBRI notes.* Washington, D.C.: Employee Benefit Research Institute.
———. 1997. Large plan lump sums: Rollovers and cashouts. *EBRI Issue Brief 188.* Washington, D.C.: Employee Benefit Research Institute.

Comment   John B. Shoven

This paper is about a very important topic for those who set public policy for pensions and retirement. The paper tries to gauge the importance of withdrawals from pension saving accounts that occur at the time of preretirement job changes. While there is some evidence that there are a large

John B. Shoven is the Charles R. Schwab Professor of Economics at Stanford University, and a research associate of the National Bureau of Economic Research.

number of such lump-sum withdrawals, closer scrutiny reveals that most of the withdrawals are for small accounts held by young participants. The bottom line of this paper is that the consequences of lump-sum withdrawals for average future 401(k) balances in retirement are relatively minor. The authors project that the impact of lump-sum withdrawals will be a 5 percent reduction in future average 401(k) retirement balances.

The authors have been responsive to the suggestions that I made as the discussant at the conference. This makes it more difficult to criticize the paper as it now stands. First, they now include administrative expenses in their 401(k) simulations and show that such expenses reduce the accumulations more than lump-sum withdrawals do. This is one of the most important results of the paper. The expenses that the authors include (35 basis points per year for the bond account and 75 basis points for the stock account) are relatively modest. Nonetheless, they can reduce the final accumulations of participants by as much as 13.3 percent. Some 401(k) accumulation vehicles impose expenses twice as high as modeled here. Clearly, participants should monitor expenses of their portfolio managers closely.

The authors calculate the average 401(k) balances for the cohort reaching age sixty-five in 2024. They project that these average balances will range from 0.5 to 2.0 times average Social Security wealth. While one can quarrel with the parameters that go into these projections, the basic message that 401(k) plans will be strikingly more important to future retirees than they are today is unassailable. Their careful treatment of cohort effects is essential in predicting the future importance of these plans.

Now that the aggregate importance of the plans and the aggregate unimportance of withdrawals are established, what is needed is a thorough examination of the risks and uncertainties of 401(k) plans both at the individual level and in aggregate. At the individual level, there is much heterogeneity in terms of contribution rates, asset allocation, length of career, management expenses, and withdrawals from plans. The issue that would be nice to address is whether the benefits of 401(k) plans are more unevenly distributed than Social Security due to the interaction of all of these effects. It would also be interesting to simulate the effect of disallowing lump-sum withdrawals on the distribution of outcomes in addition to the effect on average outcomes. Similarly, it would be interesting to know whether many participants take unnecessary risks by failing to diversify their 401(k) portfolios. At the aggregate level, there is some chance that the returns on assets over the next twenty-five or thirty-five years will not be drawn from the same random distribution that generated the returns over the last forty years. It is the nature of retirement saving plans that the late returns are more important than the early ones because the late ones apply to more of the contributions. The point estimates of average 401(k) wealth at retirement in this paper are interesting, but there is considerable uncertainty about the actual outcomes that will be observed.

Of course, to some extent the same can be said about future Social Security benefits. They also may not materialize as currently promised.

I think this is a very good paper that makes its main points effectively. Lump-sum withdrawals are not as important a problem for 401(k) plans as some people may have originally thought. Management expenses, for instance, are more important. Now, what is called for, and what seems to be on the authors' agenda, is an assessment of the individual risks that 401(k) participants bear. I look forward to the next installment of the Poterba, Venti, and Wise series of articles.

The Personal Security Account 2000 Plan, Market Outcomes, and Risk

Sylvester J. Schieber and John B. Shoven

2.1 Introduction

In early 1997, the 1994–96 Advisory Council on Social Security released its final report, which remarkably altered the nature of the debate in the United States about the reform of our national retirement system. It did so by giving legitimacy to recommendations that some element of Social Security reform should include individual accounts held by workers. The majority of the council's members actually advocated such reform. To be sure, there had been other people and groups who previously had advocated these types of Social Security reform in this country—but never before had a group of individuals assembled under an official charter by a presidential administration come close to such a recommendation. Since the Advisory Council's report was released there have been several serious proposals put forward for reforming Social Security that include some element of individual accounts. There have also been numerous criticisms of this approach to Social Security reform.

In this paper, we present a framework for assessing Social Security reform proposals by evaluating a specific reform plan. This plan is one derived from the original personal security account (PSA) plan developed by the 1994–96 Advisory Council on Social Security (Advisory Council 1997). This plan has been dubbed *PSA 2000* and its full elaboration is presented in Schieber and Shoven (1999). In part, PSA 2000 was devel-

Sylvester J. Schieber is vice president of Watson Wyatt Worldwide. John B. Shoven is the Charles R. Schwab Professor of Economics at Stanford University, and a research associate of the National Bureau of Economic Research.

We have greatly benefited from the research assistance of Davide Lombardo and Clemens Sialm, Stanford Ph.D. candidates in economics. Thank you to the National Institute on Aging and the National Bureau of Economic Research for their support.

oped to respond to some of the criticisms of the original PSA plan (see, e.g., Ball and Bethell 1998 and Aaron and Reischauer 1998). In section 2.2, a set of principles around which the plan was devised is briefly stated. In section 2.3, the proposal is developed and the underlying principles are developed in somewhat more detail. In section 2.4, we evaluate the long-term actuarial prospects of the proposal. In section 2.5, we evaluate the benefits that would be provided under the plan and the risks that individuals would bear with such a partial privatization approach. In the final section, we take measure of the plan against the principles laid out in section 2.2.

2.2   Guiding Principles

The principles underlying the PSA 2000 proposal were developed after a fairly extensive review of the history of our Social Security system in an attempt to reflect widely held values in this country about the appropriate design of a reform plan. Obviously, principles alone cannot determine the details of a proposal, but they can offer guidance to both the engineers of alternative systems and to the evaluators of proposed solutions. The principles that the PSA 2000 plan was built around are as follows:

1. The important "safety net" or progressivity of the existing Social Security system should be preserved.
2. Any redesign of Social Security should enhance the national saving rate.
3. The disability and early survivor insurance programs within Old-Age, Survivors, and Disability Insurance (OASDI) should be preserved.
4. Any reform should offer long-run solvency for the system, not simply postpone insolvency.
5. Any reform should improve equity between participants (particularly between one- and two-earner couples).
6. Economic efficiency should be increased by increasing the link between contributions and benefits.
7. The risks borne by individual participants should be diversified and kept at tolerable levels.
8. Administrative costs should be kept to reasonable levels.
9. The reforms should be determined and announced as soon as possible.

The first principle stems partially from the desire not to step back from the single greatest accomplishment of Social Security, namely, the relatively low incidence of official poverty amongst the elderly. One of the risks that Social Security insures against is a bad labor market outcome for workers during their careers. Bad labor market outcomes can be a result of poor health, a poor economy, or just lousy luck. There is a general feeling that it is unseemly for a society as wealthy as ours to force people who have been unsuccessful in their working careers to live out an impoverished old age. The current program offers those with a low lifetime earnings profile a higher replacement rate than those with above-average lifetime labor earnings. The PSA 2000 plan was designed with the intent of preserving this general pattern.

The second principle is based on the proposition that, just as saving is the only reliable way for a household to get rich, saving is also the only reliable way for our country to become wealthier. More wealth for future Americans translates to higher productivity and higher real wages for future workers. The fact that higher national saving would result in significantly higher real wages within twenty years was effectively argued by Aaron, Bosworth, and Burtless (1989). While there is no agreement as to the exact magnitudes, there is widespread acceptance of the fact that the pay-as-you-go (or PAYGO) Social Security system has depressed personal and national saving. Furthermore, providing for retirement is the most important motive for saving. It is only natural to attempt to increase saving while restoring the long-run solvency of Social Security.

The third principle, that disability and early survivor insurance should be preserved, comes from the assessment that insuring these risks is very important and that Social Security is relatively efficient in providing this coverage. The lack of any significant clamoring to replace these elements of the system with a private alternative suggests that this type of term insurance should continue to be provided by the Social Security Administration. That is not to say that the Disability Insurance (DI) program in particular shouldn't be studied carefully for inefficiencies. The DI program itself is underfunded by 20 percent over the seventy-five-year projection period used by the actuaries. Before policymakers reallocate any additional portion of the payroll tax base to the disability program, it is likely that a full-blown review of the program's operations will be undertaken.

The fourth principle was prompted by the 1983 Social Security Amendments. A nontrivial contributor to the development of a large seventy-five-year actuarial deficit since 1983 has been the mere passage of time. Even with the optimistic projections in 1983, the reformed system ran large deficits beginning in the second decade of the twenty-first century. The claim was that the program was balanced for seventy-five years with the early surpluses financing the later losses. The built-in problem was that with each passing year there was one fewer of the surplus years in the seventy-five-year window and one more deficit year. This principle suggests that we should now aspire to a system that is not only balanced over the next seventy-five years, but one that appears to be workable thereafter.

The fifth principle deals with the equitable treatment of different groups of Social Security participants. The chief concerns here are the treatment of one-earner and two-earner households and the adequacy of resources available to widows and widowers. Some of the transfers within the existing system are not only defensible but worth preserving; others are not. The large inequities among two-earner couples, one-earner couples, and single individuals should be rethought, along with other specific aspects of Social Security rules that seem convoluted and inappropriate. For instance, the cliff vesting of marriages at ten years seems arbitrary. Divorced individuals can claim benefits based on the earnings of their ex-spouses only if they were married for ten years or more. Finally, since poverty is greatest among widows, widow and widower benefits should be increased relative to those for married couples if true retirement income security is to be achieved.

The sixth principle is a very important one. There always has been a debate about whether Social Security contributions should be thought of as taxes or deferred compensation—i.e., as pension contributions. The current system has a relatively weak link between marginal contributions and marginal benefits and therefore may be viewed by most people as a tax/transfer system rather than as a deferred compensation pension system. For people with covered work histories shorter than ten years and for many whose careers are longer than thirty-five years, there is zero marginal benefit to additional marginal contributions. For secondary earners in two-earner households, the marginal connection between contributions and benefits is small or nil. If the full 15.3 percent payroll tax is viewed as a marginal tax with little or no offsetting marginal benefits, then the distortionary costs of the overall tax system are greatly increased. The total marginal tax rate for someone in the 15 percent federal income tax bracket is more than doubled and the efficiency costs of the tax system (which go up with the square of the marginal tax rate) more than quadruple due to the payroll tax. If marginal contributions and benefits are closely linked, this can lower the effective marginal tax rate and thereby enhance economic efficiency.

The seventh principle is one of the arguments against a purely privatized system, namely that such a plan has participants—some almost certainly unknowingly—who bear too much risk with their future retirement resources. Sophisticated investors can manage these risks, but many Social Security participants may be limited in this regard. This concern can be greatly reduced or even reversed for a partially privatized plan. A two-tier system in which everyone has some individual account investments would almost certainly prove a stimulus for greatly increasing the general level of financial literacy in the general population. At the same time, the tier-one or "floor" benefits provide protection from truly catastrophic financial results. Both defined benefit (DB) and defined contribution (DC) Social Security programs are risky. The DB plans bear political risks—i.e., the government can change the program at any time—as well as macroeconomic and demographic risks. Defined contribution plans carry the underlying risks of financial instruments, and we all know that stock and bond returns are highly variable. The optimal thing to do when you have a situation in which two different designs face different kinds of risk is to come up with a hybrid or "some of each" solution. This follows from the first principles of risk diversification.

The eighth principle that we should be aware of, administrative costs, is another type of efficiency consideration. Social Security will remain the primary retirement program for the majority of Americans. It is important that their contributions not be consumed with high administrative expenses. Any privatization plan or partial privatization plan must be conscious of minimizing the administrative costs of the program. That said, the current program, which is relatively inexpensively administered, provides very poor information to participants. Annual statements are still not mailed to all participants, and the statements, which are sent on request, are misleading. For instance, the only contributions shown on the statement are the half of payroll taxes attributed to the employee—the other half, those paid by the employer, are simply missing. Most economists agree that the employee bears both halves of the payroll tax, and yet the average participant sees his or her projected benefits and half of his or her payments to the system. Any private mutual fund or insurance policy prospectus would be disallowed for failing to disclose fully the cost of the investment. The PSA 2000 plan is based on a premise that we should certainly try to control administrative expenses, but better and more informative communication to participants clearly should also be a goal.

The final principle, namely, to do something as soon as possible, stems from a couple of considerations. First, the Social Security Trustees themselves report that the structure of the system is unsustainable after the third decade of the twenty-first century. The one thing we do know, however, is that there is a tremendous advantage to allowing people time to adjust to any changes in the benefit rules. Second, there still is time for the baby boomers to contribute to the solution of Social Security's solvency—but that opportunity is dwindling fast. Finally, the passage-of-time effect keeps bringing the financial problems of the system closer and making them larger with compound interest. The only way to put a check on the growth of the burden's being placed on future generations of workers is to begin making payments on the solution soon.

2.3 The Proposal and the All-Important Details

The general outline of the PSA 2000 plan is quite simple. First, the payroll tax would remain unchanged from current legislation. That means that OASDI taxes would continue to be a total of 12.4 percent of annual earnings, up to a ceiling amount of $72,600 in 1999. The percentage would stay the same for the next several decades. In the distant future it would be reduced when transition costs were paid off and the residual trust fund for the PAYGO-financed flat benefit reached 1.5 years of benefits. Just as with current law, the maximum amount of earnings subject to tax would grow with the general level of wages.

The benefit side of the program is completely redesigned under the PSA 2000 proposal. There would be two parts to Social Security's retirement benefits, a DB part and a DC part. These two parts are often referred to as the two tiers of benefits with plans such as PSA 2000. The first tier would be a flat benefit for all individuals with a full career of thirty-five years or more. The flat benefit amount for single people would be $500 per month in the year 2000. The $500 amount as an initial benefit would increase in the future by an amount reflecting the general increase in wage levels. The second tier of benefits results from the participant's accumulation in the DC part of the plan. The second tier would be financed by a combination of employee contributions matched by contributions from Social Security.

Workers would be required to contribute 2.5 percent of covered pay up to the taxable limit on which payroll taxes are due. Social Security would match the worker's contribution on a 1:1 basis, providing another 2.5 percent of covered earnings. All told, workers would be accumulating 5.0 percent of their covered earnings in a personal security account. The mandatory 2.5 percent employee contribution should not be equated to a tax increase. The money would be deposited into an account in the worker's name, which never happens with tax payments. While workers would have no discretion about making these contributions, they would have considerable control over how the moneys are invested throughout their working careers and how they are redeemed after retirement. We note that, in cases where employers offer 401(k) plans with 100 percent matching of employee contributions, the participation rates in the plans are typically around 80 percent, and are generally somewhat higher for all but the youngest and lowest-paid employees.

In retirement, workers would have the proceeds of these accounts in addition to their tier-one benefits. The government's matching contribution would not come out of thin air. In fact, it would be a rebate of the worker's 12.4 percent payroll tax. After paying the 2.5 percent rebates, Social Security would have only a net amount of 9.9 percent of covered pay to finance tier-one benefits, disability, and survivors insurance, and to honor the promises of the existing program during the lengthy transition or phase-in period.

We have just described the basics of the proposal in a few short paragraphs. Obviously, there are many details to the plan. The most important of them follow in subsections 2.3.1–2.3.13.

2.3.1   Less-Than-Full Careers

A thirty-five-year career would be required in order to receive the full flat benefit of tier one ($500 in 2000, indexed for average wage growth thereafter) at the normal retirement age. Those with a minimum-length career, ten years or forty covered quarters, would receive one-half of the flat tier-one benefit. Those with more than a ten-year covered career would get an extra 2 percent for each extra year, up to a total of 100 percent.

2.3.2   Normal Retirement Age

In order to receive the full flat tier-one benefit, or even the reduced benefit resulting from a shorter career, one would have to retire at the normal retirement age. Under the PSA 2000 plan the normal retirement age increases by two months per year for the years 2000 to 2011, reaching the age of sixty-seven years in 2011. Thereafter, further increases are indexed to improvements in life expectancies of people at the normal retirement age.

2.3.3   Early and Late Retirements

As the normal retirement age is gradually advanced, the age of eligibility for early retirement would also be advanced. Eventually, the youngest age for early retirement would reach sixty-five years. At that point, the PSA 2000 plan calls for no additional increases in the early retirement age. The adjustments for retiring at ages other than the normal retirement age (NRA) would remain as in the current law. Individuals retiring before the NRA would face reduced tier-one benefits at the rate of five-ninths of 1 percent per month. Those choosing to retire later than the NRA would have their benefits increased by two-thirds of 1 percent per month of delay in the commencement of benefits.

2.3.4   Earnings Test

Under the current Social Security system, persons who are receiving benefits have their benefits reduced if they have earnings above an exempt amount. The reduction is fifty cents for every dollar that earnings exceed the exempt amount for persons who have not attained Social Security's NRA and thirty-three and one-third cents for each dollar for persons who have. This clearly discourages part-time work for Social Security recipients. The PSA 2000 plan completely eliminates the earnings test for beneficiaries who have reached the NRA.

2.3.5   Spousal Benefits

Spouses would receive the higher of either the tier-one benefits that they would be entitled to receive based on their own earnings histories, or one-half of the tier-one benefits of their spouses. Two-earner married couples would be treated as two single persons in terms of their tier-one benefits. If both partners had full thirty-five year careers, they would receive a total of $1,000 per month in tier-one benefits. On the other hand, if one had a thirty-year career (qualifying for $450 per month) and one had a twenty-year career (qualifying for $350 per month), their total monthly tier-one benefits would be $800. Of course, all of these dollar figures would be higher in the future since the amounts are for the year 2000 and future benefits would be increased to reflect average wage growth. Since the minimum qualifying career (ten years of covered earnings) qualifies for one-half of the full tier-one benefit, all two-earner couples (where both have qualifying careers) would receive tier-one benefits (and tier-two benefits, for that matter) based on their own work records. There would be no spousal benefits for the second tier of the system (although the money would be paid out as a joint survivor annuity rather than a single life annuity). Further, we think that very few couples in the future would qualify for spousal benefits for tier one; the vast majority of married couples would receive benefits based on their own individual work records.

2.3.6   Widow's Benefits

Currently, many widows and widowers receive two-thirds the amount that the couple received before the spouse's death. Under the PSA 2000 plan, the surviving spouse would receive the highest of either her or his own tier-one benefit, the deceased spouse's tier-one benefit, or 75 percent of the combined tier-one benefits. The tier-two annuities would be a joint survivor type with the survivor receiving 75 percent of the prior amount.

2.3.7   Divorce

Tier-two PSA accumulations would be treated like any other DC pension plan in terms of dividing the assets in the event of divorce. Tier-one benefits would be available to divorced spouses only with restrictive rules similar to those in the current program. It is our expectation that the vast majority of adults will earn their own tier-one benefits with a covered work career of at least ten years.

2.3.8   Universal Coverage

The PSA 2000 plan, like existing Social Security, involves redistribution from those with higher lifetime labor earnings and those with lower lifetime labor earnings. With PSA 2000 the redistribution is transparent. The tier-one benefit is the same for everyone regardless of wage. However, total payroll taxes are higher for those who have more earnings. The well off pay more for the system than the not-so-well off. That is the nature of redistribution. However, a fair redistributionary plan means that everyone must participate. Otherwise, groups that are well off opt out, refusing to help fund the transfers to those who are less well off. The bottom line of this discussion is that PSA 2000 features compulsory universal coverage. The new group that is brought into the system is all newly hired state and local government employees.

2.3.9   Annuitization of PSA 2000 Payouts

Social Security benefits are currently paid out as inflation-indexed life annuities, meaning that once a person starts receiving benefits he or she gets that amount for the rest of his or her life, with annual increases reflecting price inflation as measured by the Consumer Price Index (CPI). The tier-one PSA 2000 benefits would be paid out in exactly the same manner. At the time of retirement, one-half of the tier-two accumulation would be automatically converted into an inflation-indexed life annuity. This half represents the government's matching contribution to the PSA accounts. The individuals would be able to choose how he or she would like to withdraw the other half of the PSA balance. Social Security would convert it into an indexed life-annuity on the same terms as the other half of the assets. On the other hand, participants could roll half of their PSA balances into individual retirement accounts (IRAs) or withdraw the money in any pattern that suits their needs.

2.3.10   Taxation of Benefits

The payroll tax would continue to be split between employees and employers. This means that workers would pay tax on half of the OASDI deductions (their own halves, but not the employers' halves). Half of the 2.5 percent mandatory contribution to the PSA account would be made with before-tax dollars and half with after-tax dollars. With this system, tax would be paid on half of all the money contributed to Social Security at the time of the earnings. In retirement, 50 percent of the payouts from both tier one and tier two would be subject to the personal income tax. This treatment means that the entire PSA 2000 system is taxed according to consumption tax principles. One way to think about it is that half of the contributions are treated like Roth IRAs (where after-tax contributions are withdrawn tax-free in retirement) and half are treated like normal IRAs (where before-tax contributions are taxable upon withdrawal). Taxing half the money going in and half coming out allows people to be diversified over two different tax regimes. It is important to note that the fact that half of the benefits constitute taxable income does not mean that all retired people will actually have to pay income taxes on this money. Take, for instance, a married couple who receives $18,000 per year from the two parts of their PSA 2000 plan. Under the plan, only $9,000 of their PSA payments would be treated as gross taxable income. However, as of 1998, a married couple with both spouses over age sixty-five was not required to file a federal income tax return unless they had gross income exceeding $14,200. Therefore, such a couple could have up to $5,200 of other income and still not owe any federal income tax. Only those with larger sources of other income (such as taxable pension distributions and dividends and interest income) would have to pay income taxes on the $9,000 of taxable PSA distributions.

2.3.11   Investment Choices and Regulation

The 5 percent tier-two PSA accounts would be funded through payroll deductions, half from the employee and half from Social Security as a rebate of the standard FICA tax. Social Security would offer a limited menu of diversified investment options: indexed stock and bond accounts, and one total market account combining stocks and bonds. It is likely that there would be considerable delays in transferring the money into the ultimate investment accounts. The government would pay interest on contributions during the delay period. In addition to the standard government-sponsored investment accounts, individuals could choose to place their money with an approved financial service provider such as Vanguard, Schwab, or Fidelity. All of these providers would be required to offer special investment funds for the PSA accounts. They would be regulated in terms of the information and service that they provided participants and the administrative costs they charged PSA account holders. The maximum administrative cost would be 1 percent per year. We expect that competition would force many vendors to provide investment products with much lower costs than that. Individuals would be required to invest all of their PSA balances with a single approved and regulated vendor, so that there would be a single centralized record keeper, and would be allowed to change vendors on an annual basis. It is possible that employers would be allowed to make direct deposits into their workers' PSA accounts, thus bypassing the need for the money to pass through Social Security's hands.

2.3.12   No Early Withdrawals Permitted

The tier-two PSA program would be an essential part of this particular proposal. No early withdrawals would be permitted from these accounts for any purpose. That means no hardship withdrawals, no withdrawals for down payments on first homes, nor for any other use for the money. The balances could not be used to collateralize loans and could not be touched even in bankruptcy proceedings. Individuals would be apt to accept these restrictions if the rationale for them were explained, namely, that the money is strictly for the purpose of retirement income provision. The 1:1 match also might make the restrictions more acceptable.

2.3.13   The Phase-In

The new program would be phased in extremely gradually. Current retirees and workers aged fifty-five and older in 2000 would be covered under the existing Social Security system. They would be subject to the accelerated increase in the normal retirement age and the change in the tax treatment of benefits. Half the benefits would be taxable income under the new program, rather than the current 85 percent for those with taxable income above $25,000 (single people) or $32,000 (married couples). The net change for those aged fifty-five and over in 2000 would be quite small. The new program would be the only program for those under age twenty-five in 2000. They would have at least forty years to accumulate assets in their 5 percent PSA accounts until becoming eligible for early retirement at age sixty-five in 2040 and beyond. Workers who are between ages twenty-five and fifty-four in 2000 would get some benefits under the new PSA 2000 plan and some under the existing Social Security rules. The fractions would be different for each age cohort. For instance, someone who was forty-five in the year 2000 would get half of the full-career tier-one benefit and half of his or her benefits from the existing primary insurance amount (PIA) formula. Someone closer to age fifty-four would have more of his or her benefits determined the old way, and someone closer to twenty-five would have more of his or her benefits determined by the new PSA 2000 plan. With the phase-in, the DB payments from the existing PIA approach would be essentially unchanged for the first ten years. Then gradually those benefits would be reduced as people began to retire with some of their benefits determined by the new plan. Benefits under the old plan would be essentially completed in seventy-five years, when the twenty-five-year-olds of 2000 hit the century mark.

2.4 Static Macroeconomic Balance

Since one of the first goals of Social Security reform is to restore the solvency of the system, the first test of any proposal is whether it accomplishes this with any degree of certainty. The PSA 2000 plan retains a largely unfunded DB component to the program. Because 2.5 percent of covered payroll is used for the 1:1 matching of the individual contributions, Social Security would have less revenues to work with to meet its DB promises than under current law. Since the proposal calls for a very gradual transition from the existing program to the new one (with everyone over the age of fifty-five retaining their full current benefits), the program's DB expenditures would not be immediately lowered. As the new system matured, current law obligations would diminish. In the very long run, the only DB promises would be the flat tier-one benefits.

The Actuarial Research Corporation (ARC) has made a seventy-five-year forecast of the PSA 2000 plan using the intermediate demographic and economic assumptions of Social Security. We refer to these forecasts as the *static macroeconomic outlook* because they do not take into account the higher productivity growth that should accompany the higher saving resulting from this program, and also from many of the other Social Security proposals. The long-run finances of the system would be more favorable with a dynamic model, perhaps significantly so. We are planning to develop such a model. For now, the direction of the bias of not including such feedback should be noted.

In developing the static projections of the PSA 2000 plan, ARC benchmarked its valuation of this type of plan by doing a seventy-five-year projection of the PSA plan that was developed by the 1994–96 Advisory Council on Social Security. The Office of the Actuary at the Social Security Administration (SSA) also valued this plan. In their work for the Advisory Council, the SSA actuaries had estimated that the PSA plan would restore actuarial balance to the OASDI system by the end of their seventy-five-year projection period. The ARC valuation of the original PSA plan suggests that the PSA proposal, as it was specified by its designers, was significantly underfunded. They estimated that the OASDI trust fund balance at the end of the projection period would be negative, with the aggregate borrowings at the time being about 7.5 years of annual benefit flows. The ARC contends that the Social Security actuaries captured adequately neither the interaction of increases in retirement ages nor the move to lower OASDI benefits in the proposal as the reasons for the difference between the two sets of projections. Social Security's actuaries do not necessarily agree with this assessment and have not conceded any problems with their earlier estimates. The point here is that the ARC valuation of the PSA 2000 proposal is being done with a model that would appear to be giving off very conservative estimates. That is, ARC's estimates make the PSA 2000 proposal look much worse than it would under the methodology used to assess the original proposal. Our analysis of the PSA 2000 plan utilizes ARC's projection of the plan supplemented with data, from the SSA Office of the Actuary, on the accumulations in the individual-account element of the system.

The basic seventy-five-year outlook for the Social Security trust fund under PSA 2000 is shown in figure 2.1. The trust fund and PSA 2000 accumulations are stated as ratios of assets to the total projected DB payments. In the initial years, the DB payments are purely current law benefits. As the transition evolves, the DB payments will increasingly become a blend between accrued benefits under the current system up to the point of transition plus the tier-one flat benefit accrued under the new system as it matures. Toward the end of the projection, the overwhelming majority of the defined benefit will be tier-one benefits paid out of the PSA 2000 system. The lowermost solid line in the figure is the OASDI trust fund balance over the projection period. The dashed line is the accumulations in the PSA accounts each year. The uppermost solid line is the aggregate of the two.

The intermediate-assumptions actuarial forecast for the PSA 2000 trust

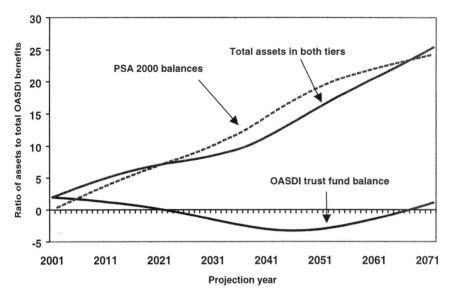

Fig. 2.1   OASDI trust fund ratios, PSA 2000 balances, and total asset levels

fund is that it would end the seventy-five-year period about where it started, with one to two years' worth of DB expenditures in assets. At the end of the seventy-five-year period, all of the current-law obligations would have been honored and the system would be running a substantial surplus. However, the ratio of trust fund assets to program expenditures would fall almost immediately upon the adoption of the PSA 2000 plan and the trust fund would be exhausted by 2022. Under current law, the Social Security trust funds do not have borrowing authority if their balances decline to zero. The projection of the trust fund balances in figure 2.1 portends a problem in that regard under the PSA 2000 proposal. Under the ARC projections, adjusted to account for the added benefits paid through the DI program, the trust funds would have negative balances of about 3.3 years' worth of benefit payments between 2045 and 2050. To deal with this potential some sort of special provisions would have to be made.

The program as a whole, including the second-tier accounts, would continue to be a net supplier of saving during this entire period, because the asset buildup in the PSA 2000 tier-two accounts, also shown in figure 2.1, would be significantly larger than the annual deficits of the DB portion of the program. The asset trajectory shown for the PSA 2000 accounts in figure 2.1 is based on the relatively conservative assumption of a net real annual rate of return of 4.5 percent on the assets in the accounts. This rate of return could be earned even if the PSA 2000 accounts accumulated most (if not all) of the bonds issued by the DB operation during the deficit years.

One conceivable way to handle the prospect that the OASDI system would have to borrow funds for some period of time is to construct a funding mechanism that is internal to the combined structure of the system. For example, over the initial years of the programs' operations, Congress might mandate that some portion of the PSA 2000 accounts must be invested in bonds issued to provide earmarked funding for the OASDI transition borrowing. The borrowing in this case would have to equal the projected trust fund debt associated with the transition to the PSA 2000 plan, plus some additional amount to finance a contingency fund to smooth financing over business cycles.

It is generally accepted that pay-as-you-go governmental retirement systems should maintain a contingency fund of around one year's worth of benefits. Social Security currently has a balance of nearly two years. In order to see how the transition might work under a plan of this type we assume that the OASDI trust fund would maintain roughly its two-year balance as long as the majority of the baby boomers continue to work. Beyond that, we assume it would be spent down to between one and one-and-a-half years' worth of benefits. Using these assumptions, we estimated how much of the PSA balances would be required to cover the transitional borrowing.

The results of our analysis are shown in figure 2.2. In the initial years, 25 percent of the PSA balances would be invested in U.S. government bonds. Starting in 2026, we increase the percentage by 1 point per year,

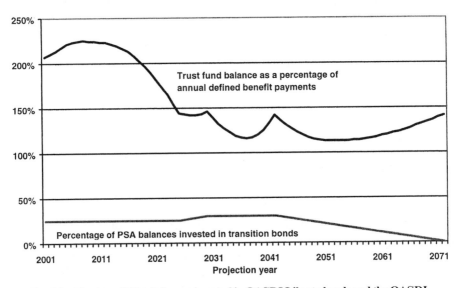

Fig. 2.2   Portion of PSA balances invested in OASDI Liberty bonds and the OASDI trust fund ratios during the full transition to the PSA 2000 plan

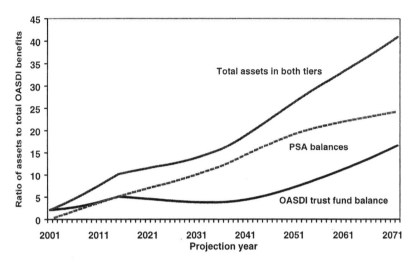

Fig. 2.3   OASDI trust fund ratios, PSA 2000 balances, and total asset levels after transferring 62 percent of the 2000–2014 projected budget surpluses to OASDI

reaching 30 percent in 2030 and holding steady there until 2043, when we begin to reduce the required bond holdings as a percentage of total PSA balances by 1 percent per year. These bonds would be completely paid off in 2070. At that point the trust fund balance would be rising steadily and it would be possible to implement a sizable payroll tax cut.

As a total stand-alone proposal, then, the PSA 2000 plan is balanced over seventy-five years and generates additional saving for the economy for every year in the forecast period. It should be noted that the assumptions behind figures 2.1 and 2.2 do not include using any of the projected federal government surpluses of the next fifteen years. Presumably, those surpluses could then be used for other valuable things such as helping Medicare's finances or permitting tax reductions. During his term, President Clinton indicated that a large fraction of the surpluses should be used to restore the financial stability of Social Security and the Republicans for the most part agreed, we developed an analysis that would dedicate the surplus to the transition to the PSA 2000 plan. We attribute the projected surplus to saving Social Security at exactly the same rate as former President Clinton recommended as estimated by the Social Security actuaries (Goss 1999a).

The results of our analysis are shown in figure 2.3. This figure shows the effect of transferring 62 percent of the 2000–2014 surpluses into the Social Security trust fund and adopting the PSA 2000 plan. Now, under the intermediate assumptions, the trust fund backing the DB promises of the system always retains a sizable positive balance. In fact, the balance between 2015 and 2045 hovers between four and five years' worth of expenditures before rising sharply as the obligations of the current system recede. The total assets in the PSA 2000 accounts and the trust fund reach rather staggering levels by the end of the seventy-five-year forecasting period—i.e., forty years of expenditures. All this indicates is that the PSA 2000 plan with the infusion of surpluses proposed by Clinton is an overfunded package.

Of course, there is no shortage of things to do with the extra cash. If we were truly going to use the budget surpluses to help in the transition funding, figure 2.4 suggests that a payroll tax could be implemented as a means to reduce the cost of the shift to the PSA 2000 plan for workers. The flat line in the figure shows the combined payroll tax rate and PSA contribution to the system without the benefit of the budget surplus financing. The line with three flat steps shows a scenario in which the basic OASDI payroll tax rate is immediately lowered by 0.5 percent because of the beneficial effect of using some of the surplus to support the transition. The rate is lowered by a total of 1.2 percent, relative to current levels, in 2038 and by a total of 2.5 percent in 2055. Since the PSA 2000 plan calls for a mandatory contribution of 2.5 percent of payroll to the tier-two accounts, that contribution would be entirely offset by the permitted payroll tax reduction beginning in 2055. Twenty percent of the contribution would be offset immediately by the 0.5 percent tax reduction. The curved line in the figure shows the cost of the current-law benefits if we attempt to provide them using the current financing mechanism. While the PSA 2000 plan would cost somewhat more in the short term, the long-term cost rates would be sig-

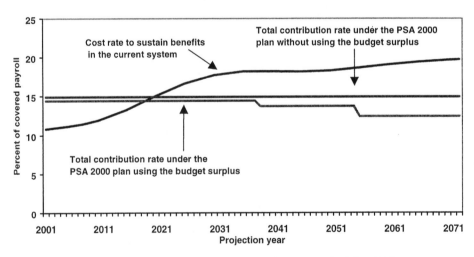

Fig. 2.4   Social Security cost rates and contributions under the PSA 2000 plan with utilization of the federal budget surpluses to help in financing the transition costs

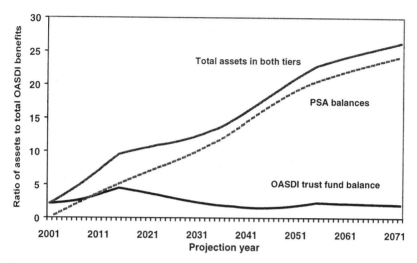

Fig. 2.5   OASDI trust fund ratios, PSA 2000 balances, and total asset levels after transferring 62 percent of budget surpluses to OASDI and reducing contribution rates

nificantly lower than staying the current course. The infusion of budget surpluses along with the series of tax cuts would result in a fairly stable trust fund, as shown in figure 2.5. The trust fund would range roughly between 2.0 and 4.0 years' worth of expenditure, a slightly higher level than the current ratio.

The results in figure 2.4 suggest that over the next twenty years or so, workers would have to contribute at higher rates than under the current system in order to get their benefits under the PSA 2000 plan. The problem with the current system is that it cannot sustain current-law benefit obligations. The 1999 OASDI trustees' report estimated that the seventy-five-year shortfall in the current payroll tax rate was 2.07 percent of covered payroll. That means the current tax rate of 12.4 percent would have to go immediately to 14.47 percent in order to meet the estimated seventy-five-year obligations. However, we know that the 2.07 percent increase in the payroll tax would likely fall short of meeting the long-term obligations of the program some five or ten years into the future. Goss (1999b) has estimated that the payroll tax would have to increase 4.7 percent of covered pay to restore actuarial balance to the system in perpetuity. The flat line in figure 2.4 is at 14.9 percent of covered payroll. If the surplus is used to help cover transition costs to the program, it would bring the total contribution rate down to 14.4 percent of payroll immediately and eventually allow it to return to 12.4 percent. In the next section of this discussion, we show how benefits under the PSA 2000 proposal fare compare to current law.

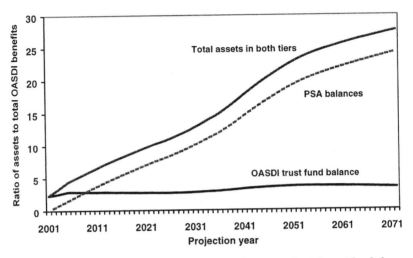

Fig. 2.6   OASDI trust fund ratios, PSA 2000 balances, and total asset levels by using part of the budget surpluses to fund DI maintaining current contribution rates

Using budget surpluses to give contribution relief to workers will preclude using them in some other fashion. Indeed, there may be other elements of Social Security that would potentially benefit from them. In the development of the original PSA plan its advocates proposed that future DI benefits be held at a level supportable by the current cost rate of these benefits stated as a percentage of covered payroll. At this rate, the current benefit structure is underfunded. The PSA proponents, however, felt that it was unfair simply to assume that additional contributions would be directed to DI without some sort of formal review of the plan. The 1994–96 Advisory Council did not undertake such a review. The net result was that the PSA plan would result in the scaling back of future DI benefit levels. This has been one of the major criticisms of the plan (Ball and Bethell 1998; Aaron and Reischauer 1998).

The baseline projections of the PSA 2000 plan also assume that future DI benefits would be financed at the rate legislated by current law. One way the federal budget surplus could be used would be to infuse excess revenues into the DI trust fund to maintain current-law benefits at current-law tax rates. The trust fund projections that would result if this were done without a tax cut are shown in figure 2.6. Over the projection period, the combined OASDI trust funds would gradually rise from their level of two times current benefits to three times annual benefits by the mid-2030s. They are projected to reach 3.6 times annual benefits by 2050 and to decline at a very slight rate beyond the mid-2050s. At the end of the projection period they would still be at about 3.4 times annual benefit levels. We believe the contention of the proponents of the original PSA proposal that DI be reviewed before revenues are added to it merits consideration.

Taken as a whole, the actuarial projections of this section show that the aggregate finances of the PSA 2000 program are feasible without counting on the dynamic gains from the additional saving and without using the projected federal government budget surpluses. Of course, if the surpluses were dedicated to a reformed Social Security program, they would permit other actions such a series of payroll tax cuts or a very substantial improvement in the finances of the disability program. Naturally, any combination of these two possibilities could be pursued.

2.5 Individual Choice and Individual Risk with Partial Privatization

In this section, we examine the choices and risks that individuals would face under a Social Security reform along the lines of the PSA 2000 plan. The outcomes are calculated under a very limited set of asset choices. We presume that the actual menu of options would be larger than those examined here. The two asset classes we consider are zero-coupon inflation-indexed government bonds and an S&P 500 index fund. We assume that the government would offer a full array of maturities of zero coupon inflation-indexed bonds. This would allow people to purchase bonds with different maturities at different points in their career, each of which matures upon retirement or upon the anticipated withdrawal date. The government or private investment companies could offer a simple program of lifecycle acquisition of inflation-indexed bonds. This would provide participants an extremely safe wealth accumulation vehicle. The other asset, the S&P 500 index fund, is examined here because of the availability of data regarding the returns on the S&P 500. Index funds have the appeal of low asset-management expenses. From a pure diversification point of view, a better offering for the actual implementation of a PSA 2000 plan would be a total market index fund that included the stocks of small capitalization and perhaps foreign companies. The S&P 500 index fund, however, will be used here to gauge the riskiness of stock accumulation in individual accounts.

We examine the outcomes for someone who is twenty-three years old in 2000 and who participates in the PSA 2000 plan for his or her entire career. The individual is assumed to work for forty-five years, retiring in 2045 at the age of sixty-eight. It is assumed that the normal retirement age has advanced to sixty-eight by 2045. The general real wage level is presumed to improve at the rate of 1 percent per year. The real wages of individual workers rise at the rate of 2 percent per year due to the accumulation of seniority and human capital. The inflation-indexed bonds are assumed to yield a real return of 3.8 percent (consistent with the returns on existing inflation-indexed coupon bonds) at all maturities. The gross real returns on the S&P 500 index fund are determined from the actual 1926–97 observations chosen in three-year blocks according to a bootstrap statistical technique. For each forty-five-year career, fifteen dates are chosen between

1926 and 1995 (with replacement, so that the same date can be chosen more than once). From these fifteen dates that each mark the first year of a three-year block of returns, we create a simulated sequence of forty-five years of real gross returns. With this procedure, we generate 10,000 sequences of stock returns for each case examined in the paper. Both stock and bond returns are reduced by 30 basis points per year to account for the costs of managing the individual accounts. This charge for 5 percent accounts is consistent with the recent estimates of Schieber and Shoven (2000), James et al. (2000), and Goldberg and Graetz (2000).

Figure 2.7 shows a simulation of the outcomes that this cohort of 2000–2045 workers would face if they chose to invest all of the money in their individual accounts in zero-coupon inflation-indexed government bonds. The assumed one percent per year growth in average covered wages means that the tier-one benefit becomes $782.40 per month (in year-2000 dollars) by 2045. Of course, the entire PIA formula is also adjusted for the growth in average real wages. The tier-two benefits are proportional to contributions. The nonlinearity in the graph for people with high average indexed monthly earnings (AIME) is due to the interaction of the ceiling imposed on covered earnings and the fact that the AIME counts only the highest thirty-five years of earnings. Consider someone who has thirty-four years

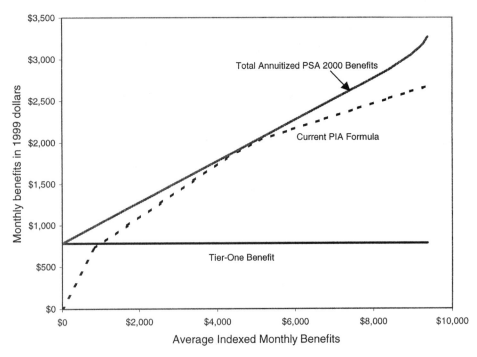

Fig. 2.7   **Monthly benefits with 100 percent inflation-indexed bonds**

of earnings at or above the cap and someone else who has thirty-five years at or above it. With our assumed smooth forty-five-year earnings histories, these two individuals will have very similar AIMEs. However, the person with thirty-five years at the cap will have eleven years of larger contributions to their tier-two account than will the person with thirty-four cap years (because of the assumed forty-five-year work career). The result is that the PSA 2000 benefits appear slightly convex when charted against AIME.

As can be seen in the figure 2.7, the PSA 2000 program would offer safe benefits at least as high as current benefits for all participants with full-length careers who choose to invest their individual accounts in safe inflation-indexed government bonds and who choose to annuitize their entire accumulation. We did not model the annuitization process in great detail. Instead we assumed a very high gender-blended life expectancy at sixty-eight in 2045 of twenty years and priced the annuities fairly for that life expectancy. In reality, life expectancy is not likely to have progressed that much by 2045. However, the conversion to annuities will not be cost-less as modeled here. We think that our overall results are reasonable predictions of the likely outcome of annuitized benefits. The results of figure 2.7 are for single individuals. Under the PSA 2000 proposal, the vast majority of married couples would receive benefits as if they were two single individuals.

Presumably most people would invest their tier-two PSA 2000 individual accounts in a diversified portfolio of stocks and bonds rather than in the all-bonds portfolio just examined. Figure 2.8 shows the outcomes for someone who consistently chooses to invest half of his or her individual account money in zero-coupon inflation-indexed bonds and half in the S&P 500 index fund. Note that the average outcome is significantly higher than current benefits for all levels of average indexed monthly earnings. The 25th percentile outcomes are also noticeably better than current benefits. The 5th percentile outcome crosses the current PIA formula at about $3,250 per month and again at about $7,000 per month, with both amounts in year-2000 dollars. That means that those whose average indexed annual earnings were between $42,250 and $84,000 would have a one in twenty chance of receiving less under the PSA 2000 plan than under current law. The poor, who benefit relatively more from the flat tier-one benefit, would enjoy higher benefits with the PSA 2000 plan with a very high degree of certainty.

Figure 2.9 charts the outcomes for people who invest their entire individual account balances in the S&P 500 index fund. Presumably, such people are less risk averse than most. On average, they do extremely well. For someone retiring in 2045 with an AIME of $5,000, the mean PSA 2000 outcome would be about 2.5 times current benefits if all of the money had always been invested in stocks and if stock returns are generated by

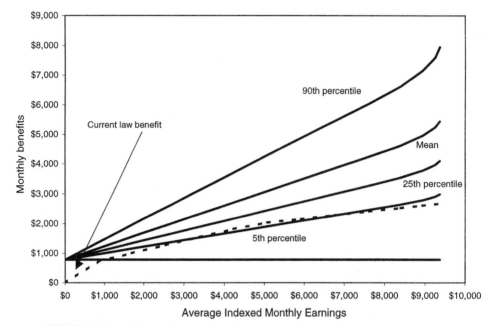

Fig. 2.8   Monthly benefits with 50-50 stocks and inflation-indexed bonds

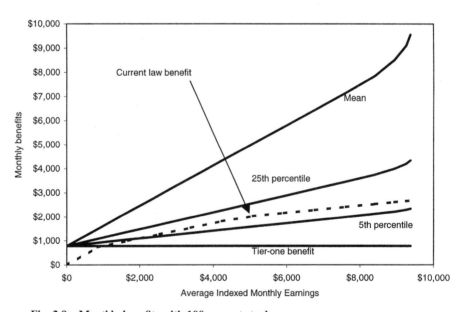

Fig. 2.9   Monthly benefits with 100 percent stocks

the bootstrap procedure just described. However, stocks are quite risky in the sense that the level of benefits under the PSA 2000 plan would be highly uncertain for people who put all of their individual account assets in the stock market. The 90th percentile outcome was so high that we couldn't include it on the chart without compressing the scale to an undesirable degree. The 25th percentile outcome is always at least 25 percent greater than current-law benefits. However, the 5th percentile outcome is as much as 20 percent less than current benefits. That means that there is a one in twenty chance that the PSA 2000 plan would leave an individual with less than 80 percent of current-law benefits if he or she invested 100 percent of the funds in his or her individual account in common stocks. The flat tier-one benefit helps reduce the overall riskiness of the plan however, particularly for low-income individuals. In fact, those whose AIME is less than $2,000 are better off with the PSA 2000 plan even if they invest all of their funds in stocks and have the bad fortune to end up with the 5th percentile outcome.

So far we have concentrated on hypothetical smooth income paths in evaluating this particular Social Security reform proposal. Of course, people face uncertainty about their labor income as well as about the return on their financial investments. Next, we evaluate how the PSA 2000 plan compares to the present Social Security system for individuals facing labor income uncertainty. The process of real labor income growth is now taken as

$$\omega(t) = 1 + \overline{\omega} + \sigma_u u(t) + \sigma_e [e(t) - e(t-1)],$$

where $\omega(t)$ is the growth rate of labor income between t and $t + 1$, ω is the average individual wage growth rate (set 1 percent above the aggregate wage growth rate for seniority reasons), and $u(t)$ and $e(t)$ are standard normal random variables (zero mean and a standard deviation of one). σ_u is interpreted as the standard deviation of the permanent shocks on the *level* of labor income, while σ_e is the standard deviation of the transitory shock (again on the level of income). This specification is a simplification of the treatment in Campbell et al. (2000). We set ω at 0.02 and obtain the magnitudes of σ_u and σ_e from Campbell et al. We separately evaluate high school graduates and college graduates. The specification for the σ_u and σ_e pair of parameters is $(0.103, 0.272)$ for high school graduates and $(0.130, 0.242)$ for college graduates. These imply that labor income is actually quite volatile.

Figure 2.10 shows the ratio of total PSA 2000 benefits to current-law benefits for college graduates who would participate in the new plan for their full careers if it were adopted. Figure 2.10 shows this ratio for those who invest solely in inflation-indexed bonds. The results for high school graduates are very similar, so much so that it is not worth showing them

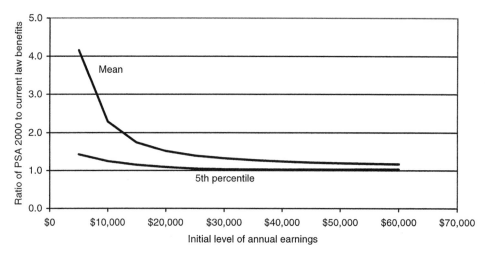

Fig. 2.10   Ratio of PSA 2000 benefits to current-law benefits for college graduates with uncertain labor earnings

separately. What the figure shows is that the benefits of the new program would be at least as great as current benefits with a high degree of certainty if the individual accounts were invested in inflation-indexed bonds.

Figure 2.11 shows the same type of information for college graduates who dedicate half of their contributions to stocks and half to indexed bonds. While this diversified investor can end up with less than current-law benefits, we had to go to the 1st percentile outcome to get this outcome. Investors who choose to invest in 100 percent stocks (not shown in the figure), of course, take more risks. For them, the 5th percentile outcome (in terms of these ratios) can be a 10 percent loss and the 1st percentile outcome is roughly a 20 percent loss relative to current-law benefits.

The final thing we look at in terms of how individuals would fare with the implementation of the PSA 2000 plan is how someone would do if he or she were in mid-career when the plan was adopted. We return to the case of smoothly rising wages and examine the outcome for someone who is forty-five years old in the year 2000 when the plan is hypothetically put into effect. This forty-five-year-old is assumed to work until 2022 when he or she retires at the then-normal retirement age of sixty-seven. This person will receive half of his or her current PIA benefits, half of his or her tier-one flat benefit, and the annuitized proceeds of his or her tier-two account. Figure 2.12 shows the person's outcomes under the reformed Social Security plan and his or her outcomes with current-law benefits. The assumption of this figure is that all of the tier-two investments are inflation-indexed bonds.

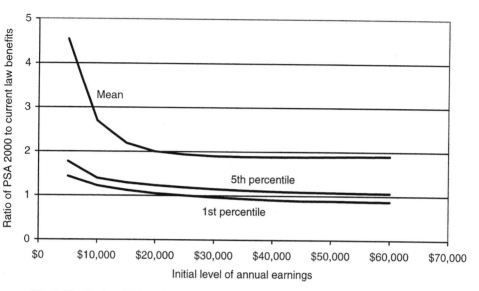

Fig. 2.11 Ratio of PSA 2000 benefits to current-law benefits for 50-50 investors with a college education and uncertain labor earnings

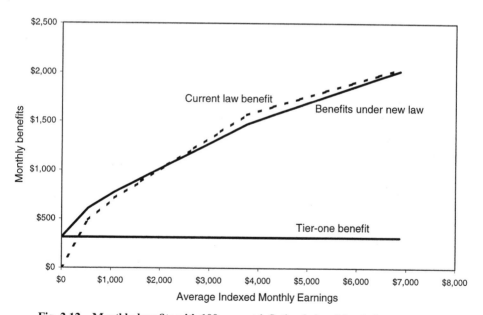

Fig. 2.12 Monthly benefits with 100 percent inflation-indexed bonds for someone aged forty-five

2.5.1   At the Time of the Reform

This person who was in mid-career at the time of the reform may get less under the reformed plan than with the current benefit structure. The reason that the mid-career individual does not do as well as those at the beginning of their careers at the time of the introduction of the new policy is that the contributions from the second half of a career are less valuable at the time of retirement than those from the first half. The transition plan of the PSA 2000 plan could be modified to phase out current benefits more slowly. For instance, this person who was forty-five when the new plan was introduced would be able to match current-law benefits if he or she qualified for 55 percent of current-law benefits rather than the 50 percent specified by the plan. This slower transition would, of course, cost more money; perhaps it is another use for the projected federal government surpluses.

Figure 2.13 shows how this same forty-five-year-old would do if he or she qualified for only 50 percent of current-law benefits and invested his or her tier-two funds 50-50 in stocks and bonds. The dotted line represents current-law benefits (the PIA formula). Also shown are the 90th percentile outcome, the mean outcome, the 25th percentile outcome, and the 5th percentile outcome. Since this person is going to get half of the PIA benefit

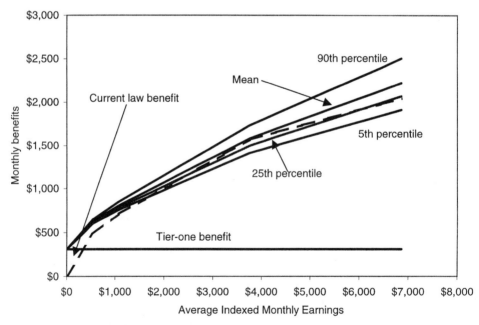

Fig. 2.13   Monthly benefits with 50-50 stocks and inflation-indexed bonds for someone aged forty-five at the time of the reform
Note: Dotted line represents benefits of the present Social Security program.

and half of the full tier-one benefit, the outcome is not as sensitive to financial market outcomes. Both the mean outcome and the 25th percentile outcomes for the individual accounts lead to total benefits closely approximating current-law benefits. The 5th percentile outcome can be approximately 10 percent less than current benefits. Of course, this 50-50 investor would also benefit if the phase-out of current law benefits were slightly slowed to reflect the fact that persons with half of their careers remaining would not be able to accumulate individual accounts half the size of full-career ones.

Our overall interpretation of the results of this section is that the PSA 2000 plan allows risk-averse individuals to retain benefits at least as high as current-law benefits. Those who choose to take the risks inherent in stocks bear some chance of having to live on lower than current-law benefits in retirement. These risks are modest, however, and the poor are significantly protected by the presence of the tier-one benefits.

2.6   Conclusions

The purpose of this paper has been to assess the riskiness of a partial privatization plan and to check how it performs with respect to the set of principles laid out in section 2.2. The main topic has been the risk evaluation. We have described a particular partial privatization plan, one that relies more heavily on individual accounts than do most proposals, and evaluated its overall actuarial soundness and the outcomes that individuals would face if it were adopted. The plan passes the actuarial soundness test and would permit individuals to enjoy safe benefits approximately equal to current-law benefits if U.S. government inflation-indexed bonds were offered and invested in. If participants invested their tier-two accounts in common stocks, they would face a small probability of having significantly less in retirement than current-law benefits. However, these risks are reduced by the presence of the flat tier-one benefits. This first tier is relatively more important for low-income households; who would enjoy benefits at least as great as current benefits with a high degree of certainty.

It is not surprising that the PSA 2000 plan performs well with respect to the principles of section 2.2. That is because these principles provided the design guidelines for the plan in the first place. To summarize briefly, the first-tier defined benefit feature provides an important safety net against poor investment returns and permits the retention of the basic progressive structure of the current program (Principle 1). A primary feature of the program is the mandatory contribution of 2.5 percent of covered payroll. While these additional contributions would be partially offset by actions of individuals, there would certainly be a significant net increase in national saving (Principle 2). The disability and early survivor programs would be retained, and if the same proportion of the projected federal government surpluses as suggested by the Clinton administration were allocated to the program, there would be enough money to cover the long-run deficit of the disability program (Principle 3). Under all of the scenarios we have examined, the PSA 2000 plan would be in balance or surplus after seventy-five years and would offer the prospects of payroll tax reductions (Principle 4). Most retiring couples would be treated as two single individuals, thereby improving the equity between these participant classes (Principle 5). The tier-two contributions and payouts would be directly connected. In fact, the tax element of payroll deductions would be reduced by the 2.5 percent rebate in the form of a 1:1 match of tier-two contributions (Principle 6). We have examined the risks borne by individuals and judge them to be tolerable. In particular, the amount of risk one bears would be a matter of personal choice. Further, the risks are least for low-income households (Principle 7). We have written elsewhere about administrative costs. Here we note simply that the PSA 2000 plan has relatively low administrative costs partly, because it has relatively large (5 percent) individual accounts (Principle 8). We cannot control when Social Security will be reformed. However, there is nothing in the PSA 2000 plan that would delay implementation seriously.

In this paper, we are not advocating the particulars of the PSA 2000 plan. We are advocating that the riskiness of all serious proposals be evaluated in a manner similar to what we have done here. What is heartening about our findings is that a plan that relies heavily on individual accounts can still be relatively safe for individual participants.

References

Aaron, Henry J., Barry P. Bosworth, and Gary Burtless. 1989. *Can America afford to grow old? Paying for Social Security.* Washington, D.C.: The Brookings Institution.

Aaron, Henry J., and Robert D. Reischauer. 1998. *Countdown to reform: The great Social Security debate.* New York: The Century Foundation Press.

Advisory Council on Social Security. 1997. *Report of the 1994–96 Advisory Council on Social Security.* Vol. 1, *Findings and recommendations.* Washington, D.C.: GPO.

Ball, Robert M., and Thomas N. Bethell. 1998. *Straight talk about Social Security.* New York: A Century Foundation/Twentieth Century Fund.

Campbell, John Y., João F. Cocco, Francisco J. Gomes, and Pascal J. Maenhout. 2001. Investing retirement wealth: A lifecycle model. Paper prepared for the NBER Conference on Risk Aspects of Investment-Based Social Security Reform. 15–16 January, Cheeca Lodge, Fla.

Goldberg, Fred T., Jr., and Michael J. Graetz. 2000. Reforming Social Security: How to implement a practical and workable system of personal retirement accounts. In *Administrative costs and Social Security privatization,* ed. John B. Shoven. 9–40. Chicago: University of Chicago Press.

Goss, Steven C. 1999a. Long-range OASDI financial effects of the president's proposal for strengthening Social Security—INFORMATION. Memorandum to Harry C. Ballantyne, Chief Actuary, Social Security Administration. January 26.

———. 1999b. Measuring solvency in the Social Security system. In *Prospects for Social Security reform,* ed. Olivia S. Mitchell, Robert J. Myers, and Howard Young, 16–36. Philadelphia: University of Pennsylvania Press.

James, Estelle, Gary Ferrier, James Smalhout, and Dimitri Vittas. 2000. Mutual funds and institutional investments: What is the most efficient way to set up individual accounts in a Social Security system? In *Administrative costs and Social Security privatization,* ed. John B. Shoven, 77–136. Chicago: University of Chicago Press.

Schieber, Sylvester J., and John B. Shoven. 1999. *The real deal: The history and future of Social Security.* New Haven: Yale University Press.

———. 2000. Administering a cost effective national program of personal security accounts. In *Administrative costs and Social Security privatization,* ed. John B. Shoven, 41–76. Chicago: University of Chicago Press.

Comments   Steven F. Venti

In the last three years no fewer than a dozen proposals have been offered to resolve the funding problems of the Social Security system. Most of these proposals include privately held individual accounts, although the details vary widely among plans. The Personal Security Account 2000 plan (PSA 2000) is one of the first (derived from the report of the 1994–96 Advisory Council on Social Security), one of the more widely known, and one of the more far-reaching of these proposals. Most of the plans incorporating individual accounts that have been advanced restore long-term balance to the system. All proposals help prefund the system. Many of these plans also increase benefits paid relative to current law in most future states of the world. Other benefits of individual accounts have been touted as well, including promoting personal responsibility, increasing awareness of the need to provide for retirement, and increased national saving and economic performance. Why has the public been so slow to embrace individual account plans?

There are several obstacles to public acceptance. The first is that many of the benefits of a privatized system of personal accounts may also be available through a variety of public sector arrangements. A second obstacle concerns the ability of an individual accounts system to maintain and protect the level of redistribution contained in the present system (I will say a few words about this problem at the end of this comment). A third obstacle, which is the primary focus of this paper, is the perceived risk associated with individual accounts. It is alleged that these accounts ex-

Steven F. Venti is professor of economics at Dartmouth College and a research associate of the National Bureau of Economic Research.

pose participants to more risk—or at least to risk of a different sort—than the present system does. This aspect of Social Security reform mirrors the ongoing debate between the merits of defined benefit (DB) and defined contribution (DC) pensions in the private sector. How risky are DC-type plans? The goal of this paper is to develop a framework for assessing the consequences of investment risk and to apply this framework to the PSA 2000.

Before turning to this framework, it is useful to highlight a few details of the PSA 2000. Unlike most other individual account proposals, the PSA 2000 fundamentally changes the Social Security system. It is neither an add-on to the existing system nor an alternative way of funding the current benefit structure. After a lengthy forty-year transition period, retirees will receive an inflation-indexed flat benefit and an annuity from an IRA-like account. Like all proposals, the PSA 2000 must somehow pay for transition costs. It does so by effectively raising the tax rate to 14.9 percent, although the authors would argue that the 5 percent of payroll deposited in the PSA is not a tax since the employee retains control over the investment. The remaining 9.9 percent covers existing obligations as they are phased out and the flat benefit that is phased in over the transition period. In the steady-state, the tax rate will be reduced to the level required to fund the flat benefit and a little more than a one-year reserve. Note that the usual transition cost problem—paying for the retirement benefits of two generations—is a less serious problem for the PSA 2000 because it never becomes fully funded.

The evaluation framework involves simulating benefit outcomes for representative individuals with different earnings histories and one of three investment choices: 100 percent indexed bonds, 100 percent equities, and a 50-50 mix. Uncertain asset returns are bootstrapped from historical distributions using three-year blocks. On average, the PSA benefit dominates the current-law benefit at all levels of earnings and for all portfolio choices (more than double in some cases). However, in some states of the world the PSA benefits fall below existing law payouts. For example, a person with average indexed monthly earnings of $5,000 would have a one in twenty chance of faring worse under the 50-50 PSA. The probability is somewhere in the neighborhood of 10 percent for the 100 percent equity case.

How should we expect most potential recipients to respond to the risks associated with the PSA 2000? The choice between current-law benefits and the PSA 2000 can be summarized as follows: There exists a safe asset that provides a rate of return B. A risky asset with the following distribution of returns is introduced. It yields more than $0.8B$ with a probability of .95, more than B with a probability of .9, more than $1.25B$ with probability .75, and more than $2B$ with a probability of .5. Moreover, losses are bounded from below (at $0.5B$) by the flat benefit. If faced with an all-or-nothing choice, most economists would probably jump at the chance to buy the risky asset. Yet, as the equity premium has taught us, the behavior of real people is not quite so easy to predict. When faced with the choice between Social Security plans, many people have (or behave as if they have) a zero tolerance for risk. Just the whiff of a bad outcome—benefits below the currently legislated level—is enough to scare them off. If this is so, there are some deeper questions about whether such behavior is fully informed, whether people correctly assess low-probability events, or even whether choices are rational. In any case, it is my sense that perceptions of bad retirement scenarios will remain an obstacle to acceptance of the PSA 2000 (although it is not an issue with some other individual account proposals). The burden is on the authors to educate people about the probability distributions of both good and bad outcomes, and the framework developed here is an important step in that direction.

There are a couple of additional issues that may marginally affect the benefit projections (and these may be addressed in the more detailed account of the PSA in Schieber and Shoven 2000). First, the simulations assume that administrative fees are a modest 30 basis points. This is a reasonable assumption for large indexed accounts. However, during the phase-in period, older cohorts will retire with only a few years of PSA contributions. Given the high fixed costs of servicing accounts, private firms may be reluctant to deal with these persons and, if they do, the costs of servicing these accounts may be quite high relative to the accumulation. Second, the PSA 2000 requires beneficiaries to annuitize one-half of their PSA balances at retirement. Disposition of the other half is at the recipient's discretion. The authors assume that the discretionary component can be annuitized at the same rate as the mandatory component. With the possibility of opt-outs, costless conversion to a fair annuity may be overly optimistic.

In addition to the investment risk addressed above, there are other kinds of risk associated with individual account arrangements. The PSA 2000 reduces the risk that political forces will change future benefit levels. However, unlike the current system, the PSA 2000 allows persons to harm themselves by making bad decisions. Thus some sort of education effort or safeguards are necessary to minimize this kind of risk. The most obvious have already been addressed: The system must be mandatory, preretirement withdrawals must be prohibited, and fund providers must meet some minimum regulations. However, persons can also harm themselves in many other ways: by making bad investment choices, by failing to draw down equity holdings gradually prior to withdrawal or annuitization, by falling for pension scams (as in the United Kingdom). It seems clear that PSA 2000 would need to be accompanied by a massive educational effort after its introduction.

Nor is the PSA 2000 likely to win political favor among persons intent on preserving the redistribution inherent in the existing system. The current system is based on a single formula that provides substantial assistance to low earners and a modest "pension" benefit to others. The PSA 2000 decouples the redistributive and nonredistributive components. The social assistance or safety net component is explicit. The pension is explicit. Each is subject to separate political bargaining. The PSA 2000 setup may make it more difficult to protect the tier-one benefit later on. Future decisions—should we increase the "base" or the "supplement"?—may erode the "insurance" component of the program over time. Certainly, when the market is booming and future retirees project high benefits from the tier-two component, there will be political pressure to lower the base.

Putting Social Security back on track will be one of the most important political and economic decisions the country will make in the next few years. The authors should be commended for their innovative long-term solution. There are a number of reasons why the PSA 2000 has not yet been more widely embraced by the public, yet my sense is that many of the objections are based more on perception than reality. Thus, providing as much information to the public as is possible about the distribution of outcomes under alternative reform proposals is critical for reform to be successful. Further analyses along the lines of this paper are a start in this direction.

References

Advisory Council on Social Security. 1997. *Report of the 1994–96 Advisory Council on Social Security.* Vol. 7, *Findings and recommendations.* Washington, D.C.: GPO.
Schieber, Sylvester J., and John B. Shoven. 2000. Administering a cost effective national program of personal security accounts. In *Administrative costs and Social Security privatization,* ed. John B. Shoven, 41–76. Chicago: University of Chicago Press.

3

Are the Elderly Really Over-Annuitized?
New Evidence on Life Insurance and Bequests

Jeffrey R. Brown

3.1 Introduction

It is well established in the economics literature that annuities ought to be of substantial value to life-cycle consumers who face an uncertain date of death. Yaari (1965) proved that a life-cycle consumer with an uncertain lifetime and no bequest motives would find 100 percent annuitization the optimal investment. More recent work has quantified the potential utility gains to such a life-cycle consumer. For example, a sixty-five-year-old male life-cycle consumer would be willing to give up nearly one-third of his wealth to gain access to an actuarially fair market for annuities (Mitchell et al. 1999).

Buying a life insurance contract is analogous to selling an annuity. Life insurance is generally viewed as an appropriate product for working-age individuals who seek to protect their families against the loss of future labor earnings (Lewis 1989). However, it appears to serve little purpose in the portfolio of a retired life-cycle consumer whose sole concern is self-financing retirement out of his or her accumulated wealth. With no labor earnings to insure, an elderly individual should be purchasing annuities in order to provide a certain consumption stream in retirement, not selling annuities through the purchase of life insurance. Even if the individual

Jeffrey R. Brown is assistant professor of public policy at the John F. Kennedy School of Government at Harvard University, and a faculty research fellow of the National Bureau of Economic Research.

For helpful comments and discussions, I wish to thank Anne Case, Courtney Coile, Peter Diamond, Jon Gruber, Jerry Hausman, Jim Poterba, Harvey Rosen, Scott Weisbenner, participants in the MIT Public Finance lunch, and participants in the NBER Aging Conference. The author gratefully acknowledges the financial support of the NBER and NIA aging Fellowship and the National Science Foundation.

wishes to leave a portion of wealth to his or her heirs in the form of gifts or bequests, this can be achieved by investing this portion of wealth in ordinary bonds or other non-annuitized assets. In fact, if life insurance premiums were higher than actuarially fair, holding riskless bonds would dominate life insurance as a form of wealth transfer.

Yet elderly households in the United States overwhelmingly hold life insurance, while only a small fraction hold privately purchased annuity contracts. In the Asset and Health Dynamics among the Oldest Old (AHEAD) survey, which consists of households aged seventy and older, privately purchased annuity contracts (excluding private pensions) are held by fewer than 8 percent of couples, while 78 percent of couples age seventy and older own a life insurance policy on at least one member. According to the Life Insurance Ownership Study (Life Insurance Market Research Association [LIMRA] 1993), ownership of individual (non-group) life insurance policies is actually higher among the group aged sixty-five and older than any other age cohort. While this difference is offset by much lower coverage by group (usually employer-based) policies, the overall incidence of coverage among the elderly is quite high by any measure.

Two major alternative hypotheses have been explored in the literature to explain the patterns of life insurance coverage among the elderly. Auerbach and Kotlikoff (1987, 1989) explored the idea that married couples use life insurance to reallocate annuity streams across survival states of the couple. However, they found virtually no support for the notion that older households were using life insurance to protect potential widows and widowers against severe drops in living standards upon the death of the other spouse.

The second hypothesis, suggested by Bernheim (1991), is that life insurance is being held by elderly households to offset an excessive level of mandated annuitization in the form of Social Security. He estimates that 25 percent of elderly households have too much of their wealth annuitized and that they are using term life insurance to sell these annuities in order to leave a bequest. To the extent that this "annuity offset model" is true, it has at least two important implications. First, this would be indicative of very strong bequest motives, which is an issue of perennial controversy in the economics literature (e.g., Kotlikoff and Summers 1981; Modigliani 1988; Hurd 1987; Laitner and Juster 1996). Second, if individuals are over-annuitized due to these strong bequest motives, this would indicate a potential welfare gain from lessening the extent of the mandated annuitization. This is potentially important in the debate about whether individuals would be required to annuitize individual account accumulations as part of a reformed Social Security system. If a significant fraction of households are over-annuitized, allowing individuals some discretion over the disposition of the assets in their individual accounts could be welfare enhancing.

This paper reexamines the annuity offset model using more recent and better data than were available for the original empirical tests. The four empirical implications of the model that this paper tests are (1) that no individual would hold both term life insurance and private annuities, (2) that the level of Social Security benefits and term life insurance ownership should be negatively correlated, (3) that term life insurance should behave as an inferior good because it is a negative annuity and annuities are normal goods, and (4) that individuals who hold term life insurance must have a Social Security benefit in excess of desired retirement consumption. These implications will be explained in more detail in the next section. This paper presents results that are inconsistent with all four of these empirical implications, and thus concludes that life insurance coverage is *not* a good indicator of the extent of over-annuitization.

This paper proceeds as follows: Section 3.2 summarizes the annuity offset model as posited by Bernheim (1991), and outlines the empirical implications of the model to be tested. Section 3.3 presents and critiques the empirical results from the previous literature, with particular attention on the distinction between types of life insurance. Section 3.4 discusses the data used in this paper, from the AHEAD study. Section 3.5 presents empirical results. Section 3.6 discusses some alternative explanations for life insurance holdings among the elderly, and section 3.7 concludes.

3.2   The Annuity Offset Model of Life Insurance Demand

The basic insight behind of the annuity offset model of life insurance demand is that individuals can purchase term life insurance in order to sell a government mandated annuity. Bernheim suggests a simple two-period model that demonstrates this point. Assume that an individual possesses total wealth W_0, which the individual is able to divide between two types of investments. It is assumed that the investment decision is taking place after consumption in period 0 has already occurred. The first type of asset, A, is a life-contingent annuity contract that yields a return of α in period 1 if the individual is alive, and 0 otherwise. The second type of asset, B, is a traditional (bequeathable) financial asset that yields a return of β in period 1 regardless of whether the individual is alive. If the individual lives, his or her period 1 resources are $W_1 = \alpha A + \beta B$. If the individual dies, his or her heirs receive βB. Because actuarially fair annuities pay a "mortality premium" equal to the probability of dying, $\alpha > \beta$. Utility of the individual is assumed to be a function of total resources and bequeathable resources in period 1, $U = U(B, W_1)$. Call A^* and B^* the quantities of the two assets that correspond to the optimal division of total wealth, subject to the constraint that $W_0 = A + B$.

Now suppose the government confiscates A^g in period 0 and returns αA^g in period 1, conditional on the individual's survival. In other words, the government mandates a minimum level of annuitization. If $A^g < A^*$, then the individual simply decreases his or her private purchase of annuities by an amount equal to A^g, or alternatively, the individual buys private annuities in the amount of $A^* - A^g$. If $A^g > A^*$, then the individual wishes to sell annuities. This can be done through the purchase of a term life insurance contract. When markets for annuities and life insurance are actuarially fair, then the government mandate has no effect on the individual's division of wealth between A and B. Private insurance contracts offset the government annuity dollar for dollar. If insurance is not actuarially fair, then the offset is less than dollar for dollar, but the basic story is unchanged. Individuals who wish to hold more annuities than the government mandates will own private annuity contracts. Individuals who wish to hold less in annuities will own private life insurance contracts. No individual will hold both private annuities and life insurance, since they are offsetting transactions, each with a positive load factor. Some individuals will hold neither, if A^g is sufficiently close to A^*.

There are four major empirical implications that must hold if the annuity offset model is the reason that the elderly hold life insurance. These are as follows.

1. *No individual will hold both private annuities and private term life insurance contracts.* Given the existence of significant load factors in annuity markets (Mitchell et al. 1999), no one would rationally purchase annuities above the actuarial cost only to sell them back below the actuarial cost.

2. *An increase in the level of the mandated annuity will increase the demand for term life insurance.* Recall that an individual will hold term life insurance in the amount of max$\{0, A^g - A^*\}$. Holding W_0 fixed, an increase in A^g will increase the total amount of life insurance coverage among those who already hold it. It will also cause some individuals who did not hold life insurance before to purchase it.

3. *Term life insurance will behave as an inferior good.* If B and W_1 are normal goods, then an increase in the individual's total resources will increase the demand for annuities. This is because a person with more resources will wish to buy more annuities in order to increase retirement consumption. Since term life insurance is a negative annuity, an increase in the demand for annuities corresponds to a decrease in the demand for term life insurance. Therefore, term life insurance will decline with total resources, and thus behave as an inferior good.

4. *The Social Security annuity income flow must exceed consumption for life insurance owners.* If an individual is over-annuitized due to bequest motives, it must be because his or her desired consumption is less than the annuity income from Social Security. So long as optimal consumption exceeds the level of the Social Security benefit, there is no need to offset Social Security. Rather, one would want to supplement Social Security through the purchase of private annuities. An equivalent way to state this

implication is that an individual who purchases life insurance to offset an annuity will not consume out of his or her non–Social Security resources. The individual will save these resources for bequests, and will in fact supplement this bequest with the term life insurance.

It should be noted some of the reasons an individual might be over-annuitized have nothing to do with bequest motives. Hurd (1987) points out that when an individual's optimal consumption path is constrained by an exogenously given annuity stream, he or she may be willing to give up annuitization at an actuarially fair rate in order to loosen this liquidity constraint. This is especially likely if the individual has little nonannuitized wealth. However, over-annuitization in this case is driven by a desire to reallocate consumption across one's lifetime, not to reallocate between consumption and bequests. Another example is the case in which an individual wishes to hold a buffer stock of assets to cover unforeseen expenditure shocks (e.g., health expenditures). In such a situation, the individual may wish to hold some of his or her wealth in a nonannuitized form. Once again, the role of the nonannuitized wealth in this case is still to provide for own consumption, not to leave a bequest to one's heirs. In this case, the way to undo the excessive annuitization, however, is not to purchase life insurance, since these proceeds will be unavailable for future consumption. Rather, the individual would wish to purchase insurance against the risky future event (e.g., health insurance) or alter his or her saving behavior in order to provide for a buffer stock. The tests that I propose in this paper are meant to test for over-annuitization that derives from bequest motives, not these other factors.

3.3 Discussion of Previous Empirical Results and Data Contamination

Bernheim tested the first three implications of the annuity offset model using the 1975 cross-section of the Retirement History Survey (RHS), and found support for two of them. The most robust finding was that higher Social Security benefits were correlated both with a higher probability of owning life insurance, and with the amount of coverage conditional on owning a policy. His interpretation of this finding is that individuals are using the life insurance to offset excessive levels of Social Security. He also found some evidence to suggest that life insurance coverage was a decreasing function of lifetime resources, which is consistent with the "inferior good" implication, though this finding was not robust across specifications.

The first implication, that no person would hold both life insurance and annuities, was clearly at odds with the data, because 36 percent of the RHS sample reported both in-force life insurance holdings and the receipt of pension annuities. He attributes this latter result to data contamination, namely, the fact that there is no way in the RHS to distinguish whole from term life insurance. Because much of Bernheim's analysis was focused on trying to overcome this data handicap, it is useful to discuss the types of life insurance in more detail.

3.3.1   Term versus Whole Life Insurance

The distinction between term and whole life insurance is quite important to the annuity offset model. The difference between the two policy types is quite simple, but has important economic implications. Term life insurance contracts provide insurance protection for a specified limited period. The face amount of the policy is payable to the beneficiaries only if the insured dies within the term specified. Common term periods include one-year, five-year, ten-year, and twenty-year. Most term policies have options allowing an individual to guarantee renewability at the end of the term specified. This means that an individual is not at risk for losing coverage if he or she is diagnosed with a serious health problem, so long as he or she pays the contract premium. Because the price of a term insurance contract is a function of the probability of the individual's dying during that term, premiums are an increasing function of the insured's age.

Whole life policies, on the other hand, are not limited in duration, but rather protect "the whole of life" (Graves 1994). Unlike term insurance contracts, which represent pure insurance, the typical whole life contract is a combination of insurance and tax-deferred savings. The typical "ordinary life" product has fixed- (nominal) level premiums and a fixed (nominal) death benefit or face value. As demonstrated in figure 3.1, the cash values of these policies rise over time, while the pure insurance component declines. The standard practice among life insurers is for the cash value to equal the face value by age ninety-five or 100 (Graves 1994). According to the 1995 Survey of Consumer Finances (SCF), the median whole life insurance policy held by individuals aged seventy and up had a cash value that was 67 percent of the face value. This means that only one-third of the reported face value of whole life policies represents insurance. Most whole life policies have provisions that enable the individual to borrow against the cash value of his or her policy, and thus provide some degree of liquidity. Importantly for the annuity offset model, the cash value of a policy is *not* a negative annuity, but rather represents a nonannuitized financial asset, much like a saving account. While it is true that the cash value of a life insurance policy may be left to one's heirs as a bequest, a large cash value policy would not be indicative of over-annuitization any more than would the holding of a large savings account.

As important as this distinction may be between term and whole life insurance, previous empirical work on the elderly was unable to distinguish between them. The RHS provided data only on the total face value

Dollars

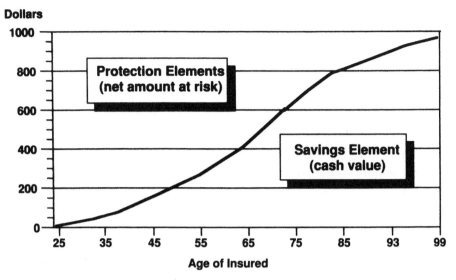

Fig. 3.1 **Proportion of saving and insurance elements in an ordinary whole life insurance contract**
Source: Graves (1994)
Note: Calculated based on issue age of twenty-five using 1980 Commissioners Standard Ordinary female lifetable and a 4.5 percent rate of interest.

of all life insurance policies. Thus, to the extent that ownership of whole life more closely resembles tax-deferred savings than it does insurance, previous researchers were unable to disentangle these two potentially different effects. For example, suppose high-income individuals are more likely to purchase whole life insurance as a form of tax-deferred savings. Because these individuals are high income, they also receive a higher Social Security benefit at retirement. This could lead to a spurious correlation between total life insurance holdings and the level of the Social Security benefits. As we shall see, this commingling of insurance and tax deferred savings has an important impact on the results.

3.3.2 Group versus Individual Coverage

Another relevant distinction between types of life insurance that may be important to this model is between group and individual coverage. Group life insurance policies are commonly provided through employers or unions. An example of a typical group life policy is one that insures an employee for a fixed multiple of his or her salary. Individual contracts, on the other hand, are purchased directly from the insurance company, most often through an insurance agent or broker.

The primary distinction between these policies is that individual life coverage is clearly a "choice" variable, whereas group coverage is often automatic with employment. While in many instances group coverage simply substitutes for individual coverage that would have been purchased anyway, it will also cover some individuals who may have chosen to hold no life insurance if not covered through their employer. Another reason this distinction is relevant is that, since group coverage is usually tied to employment, its purpose is often to protect an employee's family from the loss of future earnings. This purpose for holding life insurance is distinctly different from using life insurance to offset a retirement annuity.

Group coverage is less common among retired elderly households, since most group coverage is tied to employment. Neither the RHS, nor the AHEAD data used in this study, allow for this distinction between group and individual coverage. However, by making use of information about the current employment status of an individual, it is possible to extract some information about the effects of this difference.

3.3.3 Previous Empirical Results

Previous empirical support of the annuity offset model rests on two key results. The first is that there exists a strong positive correlation in a cross-section of households between the level of Social Security benefits and the holdings of life insurance. Bernheim estimates that approximately 25 percent of households own term life insurance, and based on his model, are therefore over-annuitized. His central results indicate that they are using term insurance to offset Social Security by roughly twenty cents on the dollar.

Second, Bernheim finds mixed evidence to suggest that a portion of the total life insurance holdings are negatively correlated with total lifetime resources, and thus represents an inferior good. Importantly, in his most direct specifications, he finds that life insurance coverage is actually increasing with resources for married couples with children. Only when he imposes more structure on the problem to overcome problems of data contamination does he find a consistently negative and significant resource effect. However, this approach is unable to identify directly the effect of resources on term life insurance, and instead relies on modeling total holdings as the sum of two separate processes (one representing term and one representing whole, but each unidentified in advance) and testing the sign of various coefficient combinations.

The difficulty with these results is that the potential for bias is quite high due to the inability to identify directly the term insurance component of total life insurance holdings. Suppose that individuals purchase insurance during their working lives in order to protect their spouses and children from the loss of their human capital in the event of an early death. Individuals can choose between term and whole life insurance to meet this insurance need. The annual premium on a whole life contract is higher than the premium on a term life contract because some of the additional premium essentially goes into a savings account that benefits from tax-deferred inside buildup. Because of this, the whole life contract is more attractive, all else equal, to an individual in a higher marginal tax bracket. Therefore, high earners (who therefore face higher marginal rates) have the most to gain from purchasing whole life contracts. High earners will also be paying more in Social Security payroll taxes, and will thus have a higher benefit upon retirement. Thus, to the extent that whole life contracts held by the elderly represent "residue" from decisions made early in life to protect human capital, this would induce a spurious positive relationship between Social Security benefits (SSB) and whole life insurance coverage.

Two pieces of evidence suggest that this scenario is a strong possibility. First, according to a life insurance ownership study conducted by LIMRA, the median age of the oldest life insurance policy held by individuals aged seventy and up was forty-two years, suggesting that most policies were in fact purchased during the individual's working life. Second, there is a clear positive relationship between ownership of whole life insurance and income during one's working life. For example, if we focus on working-age individuals (aged twenty-two to sixty-five) in the 1995 SCF, we find that only 20 percent of individuals with incomes under $30,000 own a whole life insurance policy. Of those with annual incomes between $30,000 and $60,000, 33 percent own a whole life policy. Nearly half (48 percent) of those earning over $60,000 per year own a whole life policy. This relationship is not biased by the age-earnings profile, as a nearly identical trend emerges when one examines ownership patterns conditional on age. Thus, whole life insurance ownership during one's working life is clearly correlated with income, and thus with OASDI contributions. If individuals continue to hold these policies after retirement, this will lead to a positive correlation between the level of Social Security benefits and whole life insurance ownership. Newly available data allow for a separation of total life insurance into whole versus term life policies, and as such provides a more direct test of the model.

A second potential source of spurious correlation is that some individuals in the Bernheim study were still in the work force. His 1975 RHS sample was comprised of individuals aged sixty-five to sixty-nine. According to Department of Labor statistics, in that year the labor force participation rate of individuals aged sixty-five to sixty-nine was 31.7 percent. High labor force participation can lead to bias in the annuity offset test for two reasons. First, individuals still in the workforce still have positive human capital to protect, and may hold life insurance for this reason. If these individuals also have higher Social Security benefits due to their strong attachment to the labor force, this could induce a positive correlation between benefits and insurance coverage. Second, employed workers are more likely to be automatically covered by group insurance plans.

Therefore, even if the person has no demand for insurance, he or she may be insured. If employed workers are more likely to have higher Social Security benefits, a spurious positive correlation would result.

3.4   Data and Methodology

This paper uses data on elderly households from the first wave of the AHEAD survey. Fielded in 1993–94, this survey collected detailed financial and demographic data on community-based individuals born in 1923 or earlier, so they were aged seventy and up at the date of the survey. The questionnaire collects detailed information on economic and demographic variables, health, work status, and importantly for this study, life insurance coverage.

There are several advantages to the use of this data over the earlier work completed using the RHS. First, the data allow for the important distinction between term life and whole life insurance coverage. While they still do not permit the decomposition of whole life into its cash versus insurance value, the fact that we can distinguish between pure term policies and whole policies represents an important improvement over the total face value of all insurance. Second, because the data consist of individuals aged seventy and up, nearly all of them are retired. This is important both because this means that the individuals no longer carry life insurance to protect against the loss of human capital, and because it is significantly less likely that the individual will be covered by a group life insurance plan through the employer. Therefore, a test of the annuity offset hypothesis will not be contaminated by work-related reasons for insurance coverage. Third, the data are much more recent than the RHS, which is potentially important due to the clear long-term decline in the life insurance coverage of households over the past three decades (LIMRA 1993). Fourth, because of the advanced age of the cohorts, there are large enough samples to investigate the behavior of widows and couples separately. This may be an important distinction because at least one alternative to the annuity offset hypothesis is relevant to couples but not to widows. This is the notion that elderly couples may use life insurance to reallocate wealth across states of spousal survival.

The primary disadvantage of the AHEAD data is the fact that they do not currently contain information on the earnings histories of respondents. As a result, it will not be possible to replicate precisely the specification of lifetime resources as used in Bernheim's work on this subject. However, the information on current income from Social Security and pension plans is quite detailed, and along with information on financial assets it is possible to construct a very good measure of resources available to the household from the date of the survey forward.

This analysis will focus on two subsets of households in the AHEAD data set. The first is married couples in which both spouses were interviewed, and for which we therefore have complete information about important characteristics of both spouses. The second set consists of male widowers and female widows (hereafter often referred to collectively as widows), i.e., formerly married individuals who lost their spouses to death. Excluded from this analysis are never married individuals, both because of small sample sizes and because they are less likely to have children or grandchildren to which they may wish to bequeath. Also excluded are single divorcees, due to small sample sizes and the fact that the survey lacks important information about their former spouses. The resulting sample size for married couples ranges from 1,750 to 1,950 households, and from 2,600 to 2,800 widows and widowers. The range of households arises from missing data for some versions of the dependent variable. For example, an individual may state that he or she does not own a whole life policy, but that he or she does own a term life policy with an unknown face value. My decision rule was to include the maximum number of households possible, so this person would be included in the whole life regressions, but excluded from the term life and total life regressions due to missing data. I have conducted extensive checks to ensure that the results were not sensitive to this selection process, and found that the basic results are unchanged.

In order to test for the effect of Social Security benefits and total resources on the holdings of life insurance, I use the following econometric specification:

(1) $LI_i = \max\{0, \beta_0 + \beta_1 SSB_i + \beta_2 LR_i + \beta_3 X_i + \varepsilon_i\}$

LI is the face value of life insurance. In some specifications, this will represent total face value, while in others I will limit it to term life or whole life only, in order to account for the cash value bias discussed earlier. SSB represents the annual flow of benefits from Social Security. LR is a vector of characteristics that attempts to capture components of lifetime resources. It includes the variable PVR (present value of resources), which equals the expected discounted present value of resources, including net worth, social security wealth, and pension wealth. Because lifetime earnings records are not yet available in the data set that I use, the LR vector also includes a number of variables which proxy for the effect of lifetime earnings. These include nine occupation indicators and four educational attainment indicators. For specifications involving couples, these indicator variables are all included separately for each spouse. X is a vector of other relevant demographic characteristics, including age, gender, race, and whether the respondents have any living children.

I will show results using two different estimation procedures. For comparability with Bernheim's study, I will first assume the normality of ε and report results from a tobit specification. One might be concerned about the possibility of heteroscedasticity in the unobservables in the demand for life insurance, which would render the tobit results inconsistent. Therefore, I will also report results using simple ordinary least squares (OLS) regressions with White-corrected standard errors. As the results will indicate, to the extent that heteroscedasticity biases the tobit results, it appears to do so in a direction that favors the annuity offset model. Further specification checks using a censored least absolute deviations (LAD) estimator, or modeling the heteroscedasticity in a multiplicative form, similarly indicate that any such biases tend to work in favor of the annuity offset model. This phenomenon is captured by the OLS estimates, so I limit reported results to tobit and OLS.

Equation (1) closely approximates the main specification used by Bernheim in his test of the annuity offset model in the RHS, with three primary differences. The first is that Bernheim was restricted to using total face value of all life insurance as his dependent variable, whereas the current study can examine whole and term separately. The second difference is in the construction of the measure of total resources. The definition used here, PVR, is net worth plus the present value of future income from Social Security and pensions, and thus represents resources available from today forward. Bernheim's measure was the present value of lifetime earnings plus the present value of Social Security and pensions, and thus represented total lifetime resources. The third difference is that the current study examines behavior of widows and couples in separate regressions. Bernheim ran his model on all households, with appropriate indicators for marital status, but excluded individuals who had been widowed more than six years.

3.5   Results

Table 3.1 presents summary statistics on life insurance ownership among households aged seventy and up in the AHEAD data. Several features of the data are worth noting. First, men are more likely to hold all types of life insurance than are women. Nearly 62 percent of widowed men own a life insurance policy, versus only 49 percent of widowed women. Among currently married couples, 72 percent of men are covered by at least one policy, versus only 55 percent of married women. Looking at term and whole life ownership separately, the same basic pattern emerges, in that men are always more likely to hold insurance than women. In addition, men always hold more insurance conditional on owning, than do women.

A second feature of the data is that most policies tend to be quite small, though the distribution is fairly skewed. The median married household owns a total of $10,756 of life insurance, a figure that includes all types of

Table 3.1   Life Insurance Coverage in the AHEAD Data

	Widows/widowers		Married Couples		
	Men	Women	Men	Women	Household
Pr(Owns Any LI)	0.6184	0.4868	0.7176	0.5540	0.7791
Amount | Owns Any					
Median ($)	5,000	2,500	9,000	3,000	10,756
Mean ($)	14,280	5,250	25,481	10,718	31,541
Pr(Owns Term LI)	0.3730	0.3310	0.4174	0.3014	0.4958
Amount | Owns Term					
Median ($)	5,000	2,000	5,000	3,000	7,000
Mean ($)	9,028	3,841	12,238	7,564	15,313
Pr(Owns Whole LI)	0.2749	0.1505	0.4940	0.2577	0.5659
Amount | Owns Whole					
Median ($)	6,000	3,000	10,000	4,500	14,000
Mean ($)	18,297	7,189	33,503	13,221	36,119

Source: Authors' tabulations from AHEAD survey, using household weights.

Notes: PR(Owns LI) is the fraction reporting ownership of that life insurance contract type. Amount | Owns LI is the mean or median policy size conditional on ownership.

life insurance on both spouses. Among widowed households, it is even smaller, with a median value of $5,000 for men, and $2,500 for women. However, the means are roughly two to three times larger than the medians, which is driven by the fact that a small fraction of households own very large policies. For example, the 95th percentile of total household coverage among married couples (conditional on owning) is $113,000. The 95th percentile of coverage for male widowers is $50,000.

The third broad pattern to recognize is that marital status is an important margin along which insurance coverage differs. Married individuals are much more likely to own life insurance than are widows or widowers of the same gender, and hold more of it conditional on owning. There are many reasons that this could be true, including reasons that might bear upon the relative importance of using life insurance to protect a spouse versus providing a bequest. However, a large part of these differences is undoubtedly attributable to differences in the financial status of married versus widowed households, which is not captured in these simple tabulations.

3.5.1   Test of Implication no. 1: No Simultaneous Holdings

The first implication of the annuity offset model, and the one easiest to test in the data, is the notion that no individual would choose to hold life insurance and annuities simultaneously. This is because they are offsetting transactions, each of which may cause the individual to incur transactions costs due to the fact that private insurance markets are not actuarially fair.

This assumption is clearly violated by the data in table 3.2. This is par-

Table 3.2   **Cross-Ownership Patterns for Life Insurance and Annuities**

	Owns Private Pension		Owns Private Annuity (excludes pensions)	
	Yes	No	Yes	No
Married Couples (total household coverage)				
Owns any life insurance				
Yes	.501	.278	.066	.713
No	.093	.128	.011	.210
Owns term life insurance				
Yes	.332	.164	.038	.458
No	.260	.244	.038	.466
Widows and Widowers				
Owns any life insurance				
Yes	.211	.298	.030	.479
No	.137	.354	.026	.465
Owns term life insurance				
Yes	.133	.192	.039	.309
No	.216	.460	.017	.636

Source: Authors' tabulations from AHEAD survey, using household weights.
Note: Proportion of population holding both products.

ticularly notable if one follows the Bernheim approach of treating annuities from pension plans as voluntarily purchased. Of all married households, 50 percent own both a private pension and some form of life insurance. Among widows and widowers, 21 percent own both private pension annuities and life insurance. There are reasons to suspect that private pensions are not strictly voluntary, especially among those aged seventy and up who were likely covered for most of their careers in traditional defined benefit plans. However, even if we restrict ourselves to privately purchased, nonpension annuities, 6.6 percent of married couples own both. Since only 7.7 percent of the sample own such an annuity, however, this means that 86 percent of those married households who have purchased a private, nonpension annuity also own life insurance.

These numbers are not surprising, since in Bernheim's own sample 36 percent of households, which included both married and widowed individuals, owned both pensions and life insurance. He attributed this finding to data contamination, namely the fact that he was unable to distinguish between term and whole life insurance. If the 36 percent of people holding both were really holding whole life policies with cash values approaching their face values (i.e., they contained very little insurance), then this finding would not be inconsistent with the annuity offset model. However, using the AHEAD data, we can see that this is not the explanation. Roughly one-third of married households own both straight term life insurance policies and a private pension, as do 13 percent of widows. Perhaps the purest test of the model is to use term life insurance and nonpension annuities. In this case, 3.8 percent of couples hold both. Importantly, one-half of all married households that own a nonpension annuity also have life insurance coverage. This is clearly inconsistent with the annuity offset model.

3.5.2   Test of Implication no. 2: Positive Correlation between Insurance and Social Security

The second, and arguably the most important, implication of the annuity offset hypothesis is that there should exist a positive correlation between term life insurance coverage and the level of SSB. The heart of this hypothesis, as outlined in section 3.2, is that when individuals have higher SSB, they want to buy fewer private annuities and more life insurance.

Table 3.3 reports tobit results for equation (1) in the combined sample of widows and widowers. Column (1) reports tobit coefficients for the case in which total face value of all life insurance holdings (term plus whole) is the dependent variable. Column (2) reports coefficients for the OLS specification. Columns (3) and (4) repeat this analysis with the dependent variable limited to term life insurance, and columns (5) and (6) limit the dependent variable to the face value of whole life insurance.

The coefficient on annual SSB is the coefficient of interest for testing this implication of the model. If the annuity offset model is correct, the coefficient should be significantly positive. Looking first at column (1), we can see that this relationship does hold for total life insurance coverage in the tobit specification, with a coefficient of 0.48 that is highly significant. Using the well-known approximation that the marginal effect can obtained by scaling the parameters by the probability in the uncensored region yields a marginal effect of another dollar of SSB of approximately $0.22 of life insurance coverage. Column (2) repeats the analysis using OLS, and finds a nearly identical marginal effect of 0.22, though the large (White-corrected) standard errors render this coefficient insignificant.

We can translate the life insurance face value into an annuity flow by dividing by the appropriate annuity factor, i.e., the actuarial present value of a $1.00 annuity flow. Using a real interest rate of 3 percent, this factor is approximately 10 for the average individual in the AHEAD sample. Therefore, we find that life insurance is offsetting the flow of SSB on the margin by approximately 2.2 cents on the dollar. This offset is much lower than the 10–20 cent offset that Bernheim found because the current sample is of widows and widowers only, while Bernheim's results were for a mixed sample. Results for couples, discussed below, show a somewhat larger offset that falls in the lower end of the Bernheim offset range.

Columns (3) through (6) of table 3.3 make the important distinction between term and whole life insurance. Columns (3) and (4) report the

Table 3.3   Tobit and OLS Results for Widows and Widowers

Dependent Variable Model	Total Tobit (1)	Total OLS (2)	Term Tobit (3)	Term OLS (4)	Whole Tobit (5)	Whole OLS (6)
SSB	0.4751***	0.2163	0.0440	0.0285	1.2214***	0.1680
	(0.1530)	(0.1621)	(0.1028)	(0.0324)	(0.3020)	(0.1433)
PVR	0.0093***	0.0078**	-0.0012	0.0000	0.0122***	0.0068
	(0.0019)	(0.0037)	(0.0013)	(0.0003)	(0.0032)	(0.0035)
Working	2,178.6	1,363.0	-147.37	-114.88	3,936.3	1,155.5
	(1,855.6)	(1,427.4)	(1,250.3)	(446.70)	(3,527.2)	(1,315.2)
Age	-441.40***	-99.683**	-310.39***	-80.387***	-448.34***	-16.375
	(78.97)	(49.534)	(52.850)	(19.030)	(1672.02)	(43.593)
Female	-8,181.7***	-4,836.5***	-3,257.7***	-1,898.3***	-12,538.7***	-2,738.1***
	(1,366.8)	(1,056.9)	(917.73)	(532.95)	(2,635.1)	(837.44)
Nonwhite	1,640.2	644.77	1,184.1	167.22	-3,500.7	140.78
	(1,302.9)	(619.89)	(848.02)	(245.36)	(2,778.8)	(521.08)
Kids	3,078.4**	653.55	1,616.1	311.77	3,076.3	158.92
	(1,401.5)	(685.74)	(932.16)	(309.70)	(2,858.7)	(565.06)
N	2,605	2,605	2,738	2,738	2,811	2,811

Source: Authors' calculations from the AHEAD survey.

Notes: Standard errors in parentheses (OLS standard errors are White-corrected). Specifications also include indicator variables for occupation and education. Dependent variable is the dollar value of total, term, or whole life insurance coverage. "SSB" is the annual Social Security benefit, and "PVR" is the present value of resources, including the actuarial value of pensions, Social Security, housing wealth, and financial net worth. "Working" is an indicator variable that equals 1 if respondent is employed.

***Significant at the 1 percent level.

**Significant at the 5 percent level.

results for the case in which only term life insurance is treated as the dependent variable. Relative to the results for columns (1) and (2), the difference is striking. The tobit coefficient falls to 0.04, and is statistically no different from zero. The tobit coefficient for SSB in the whole life insurance specification in column (5), on the other hand, is large and significant—the tobit coefficient on SSB is 1.22 and is highly significant. The OLS results are again similar to the marginal effects that arise out of the tobit coefficients, but are not significant. It therefore appears, at least in the sample of widows and widowers, that the central implication that SSB will be positively correlated with term life insurance coverage does not hold. While there is a significant positive relationship found between total life insurance coverage and Social Security in the tobit specifications, this relationship appears to be driven more by whole life insurance than by term coverage, and even this relationship is not always significant.

As discussed by Bernheim and earlier in this paper, the annuity offset model is really a model about term life insurance. Yet the primary implication of this model, that term life insurance ownership will be an increasing function of the level of SSB, is clearly rejected by the data. The relationship between whole life insurance and Social Security, on the other hand, is much stronger but subject to numerous sources of bias. As discussed, by age seventy, whole life insurance consists primarily of tax-advantaged savings, and therefore does not serve to undo annuitization any more than holding other financial assets. Since the individuals who have the most to gain from the inside build-up associated with whole life policies are people who were in higher tax brackets while younger (and who therefore are also likely to have higher Social Security earnings), the observed relationship may be driven more by tax consequences than by a desire to offset a government annuity.

Table 3.4 repeats the analysis for the male widowers only, and finds a similar pattern. In the specification using total life insurance as the dependent variable, there is a significant positive effect of SSB in the tobit specification, and it is much larger in magnitude. Once again, however, when we decompose total life insurance holdings into the two types, we find that the positive relationship is being driven entirely by whole life policies. The OLS results again show similar, though insignificant, marginal effects. Table 3.5 repeats the same analysis for female widows. In this case, the coefficient on SSB in the total life insurance regression falls short of significance, and is smaller in magnitude than for males. More importantly, the coefficient on SSB in the term life insurance specifications continues to be small and insignificant. The only specification in which the SSB coefficient is significant is for the tobit specification in the whole life insurance regression.

Table 3.6 presents results for married couples. Focusing on column (1), we again see that the coefficient on SSB in the "total life insurance"

Table 3.4   Tobit and OLS Results for Male Widowers Only

Dependent Variable Model	Total Tobit (1)	Total OLS (2)	Term Tobit (3)	Term OLS (4)	Whole Tobit (5)	Whole OLS (6)
SSB	1.1216***	0.7016	−0.0905	0.0536	2.4462***	0.6040
	(0.4331)	(0.5906)	(0.3289)	(0.0823)	(0.6940)	(0.5502)
PVR	0.0159***	0.0136	0.0006	−0.0001	0.0155***	0.0109
	(0.0044)	(0.0092)	(0.0027)	(0.0007)	(0.0060)	(0.0085)
Working	−7,381.7	−5,561.8	−13,058**	−4,333.8**	−824.04	−2,672.8
	(6,359.4)	(3,414.7)	(5,232.0)	(2,107.5)	(9,310.5)	(2,982.9)
Age	−612.18**	−186.26	−727.18***	−242.08***	−290.26	58.199
	(265.73)	(228.62)	(204.82)	(82.403)	(417.16)	(195.12)
Nonwhite	−2,853.6	−495.99	−3,212.2	−1,170.1	−12,367	−983.99
	(4,496.5)	(1,382.7)	(3,319.4)	(780.10)	(7,414.0)	(1,012.2)
Kids	8,625.4	3,201.0	9,285.2**	1,754.8***	−2,253.6	−13.368
	(4,473.3)	(2,460.2)	(3,647.9)	(594.73)	(6,728.3)	(2,357.1)
N	453	453	472	472	487	487

Note: See table 3.3 for source, notes, and significance levels.

Table 3.5   Tobit and OLS Results for Female Widow Only

Dependent Variable Model	Total Tobit (1)	Total OLS (2)	Term Tobit (3)	Term OLS (4)	Whole Tobit (5)	Whole OLS (6)
SSB	0.2402	0.0543	0.0778	0.0139	0.6842**	0.0339
	(0.1434)	(0.0963)	(0.0961)	(0.0342)	(0.3100)	(0.0748)
PVR	0.0036	0.0037	-0.0034	-0.0001	0.0081**	0.0035
	(0.0021)	(0.0027)	(0.0019)	(0.0002)	(0.0039)	(0.0024)
Working	3,848.9**	2,589.0	1,642.4	706.83	5,025.3	1,869.2
	(1,631.9)	(1,573.8)	(1,074.3)	(427.54)	(3,413.0)	(1,467.9)
Age	-381.36***	-96.511***	-213.34***	-46.397***	-480.66***	-42.135**
	(69.716)	(26.810)	(45.934)	(15.778)	(158.66)	(19.736)
Nonwhite	2,289.5**	964.84	1,675.1**	474.24	-932.74	454.24
	(1,138.2)	(697.72)	(729.73)	(257.79)	(2,668.6)	(608.16)
Kids	2,033.6	287.91	471.99	-31.699	4,630.9	294.18
	(1,247.0)	(553.19)	(802.27)	(352.60)	(2,888.5)	(387.59)
N	2,152	2,152	2,266	2,266	2,324	2,324

Note: See table 3.3 for source, notes, and significance levels.

Table 3.6   Tobit and OLS Results for Married Couples with Total Household Coverage

Dependent Variable Model	Total Tobit (1)	Total OLS (2)	Term Tobit (3)	Term OLS (4)	Whole Tobit (5)	Whole OLS (6)
SSB	0.9087***	0.5744	0.2668	0.1036	1.4557***	0.4745
	(0.3225)	(0.3768)	(0.1644)	(0.1459)	(0.4526)	(0.2910)
PVR	0.0289***	0.0255***	0.0001	0.0014	0.0327***	0.0209***
	(0.0038)	(0.0082)	(0.0017)	(0.0013)	(0.0051)	(0.0071)
Working husband	6,502.8	6,889.3	−1,602.4	956.93	9,439.2	4,744.8
	(4,646.6)	(4,739.7)	(2,468.6)	(1,583.4)	(6,478.5)	(4,016.6)
Working wife	9,676.4	6,512.9	5,635.4**	2,984.2	2,217.8	3,270.9
	(5,537.6)	(7,429.9)	(2,868.0)	(1,922.0)	(7,905.2)	(6,234.8)
Age of husband	−1,035.9***	−294.27	−750.98***	−284.04***	−559.88	5.7910
	(349.25)	(249.98)	(180.27)	(76.812)	(528.26)	(217.85)
Age of wife	−257.55	−309.40	66.711	−10.409	−501.19	−277.42
	(312.22)	(295.41)	(162.37)	(79.747)	(467.29)	(268.06)
Nonwhite	−7,728.8	−3,864.2**	1,244.8	−269.17	−50,519***	−4,134.2***
	(5,774.9)	(1,758.1)	(2,868.3)	(715.50)	(10,364)	(1,378.5)
Kids	7,910.6	6,200.2***	1,091.7	819.06	7,681.5	5,065.3***
	(5,976.5)	(2,268.0)	(3,128.3)	(1,033.0)	(8,835.8)	(1,848.8)
N	1,751	1,751	1,893	1,893	1,937	1,937

Note: See table 3.3 for source, notes, and significance levels.

specification is a positive and significant 0.91. This offset is similar to what Bernheim found, though at the lower end of his range. Once again, however, the split of total insurance into its two types yields dramatically different results. The coefficient for term insurance in column (2) is only 0.27, and is not significant at the 95 percent level. The coefficient on SSB in the whole insurance specification (column [3]), on the other hand, is a significant 1.46. Repeating the analysis with OLS regressions, we again find no significant correlation between SSB and life insurance ownership. As in the case with widows and widowers, the significant tobit results appear to be driven primarily by a whole life insurance, not the term insurance that the model is meant to represent.

Table 3.7 repeats the analysis on the subsample of married couples in which neither spouse is currently in the workforce. This distinction is quite important, as even the tobit coefficient on total life insurance is no longer significant. There are two important reasons to think that working couples may differ from nonworking. First, an employed individual still has some (albeit small) human capital to protect, just as a younger working-age individual does. Second, a worker is more likely to be covered by a group insurance plan through the employer. In either case, if workers also have higher Social Security benefits because of a stronger attachment to the labor force, this will induce a positive correlation between SSB and life insurance, even in the absence of a desire to undo annuitization.

Table 3.8 reports results similar to those in table 3.6, except that the dependent variable is life insurance coverage on the husband only. The pattern of coefficients on SSB is similar to those found in table 3. 6. Again, any positive correlation is limited to the total or whole life specifications, and is significant only in the tobit specifications. Table 3.9 shows the results for the sample of married women, and again we see the familiar pattern of coefficients.

In short, there is no evidence to suggest that term life insurance ownership among retired elderly households exhibits the correlation with SSB levels that the annuity offset model demands.

3.5.3   Test of Implication no. 3: Term Insurance as an Inferior Good

The third implication of the annuity offset model is that term life insurance will behave as an inferior good with respect to lifetime resources. This is simply because retirement consumption is viewed as a normal good, and therefore the demand for annuities should be an increasing function of resources. Since term insurance is to behave as a negative annuity, this means that the demand for term insurance should be declining with total lifetime resources.

I am unable to replicate exactly Bernheim's measure of lifetime resources because access to Social Security earnings records is unavailable. However, we can observe other components of resources, including the

Table 3.7   Tobit and OLS Results for Married Couples with Total Household Coverage (nonworking sample only)

Dependent Variable / Model	Total Tobit (1)	Total OLS (2)	Term Tobit (3)	Term OLS (4)	Whole Tobit (5)	Whole OLS (6)
SSB	0.0514	-0.1214	0.0850	-0.0426	0.4301	-0.0359
	(0.3146)	(0.3152)	(0.1722)	(0.1103)	(0.4412)	(0.2594)
PVR	0.0245***	0.0216***	0.0001	0.0017	0.0308***	0.0190**
	(0.0038)	(0.0083)	(0.0023)	(0.0013)	(0.0052)	(0.0078)
Age of husband	-1,029.7***	-348.94	-704.88***	-277.62***	-500.96	-1.4535
	(331.78)	(277.59)	(184.08)	(76.702)	(502.45)	(249.83)
Age of wife	-481.67	-533.43	3.0825	-36.418	-724.23	-484.06
	(300.29)	(284.52)	(166.94)	(71.699)	(451.59)	(259.29)
Nonwhite	-10,281	-5,453.6***	-170.96	-835.96	-48,199***	-5,221.2***
	(5,301.6)	(1,773.4)	(2,799.5)	(732.26)	(9,721.2)	(1,389.7)
Kids	3,042.9	3,961.5	-1,374.8	-317.32	2,415.4	3,593.9**
	(5,466.9)	(2,307.3)	(3,035.8)	(1,148.5)	(8,135.7)	(1,679.1)
N	1,393	1,393	1,505	1,505	1,536	1,536

Note: See table 3.3 for source, notes, and significance levels.

Table 3.8   Tobit and OLS Results for Married Men

Dependent Variable Model	Total Tobit (1)	Total OLS (2)	Term Tobit (3)	Term OLS (4)	Whole Tobit (5)	Whole OLS (6)
SSB	0.7851***	0.4080	0.1934	0.0370	1.4209***	0.3889
	(0.2640)	(0.2674)	(0.1448)	(0.0960)	(0.4154)	(0.2221)
PVR	0.0208***	0.0181***	−0.0006	0.0009	0.0259***	0.0154***
	(0.0031)	(0.0061)	(0.0016)	(0.0009)	(0.0046)	(0.0057)
Working husband	7,700.2**	7,240.7	168.17	1,259.7	11,689**	5,092.5
	(3,827.4)	(4,047.6)	(2,171.6)	(1,235.7)	(5,883.0)	(3,582.7)
Working wife	−3,929.9	−1,769.2	2,128.6	975.72	−11,394	−2,225.4
	(4,593.4)	(4,318.2)	(2,543.2)	(1,197.2)	(7,368.1)	(3,810.9)
Age of husband	−1,041.5***	−270.94	−744.40***	−252.96***	−791.92	0.8571
	(294.07)	(210.71)	(161.99)	(63.281)	(492.02)	(189.65)
Age of wife	−184.67	−236.69	252.68	89.866	−547.23	−324.11
	(260.38)	(246.53)	(145.05)	(50.504)	(432.07)	(229.46)
Nonwhite	−10,877**	−3,678.9***	454.91	−568.51	−50,921***	−3,155.0***
	(4,798.9)	(1,236.4)	(2,504.2)	(471.63)	(10,142)	(1,042.6)
Kids	6,575.6	5,123.3***	877.24	831.61	6,074.2	4,188.6***
	(4,997.1)	(1,676.8)	(2,762.8)	(848.74)	(8,231.1)	(1,402.9)
N	1,841	1,841	1,946	1,946	1,979	1,979

Note: See table 3.3 for source, notes, and significance levels.

Table 3.9   **Tobit and OLS Results for Married Women**

Dependent Variable Model	Total Tobit (1)	Total OLS (2)	Term Tobit (3)	Term OLS (4)	Whole Tobit (5)	Whole OLS (6)
SSB	0.3202	0.2037	0.0562	0.0619	0.6058**	0.1420
	(0.1687)	(0.1552)	(0.1173)	(0.0654)	(0.2771)	(0.1163)
PVR	0.0045***	0.0035	0.0000	0.0004	0.0060***	0.0030
	(0.0016)	(0.0022)	(0.0013)	(0.0005)	(0.0023)	(0.0018)
Working husband	1,373.4	828.63	−2,215.4	−251.48	4,510.9	973.33
	(2,503.8)	(1,497.5)	(1,794.2)	(683.79)	(3,959.9)	(1,229.1)
Working wife	9,016.2***	5,942.7	4,203.2**	1,730.3	9,043.8	3,937.9
	(2,896.4)	(3,335.7)	(1,988.4)	(1,038.0)	(4,719.6)	(2,924.3)
Age of husband	−365.95	−12.422	−237.89	−23.745	−296.10	18.801
	(188.88)	(84.895)	(128.56)	(31.576)	(321.91)	(74.479)
Age of wife	−232.24	−143.55	−160.91	−98.718**	−112.64	−33.212
	(170.72)	(113.04)	(115.72)	(46.716)	(291.01)	(98.039)
Nonwhite	−1,548.3	−1,170.1	3,330.4	284.84	−25,548***	−1,426.5***
	(2,983.3)	(688.73)	(1,898.2)	(378.71)	(6,410.8)	(516.74)
Kids	2,183.6	1,302.6	364.61	133.78	−1,333.0	1,012.2
	(3,199.7)	(865.54)	(2,207.3)	(406.76)	(5,295.1)	(670.07)
N	1,896	1,896	1,982	1,982	2,008	2,008

Note: See table 3.3 for source, notes, and significance levels.

actuarial present value of pensions, Social Security, housing wealth, and financial net worth. I construct the variable PVR to be the sum of these resource variables. In addition, I am able to use indicator variables for education and occupation to proxy for lifetime earning effects.

Using a measure of lifetime resources that included lifetime earnings and the present value of pensions and Social Security, Bernheim found mixed results in his test of this implication. Specifically, in his basic tobit results, he found that the lifetime resource effect was negative for the average childless couple, but positive and insignificant for couples with children. He finds better support for the notion that at least some portion of total life insurance demand behaves as an inferior good by conducting refined estimates that model total life insurance holdings as the sum of two distinct, but separately unidentified, processes. Based on these refined estimates, he concludes that the term part of total life insurance ownership is the component that is behaving like an inferior good.

Looking at the coefficient on PVR among widows and widowers (tables 3.3, 3.4, and 3.5) and among married couples (tables 3.6–3.9), we find no significant relationship between PVR and term life insurance. While the sign of the coefficient is negative in some of the term life insurance specifications, it is not even approaching significance at any standard level of confidence. The coefficient on PVR in the whole life insurance specifications, and as a result in some of the total life insurance specifications, is strongly positive. This latter finding is consistent with Bernheim's conclusion that term and whole life insurance respond rather differently to variation in total resources. In the AHEAD data, however, there is no evidence that term insurance is behaving like an inferior good.

3.5.4   Test of Implication no. 4: Term Insurance Owners Consume Less than Social Security Income

The fourth and final empirical implication of the annuity offset model derives from the definition of being "over-annuitized" by Social Security. The basic notion behind this model is that household bequest motives are sufficiently strong that their desired consumption level is less than the annuity provided by Social Security, and that they would therefore prefer to keep some of their wealth unannuitized in order to leave it to their heirs.

Conceptually, this is a straightforward implication to test, since it requires the simple comparison of consumption to the income provided by Social Security. If households consume more than the Social Security benefit, then they are not over-annuitized. However, this implication is difficult to test directly in the AHEAD data due to the fact that a good measure of consumption is difficult to construct with currently available data. Therefore, I will rely on less direct methods to infer the extent to which households wish to consume less than their Social Security income.

It is useful first to consider a household's dynamic budget constraint:

(2) $$W_{t+1} = (W_t - C_t + \text{SSB}_t + Y_t)(1 + r),$$

where W_t represents financial wealth at period t, C_t is consumption in period t, SSB_t is the income flow from Social Security, and Y_t is the income flow from other (non–Social Security) sources. If it is true that individuals are over-annuitized by Social Security, it must be the case that $\text{SSB}_t \geq C_t$. If not, then the constraint of the mandated Social Security annuity is nonbinding, and it need not be offset by life insurance. Since we do not directly observe consumption in the AHEAD survey, this test must necessarily be indirect. To be over-annuitized by Social Security requires $\text{SSB}_t - C_t \geq 0$. This implies

(3) $$W_{t+1} - W_t(1 + r) \geq Y_t.$$

In other words, we need the amount of net saving done by households to exceed the levels of non–Social Security income that they receive during the period. That is, they must be saving some fraction of their Social Security payments in addition to all non–Social Security income. According to the annuity offset model, households that own term life insurance should be saving all non–Social Security income, and then supplementing this bequeathable saving with life insurance.

One simple way to test for this is to make use of a question asked in the first wave of the AHEAD survey:

> Not counting any money or assets that you may have given children or others, did you [and your (husband/wife/partner)] use up any of your investments or savings during (1992/1993) to pay for expenses?

If households are spending down their existing nonannuitized assets in order to pay for current consumption expenses, then they must be consuming at least as much as their current *total* income, and therefore at least as much as their Social Security income. Therefore, these individuals would have no reason to hold life insurance.

Table 3.10 shows that approximately one-fourth of all households spent down assets in 1992–93. Importantly, the overwhelming majority of these households own life insurance, and in particular, term life insurance. In fact, the proportion of those owning term life insurance who spent down assets does not appear to be very different from the proportion of those not owning term insurance who spent down assets, for both widows and couples. Specifically, 24 percent of widows and 25 percent of couples who own term life insurance engaged in a spend-down of financial assets. This test clearly understates the proportion of term life insurance owners who are consuming more than their SSB levels, as it does not account for consumption out of non–Social Security income. If a person also has pension or investment income, for example, the individual may consume in excess of Social Security, and yet still be a net saver.

Table 3.10   **Asset Spend-Down Versus Life Insurance Ownership (fraction of population)**

	Own Any Life Insurance?		Own Term Life Insurance?	
	No	Yes	No	Yes
Widows/Widowers				
Spend-down?				
No	.383	.383	.516	.250
Yes	.105	.128	.157	.078
Married Couples				
Spend-down?				
No	.173	.590	.389	.371
Yes	.047	.190	.115	.125

Source: Author's tabulations from the AHEAD survey.

3.5.5   Summary of Annuity Offset Tests

All four of the major implications of the annuity offset model fail empirical testing in the AHEAD data. As a result, it seems clear that this model does not explain life insurance behavior of elderly households. This leads to the obvious next question, "What is the alternative hypothesis?" This is the subject of the next section.

3.6   Alternative Explanations

There are a number of plausible alternative hypotheses that could explain why elderly individuals and couples hold life insurance. These alternatives share the common feature that none of them rely on the four empirical implications of the annuity offset model. That is, these hypotheses are still quite plausible even knowing the results of section 3. 5. It is not the goal of this paper to conduct a definitive test to select from among these alternative hypotheses. I will, however, present some suggestive evidence to provide direction for further research. The four alternative hypotheses I discuss below include

1. *Couple protection.* Elderly couples use life insurance to insure against loss of pension or Social Security benefits upon the death of the first spouse.
2. *Inertia.* Life insurance holdings are simply "residue" from attempts earlier in life to insure human capital.
3. *Estate tax planning.* Life insurance is used to assist with estate tax planning (e.g., to provide liquidity) in wealthier households.
4. *Funeral expenses.* Many elderly view life insurance as their burial money.

3.6.1 Couple Protection

The first of these alternatives, the couple protection model, assumes that married couples are purchasing life insurance in order to reallocate life-contingent incomes. For example, suppose a husband has a pension plan which is being paid out as a "joint and 50 percent contingent" annuity. This type of annuity treats the spouses asymmetrically. If the wife dies first, the husband continues to receive the full benefit. If the husband dies first, on the other hand, the pension income paid to the wife drops by 50 percent. If the couple decide that they would like to reallocate income from the husband-only state to the wife-only state, one way to do this is to purchase a term life insurance policy on the husband.

The evidence on this alternative is mixed. First, it cannot explain the fact that 62 percent of widowers and 49 percent of widows hold life insurance policies. Second, Auerbach and Kotlikoff (1987, 1989) tested this model of couples using several data sets, including the RHS, and found little support for the model's implications. Specifically, they calculated the decline in resources that a married individual would face upon the death of his or her spouse, and used this variable as a predictor of life insurance ownership on the spouse. They found that most households do not adequately insure spouses against the potential resource loss associated with widowhood.

On the other hand, 95 percent of husbands in the AHEAD sample who own term life insurance name their spouses as the policy beneficiaries. If the insurance is truly being held to leave as a bequest to children, there is no obvious reason to leave the policy to the surviving spouse instead. Further exploration of this alternative hypothesis is left for future research.

3.6.2 Inertia

The second alternative hypothesis is that the elderly hold life insurance while old only because they held it when they were young. This could reflect irrational or rational behavior, as when an individual rationally keeps a policy because it represents a good value from today forward. This could be because the policy is already paid up, or because someone else is paying for the policy (e.g., a child or a former employer). For example, roughly 40 percent of the individuals in the AHEAD data who are covered by a term life insurance policy are currently paying no premiums. Alternatively, many have had a multiyear term policy with flat or level premiums, and therefore the policy is a better than actuarially fair deal from this time forward because the individual has essentially prepaid.

There are also nonrational reasons that one might hold on to a policy that was bought earlier in life. Samuelson and Zeckhauser (1988) provide evidence of status quo bias in decision making. They point out that almost every decision, such as an elderly individual's decision about how much life insurance to hold, has a status quo alternative of "doing nothing" or "maintaining one's current or previous decision." Using evidence from a series of experiments, as well as data on retirement plan choice, they show that individuals have a strong propensity to stick with the status quo. They attribute this to the presence of "(1) . . . transition costs and/or uncertainty; (2) cognitive misperceptions; and (3) psychological commitment stemming from misperceived sunk costs, regret avoidance, or a drive for consistency."

There are several pieces of evidence that suggest inertia may affect a significant fraction of the sample. First, data from LIMRA's Life Insurance Ownership Study indicates that most policies held by the elderly are quite old. When asked the age of the newest life insurance policy held, the median response among those aged seventy and up was thirty-two years. The median age of the oldest policy was forty-two years. Fully 30 percent of these elderly individuals bought their *newest* insurance policies before the age of thirty, and have not purchased any additional insurance since that time. Half of those owning insurance have not bought a policy since the age of forty-three. It thus appears that the majority of policy owners have not purchased any insurance for many decades, at least raising the possibility that their continued ownership is due to a failure to cancel.

On the other hand, 17 percent of those who own life insurance bought their most recent policies since the age of sixty-five. According to a LIMRA Buyer Study (1996), only 8 percent of all life insurance policies sold by agents to individuals aged sixty-five and up were term policies. Most of the rest were whole life policies, which are commonly used for estate planning purposes. The average size of the policies sold to those aged sixty-five and up was $92,800, with an annual premium of $4,698. These are quite large policies compared to the average policy size found in the AHEAD data, indicating that these individuals are likely to be wealthier than average and more concerned with estate planning. While these households may well be concerned about bequests, it is highly unlikely that they would be purchasing large cash-value policies in order to offset Social Security.

3.6.3   Estate Tax Planning

The third alternative hypothesis is that individuals hold life insurance to aid in estate planning. There are several reasons that a wealthy household that would be subject to estate taxation upon death would use life insurance as part of an estate planning strategy. First, the owners of a family business may wish to provide heirs with sufficient liquidity to pay for the estate taxes associated with the value of the business operation, in order to avoid the need to liquidate business assets. Holtz-Eakin, Phillips, and Rosen (1999) explore this point in detail. They find that, other things equal, business owners purchase more life insurance than other individuals.

While it is undoubtedly true that some high-wealth households use life insurance as an effective estate planning tool, this simply cannot explain more than a small fraction of households in the AHEAD data. Fewer than 5 percent of households in the data have a combined net worth and life insurance face value in excess of $600,000, which was the point at which the estate tax became an issue for households at the survey date.

3.6.4   Funeral Expenses

The fourth alternative hypothesis is that elderly individuals view life insurance policies as their "burial money." This could be a mental-accounting approach to portfolio choice (Thaler 1985) or a rational way to circumvent the probate process. Either way, this burial money notion may explain the preponderance of small face value policies in the sample, since according to the National Funeral Directors Association, the average cost of a funeral in 1997 was $4,782. Hurd and Smith (this volume) show that total out-of-pocket death expenses (which include out-of-pocket medical and funeral expenses) for decedents in the AHEAD data average $8,934. For comparison, the median amount of total life insurance coverage is $5,000 among male widowers, $2,500 among female widows, $3,000 among married women, and $9,000 among married men. It seems reasonable to suspect that many of these small policies are held for the purpose of paying for final death-related expenses. This notion is present in popular financial planning books as well. The author of one such book tells the story of a conversation with a widow who asked him to review her finances. She was financially well off, with more than $600,000 in net worth and annual living expenses of only $30,000. When he asked her why she was carrying a term life insurance policy that was costing her several hundred dollars a month in premiums, she replied, "That is to bury me" (Gardiner 1997).

A LIMRA study confirms that life insurance is frequently purchased with the intention of using the proceeds to pay for one's burial. Eighty-three percent of widows report using the life insurance proceeds of their deceased spouses primarily to pay for death-related expenses. The LIMRA also reports that paying for death-related expenses is the most commonly cited reason that consumers give for purchasing life insurance.

One reason that life insurance is a popular device for paying for death expenses is that it avoids probate if paid to a named beneficiary (Graves 1994). Probate proceedings can tie up ordinary assets for many months, so that family members are unable to use these assets to pay for funeral or other death-related expenses. The proceeds from a small life insurance policy, because it avoids the probate proceedings, can provide the decedent's family with timely access to funds with which to pay for these expenses.

Table 3.11   **Determining Fraction of Sample Subject to Over-Annuitization Due to Bequests**

	Widows/Widowers (%)	Married Men (%)
Full sample	100.0	100.0
Fraction holding any insurance	49.9	70.7
Fraction holding term insurance	31.5	41.6
Minus those purchasing private annuity	29.9	39.3
Minus those with private pension annuity	17.7	14.5
Minus those spending down financial assets	13.9	10.7
Minus those with zero term premium	9.2	8.6
Minus those with term premium < 0.5 actuarially fair	8.9	7.7
Minus those naming spouse as beneficiary	—	0.8
Minus policies under $5,000 (funeral expenses)	2.0	0.5

Source: Author's tabulations from the AHEAD survey.

3.6.5   Putting It All Together

Once we account for all the behavior that is directly inconsistent with the annuity offset model or is potentially explained by alternative hypotheses, what fraction of households exhibit behavior that can be explained only by the desire to offset annuities? A simple running tabulation presented in table 3.11 shows that it is likely to be a trivial fraction of the population—far less than the 25 percent figure resulting from earlier analyses.

Table 3.11 starts with the full population of widows and widowers in the left-most column, and married men in the right. As the chart shows, approximately half of all widows and 71 percent of married men own life insurance policies. However, the annuity offset model is really a model of term life insurance, which means we are really concerned about the 31.5 percent of widows and the 41.6 percent of married men who own term policies. Next we can subtract those households which purchase a life annuity, since these households would clearly not purchase life insurance to offset Social Security only to turn around and annuitize additional resources. If we follow Bernheim's lead in treating life-contingent pension annuities as a choice variable, we can further reduce the sample to only 17.7 percent of widows and 14.5 percent of married men.

Next, we can eliminate those households who are spending down their financial assets for consumption, since these individuals are also clearly not constrained by the Social Security income floor. At this point, we have 13.9 percent of widows and 10.7 percent of married men still in the pool. Now let us account for individuals whose term life insurance coverage costs them nothing. The reasoning here is that if an individual can receive a policy at zero marginal cost, then it is perfectly rational for him or her to keep it regardless of whether he or she has bequest motives. In any case, since they do not have to use the Social Security benefits to pay for the premium, they are not offsetting the annuity in any direct way. This leaves us with 9.2 percent of widows and 8.6 percent of married men. Using similar logic, we can eliminate those for whom the term premium is an actuarially advantageous deal. Specifically, I exclude those whose term premiums are less than half of the actuarially fair term premium of a seventy-year-old in 1993.

For married couples, I eliminate those who name their spouses as the beneficiaries, since such policies may be held more for spousal protection than for bequest purposes. Finally, let us take the funeral expense notion seriously, and assume that any policy with a face value of under $5,000 is essentially the individual's burial money. This reduces the sample to 2.0 percent of widows and 0.5 percent of married men.

The calculations in table 3.11 are meant to be illustrative only, and one can certainly quibble with any one of the above exclusion restrictions. These figures demonstrate, however, that one can explain away the finding that individuals use life insurance to offset Social Security. In short, with a few simple assumptions one can show that only a small fraction of households may be over-annuitized by Social Security because they have strong bequest motives.

3.7   Summary and Future Directions

This paper has presented substantial evidence that the reason the elderly hold life insurance is *not* to offset mandated annuitization in the form of Social Security in order to leave a bequest. Four empirical implications of the annuity offset model were developed and tested, and all four were found to be inconsistent with the behavior of elderly households in the AHEAD data set.

This finding is relevant to the current debate over the future of the Social Security system because it bears upon the question of whether mandatory annuitization is desirable. Were it the case that a substantial fraction of elderly households were over-annuitized by the existing Social Security system due to the existence of strong bequest motives, this would be evidence in favor of allowing choice over the annuitization decision. The results of this paper suggest that households are not over-annuitized by Social Security for bequest reasons. Therefore, the simple fact that many elderly households own term life insurance is not a sufficient reason to argue against mandatory annuitization of retirement resources. This finding is consistent with the idea that annuities are of substantial value in the retirement portfolios of elderly individuals (Mitchell et al. 1999; Brown 1999; Friedman and Warshawsky 1988). As a result, mandatory annuitization may be desirable to overcome adverse selection in the annuity market.

However, this conclusion should be tempered by the acknowledgment that individuals can be over-annuitized for reasons other than bequest motives, as suggested in work by Hurd (1987, 1989).

This paper then suggests several alternative hypotheses for explaining the large fraction of elderly households who own life insurance. While these alternatives were not subjected to formal empirical testing in this paper, informal evidence suggests that some of these alternatives may be relevant. For example, the fact that the vast majority of policies have been held for several decades suggests that many holdings may be due to inertia from insurance decisions earlier in life. This would be consistent with the "status quo bias" in decision making that has been documented by Samuelson and Zeckhauser (1988), among others. It may also be the case that many small policies are held as a method of prepaying death expenses, such as funeral expenses.

It has also been found that the majority of policies held by married individuals name the spouses as the beneficiaries rather than the children. This is at least suggestive that the purpose of these policies may be to provide an adequate consumption stream for a widowed spouse. While this hypothesis found little support in earlier empirical work by Auerbach and Kotlikoff, those authors suggested that this might be due in part to the poor quality of their data. Further investigation of these and other alternative hypotheses are left to future research.

References

Auerbach, A. J., and L. J. Kotlikoff. 1987. Life insurance of the elderly: Its adequacy and determinants. In *Work, health, and income among the elderly,* ed. Gary Burtless. Washington, D.C.: Brookings Institution.
———. 1991. The adequacy of life insurance purchases. *Journal of Financial Intermediation* 1 (3): 215–41.
Bernheim, B. D. 1991. How strong are bequest motives? Evidence based on estimates of the demand for life insurance and annuities. *Journal of Political Economy* 99:899–927.
Brown, J. R. 2001. Private pensions, mortality risk, and the decision to annuitize. *Journal of Public Economics,* forthcoming.
Friedman, B. M., and M. J. Warshawsky. 1988. Annuity prices and saving behavior in the United States. In *Pensions and the U.S. economy,* ed. Z. Bodie, J. Shoven, and D. Wise, 53–77. Chicago: University of Chicago Press.
Gardiner, R. M. 1997. *Dean Witter guide to personal investing.* New York: Penguin.
Graves, E., ed. 1994. *McGill's life insurance.* Bryn Mawr, Penn.: The American College.
Holtz-Eakin, D., J. Phillips, and H. Rosen. 1999. Estate taxes, life insurance, and small business. NBER Working Paper no. 7360. Cambridge, Mass.: National Bureau of Economic Research, September.

Hurd, M. D. 1987. Savings of the elderly and desired bequests. *The American Economic Review* 77:298–312.

———. 1989. Mortality risk and bequests. *Econometrica* 57 (4): 779–813.

Kotlikoff, L. J., and L. H. Summers. 1981. The role of intergenerational transfers in aggregate capital accumulation. *Journal of Political Economy* 89 (4): 706–32.

Laitner, J., and T. Juster. 1996. New evidence on altruism: A study of TIAA-CREF retirees. *The American Economic Review* 86 (4): 893–908.

Lewis, F. D. 1989. Dependents and the demand for life insurance. *The American Economic Review* 79:452–67.

Life Insurance Market Research Association [LIMRA]. 1993. Profiles in coverage: The widening gap in U.S. life insurance ownership. Windsor, Conn.: LIMRA.

———. 1996. The 1995 Buyer Study: A market study of new insureds and the ordinary life insurance purchased. Windsor, Conn.: LIMRA.

Mitchell, O., J. M. Poterba, M. J. Warshawsky, and J. R. Brown. 1999. New evidence on the money's worth of individual annuities. *The American Economic Review,* 89 (5): 1299–1318.

Modigliani, F. 1998. The role of intergenerational transfers and life cycle savings in the accumulation of wealth. *Journal of Economic Perspectives* 2 (2): 15–40.

National Funeral Directors Association. 1998. Funeral price information from the NFDA 1997 general price list survey. Available at [http://www.nfda.org].

Samuelson, W., and R. Zeckhauser. 1988. Status quo bias in decision making. *Journal of Risk and Uncertainty* 1:7–59.

Thaler, R. H. 1985. Mental accounting and consumer choice. *Marketing Science* 4:199–214.

Yaari, M. 1965. Uncertain lifetime, life insurance, and the theory of the consumer. *Review of Economic Studies* 32:137–50.

Comment   Anne Case

This is a sensible, straightforward paper that answers some old questions, and raises interesting new ones. Brown brings new data to an old question—whether we can find evidence of Social Security's causing the elderly to hold more annuities than they would otherwise choose, forcing them to offset their annuitization by purchasing life insurance. Using newly available data from the Asset and Health Dynamics of the Oldest Old (AHEAD) survey, Brown finds no evidence in favor of the hypothesis that households are over-annuitized by Social Security.

Brown is able to revisit evidence presented in Bernheim (1991), evidence that, according to Bernheim, "strongly suggests that an increase in Social Security old-age insurance (OAI) benefits tends to shift household resources from a regime in which they obtain annuities from private sources . . . and ultimately into a regime in which they purchase life insurance" (900). The statistic often cited from the Bernheim paper is that for "more

Anne Case is professor of economics and public affairs at Princeton University and a research associate of the National Bureau of Economic Research.

than one-fourth of all households, transfer motives are so strong that the compulsory provision of annuities through Social Security actually reduces bequests below the first-best levels" (900). As Brown lays out quite coherently, there are many reasons that the Bernheim results may not be robust. Bernheim, using the Retirement History Survey (RHS), did not have the ability to separate term life insurance from whole life insurance, and the latter often represents a tax-deferred savings instrument to wealthier people. Even without details on data deficiency, the Bernheim results seem rather implausible. The part of the income distribution most concerned with bequests would be the part *least* likely to be over-annuitized by Social Security. Social Security income represents only a small fraction of consumption for wealthy households.

While Brown's results seem reasonable in their totality, they are more problematic in some of their details. In the conference version of the paper, the results presented in the key tables had been estimated using tobits. It is highly likely that there will be heteroscedasticity in the unobservables in the demand for life insurance equation, which would bias the coefficient estimates. Wealthy households have greater scope for idiosyncratic behavior, and it would be surprising if we did not see a fanning out of the variance of unobservables with household income or wealth. In tables 3.3–3.9, Brown presents results on the demand for whole life insurance, term life insurance, and total life insurance for different groups of interest (widowers and widows, married couples, nonworking married couples). If the variance of the unobservable component of the demand for insurance differed between these groups, or between whole and term insurance, then we would expect to see differences in the Social Security benefit (SSB) coefficient due to differences in the variances, and not necessarily due to behavioral differences. (I think the next version of the paper will speak to this, so there seems little point in belaboring it here.)

There are some puzzles in the results presented in tables 3.3–3.9. For example, Brown suggests that because the coefficient on whole life insurance is positive and significant, while that on term insurance is smaller and insignificant, that whole insurance is driving the relationship between the level of SSB and life insurance that one finds when one looks at total insurance and SSB. However, something here does not quite add up. Fifty-seven percent of married couples own whole life insurance, and 50 percent own term insurance. Thus it would seem that one should find the tobit estimate of the effect of SSB on life insurance holdings for married couples to be *larger* than either of the two estimates taken individually, all else equal. That the effect is smaller than that for whole insurance estimated separately (0.91 in place of 1.46) suggests there are other forces at work here, making it difficult to state that whole insurance is driving the relationship between SSB and total life insurance.

There are many interesting findings in Brown's results that he does not discuss in the paper. For example, nonwhite widows appear to hold a good deal of term life insurance. Why would this be the case? Are these women living with children and grandchildren for whom they are the main providers?

The variable "Kids" is an indicator that the respondent has any living children (although it is unclear why one would not use the number of living children in these tables rather than an indicator variable). In tables 3.6 and 3.7, the "Kids" indicator is generally an insignificant predictor of life insurance holdings. This seems surprising. I would have thought we would see whole life insurance holdings respond to children.

In the term life insurance equations for the full sample of married couples, an indicator that the husband is working is not a significant predictor of holding term life insurance, while an indicator that the wife is working is. What explains this? I would have thought term insurance was there to protect the income flow into the household upon the unexpected demise of a working person. If, as is likely to be the case, a husband is earning more than a wife, it would seem that that source of income would be more likely to merit protection.

The paper promises that there will be a lot of interesting work ahead. There is a need to examine life insurance in a coherent model. (Brown mentioned at the conference that the saying in the business is that "life insurance isn't bought, it's sold." That seems an important part of the story still to be incorporated.) Even for a conference of economists researching aging, Brown spent two pages of his paper clarifying the difference between whole and term insurance. It seems both confusion and market imperfections may be worth modeling.

Finally, it seems the time has come to revisit the literature on spousal (and family) protection. Some of the Auerbach and Kotlikoff work cited analyzes data from the late 1960s. Much has changed—both in terms of those savings mechanisms that are available and in use, and in terms of the data available with which to analyze decisions made. It would seem an ideal time to pursue this work.

Reference

Bernheim, B. D. 1991. How strong are bequest motives? Evidence based on estimates of the demand for life insurance and annuities. *Journal of Political Economy* 99:899–927.

II

Wealth and Health

4

Mortality, Education, Income, and Inequality among American Cohorts

Angus Deaton and Christina Paxson

4.1 Introduction

Trying to understand why mortality is so strongly related to socioeconomic status (SES) has been a major concern in demography, epidemiology, and public health for many years, and is beginning to attract the attention of economists. Data from the National Longitudinal Mortality Study (NLMS) show that people aged twenty-five whose family income was $5,000 or less in 1980 (and in 1980 prices) could expect to live ten years less than those whose family income was more than $50,000 (Rogot et al. 1992). The concept of SES is more widely used outside economics than within it, and one of the issues that remains to be settled is the extent to which these health differences are caused by income or by other factors correlated with income, education being the most obvious (see, e.g., Fuchs 1989, 1993; Garber 1989). Many writers believe that there is at least some direct protective effect of income, and in a recent literature much identified with the work of Richard Wilkinson (1996), it is argued that, while the first moment of income is protective, at least at the individual level, the second moment is a health hazard, so that income inequality raises mortality, if not at the individual level at least in populations or large subpopula-

Angus Deaton is the Dwight D. Eisenhower Professor of International Affairs and professor of economics at Princeton University, and a research associate of the National Bureau of Economic Research. Christina Paxson is professor of economics and public affairs at Princeton University, and a research associate of the National Bureau of Economic Research.

We gratefully acknowledge financial support from the National Institute on Aging and from the John D. and Catherine T. MacArthur Foundation for support through their network on poverty and inequality in broader perspectives. We would like to thank Anne Case, David Cutler, Finis Welch, and especially James D. Smith, for helpful comments on the first draft.

129

tions. Wilkinson distinguishes his hypothesis from the mechanical consequence of Jensen's inequality, that a convex relationship between mortality
risk and dying means that aggregate mortality will be higher in more unequal societies. Instead he postulates that inequality itself is a health hazard and that it is less healthy for both rich and poor to live in a more unequal society. It is hardly necessary to emphasize the importance of such a
link, if it indeed exists, though economists are particularly likely to mourn
the loss of the Pareto criterion. The proponents of some changes, such as
improvement in school quality, or raising the return on social security,
make a plausible case that such changes will make everyone better off,
though some more so than others. If such changes increase inequality, as
almost certainly they would, the cost of lives lost would have to be offset
against the economic benefits.

The original empirical support for the Wilkinson hypotheses comes
from Wilkinson's cross-country comparisons within the Organization for
Economic Cooperation and Development (OECD), where some measures
of inequality are much more closely related to mortality levels and mortality changes than is either the level or rate of growth of national income.
There are also a number of studies in the United States that find a relationship across states between income inequality and mortality (see Kaplan
et al. 1996; Kennedy, Kawachi, and Prothrow-Stith 1996). Although this
work has been challenged on a number of grounds (e.g., Judge 1995; Fiscella and Franks 1997; Mellor and Milyo 1998), and in some cases has
been substantially modified (see Judge, Mulligan, and Benzeval 1998; Mc-
Isaac and Wilkinson 1997; Lobmayer and Wilkinson 1999), what was initially perceived as implausible seems most recently to be commanding acceptance from careful and unbiased researchers in the field (e.g., Marmot
1997 and the survey by Robert and House 1999). While we have reserva-
tions about the robustness of many of the positive findings, our main purpose in this paper is not to try to come to judgment based on the review
of the evidence—we suspect that it is too early to try to do so—but to
offer some new evidence based on income, income inequality, and mortality data for birth cohorts of Americans observed over the two decades
from 1975 to 1995. As far as we are aware, birth cohorts have not previously been used in this context—as opposed to individual data, state
data, or country data—and unlike these other sources, they offer both a
cross-sectional and time series dimension in the same data.

The next section of the paper summarizes and substantially extends a
simple model first developed in an earlier paper by one of us (Deaton
2001). The model is designed to provide a framework for empirical application, and provides a way of thinking about the effects of income and
income inequality in a framework in which causality runs from income to
health, but where it is not absolute income that matters for health, but
income relative to the average of an (unobservable) reference group. Al-

though inequality has no direct effect on health, the fact that reference groups are not observed means that the slope of the observed relationship between health and income varies with the ratio of between- to within-group inequality. The model can be readily extended to incorporate a direct effect of inequality by making health depend on the absolute size of income differences within the reference group, but equally plausible specifications give different results so that, according to the theory, income inequality can be either protective or hazardous. We give detailed consideration to the *aggregation* of the relationship between health and income, and how it can be expected to change as it is examined with different sources of data, such as individual records, averages of states or countries, or averages of birth cohorts.

Section 4.3 presents our empirical evidence. Data on mortality for birth cohorts are combined with data on income, income inequality, poverty, and education for 1975 through 1995 from each successive Current Population Survey (CPS) from 1976 to 1996. Deaton's (1999) preliminary analysis used the same general approach, but worked with a shorter sample period (1981–93), different timing, and a more limited range of variables, and merged the mortality and CPS data on a household basis rather than on the much more satisfactory individual basis used here. Deaton found that income reduced the risk of mortality, and that while the slope of the gradient was steepened when inequality was higher, there was no direct effect of inequality at the mean. In the current paper, we again document the strongly protective effects of income, and we examine how those effects vary at different points in the life cycle. When we turn to inequality, we not only fail to find that it increases the risk of mortality, but we find that there is actually a *protective* effect, in apparent contradiction not only with the Wilkinson hypothesis but with much of the theory developed in this paper. The basis for the result is the fact that when mortality was falling the most rapidly, in the late 1970s and early 1980s (years not included in the preliminary study), inequality of income was also rising rapidly. Note that because the mortality and inequality changes affected so many birth cohorts simultaneously, our results are based on more than a correlation for a few years of data. It is hard to understand why, if income inequality is so important in explaining mortality differences across states in the United States, as well as differences between the United States and other developed countries, mortality should have fallen most rapidly just when inequality was rising most rapidly.

We also give a good deal of attention to the role of education, whether income is a mask for education, how income and education affect mortality in the cross-section and over time, and whether the treatment of income and education affects our results on the role of inequality. In a cross-section of birth cohorts, income and education are closely correlated so that, in order to disentangle their effects, we rely on the time series dimension of the cohort data, supplemented by individual-level data from the NLMS. The individual-level data show that both income and education are separately protective against mortality and that only some of the effect of income is removed when we attempt to allow for reverse causality from nearing death to income. In the cohort data, by contrast, income appears to increase the risk of mortality conditional on education, a result that we tentatively ascribe to the short-run or business-cycle effects of income on mortality.

4.2   Income, Health, and Inequality

The public health and epidemiological literatures, although richly suggestive of mechanisms, do not currently provide a precise characterization of the way in which inequality affects health. In consequence, it is difficult to know how to test the model, or how to interpret results. In this paper, we start from the framework in Deaton (2001), and show how it can be used as a basis for empirical analysis of individual level as well as aggregated data. The model is one in which the link runs from income to health, although, in this context, there is nothing to stop the reinterpretation of "income" as years of schooling so that, for the moment, we are not addressing the issue of whether it is income or education that is ultimately protective. However, we are not considering reverse causation, from health to income, a link that undoubtedly plays a part, although only a part, in accounting for the relationship between income and health. That income should cause health through a health Engel curve is consistent with standard health capital approaches in economics in which health is produced with health care and behavioral inputs that have to compete with leisure and other expenditures for a limited budget of time and money. However, identifiable health behaviors appear to explain only about a quarter of the relationship between health and income (Marmot 1994; Lantz et al. 1998), and medical care probably a good deal less, perhaps 10 percent or so (Adler et al. 1993; House and Williams 1995), so that this approach does not seem very promising. Perhaps the most promising line of investigation implicates the biochemical effects of psychosocial stress as a risk factor, linking this stress to social status; see, for example, Sapolsky (1993), Cohen, Tyrell, and Smith (1991), and Cohen et al. (1997) for some of the results, and Sapolsky (1996) and Adler et al. (1992) for reviews.

In the spirit of this work, suppose that health status (measured positively) is an increasing function of income relative to the average income in the reference group to which the individual belongs. Write h for health, y for (the logarithm of) individual income, and z for the mean (logarithm of) income in the reference group. Once again, note that we are using income as a measure of social status, which could just as well be thought of as education, or as any other (absolute) measure of achievement. We assume that the relationship is linear, so that for $\beta > 0$,

(1) $E(h \mid y, z) = \alpha + \beta(y - z).$

If we knew the reference group to which each individual belonged, we could estimate equation (1) directly using individual-level data. However, such information is rarely available, and there can be no presumption that individuals relate to any clearly identifiable group, such as neighbors, birth cohorts, or members of the same educational or occupational groups. Health may be determined by status at work, status in the local (geographical) community, or status at church or in some community organization. As a result, z must be treated as an unobservable, and health conditioned only on (own) income, so that equation (1) becomes

(2) $E(h \mid y) = \alpha + \beta[y - E(z \mid y)].$

The conditional expectation on the right-hand side of equation (2) can be calculated from knowledge of the joint distribution of z and y. Given the linear structure, the most convenient assumptions are that z and y are joint normally distributed (recall that incomes are measured in logarithms). We write the marginal distribution of z as $N(\mu, \sigma_z^2)$, and the distribution of y conditional on z as $N(z, \sigma_\varepsilon^2)$, so that σ_ε^2 and σ_z^2 are measures of within-reference-group and between-reference-group inequality, respectively.

Given the normality assumptions and the linearity of the original expectation, the expectation of health conditional on income takes the convenient form (see the appendix for this and other useful results on the normal distribution)

(3) $E(h \mid y) = \alpha + \dfrac{\beta \sigma_\varepsilon^2}{\sigma_\varepsilon^2 + \sigma_z^2}(y - \mu),$

so that the slope of the "gradient," the relationship between health and income, is a function of the ratio of within-group to between-group inequality. When reference groups are internally homogeneous relative to the disparity across groups, differences in individual income largely reflect intergroup disparity, which is irrelevant for health, so that the effect of income is attenuated. When inequality within reference groups is relatively high, individual income is a good indicator of relative income, and a good predictor of health. Another useful way of thinking about equation (3) is that income is an error-ridden estimate of relative income, so that the slope of the regression function is attenuated in the usual way. Note, however, that the convenient form in equation (3) depends, not only on the linearity of equation (1), but also the normality assumptions about reference-group and within-reference-group incomes.

Equation (3) does not assign to inequality any direct role in the determination of health. To the extent that changes in inequality change the relationship between intragroup and intergroup inequality, the observed relationship between health and income will become more or less steep. Yet even here, there is no structural effect of inequality on health. For example, if within-group inequality increases, some people in each group will become less healthy, and some more healthy, but the average health of each group will not change. If intergroup inequality changes, leaving intragroup inequality the same, no one's health changes, even though the relationship between health and income changes. The gradient is driven, not by changes in health, but by changes with inequality in the relative income composition of each absolute income group.

The relative income model can be extended to incorporate a direct role for inequality. In some of the literature, there are suggestions that it is the absolute income differences that matter, so that each person's health is determined by, for example, the difference between their income and the income of the best-off person in the reference group. If the best-off person is θ standard deviations from the group mean, health responds, not to the difference between y and z, but to the difference between y and $z + \theta\sigma_\varepsilon$, so that equation (1) becomes

(4) $$E(h \,|\, y, z) = \alpha + \beta(y - z - \theta\sigma_\varepsilon).$$

Following through the argument as before, and assuming that σ_ε is orthogonal to income, gives a new version of equation (3),

(5) $$E(h \,|\, y) = \alpha + \frac{\beta\sigma_\varepsilon^2}{\sigma_\varepsilon^2 + \sigma_z^2}(y - \mu) - \beta\theta\sigma_\varepsilon,$$

so that inequality plays a direct negative role on health as well as playing the indirect role originally assigned to it. This appears much closer to the kind of effect discussed by Wilkinson (1996) and of much of the related literature.

However, this account of inequality and health contains no fundamental reason that the effect not be *negative*. In the original equation (1), individual health depends on relative income, so that a mean preserving spread of income within the reference group hurts some but helps others, so average health is unaffected. In the modified equation, people are hurt by their distance from the tops of their reference groups, so that a mean preserving spread hurts everyone except the person at the top, who is unaffected, and the healthiness of the group falls. Yet this is not the only way of measuring relative income effects. Instead of looking to the top, people might look to the bottom, and become healthier the further they are above the reference group floor. Just as in the upward-looking model, health is determined by relative standing, and both approaches seem equally consistent with findings that people with higher social status are healthier. The downward looking specification, however, gives exactly the opposite effect of inequality on health. A mean preserving spread improves everyone's health except that of the poorest person, which remains unchanged, and the group becomes healthier. This model leads to exactly the same functional form as equations (4) and (5), but with the sign on the last term reversed. Without more content, linking health to relative economic status delivers no prediction for the direction of the effect of inequality on health.

Ambiguous though it may be, equation (5) is a convenient basis for empirical estimation, at least on individual-level data. Health is linearly related to income, to inequality, and to an interaction term between inequality and income. For the analysis of individual level data, equation (5) can be used directly—for example, as a probit or logit. Taking the former as an example, suppose that someone dies when h falls below some critical level h_0, then the probability of death is

$$(6) \qquad p = \text{prob}(h \le h_0) = \Phi\left(\frac{h_0 - \tilde{\alpha} - \tilde{\beta}y}{\sigma_u}\right),$$

where Φ is the cumulative density function of the standard normal, σ_u is the standard deviation of health conditional on income (see equation [15]), and $\tilde{\alpha}$ and $\tilde{\beta}$ are given by

$$(7) \qquad \tilde{\alpha} = \alpha - \frac{\beta \sigma_\varepsilon^2 \mu}{\sigma_\varepsilon^2 + \sigma_z^2} - \beta \theta \sigma_\varepsilon$$

$$(8) \qquad \tilde{\beta} = \frac{\beta \sigma_\varepsilon^2}{\sigma_\varepsilon^2 + \sigma_z^2}.$$

Note that the within-reference-group inequality term σ_g is being taken as a constant and absorbed into the intercept; even though we do not know the reference groups, or their mean incomes, we may have a proxy for reference group inequality—such as inequality over some observable group—in which case σ_g could be included as a variable.

Although there are a number of microeconomic data sets on which equation (6) might be estimated, from one of which we will show results below, we are faced with the usual choices in work linking health and economics: between data sets that are rich on economic measures but poor on health, and data sets that are strong on health but weak on economics. One way of solving the dilemma is to merge information from multiple data sets, not at the level of the individual, but at the level of some group that is represented in more than one survey. In this paper, we group at the level of birth cohorts observed in a particular year, and we merge mortality data from the vital registration system with income, income inequality, and education data from the CPS. Before discussing the empirical results, we therefore need to consider the effects of cohort-level aggregation on equation (5). We do this in a fairly general way, so as to allow other kinds of aggregation (e.g., by occupation, or by region). Since some of the previous work on inequality and health has used either state-level or international aggregates, we need some aggregation framework if we are to compare results.

Return to equation (4) in the form

$$(9) \qquad E(h\,|\,y, z) = \alpha + \beta(y - z) - \beta\theta\sigma_\varepsilon$$

and suppose that we observe neither y nor z, but some conditional average, denoted x. In our empirical work, x is the average (log) income of a birth cohort in a particular year, but it might just as well be an average conditioned on state or occupation. Conditional on x, y is $N(x, \sigma_c^2)$, where c refers to the aggregation group. If x is jointly normally distributed with both y and z, with common mean μ, then the expectation of h conditional on x is given by (again using the normal formulas)

$$(10) \qquad E(h\,|\,x) = \alpha + \beta\left(1 - \frac{\sigma_{zx}}{\sigma_x^2}\right)(x - \mu) - \beta\theta\sigma_\varepsilon ,$$

where σ_{zx} is the covariance of x and z, mean incomes in aggregation and reference groups, respectively. Once again, we have assumed that the within-reference-group inequality σ_ε is orthogonal to the aggregation group income. Equation (10) is analogous to equation (5) and both come from projection of the fundamental behavioral relationship in equation (1) onto different variables. They are identical if each person is her or his own aggregation group, so that individual income y and group income z coincide. More generally, however, equations (10) and (5) are different; the bias to the slope now depends, not on the ratio of within- to between-reference-group variance, but (negatively) on σ_{zx}/σ_x^2, the slope of the regression of reference group on aggregation group income. When aggregation group income moves one-for-one with reference group income, as when the reference and aggregation groups coincide, the relationship between health and group income is lost. To get an unattenuated slope, we need to select aggregation groups whose average incomes are uncorrelated with reference group incomes.

Some examples clarify the implications of equation (10). While in principle it is possible for health to be negatively related to income at the aggregation group level, this seems unlikely in practice. Consider a component model of income, written as

$$(11) \qquad y = \mu + \theta_a + \eta_t + \gamma_g + \varepsilon ,$$

where, as always, μ is the grand mean, and the other components are zero-mean random terms associated with the effects of age (a), time (t), occupational group (g), and an individual idiosyncratic term. In Case A, suppose that the reference group is people of the same age, in the same occupation, today. In Case B, the reference group is all members of the profession today, irrespective of age. In both cases, the aggregation groups are birth cohorts, people of the same age today, so that the aggregation group income is $\mu + \theta_a + \eta_t$. In Case A, the reference income is the sum of the first four terms on the right-hand side of equation (11), so that $y - z$ is simply the idiosyncratic residual ε which, by assumption, is orthogonal to z, so that the coefficient on x in equation (10) is zero. In terms of that equation, as is easily checked, we have

$$(12) \qquad \operatorname{cov}(x, z) = \sigma_{zx} = \sigma_a^2 + \sigma_t^2 = \sigma_x^2 = \operatorname{var} x,$$

so that x has no effect in the regression, and aggregation group income does not predict aggregation group health. Even though income predicts health in the microdata, only inequality predicts health in the aggregate. Case B is different. Because the age component is included in aggregation group income, but not in reference group income, the covariance of x and z is only σ_t^2, so that with the variance of x unchanged, equation (10) becomes

$$(13) \qquad E(h \mid x) = \alpha + \beta \left(\frac{\sigma_a^2}{\sigma_t^2 + \sigma_a^2} \right)(x - \mu) - \beta\theta\sigma_\varepsilon,$$

so that aggregation group income matters for aggregation group health, albeit with an attenuated effect. In this case, there will be attenuation except in the implausible case where $\sigma_t^2 = 0$ and there are no common aggregate shocks to income.

In general, if the reference groups are more finely defined than the aggregation groups (e.g., economists of the same age observed at the same time versus an age cohort), aggregation will annihilate the relationship between income and health in the aggregated data. If neither group is more finely defined—economists of all ages versus birth cohorts—or if the reference group is less finely defined than the aggregation group—the whole population versus birth cohorts—income of the aggregation groups will predict average health in the aggregation groups. Note that if the reference group is the whole population, so that reference group income is the population mean, the covariance of x and z is zero so that, by equation (10), there is no attenuation, and the microeconomic relationship carries through directly to the aggregate relationship. Finally, if the aggregation groups are individuals, so that $x = y$, it is easily checked that equation (10) reduces to the attenuated microrelationship equation (5). This kind of analysis seems to capture some (although not all) of the discussion in Wilkinson (1997), who argues that looking across small geographical areas, income will be more important than inequality, while the opposite will be true in comparisons over aggregates for large areas, such as states or regions.

In applications such as the present, where health is measured only to the extent that it does or does not fall beneath a threshold and results in

death, the parameters in equations (5) or (10) can be estimated only up to
scale, where the scale is the standard deviation of health around the two
regression equations (5) and (10). As was the case for the slopes, the residual variances come from standard results on the normal distribution. If we
write σ_h^2 for the variance of health conditional on both y and z in equation
(1), then the residual variance of the regression equation (10) is

$$(14) \qquad \sigma^2 = \sigma_h^2 + \beta^2\left[\sigma_\varepsilon^2 - \frac{(\sigma_x^2 - \sigma_{zx})^2}{\sigma_x^2}\right].$$

When the model is estimated on group-aggregated data, here on age cohorts, the slope of the income relationship should be the ratio of $\beta(1 -
\sigma_{zx}/\sigma_x^2)$ to the square root of equation (14). In the microdata, correspond-
ing to equation (4), equation (14) also holds but with $x = y$, so that rear-
ranging, we have

$$(15) \qquad \sigma_u^2 = \sigma_h^2 + \frac{\beta^2\sigma_\varepsilon^2\sigma_z^2}{\sigma_z^2 + \sigma_\varepsilon^2}.$$

Unfortunately, without knowledge of the variances, there is no general
inequality that holds between equations (14) and (15), nor indeed between
the coefficients on income in the micro- and macro-regressions, equations
(5) and (10). The theory does not deliver any general basis for comparing
estimated gradients at different levels of aggregation.

Nevertheless, there are two polar cases in which the results are straightforward and are worth keeping in mind when interpreting the results.
These are (1) when the reference groups are small, and are contained
within the aggregation groups, and (2) when reference groups are universal, so that reference income z is the same for all people and equal to mean
income. Case 2 would arise if health is a function of relative income, but
all people are members of the same reference group, or if health is simply
a function of absolute income rather than relative income. In these two
cases the gradients from micro- and macrodata can be compared. In Case
1, with individual data, the gradient will be the ratio of equation (8) to the
square root of equation (15), an attenuated but still positive effect. In the
same case, but with aggregation group data, there will be no relationship
between aggregation group income and mortality, so that only inequality
matters. In case (2), when z is common to everyone, σ_z^2 and σ_{zx} are both
zero. In the individual-level data, by substituting $\sigma_z^2 = 0$, the ratio of equation (8) to the square root of equation (15) reduces to

$$(16) \qquad \frac{\beta}{\sigma_h}.$$

By contrast, in the aggregation group data, by substituting $\sigma_{zx} = 0$ we get, for the ratio of the slope in equation (10) to the square root of equation (14),

(17)
$$\frac{\beta}{\sigma_h\sqrt{1 + \beta^2\sigma_c^2/\sigma_h^2}},$$

where σ_c^2 is the within-aggregation-group variance $\sigma_\varepsilon^2 - \sigma_x^2$. Probits run at the aggregation group level will therefore be attenuated compared with those run on the individual-level data. In our econometric analysis below, β/σ_h from the microdata is around -0.3, while the mean within-cohort variance of log income is about 0.6, so that the factor in the square root of the denominator of equation (17) is 1.054, and the two sets of estimates should be close.

What can be said about the relationship between inequality and the probability of dying at the cohort or other group-aggregate level? The formulas are sufficiently complex to permit a wide variety of results. However, if all the variances (and covariances) were to increase in proportion, which is one way in which inequality might increase, there would be two distinct effects. The first acts through the last term on the right-hand side of equation (10); when people are less healthy when they are lower in the reference group, average health declines with inequality, and this effect is not altered by the aggregation. The second effect can be seen by noting that the slope in equation (10) is unaffected by a proportional change in variances, while the variance in equation (14) will move with the other variances. This is an aggregation effect that, in the aggregate data, acts to attenuate further the estimate of slope but, provided the probability of death is less than a half, will raise the probability of death. When mortality risk is small, we are on the convex portion of the relationship between the probability of death and (log) income, so that Jensen's inequality makes the aggregate probability an increasing function of the variance. Of course, this effect could be weakened (or strengthened) by relaxing the original linearity assumption between health and income. The possibility remains that changes in inequality, by changing the ratio of σ_{zx} to σ_x^2, will alter the slope itself, but the formulas are complicated enough to prevent further conjecture.

4.3   Data and Results

Our empirical analysis is based on merging data on all-cause mortality for the United States as a whole with data on incomes from the successive years 1975–95 from the 1976–96 CPS. (Note that the March CPS collects data on the previous year's income.) Merging is at the level of birth cohorts by sex so that, for example, we will be relating the fraction of men or women born in year b who died in year t, to the incomes of that same cohort in year t (or possibly earlier). The data on mortality are taken from the Berkeley Mortality Database (BMD); we use the 1×1 table, i.e., fractions dying by sex, by single year of age, and in each year from 1900 (see Wilmoth 1999). The CPS data are used to attribute to each individual a family income per adult equivalent, say, y, and we then calculate various characteristics of the distribution of y over individuals for each birth cohort. In particular, we work with the cohort average of ln y, with the variance of the logarithm of y within the cohort, with the Gini coefficient, and with the proportion of people below the poverty line. Household income is the CPS measure of total household income, and adult equivalents are measured as the number of adults plus half the number of children, defined as those under eighteen years of age. Note that, although y is family income per adult equivalent, identical values of which are assigned to all members of each household, the mean and other statistics will generally differ by sex if, for example, women on average live in families with lower income. We also use data on education from the CPS, calculating years of education for each person, as well as dummies for various attainment levels so that, at the cohort level, we have data on average years of education as well as on the fraction who have graduated from high school, college, and so on. After 1991, the CPS reports education in bracketed intervals rather than in years. We use means within brackets from 1991 to attribute years of education in the later surveys. With an age restriction from twenty-five to eighty-five, and with CPS data from 1975 through 1995, our data set consists of 1,281 age-year cohort averages.

Given that we have drawn a direct link from the theory at the individual level to its implications for birth cohorts, estimation at the cohort level is a viable alternative to estimation using individual records. Cohort data also have some distinct advantages of their own, as well as some disadvantages. On the positive side, because deaths are rare events, very large numbers of individuals need to be sampled to make individual data useful. By contrast, the cohort data use the data on all deaths in the United States, eliminating the need for sampling. Cohort data also overcome one of the major difficulties in linking mortality to SES, which is the lack of individual-level surveys that record adequate economic data together with information on deaths. In this paper, we link mortality information from the vital registration system with the CPS, which is probably the best source of data on incomes and education. It would be possible to extend this principle further, bringing in information on risk factors, such as smoking, drinking, and obesity, from other sources, such as the Behavioral Risk Factor Surveillance System, something we plan to do in our future work.

There are also disadvantages of cohort data, primarily the impossibility of separating genuine individual effects from those that result from aggregation. Using individual data that include community characteristics, we could in principle test directly for effects of community means or community inequality, in addition to controlling for individual income. With aggregate data, we have to face the problem of identifying the direct effects from the aggregation effects, and such identification will not always be possible. One of our (subsidiary) aims in this paper is to assess the cohort approach, and to test whether it yields results that are similar to those from individual record data. If so, we will have more confidence in using it in situations where individual data cannot be used.

Figure 4.1 shows the log odds of dying, by age, for a selection of birth cohorts born from 1870 through 1970. Although we can use only a fraction of this information in the analysis, the long-run information is important for interpreting recent events. One immediate feature of the patterns in figure 4.1 is the age profile of mortality. The risk of death is high immediately after birth, falls to low levels in the mid-teens, and then rises with age thereafter. After about age thirty, the log odds of death is approximately linear in age (see also Elo and Preston 1996), albeit with a time-dependent slope. Mortality has also been falling over time, so that the age profiles for the later-born cohorts are below the profiles for those born earlier. However, these two obvious features are far from exhausting these data; the log odds are far from being completely explained by a sum of age and cohort effects. For example, there are clear traces of specific events, such as the 1919 influenza pandemic on the cohort born in 1890. Note also that the proportional reduction in mortality is larger at younger ages—which in the limit must be true because everyone dies eventually—but that the reductions differ by sex; note for example the large reduction in female mortality during child-bearing years. The reduction in mortality among young males is much less than among young females, and for recent cohorts, there has been little or no reduction in the mortality of males in their early twenties. As a result, for the cohort born in 1973, the ratio of mortality rates for males to females in 1995, at age twenty-two, is 3.25:1. For recent cohorts, male mortality rates fall with age from the early twenties to the mid thirties. The causes of these deaths—violence, accidents, and AIDS—are quite different from those at higher ages, and it is implausible that a single explanation in terms of income and income inequality will do for both.

Figure 4.2 shows the mortality data in a way that is more immediately relevant to the task at hand. The graphs show estimated year and cohort effects in the log odds of mortality for males and females separately. These figures use only the birth cohorts that are observed in at least one year between 1975 and 1995 (inclusive), and that can therefore be matched to the CPS data. Panel *A* shows the year effects estimated from a regression of the log odds of dying on a set of year and age dummies, one for each

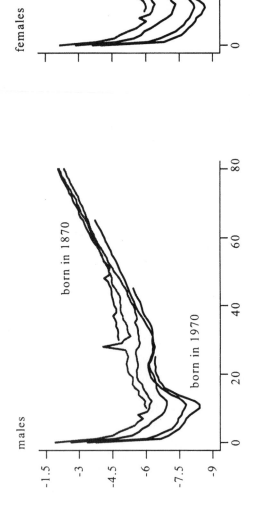

Fig. 4.1 Log odds of mortality, every twentieth cohort
Source: BMD.

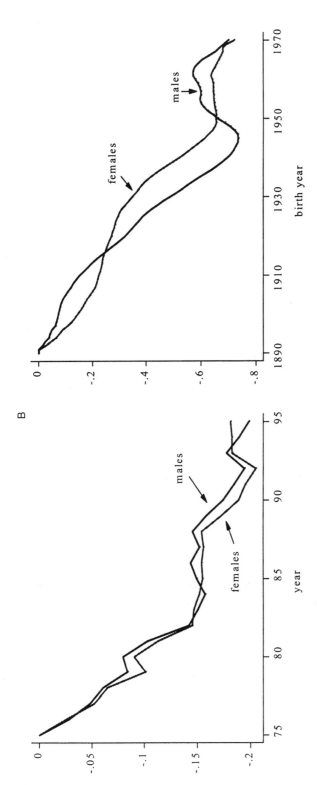

Fig. 4.2 Year and cohort effects in log odds of mortality, from (*A*) regressions of log odds on age and year effects, and (*B*) on age and cohort effects

Source: Authors' calculations using the BMD

year and one for each year of age. Panel *B* is obtained in the same way, but with cohort (date of birth) effects replacing year effects. Panel *A* corresponds to a fitted model in which the age profile remains constant, but drifts down with time, so that all people alive at any given date benefit from that year's reduction in mortality. It shows that the rate of mortality decline was relatively rapid from 1975 through the early 1980s, but has been a good deal slower since then. The timing of the increase in income inequality is not identical to the timing of the slowdown in mortality decline; the largest increase took place in the late 1970s and early 1980s, and the increase since then has been more modest. The cohort effects in Panel *B* do not tell a picture of continuing progress. In particular, males born since 1950 show sharply higher mortality rates than those born in the 1940s. Note that those born most recently are observed only in the early periods of their lives, so that these graphs give undue weight to the recent mortality experience among young adults, for whom deaths are due to violence, accidents, and AIDS, and thus do not share the long-run downward trend.

Table 4.1 presents a first set of results focusing on the relationship between income and mortality. The dependent variable is the log odds of dying while the independent variables are dummy variables for each age from twenty-five to eighty-five and the logarithm of income per adult equivalent. Because the age effects are removed, identification comes from the relationship between cohort (and interaction) components of mortality and income less its age profile. One hypothesis is that all of the trend reduction in mortality is potentially attributable to income, but the historical and international evidence suggests that this is not the case (see, in particular, Preston 1975). In consequence, and in order to avoid the risk of spurious correlation between time trends, we present results with and without the inclusion of a time trend. In the ordinary least squares (OLS) regressions in the upper half of the table, the coefficient on the logarithm of family income per equivalent is -0.559 for men, and -0.528 for women; with the introduction of a time trend, these numbers become -0.281 and -0.125, respectively. Since the log odds is approximately the log-probability when the probability is small, these estimates can be thought of as elasticities. If the coefficient were -0.5, a fourfold increase in income would cut the risk of death in half.

In order to compare the cohort results with those from individual-level data, we estimated logits for the probability of dying using the National Longitudinal Mortality Study (NLMS). This is a survey of individuals originally sampled in CPS surveys and in the census around 1980, into which death certificates have been retrospectively merged. For all individuals from age twenty-five to eighty-five, we constructed an indicator of whether the individual had died within 365 days of the interview, and estimated a logit model in which the independent variables are a set of age

Table 4.1 Log Odds of Dying as a Function of Income, by Age Group

	Men			Women		
		IV			IV	
	OLS	Years of Education	Years of Education (cohort dummies)	OLS	Years of Education	Years of Education (cohort dummies)
			No Time Trend Included			
All age groups	-0.559	-0.923	-0.826	-0.528	-0.840	-0.838
	(24.1)	(29.1)	(28.6)	(27.4)	(31.1)	(32.7)
Ages 25-39	0.452	-0.940	0.646	-0.362	-0.995	-0.850
	(5.1)	(3.2)	(4.7)	(6.1)	(9.7)	(9.8)
Ages 40-54	-0.770	-1.046	-0.996	-0.850	-1.114	-1.081
	(17.8)	(19.6)	(19.6)	(23.5)	(24.9)	(25.3)
Ages 55-69	-0.559	-0.923	-0.826	-0.528	-0.840	-0.838
	(24.1)	(29.1)	(28.6)	(27.4)	(31.1)	(32.7)
Ages 70-85	-0.430	-0.637	-0.603	-0.370	-0.671	-0.637
	(19.0)	(20.2)	(20.9)	(14.6)	(16.8)	(17.1)
			Time Trend Included			
All age groups	-0.281	-1.224	-0.877	-0.125	-0.619	-0.686
	(8.8)	(15.6)	(15.1)	(5.4)	(9.8)	(13.8)
Ages 25-39	0.168	-1.363	-0.189	-0.174	-1.150	-0.809
	(1.8)	(4.1)	(1.0)	(2.7)	(7.2)	(7.1)
Ages 40-54	-0.261	-1.379	-0.918	-0.022	-0.547	-0.466
	(3.9)	(6.7)	(7.0)	(0.5)	(3.6)	(4.9)
Ages 55-69	-0.281	-1.224	-0.877	-0.125	-0.619	-0.686
	(8.8)	(15.6)	(15.1)	(5.4)	(9.8)	(13.8)
Ages 70-85	0.035	-0.118	0.037	0.059	-0.194	-0.035
	(1.7)	(1.40)	(0.8)	(2.8)	(1.8)	(0.6)

Sources: Authors' calculations based on CPS and BMD.

Notes: Coefficients on mean ln(income/adult equivalent); *t*-statistics in parentheses. Each regression includes the mean of the logarithm of household income per adult equivalent (mean ln[y/ae]), and a set of age dummies. The regressions are estimated for the full sample, and for subsets of cohorts in different age groups. Each cell in the table reports a coefficient on the mean of log of income per adult equivalent from a single regression. The instrumental variable (IV) estimates instrument mean ln(y/ae) with the mean years of education (in the Years of Education columns) or with mean years of education and a set of birth-cohort dummies (in the Years of Education [cohort dummies] columns).

dummies, one for each age, and the logarithm of real family income per adult equivalent. (The public-use version of the NLMS provides only real-income classes, not actual income, and we have used the classes to construct a [rough] measure of the logarithm of total family income. We use the 1981 CPS to calculate mean log income by age and sex within each of the NLMS income brackets, using the results to impute log income to each person in the NLMS within his or her reported income bracket. In practice, this gives very similar results to the simpler method of setting income to the middle of the bracket. Adult equivalents were computed by linking individuals to households and counting the numbers of adults and children.) Figure 4.3 shows the one-year log odds of mortality from the NLMS, computed from the fractions in the sample who died at each age, together with the age profile of the log odds of mortality from the BMD for 1982. The NLMS mortality figures, which exclude deaths among the institutionalized population, are somewhat lower among the elderly, although the major effect is presumably beyond age eighty-five and is noisier, especially at young ages. However, the two data sets are clearly measuring the same thing, so that the NLMS results are a useful comparison. The coefficient on the (log) income term in the logit is -0.352 for men (161,472 observations, $t = 10.8$) and -0.262 for women (177,953 observations, $t = 6.3$), close to the estimates in Elo and Preston (1996, using the same data but a different specification). As we have seen, there are a number of reasons that these numbers should *not* be the same as those in table 4.1. In addition to the aggregation issues, note that the NLMS records only a single estimate of family income so that, if permanent income is a better predictor of mortality than current income, or if income is measured with error, the NLMS estimate will be attenuated relative to the cohort based estimates to the extent that averaging over cohorts limits measurement error or proxies permanent income. Note also that the NLMS relates only to income in a few years around 1980, so that the two sets of calculations cover quite different periods. Given this and the aggregation differences, we find the estimates surprisingly similar!

Table 4.1 shows a number of other results, including breakdowns by age, and using two alternative instrumental variable strategies to estimate the income effect. In the four OLS columns, with results for four age groups, we obtain the now-standard results that income matters most for health in middle age, in the forty to fifty-four age range, and that the effect diminishes with age. Even so, income is still protective for the oldest group of both men and women, though the result vanishes (and indeed income becomes mildly hazardous for women) if time trends are included in the regressions. Perhaps most striking is the *positive* effect of income on mortality among young men; the effect is large and negative among young women. This result is associated with the recent increase in mortality rates among young men, which appears to be greater among cohorts with higher

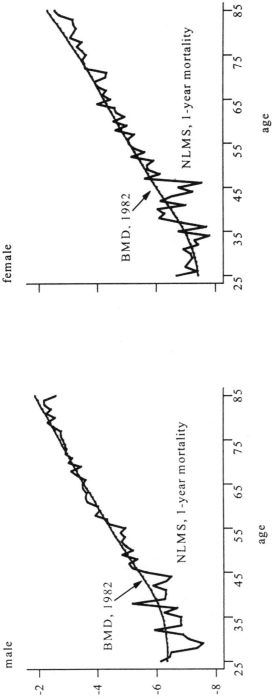

Fig. 4.3   Log odds of mortality, National Longitudinal Mortality Study and Berkeley Mortality Database
Source: Authors' calculations using the BMD and NLMS

average incomes. Plausible arguments can be made for a positive association between income and the specific causes of mortality in this age group—AIDS, violence, and accidents—and there is good evidence from pooled state and time series evidence that gives very similar results (Ruhm 2000).

The way in which the protective effect of income varies with age can also be assessed directly, by entering age into the regressions not only in levels, but also interacted with income. We have done this for both the cohort and NLMS data, in the latter by running a logit on age dummies, the log of income per adult equivalent, and on age dummies interacted with the income term. The results are shown in graphical form in figure 4.4, for males in the left-hand panel and for females in the right-hand panel. These graphs are noisy, particularly for the NLMS, which is to be expected given the very large number of age coefficients in the regressions. Nevertheless, for women, we see the familiar pattern whereby protection increases with age to around age forty-five and decreases thereafter. For men, the two graphs are not the same. In particular, the cohort data again show a positive association of mortality and income among young men, a phenomenon of which there is no trace in the NLMS data. The obvious explanation here is the fact that the NLMS measures mortality in the early 1980s, before the youth mortality phenomenon had become so pronounced. More disappointing is the failure of the NLMS to show any other age pattern; perhaps we are asking too much of single-year mortality data.

The instrumental variable (IV) estimates in table 4.1 are motivated by an attempt to replace current income with a longer-term or permanent measure. One strategy is to instrument income with years of education, on the assumption that education does not affect health directly—a controversial supposition that we shall investigate more directly below. Another is to use cohort dummies as instruments; this would be correct if we wanted to measure lifetime resources, which remain constant over time at the cohort level. These instrumentation schemes are likely to work better for people of working ages than for the elderly, whose current income is less well predicted by their education, and whose lifetime income will not be adequately captured by averaging over the maximum of twenty years in our sample. Nevertheless, the estimated income effects move as would be expected if long-run income is a better predictor of health than current income. In the top half of the table, instrumentation of income by years of education moves the coefficient for men from -0.56 to -0.92, and for women from -0.53 to -0.84. Instrumentation also removes much of the difference between the estimates with and without time trends. Most remarkably, when years of education (but not education and cohort dummies) is used as an instrument, the protective effect of income for young men is restored. If this result is accepted—and there are reasons for not

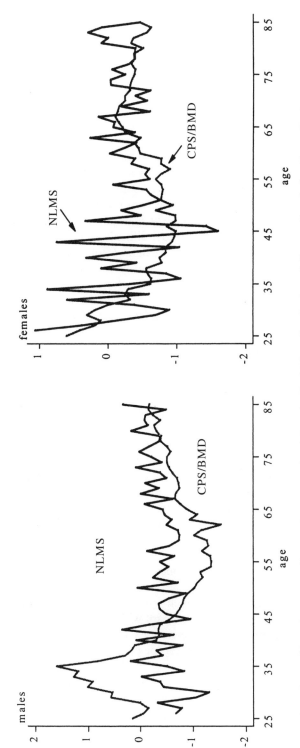

Fig. 4.4 Effects of income on mortality at each age, National Longitudinal Mortality Study and Current Population Survey/Berkeley Mortality Database

Source: Authors' calculations using the BMD, CPS, and NLMS

doing so, including the possible direct role of education, and the different result when cohort dummies are added to the set of instruments—it indicates that mortality among young men is procyclical, again in line with Ruhm's (2000) result that unemployment is good for health.

Figure 4.5 shows one aspect of the partial correlation between ln y and mortality. These graphs show the residuals of regressions of mortality, years of education, and ln y on a set of age dummies, averaged over birth cohorts in the top two panels, and over years in the bottom two panels. The very clear inverse variation is clear for both men and women, as is the fact that education is a very good predictor of income at the cohort level (though less so on the time series), which helps in instrumentation but which, in our later tests, will also make it difficult to separate out the roles of income and education on the cohort data. (Note that the regressions contain more information than shown in the figures, since the observations are cohort-year pairs, with interactions, not cohort or year averages.)

Table 4.2 is similar to table 4.1, but with the addition of two within-cohort inequality measures, the variance of log income and the Gini coefficient. (These regressions were also run with time trends, but the results are not much affected.) The introduction of either the variance of log income or the Gini coefficient produces an estimated *protective* effect of inequality on health. To see the size of the coefficients, we note that, averaged over all cohorts, log odds of male mortality declined by 0.20 from 1975 to 1995. The mean of the logarithm of income per adult income rose by 0.20, and its variance by 0.196. Using the coefficients for all age groups combined, then the rise in income equal would be predicted to reduce the log odds by about half of the actual decline, 0.10 (OLS) and 0.12 (IV). The rise in the variance would lead to a decline in the log odds of death by 0.03 (OLS) and (an absurd) 0.12 (IV). The changes in mortality, income, and inequality were much the same for females as for males, but the coefficients are different. The predicted effect of the rise in income is a decline in the log odds of female mortality of 0.08 (OLS) and 0.07 (IV), while the predicted declines from the increase in inequality are 0.03 (OLS) and 0.11 (IV). In the four OLS regressions (men versus women, variance of logs versus Gini), the introduction of the inequality measure has very little effect on the income coefficient, which remains protective as before, but in all cases the inequality measure appears with a significant negative coefficient. The protective effect of inequality is about the same for males and females, and is a good deal larger for people aged thirty-five to fifty-nine than for those aged sixty and over. For the elderly, the estimated coefficient on the Gini is insignificantly or barely significantly different from zero. While the theory allows for the possibility that inequality is protective—for example, if individuals look to the bottoms of their reference groups in assessing their health, or if the covariance of mean cohort and mean reference group income is large enough—the result remains implausible.

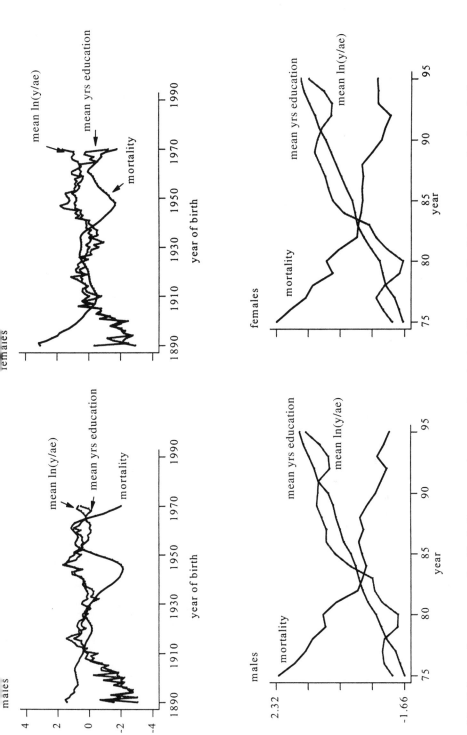

Fig. 4.5   Cohort and year averaged residuals from regressions on age dummies (variables standardized to have mean = 0 and standard deviation = 1).

Source: Authors' calculations using the CPS and BMD

Table 4.2   **Log Odds of Dying as a Function of Income and Income Inequality by Age Group**

	Men		Women	
	OLS	IV	OLS	IV
Inequality Measure Is Variance of ln(y/ae)				
All age groups				
mean ln(y/ae)	−0.520	−0.606	−0.479	−0.417
	(22.7)	(8.1)	(26.2)	(4.5)
var ln(y/ae)	−0.157	−0.655	−0.180	−0.656
	(8.7)	(4.9)	(13.6)	(5.1)
Ages 35–59				
mean ln(y/ae)	−0.621	−1.368	−0.726	−0.307
	(14.6)	(4.9)	(26.2)	(1.5)
var ln(y/ae)	−0.236	0.353	−0.240	−1.066
	(8.0)	(1.0)	(11.4)	(3.9)
Ages 60–85				
mean ln(y/ae)	−0.506	−0.594	−0.298	−0.380
	(21.6)	(9.4)	(15.9)	(5.7)
var ln(y/ae)	−0.123	−0.475	−0.084	−0.375
	(5.7)	(3.3)	(5.7)	(3.0)
Inequality Measure Is Gini Coefficient of y/ae				
All age groups				
mean ln(y/ae)	−0.505	−0.596	−0.440	−0.631
	(20.3)	(8.0)	(21.7)	(12.4)
Gini y/ae	−0.525	−2.910	−0.819	−1.522
	(5.5)	(5.1)	(10.5)	(5.2)
Ages 35–59				
mean ln(y/ae)	−0.504	−1.370	−0.625	−0.588
	(10.6)	(6.6)	(18.9)	(3.4)
Gini y/ae	−1.563	1.476	−1.398	−2.624
	(8.3)	(1.4)	(9.8)	(2.8)
Ages 60–85				
mean ln(y/ae)	−0.518	−0.694	−0.308	−0.435
	(20.3)	(15.3)	(15.1)	(7.0)
Gini y/ae	−0.154	−0.870	−0.105	−1.514
	(1.5)	(2.4)	(1.2)	(2.2)

Sources: See table 4.1.

Notes: Each regression includes the mean of the logarithm of household income per adult equivalent (mean ln[y/ae]), a set of age dummies, and an inequality measure. The instrumental variable (IV) estimates instrument mean ln(y/ae) and the inequality measure with the mean years of schooling, and the fraction of people in education categories. The education categories are years of schooling equal to 5–8, 9–11, 12, 13–15, and 16 or more. Years of education from 0 to 4 is the omitted category. Numbers in parentheses are *t*-statistics.

Figure 4.6 provides some insight into the source of these results, as well as an explanation for the difference with Deaton (2001), whose similar regressions yielded essentially no effect. The top two panels of the figure show the raw income inequality data, on the left for the Gini coefficient and on the right for the variance of logarithms. Each of these has a male

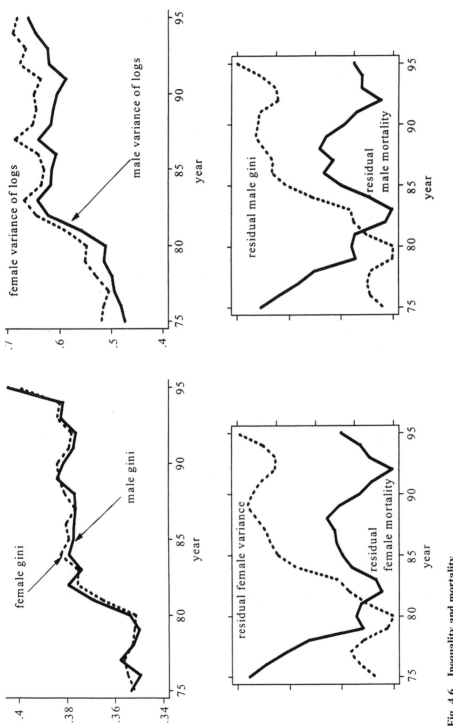

Fig. 4.6   Inequality and mortality
Source: See fig. 4.5.

and a female variant because we use the CPS data to assign (the same) family income per equivalent to each person in the household, so that differences in inequality by sex reflect the distribution of men and women across households. As far as trends are concerned, there is no important difference by sex. Note also that the inequality measures are not the usual inequality measures for the whole country, but the average over all the cohorts in a given year of the inequality measure within the cohort. Such measures exclude the contribution of between cohort inequality to the national aggregate. Even so, the trends are similar to the national trends. Family income inequality rises rapidly from the late 1970s to the mid 1980s, with relatively little change thereafter. (The sharp increase in the Gini in 1995 is not mirrored in the variance of logs, because it is associated with inequality at the very top of the distribution, and is probably distorted by top-coding effects and by other changes in interview protocols.)

The bottom panels of the figure are constructed by calculating the residuals of the regression of the log odds of death on age effects and on the mean of log income per equivalent, averaging by year, and plotting them against the similarly averaged residuals of the inequality measure on age effects and the mean of log income per equivalent. Without the averaging, the regression of the mortality residuals on the inequality residuals would reproduce the coefficients in table 4.2, and the averaging is used only to produce uncluttered graphs. The negative (partial) relationship between inequality and mortality is transparent in both figures. When inequality was low, mortality was high (and falling), and when inequality was high, mortality was low. The timing of mortality change and income inequality in the United States is not supportive of the hypothesis that inequality increases the risk of death in the aggregate. The estimated protective effect of inequality is reduced if time trends are included in the regression, but neither the sign nor the statistical significance is altered. Nor are the results affected by introducing one- or two-period lags between inequality and mortality.

Table 4.2 also shows the consequences of instrumenting both inequality and income, on the same grounds as before: that it is possibly the long-term experience of high income and high inequality, not their year-to-year variations, that conditions mortality. Also as before, we use education as instruments, not only the mean years of education in the cohort, but also the fractions of the cohort with various educational attainment levels. The inclusion of the latter captures the distribution of educational attainment within the cohort, and generates excellent instruments for income inequality. Generally, the results are what might be expected, that moving to a long-term basis reduces attenuation and makes the estimates absolutely larger, for both mean income and inequality. There is one exception, for men aged thirty-nine to fifty-nine, where the protective effect of inequality is reversed, so that we get the (originally expected) positive coefficient, though for neither the Gini nor the variance of logs is the estimate significantly different from zero. (One line of investigation that needs to be pursued with different data is the extent to which these results reflect mortality among young men, and its relationship to the business cycle on the one hand, and with income in the cross-section through AIDS, an effect that has almost certainly changed sign over time.)

Table 4.3 investigates another possibility that is often raised in the literature, that the effects of inequality might be a mistaken attribution of the effects of poverty. The first two rows of the table show the OLS and IV results for men and women, first including only the fraction of people below the official U.S. poverty line, and in the next row, including both the fraction who are poor and the variance of log income. These results serve merely to deepen the puzzle. Poverty, like inequality, is estimated to be

Table 4.3   **Poverty and Interactions between Income and Inequality**

	Men		Women	
	OLS	IV	OLS	IV
mean ln(y/ae)	−0.646	−1.101	−0.670	−0.970
	(25.0)	(24.3)	(33.6)	(34.0)
Fraction poor	−0.825	−1.774	−1.181	−1.447
	(7.1)	(5.4)	(15.2)	(7.0)
mean ln(y/ae)	−0.580	−0.688	−0.603	−0.700
	(21.1)	(2.9)	(28.7)	(4.9)
var ln(y/ae)	−0.125	−0.552	−0.117	−0.333
	(6.4)	(1.8)	(8.4)	(1.9)
Fraction poor	−0.490	−0.321	−0.884	−0.853
	(3.9)	(0.4)	(10.6)	(2.3)
mean ln(y/ae)	−0.263	−0.274	−0.215	−0.261
	(5.5)	(1.8)	(5.2)	(2.4)
var ln(y/ae)	4.165	8.191	3.769	3.215
	(5.9)	(2.3)	(6.7)	(1.7)
mean * var	−0.474	−0.929	−0.438	−0.413
	(6.1)	(6.1)	(7.0)	(7.0)
∂/∂mean ln(y/ae)	−0.539	−0.815	−0.485	−0.515
	(23.6)	(7.7)	(27.0)	(5.6)
∂/∂var ln(y/ae)	−0.160	−0.299	−0.188	−0.518
	(9.0)	(1.6)	(14.3)	(4.0)

Sources: See table 4.1.

Notes: Each regression also includes a set of age dummies. The IV estimates instrument mean ln(y/ae), poverty, and inequality with the mean years of schooling, and the fraction of people in different education categories. The education categories are years of schooling equal to 5–8, 9–11, 12, 13–15, and 16 or more. Years of education from 0 to 4 is the omitted category. The derivatives are evaluated at the sample means of var ln(y/ae) and mean ln(y/ae), respectively. The means for var ln(y/ae) are 0.583 (men) and 0.617 (women). The means for mean ln(y/ae) are 9.135 (men) and 9.039 (women). Numbers in parentheses are t-statistics.

protective of health, and when both poverty and inequality are included, both are separately protective.

The last row of the table investigates whether the slope of the gradient between income and mortality is affected by mortality. As we saw in the theoretical development, except when we observe individual and reference group income, the effect of income on health is a function of inequality, and is predicted to increase with general increases in inequality in the individual-level data if such changes increase within-group inequality more than between-group inequality. In the cohort data, the same effect is caused by an increase in the variance of aggregation group income relative to reference group income, which is itself a plausible consequence of an increase in within-reference-group inequality. (For example, see equation [11], and take $z = \mu + \eta_i$ and $x = \mu + \theta_a + \eta_i$, so that increases in the variance σ_a^2 will simultaneously increase the slope of the gradient as well as the ratio of within-reference-group to between-reference-group inequality.) The interaction terms in the third section of the table are estimated to be negative, so that the gradient of mortality with income is steeper when inequality is larger. This is again a plausible result, but it does not remove the implausible (and significant) protective effect of inequality at the mean (see the derivatives at the bottom of the table).

In the results so far, we have adopted the position that the underlying determinant of health is income rather than education, and have used education to instrument income and income inequality. This is a controversial position, however; many would argue that it is not income, but education—or at least some personal attribute that is strongly related to education—that is the ultimate determinant of health. It is also possible, in the immediate context, that our misspecification of the role of education is responsible for our unexpected results on the role of inequality. Americans have been becoming more educated on average, and the rate of return to education has been rising, so that changes in income inequality are due in part to changes in the relationship between income and education.

Before looking at the cohort data, it is worth using the individual-level data in the NLMS to give another assessment of income versus education, and one that is not affected by the time series effects that are potentially important in the cohort data. Table 4.4 shows results from logit estimation of the probability of death on men and women in the NLMS within a year of interview. Age effects by single years of age were included but are not shown. In the first row are the results already discussed, on the effects of the logarithm of income per adult equivalent on the log odds of dying. The second row shows what happens if we replace income by years of education; like income, education has a strong and significant effect on mortality; an additional five years of education, from, say, high school to a master's degree, reduced the probability of death by around 20 percent for men and about 25 percent for women. In the final row of the table, the logits are run with both education and income. For men, the income co-

	Men	Women
Table 4.4 — The Effects of Education and Income on Mortality in the National Longitudinal Mortality Study		

	Men	Women
ln(y/ae)	−0.3524	−0.2620
	(10.8)	(6.3)
Years of Education	−0.0374	−0.0483
	(6.2)	(6.0)
ln(y/ae)	−0.3254	−0.1968
	(9.1)	(4.3)
Years of Education	−0.0121	−0.0336
	(1.8)	(3.8)

Sources: Authors' calculations based on NLMS.

Notes: Coefficients from logit regressions in which dependent variable is whether the respondent died within 365 days of interview. A full set of age dummies, one for each year from twenty-five to eighty-five, are included but not shown. There are 161,472 males in the sample and 183,282 females. The income and education variables are entered separately (the first two rows) and then together (last two rows). Numbers in parentheses are t-statistics.

efficient is reduced hardly at all, while the coefficient on education is reduced threefold, and is no longer significantly different from zero. According to these estimates, to a first approximation, it is income, not education, that is protective of health. These results are not replicated for women, whose combined regression shows effects of both income and education separately, each protective, and each with a coefficient somewhat smaller than when they are included alone.

Income is much less well predicted by education for women than for men, but this does not explain why it is income, not education, that plays the dominant role in male mortality. Although others in the literature have found that income drives out education—see Lantz et al. (1998), who use the (much smaller) American Changing Lives Survey, which also allows controls for behavioral factors—we find the result quite surprising. Even if it is ultimately income that matters, it is astonishing that a single observation of a year's income, with all the usual measurement error, should predict mortality better than a longer-term measure as predicted by education, in which case both income and education should show up in the reduced form regression. The obvious possibility is that there is causality running from health to income for people about to die. There is some evidence for this in the results reported by Elo and Preston (1996), who also find marked reductions in the education effects on five-year mortality when income is introduced, with reductions larger for men. However, even after allowing for income—and for a range of other covariates, but with age effects restricted to entering linearly—male education is still significant, and twice as large as in table 4.4.

Tables 4.5 (men) and 4.6 (women) report results from the NLMS is the

Table 4.5   **Effects of Income and Schooling on Male Mortality, National Longitudinal Mortality Study (logits)**

	Died in 0–1 Years	Died in 1–2 Years	Died in 2–5 Years	Died in 5–9 Years
	A. Men Aged 25–59 at Time of Survey			
ln(y/ae)	−0.456	−0.397	−0.415	−0.325
	(8.14)	(7.32)	(14.01)	(13.43)
Years school	−0.072	−0.054	−0.076	−0.063
	(5.70)	(4.47)	(11.62)	(11.85)
ln(y/ae)	−0.390	−0.357	−0.328	−0.248
	(6.25)	(5.94)	(9.95)	(9.24)
Years school	−0.035	−0.021	−0.045	−0.040
	(2.50)	(1.55)	(6.27)	(6.81)
N	123,806	123,298	122,740	120,811
Number of deaths	508	558	1,929	3,059
	B. Men Aged 60–85 at Time of Survey			
ln(y/ae)	−0.302	−0.197	−0.224	−0.202
	(7.62)	(5.10)	(9.43)	(9.29)
Years school	−0.028	−0.034	−0.028	−0.026
	(4.06)	(5.14)	(6.73)	(6.62)
ln(y/ae)	−0.285	−0.138	−0.191	−0.172
	(6.54)	(3.23)	(7.26)	(7.11)
Years school	−0.007	−0.024	−0.013	−0.012
	(0.88)	(3.26)	(2.91)	(2.75)
N	37,666	36,123	34,514	29,705
Number of deaths	1,543	1,609	4,809	6,061

Sources: See table 4.4.

Notes: For men aged twenty-five to fifty-nine, age at the year of the survey was also included. For men aged sixty to eighty-five, a complete set of age dummies was included. The sample for each logit includes individuals who either died in the time period at the head of column or died later; individuals who died earlier than the time period specified are excluded. Numbers in parentheses are *t*-statistics.

same format as in table 4.4, but using deaths in periods at various lengths after the interview; in the first column for death in the first year, as in table 4.4, in the second column for the second year, the third column between two to five years after the interview, and in the last column, for deaths from five to nine years after the interview. (For the results in the second, third, and fourth columns, the logits are estimated only over the group of individuals who survived to the beginning of the period, so that the samples become successively smaller across the panels.) Although moving forward in time will not eliminate the effect of prospective death on income—some conditions will produce low income for many years prior to death—it should certainly reduce the influence of reverse causality. And indeed, the results in the table are supportive of such an interpretation. For men under sixty, in the last two lines under heading A, the effects of

Table 4.6   **Effects of Income and Schooling on Female Mortality, National Longitudinal Mortality Study (logits)**

	Died in 0–1 Years	Died in 1–2 Years	Died in 2–5 Years	Died in 5–9 Years
	A. Women Aged 25–59 at Time of Survey			
ln(*y/ae*)	−0.409	−0.340	−0.344	−0.332
	(5.75)	(4.78)	(9.03)	(11.41)
Years school	−0.076	−0.060	−0.066	−0.065
	(4.13)	(3.26)	(6.74)	(8.66)
ln(*y/ae*)	−0.348	−0.296	−0.287	−0.276
	(4.41)	(3.75)	(6.80)	(8.54)
Years school	−0.037	−0.027	−0.035	−0.035
	(1.82)	(1.34)	(3.16)	(4.17)
N	134,355	134,041	133,721	132,581
Number of deaths	314	320	1,140	1,995
	B. Women Aged 60–85 at Time of Survey			
ln(*y/ae*)	−0.190	−0.074	−0.174	−0.133
	(3.75)	(1.52)	(6.50)	(6.01)
Years school	−0.042	−0.017	−0.024	−0.019
	(4.67)	(1.96)	(4.95)	(4.56)
ln(*y/ae*)	−0.118	−0.044	−0.145	−0.111
	(2.16)	(0.84)	(5.01)	(4.60)
Years school	−0.034	−0.014	−0.014	−0.011
	(3.50)	(1.49)	(2.64)	(2.37)
N	48,927	47,900	46,789	42,789
Number of deaths	1,027	1,111	4,000	6,202

Sources: See table 4.4.

Notes: For women aged twenty-five to fifty-nine, age at the year of the survey was also included. For women aged sixty to eighty-five, a complete set of age dummies was included. The sample for each logit includes individuals who either died in the time period at the head of column or died later; individuals who died earlier than the time period specified are excluded. Numbers in parentheses are *t*-statistics.

education on the log odds hold fairly steady, but the effects of income are reduced. Some such effect is also to be expected from the increasing irrelevance of an increasingly remote measure of income, so it is not clear how much of the reduction should be attributed to reverse causality. For women, however, in table 4.6, where the reverse causality is weaker, the initial income estimates are lower, and are less affected as the mortality window is moved forward. On this evidence, while the initial male estimate of −0.4 is probably too large (in absolute value), a case can be made for defending an estimate of around −0.3. Even for the elderly, and even five to nine years after interview, income exerts a protective effect against mortality, and the effect is not removed by controlling for education.

The cohort data are perhaps less well suited to investigating the question of whether it is income or education that matters for health. As we saw in figure 4.5, the cohort average of the mean of the logarithm of income per equivalent adult is closely related to the mean years of education, even after removing age effects from both. As a result, attempts to include both variables in the cohort regressions lead to a good deal of instability in the results. Nevertheless, the cohort data allow us to investigate the possibility that there are dynamic effects of income on mortality, with differences in short- and long-run responses. Table 4.7 shows the results of trying to investigate education versus income, and the effects on the estimates of variance. The first two rows, labeled "Regression 1," shows the results of OLS regressions on age effects and on mean income and mean years of education. For both men and women, and whether or not time trends are included, income is either hazardous (or insignificant), and education is protective. The absence of a protective role for income is in sharp contradiction to the cross-sectional results from the NLMS, and for males, that education drives out income is exactly the opposite of the NLMS result. That income might actually be harmful once education has been controlled for has been argued by Fuchs (1974, 1993) and by Garber (1989), but the studies cited either do not support the conclusion (Grossman 1975; Leigh 1983; Newhouse and Friedlander 1980), or are unpersuasive, as in Auster, Leveson, and Sarachek (1969), who estimate regressions across states in 1960 with results that are frequently statistically insignificant and that are not robust across specifications. What is more plausible is the existence of dynamic effects, whereby mortality is positively related to transitory income and (positively) follows the business cycle, but is negatively related to permanent income. (There is a parallel here with the argument that "new" causes of mortality—cigarette smoking, obesity, lack of exercise, AIDS—first affect the rich but eventually settle down into the traditional pattern of differentially harming the poor. Income brings health risks in the short run, but ultimately the also the ability to understand and overcome them.) Even so, we must note that these results are not very robust; the correlation between the two parameter estimates is -0.80 for men and -0.78 for women. Instrumental variable results using cohort dummies as instruments (not shown here) show very different (and sometimes bizarre) patterns. Clearly, much work remains to be done, perhaps with data that are less collinear than those used here.

Table 4.7 also shows the results of entering education, not as average years of education, but as the proportions of the population with various levels of educational attainment ("Regression 2"). These results do not differ in any major way from those in regression 1; the estimated effects of income on mortality are still positive or insignificant, and education is strongly protective, especially years of education beyond high school. Interestingly, those with "some college," shown here as thirteen to fifteen years of school, are consistently at higher risk of mortality than those with only a high-school diploma. (This effect, possibly attributable to selection,

Table 4.7   Mortality, Income, and Education (cohort data)

	Men			Women		
	All Ages	Ages 35–59	Ages 60–85	All Ages	Ages 35–59	Ages 60–85
Regression 1						
mean ln(y/ae)	0.088	0.285	0.002	−0.022	−0.001	0.090
	(2.9)	(4.7)	(0.1)	(0.9)	(0.0)	(4.71)
mean years education	−0.117	−0.192	−0.088	−0.097	−0.159	−0.071
	(26.2)	(19.6)	(22.7)	(25.6)	(23.2)	(27.7)
Regression 2						
mean ln(y/ae)	0.079	0.173	−0.018	0.065	0.019	0.081
	(2.8)	(3.2)	(0.7)	(2.9)	(0.5)	(4.2)
5–8 years school	0.205	−0.236	0.330	−0.356	−0.300	−0.402
	(1.7)	(0.5)	(3.8)	(3.1)	(0.8)	(5.2)
9–11 years school	0.142	−1.430	0.245	−0.003	−0.319	−0.661
	(1.3)	(3.4)	(2.9)	(0.0)	(0.9)	(9.5)
12 years school	−0.463	−2.029	−0.160	−0.704	−1.452	−0.749
	(4.5)	(5.1)	(2.1)	(7.7)	(4.5)	(12.2)
13–15 years school	−0.107	−0.996	−0.483	−0.513	−0.779	−0.798
	(1.0)	(2.5)	(5.7)	(5.2)	(2.4)	(10.4)
16+ years school	−1.502	−2.911	−0.795	−1.782	−2.255	−1.045
	(12.8)	(7.4)	(8.4)	(17.1)	(6.8)	(12.7)
Regression 3						
mean ln(y/ae)	0.077	0.267	−0.003	−0.053	−0.043	0.087
	(2.5)	(4.3)	(0.1)	(2.1)	(1.0)	(4.6)
mean years education	−0.112	−0.186	−0.086	−0.087	−0.148	−0.070
	(24.4)	(16.9)	(21.7)	(21.6)	(18.3)	(26.4)
var ln(y/ae)	−0.061	−0.027	−0.051	−0.079	−0.052	−0.011
	(4.0)	(1.0)	(3.2)	(6.5)	(2.7)	(1.1)

Sources: See table 4.1.

Notes: Each regression includes the mean of the logarithm of household income per adult equivalent (mean ln[y/ae]), and a set of age dummies. The regressions are estimated for the full sample, and for subsets of cohorts in different age groups. Numbers in parentheses are *t*-statistics.

also reappears in the NLMS, albeit in a much weaker form; see Elo and Preston 1996). Apart from this, there is no evidence here that there is a problem with using mean years of education to predict mortality. In the final regression in the table, regression 3, we repeat the first regression but with the addition of the variance of the logarithm of income per adult equivalent. The coefficients on inequality are much reduced compared with those in table 4.2, typically by a factor of more than two, but the estimated protective effect remains. Allowing for the possible separate effects of education and income much reduces the size of the estimated protective effect of inequality, but it does not eliminate it.

4.4   Conclusions

Our original purpose was to use birth-cohort data to examine the links between mortality and inequality. Controlling for income, we find that higher inequality is associated with lower mortality, a conclusion that comes from negative association of mortality and inequality in the United States in the late 1970s and early 1980s. While it is possible that such a result has some real basis—and there are theoretical mechanisms that could produce it—it is hardly established by these results. In particular, the sign of the effect is implausible, if only because of the expected operation of Jensen's inequality, and the magnitude of the effect is quite sensitive to the way in which other variables are introduced, particularly income and education. Indeed, we suspect that the current priority should not be the investigation of the effects of inequality, but the unpacking of "socio-economic status" into its components, particularly education and income, as well as the disaggregation of mortality into its different components so as to allow them to respond to income and education in different ways. The results reported here make it clear that this is no easy task; the way in which education and income affect mortality is not the same for men as for women, nor for young adults as for older adults; it is different over long time periods and over the business cycle, and it is different in the cross-section from over time. We find evidence that short-term increases of income may raise the risk of mortality, particularly for young men. In the cohort data, however, the longer-term effects of income, or of income linked to education, are protective. Yet this evidence needs to be reconciled with the individual-level data from the follow-up studies, which show that, especially for men, income plays a role as large as or larger than that of education. Work on these issues has hardly begun.

Appendix

In the text, we make repeated use of a standard result from the normal distribution, which is stated here for convenience. In words, if two variable are jointly normally distributed, the conditional expectation of one given the other—the regression function—is linear and homoscedastic, with coefficients and residual variance equal to the coefficients and residual variance of a large sample OLS regression. Formally, suppose that

(A.1)
$$\begin{pmatrix} x_1 \\ x_2 \end{pmatrix} \sim N \begin{pmatrix} \mu_1, \sigma_{11}\ \sigma_{12} \\ \mu_2, \sigma_{21}\ \sigma_{22} \end{pmatrix}$$

then

(A.2)
$$E(x_1 \mid x_2) = a + bx_2$$

(A.3)
$$a = \mu_1 - \frac{\sigma_{12}}{\sigma_{22}}\mu_2$$

(A.4)
$$b = \frac{\sigma_{12}}{\sigma_{22}}$$

and for the variance,

(A.5)
$$V(x_1 \mid x_2) = \sigma_{11} - \frac{\sigma_{12}^2}{\sigma_{22}}.$$

The same results hold for the expectation of x_2 conditional on x_1 with 1 and 2 transposed.

References

Adler, Nancy E., Thomas Boyce, Margaret A. Chesney, Sheldon Cohen, Susan Folkman, and S. Leonard Syme. 1994. Socioeconomic status and health: The challenge of the gradient. *American Psychologist* 49:15–24.

Adler, Nancy, W. Thomas Boyce, Margaret A. Chesney, Susan Folkman, and Leonard Syme. 1993. Socioeconomic inequalities in health: No easy solution. *Journal of the American Medical Association* 269:3140–5.

Auster, Richard, Irving Leveson, and Deborah Sarachek. 1969. The production of health, an exploratory study. *Journal of Human Resources* 4:411–36.

Cohen, S., S. Line, S. B. Manuck, B. S. Rabin, E. R. Heise, and J. R. Kaplan. 1997. Chronic social stress, social status, and susceptibility to upper respiratory infections in nonhuman primates. *Psychosomatic Medicine* 59:213–21.

Cohen, S., D. Tyrrell, and A. Smith. 1991. Psychological stress and susceptibility to the common cold. *New England Journal of Medicine* 325:606–12.

Deaton, Angus. 2001. Inequalities in income and inequalities in health. In *The causes and consequences of increasing inequality,* ed. Finis Welch, 285–313. Chicago: University of Chicago Press.

Elo, Irma T., and Samuel H. Preston. 1996. Educational differentials in mortality: United States, 1979–85. *Social Science and Medicine* 42:47–57.

Fiscella, Kevin, and Peter Franks. 1997. Poverty or income inequality as predictor of mortality: Longitudinal cohort study. *British Medical Journal* 314:1724–8.

Fuchs, Victor R. 1974. *Who shall live? Health, economics, and social choice.* New York: Basic Books.

———. 1989. Comments. In *Pathways to health: The role of social factors,* ed. John P. Bunker, Deanna S. Gombey, and Barbara Kehrer, 226–29. Menlo Park, Calif.: Kaiser Family Foundation.

———. 1992. Poverty and health: Asking the right questions. *The American Economist* 36:12–18.

Garber, Alan M. 1989. Pursuing the links between socioeconomic factors and health: Critique, policy implications, and directions for future research. In *Pathways to health: The role of social factors,* ed. John P. Bunker, Deanna S. Gombey, and Barbara Kehrer, 271–315. Menlo Park, Calif.: Kaiser Family Foundation.

Grossman, Michael. 1975. The correlation between health and schooling. In *Household production and consumption,* ed. Nestor E. Terleckyj, 147–211. New York: Columbia University Press.

House, James S., and David R. Williams. 1995. Psychosocial pathways linking SES and CVD. In *Report on the conference on socioeconomic status and cardiovascular health and disease,* 119–24. Bethesda, Md.: National Heart, Lung, and Blood Institute, NIH.

Judge, Ken. 1995. Income distribution and life expectancy: A critical appraisal. *British Medical Journal* 311:1282–5.

Judge, Ken, Jo-Ann Mulligan, and Michaela Benzeval. 1998. Income inequality and population health. *Social Science and Medicine* 46:567–79.

Kaplan, George, Elsie R. Pamuk, J. M. Lynch, Richard D. Cohen, and Jennifer L. Balfour. 1996. Inequality in income and mortality in the United States: Analysis of mortality and potential pathways. *British Medical Journal* 312:999–1003.

Kennedy, Bruce P., Ichiro Kawachi, and Deborah Prothrow-Stith. 1996. Income distribution and mortality: Cross sectional ecological study of the Robin Hood index in the United States. *British Medical Journal* 312:1004–7.

Lantz, Paula M., James S. House, James M. Lepkowski, David R. Williams, Richard P. Mero, and Jieming Chen. 1998. Socioeconomic factors, health behaviors, and mortality. *Journal of the American Medical Association* 279:1703–8.

Leigh, J. Paul. 1983. Direct and indirect effects of education on health. *Social Science and Medicine* 17:227–34.

Lobmayer, Peter, and Richard G. Wilkinson. 1999. Income, inequality, and mortality in 14 developed countries. University of Sussex, Trafford Center for Medical Research.

Marmot, Michael G. 1994. Social differences in health within and between populations. *Daedalus* 123:197–216.

———. 1997. Inequality, deprivation, and alcohol use. *Addiction* 92:S13–S20.

McIsaac, Sandra J., and Richard G. Wilkinson. 1997. Income distribution and cause specific mortality. *European Journal of Public Health* 7:45–53.

Mellor, Jennifer M., and Jeffrey Milyo. 1999. Income inequality and individual health: Evidence from the Current Population Survey. Robert Wood Johnson Health Policy Scholars Working Paper no. 8. Boston: Boston University School of Management.

Newhouse, Joseph P., and Lindy J. Friedlander. 1980. The relationship between medical resources and measures of health: Some additional evidence. *Journal of Human Resources* 15:200–18.

Preston, Samuel H. 1975. The changing relation between mortality and level of economic development. *Population Studies* 29:231–48.

Robert, Stephanie A., and James S. House. 2000. Socioeconomic inequalities in health: Integrating individual-, community-, and societal-level theory and research. In *Handbook of social studies in health and medicine,* ed. Gary L. Albrecht, Ray Fitzpatrick, and Susan C. Scrimshaw, forthcoming. London: Sage Publications.

Rogot, E., P. D. Sorlie, N.J. Johnson, and C. Schmitt, eds. 1992. *A mortality study of 1.3 million persons by demographic, social, and economic factors: 1979–1985 follow-up.* Bethesda, Md.: NIH.

Ruhm, Christopher J. 2000. Are recessions good for your health? *Quarterly Journal of Economics* 115 (May): 617–50.

Sapolsky, Robert M. 1993. Endocrinology alfresco: Psychoendocrine studies of wild baboons. *Recent Progress in Hormone Research* 48:437–68.

———. 1998. *Why don't zebras get ulcers? An updated guide to stress, stress-related diseases, and coping.* New York: Freeman.

Wilkinson, Richard G. 1996. *Unhealthy societies: The afflictions of inequality.* London: Routledge.

———. 1997. Commentary: Income inequality summarises the health burden of individual relative deprivation. *British Medical Journal* 314:1727–8.

Wilmoth, John. 1999. The Berkeley Mortality Database. Available at [http://demog.berkeley.edu/wilmoth/mortality].

Comment   James P. Smith

This is a very good paper—but staying within the spirit of the thesis advanced here, very good relative to what? We clearly are in need of a reference group. The reference group could be all economic papers written during the last ten years, but, alas, that would be faint praise indeed. Another reference group could be all the papers delivered at this NBER economics of aging conference, but given my desire to receive an invitation to the next conference in this splendid Boulders setting I will not go down that particular route. Perhaps it would be safer to stay close to home and simply compare this paper to all joint papers of Deaton and Paxson. If I rank it toward the top, however, will Angus and Chris think that I do not like their other papers all that much? If I place it toward the bottom, will they feel that I really don't regard this as an important contribution? The very process of ranking clearly creates psychosocial stress, which may be an additional piece of evidence that they are onto something quite important.

The truth of the matter is that this is an outstanding paper no matter what the reference group is. There is an exploding literature on the relationship between economic inequality and health. The reasoning behind

James P. Smith is a senior economist at RAND Corporation.

the assumed relationship takes many forms, but one of most prominent variants states that through psychosocial stress mechanisms, inequality is a health risk for those at the bottom of the social pecking order. This is clearly an important scientific topic that needs original and balanced thinking and testing. Unfortunately, a good deal of the existing work is heavily ideological (by proponents and opponents alike) with a compelling desire to prove (or disprove) a result.

One reason ideology has such free rein is that the theory beyond the link between economic inequality and health has, to date, almost no formal structure, so that it is unclear how one could rigorously test (in the sense of rejecting) the hypothesis. The absence of structure appears in many forms, but perhaps the most important concerns the reference group. Without specifying what the appropriate reference group is, the theory is not testable. Advocates of the link between economic inequality and health status have been all over the map on the correct reference group—nation, state, neighborhood, birth cohort, fellow economists—would be only a partial list of options used. Some researchers simply go back and forth among them picking out whatever happens to be consistent with the particular result of the moment.

The lack of consensus about the appropriate reference group is not surprising. All choices seem quite ad hoc, justified mainly by casual intuition. As soon as you convince yourself that one option makes sense, you easily think of a dozen flaws in the argument. In my view, the inherent arbitrariness involved in selection of an appropriate reference group has been the main stumbling block in making new scientific advances on the link between inequality and health.

The powerful insight that motivates the Deaton-Paxson paper is that the authors do not have to prespecify any particular reference group. Instead, they argue that all data contain variation in economic status that is partly within-reference-group variance and partly variance across reference groups. The health–economic status (however measured) gradient that emerges then depends on how much of the variation in economic status is within rather than across reference groups. For example, suppose only relative (to the median) rank matters. If all variation in economic status is across reference groups, there would be no health–economic status gradient at all. If instead all dispersion in economic status is within reference groups, the health–economic status gradient may be quite steep.

More generally, the greater the extent to which economic status variation is within rather than between reference groups, the steeper the social health gradient will be. This insight may help explain the old puzzle of why the health–grade of employment gradient was steeper in the Whitehall sample of civil servants than it appeared to be in the population at large (Marmot et al. 1991). Based on the same reasoning, one would also speculate that the health gradient would be steeper in data from small towns than for the nation as a whole. To my knowledge, that particular idea has not been tested, but the general framework outlined by Deaton and Paxson suggests that any time we can narrow variation to within-reference-group variance, the social health gradient should be steeper.

This formal structure provided by Angus and Chris as a way of thinking about the effects of inequality on health is extremely important and will have a major impact on the field. As an aside, I must admit that I prefer their earlier specification, which ranks relative to the median rather than what seems like their current favorite, relative to the top dog. In the top-dog model, everyone's health will deteriorate if the wealthiest person gets richer. That seems a particularly dreary view of human nature, although I must admit that there are some economic departments that seem to fit it.

However, their contribution is not yet done. Another important insight comes from their discussion of the implications of aggregation. Rather than simply jumping to test the model on data aggregated into birth cohorts, in typical fashion, they first work out analytically the implications of doing so. It turns out that the type of aggregation matters a lot in testing the implications of the theory of the effects of economic inequality on health. Deaton and Paxson demonstrate that what happens to the slope of the social health gradient depends on the fineness of the reference group relative to the fineness of the aggregation. For example, if the reference group is very broad (say, the nation) relative to aggregation across groups, the relation between health and income will be preserved. If instead the reference group is narrow relative to any aggregation, the health-income relation can be lost completely.

This is an important insight with significant implications for interpreting the vast number of existing studies on this topic. In some ways, the authors may not be making enough of this idea, which can be used to evaluate whether a particular group is a likely candidate for a reference group. For example, in their own work, they find a preserved relation suggesting that reference groups are much broader than birth cohorts, which further suggests that something akin to nations may be close to the mark.

The second part of the paper shifts gears and becomes decidedly empirical. This part of the paper has the attribute in applied work that I most value. After reading their paper, I believe I know pretty much everything that such data aggregated across cohorts will tell us about the relationship between economic status and health. The reasons I feel so informed are that Chris and Angus leave no stone unturned and that they believe in full disclosure. We are told about all results whether they conform to priors or not, and we are also informed about the robustness of the main findings. That is how scientific progress is eventually possible and is a step toward restoring the good name of applied work.

What are their principal findings? First, they report that income is protective of health (higher income leads to improvements in health). Somewhat surprisingly, they find that income may be more protective of health than education is, which certainly runs counter to the accepted wisdom on this subject. This finding is intriguing and fortunately Deaton and Paxson plan to do more work on this important topic.

There is another relation implicit here that they do not emphasize at all, which may be even more surprising—your kids will kill you! In their empirical specification, economic resources of the household are defined as adjusted household income in which the adjustment is an equivalence scale correction where adults are counted as one and children as one-half. Household economic resources can decline either because household income falls or because there are more children present—both have the identical effect of reducing health. Without getting into a debate about the theoretical justification of doing an equivalence scale adjustment (which I personally do not find plausible), there is a legitimate concern about how much of the protective effect of income comes through the numerator (household income) and how much through the denominator (family size). This is an especially relevant concern given how much variation in family size exists during this time period. During these years, variation in family size stems not only from the significant variation over life cycles as families are formed, but also from the fact that these data span the years of both the baby boom and, especially, the sharp baby bust. Since it is testable whether income or family size is driving their results, at a minimum they should provide such tests by separately entering into their empirical models the numerator (income) and the denominator (family size). I doubt that they will have equivalent effects.

There is another issue regarding the protective effect of income on health lurking in the background. While Deaton and Paxson mention a number of times the possibility of reverse causation from health to income, a full accounting of the impact of income on health is not possible without taking reverse causation into account. For example, in a recent paper (Smith 1999), I show that the full correlation between income and health among men in their fifties is due to the effect of health on income, leaving nothing left over for income to affect health. A good deal of the association between health and income apparently is reverse causation. Unless reverse causation is isolated and controlled, one must be extremely cautious before interpreting any age or gender patterns that emerge on the protective effect of income on health.

Second, and perhaps even more shocking to them, they find that income inequality is also protective! Your health is better if you live in a very unequal society. Of course, this runs counter to the spirit, letter, and the law of the hypothesis advance by Wilkinson (1996) and others and will certainly be greeted with much dismay. Angus and Chris do not accept this result at face value, finding it implausible, but they never really make it disappear. Before talking about why it may not be so surprising empirically to find this result in the recent U.S. experience, one should stop for a moment and ask whether finding income inequality to be protective is any more implausible than finding inequality to be harmful for health. If one were to decide, based only on the implications for one's own health, between living in two societies that were identical, except that the top 25 percent in the economic hierarchy had higher incomes in one society, which would one choose? I would favor the society where the top 25 percent had higher incomes (and thus more inequality). Those very rich people with fears for their own mortality might invest more in medical research or hospitals seeking a cure to spare them at least for a while from some dreaded diseases. These investments are very much in the nature of public goods so I should benefit from them as well. Now, I would not push this argument very strongly since the most likely outcome (until there is strong evidence otherwise) is that my health would be the same in both societies. At this point, however, I do not think we should have strong directional priors about the impact of inequality on health.

Whatever our theoretical expectations, is it empirically surprising to find that rising inequality is correlated with better health in recent U.S. history? I think not. Before coming to that, I would like to raise a related point. Deaton and Paxson's mortality measure includes death from all causes, but I think that the inequality hypothesis with its emphasis on psychosocial stress deals principally with mortality from only a subset of causes, such as deaths related to heart disease. For example, the inequality hypothesis has little to do with deaths from AIDS. To explain AIDS-related deaths, we want to understand the causes of the spread of HIV through unprotected sex and unsanitary needles among drug users. It would be a real stretch to believe that AIDS-related deaths had much to do with rising economic inequality. Therefore, a more relevant test of the inequality hypothesis would limit mortality to certain diseases, with heart disease being the most prominent.

Heart disease is an interesting case since it is generally agreed that, at least among adults, reduction in mortality from heart disease is the major reason for the recent extension in the length of life. However, the reasons for heart disease–related improvements in life expectancy appear to be related to new drug treatments for hypertension, better health behaviors (especially exercise and diet), and new surgical procedures following heart attacks. Who would seriously argue that this heart disease–related improvement in life expectancy was due to lower economic inequality?

As we know, economic inequality in the United States was not falling during these years, but was increasing rather sharply. The sharpest drops in mortality reported by Deaton and Paxson took place during the mid-1970s to early 1980s—the very years when economic inequality was rising most rapidly (and income was relatively constant). It should come as no surprise, then, that data based on the U.S. experience will produce a positive correlation between inequality and health. As I argued above, the reasons for this correlation lie outside the inequality-health transmission mechanism which at best can be only a bit player in a much larger story.

What then do I take from the empirical work in this fine paper? My bottom-line conclusion is that this organization of the data with aggregation across birth cohorts or calendar year is unlikely to answer conclusively the question of the effect of economic inequality on health, or possibly even whether income or education is more protective for health. I do not regard this as a negative assessment of the value of the work presented here. Much of the evidence by others purporting to demonstrate the effects of inequality on health is based on some type of data aggregation. After reading Deaton and Paxson's paper, I would regard such evidence with a good deal more skepticism. That is contribution enough for any paper.

References

Marmot, Michael G., George Davey Smith, Stephen Stansfeld, Chandra Patel, Fiona North, J. Head, Ian White, Eric Brunner, and Amanda Feeny. 1991. Health inequalities among British civil servants: The Whitehall II Study. *Lancet* (June 8): 1387–93.
Smith, James P. 1999. Healthy bodies and thick wallets: The dual relation between health and economic status. *Journal of Economic Perspectives* 13 (2): 145–166.
Wilkinson, Richard G. 1996. *Unhealthy societies: The afflictions of inequality.* London: Routledge.

Predictors of Mortality among the Elderly

Michael D. Hurd, Daniel McFadden, and
Angela Merrill

5.1 Introduction

Mortality risk is a fundamental determinant of consumption and saving in a life-cycle model. Understanding the behavioral reactions to variation in mortality risk is important from a scientific point of view and from a policy point of view. The reaction will reveal the degree of risk aversion, which is an important behavioral parameter. The economic status of the oldest old will depend on their consumption and saving choices in the years closely following retirement. Under the life-cycle model, the predicted changes in life expectancy will have an effect on national saving beyond what would be forecast from a compositional effect.

Mortality risk in the population may be adequately measured by lifetables; however, individuals are likely to have additional information about their life chances and use that information in making consumption and saving decisions. Some of that information may be related to observable characteristics such as health status and socioeconomic status (SES). Accounting for the relationship between SES and mortality (the SES gradient) is particularly important. The gradient is important because it causes difficulties in predicting the economic status of a cohort and in under-

Michael D. Hurd is senior economist and director at the RAND Center for the Study of Aging and a research associate of the National Bureau of Economic Research. Daniel McFadden is the E. Morris Cox Professor of Economics and director of the econometrics laboratory at the University of California, Berkeley, a 2000 Nobel Laureate in economics, and a research associate of the National Bureau of Economic Research. Angela Merrill is a researcher at Mathematica Policy Research.

Financial support from the National Institute on Aging through a grant to the National Bureau of Economic Research is gratefully acknowledged.

standing life-cycle behavior from cross-sectional variation in wealth. Besides cohort effects that would, by themselves, cause wealth to decline with age in cross-section, the mortality gradient will cause wealth to increase both in cross-section and in panel. As a cohort ages those with less wealth die, leaving survivors from the upper part of the wealth distribution. Thus, even if no couple or single person dissaves after retirement, the wealth of the cohort would increase with age. This makes it difficult to study life-cycle wealth paths based on synthetic cohorts, which will eliminate cohort differences in lifetime time resources but not differential mortality. These difficulties carry over to studies of income and consumption in synthetic cohorts.

Yet it is likely that individuals have subjective information about their own survival chances that cannot be discovered from mortality rates stratified by observable covariates such as SES. First, some personal characteristics are not easily measured, so they cannot be used as stratifying variables. Second, individuals may misperceive their survival chances, choosing consumption based on subjective yet biased life expectancy. If we are to understand consumption choices we need to have observations on the subjective variables that individuals use in making their choices. Third, even if we could stratify by many characteristics and understand average bias, there surely would remain considerable heterogeneity in subjective survival probabilities: Understanding that heterogeneity would help in the estimation of life-cycle models.

To model and use heterogeneous information about survival chances in life-cycle models is a multistep process. First, we need to find the observable correlates of mortality and measure their effects. Second, we need to measure the perceptions of individuals about their own mortality risk, and, given observable characteristics, to find if these perceptions have explanatory power for mortality. Third, we need measures of mortality risk that embody all of our knowledge about heterogeneity in models of decision making. This paper addresses the first two of these steps.

Differential mortality by SES has been observed over a wide range of data and populations: Mortality rates are high among those from lower SES groups (Kitagawa and Hauser 1973; Shorrocks 1975; Hurd 1987; Hurd and Wise 1989; Jianakoplos Menchik and Irvine 1989; Feinstein 1992). However, because of data limitations the measures of SES have typically been occupation or education. In the Health and Retirement Study (HRS) and the Asset and Health Dynamics of the Oldest Old (AHEAD) study there is scope for expanded studies of differential mortality because these are panel surveys with considerable age density and they obtain extensive data on income, wealth, and health conditions in addition to occupation and education. The AHEAD data in particular offer opportunities for increasing our knowledge of the gradient because the population (aged seventy or over at baseline) has not been studied to the extent to which younger populations have been. Furthermore, the fact that the

AHEAD population is almost completely retired means that a very strong confounding effect of health on income via work status is practically eliminated. Finally, almost the entire AHEAD population is covered by Medicare: Therefore, an important causal pathway linking SES to mortality via access to health care services is reduced and even possibly eliminated.

The HRS and AHEAD asked each respondent to give an estimate of his or her chances of surviving to a target age, which was approximately twelve years in the future. In the HRS this variable is a significant predictor of mortality between waves 1 and 2 (Hurd and McGarry forthcoming). Here we aim to find if it has predictive power for mortality in the AHEAD population both unconditionally and conditionally on observable characteristics.

In this paper we will verify that SES is related to mortality in the AHEAD data. Then we will give evidence about the validity of the subjective survival probabilities. The evidence will be of three kinds: whether the subjective survival probabilities vary in cross-section in a way that is appropriate given the variation in actual mortality; how the subjective survival probabilities change in panel in response to new information such as the onset of an illness; and whether they predict actual mortality. We will then examine whether, conditional on health status and SES, the subjective survival probabilities have explanatory power for predicting mortality.

5.2   Data

Our data come from the AHEAD study (see Soldo et al. 1997), a biennial panel survey of individuals born in 1923 or earlier and their spouses. At baseline in 1993 it surveyed 8,222 individuals representative of the community-based population except for oversamples of blacks, Hispanics, and Floridians. Wave 2 was fielded in 1995.

The main goal of AHEAD is to provide panel data from the three broad domains of economic status, health, and family connections. Our main interest in this paper is to understand the predictors of mortality between waves 1 and 2, especially education, income, wealth, and the subjective probability of survival. In wave 1, individuals and couples were asked for a complete inventory of assets and debts and about income sources. Through the use of unfolding brackets, nonresponse to asset values was reduced to levels much lower than would be found in a typical household survey such as the Survey of Income and Program Participation (SIPP).[1]

Both HRS and AHEAD have innovative questions about subjective

---

1. To handle nonresponse to asset and total income questions, we use a nested composite imputation procedure. We impute nonresponse to asset ownership, unfolding brackets, and asset amounts sequentially. Ownership and complete brackets are imputed using stepwise logistic regression on a number of demographic characteristics. Dollar amounts are then imputed, conditional on a complete bracket, using a nearest neighbor which makes extensive use of covariates (Hoynes, Hurd, and Chand. 1998).

probabilities, which request the subject to give the chances of future events. We will use observations on the subjective probability of survival. The form of the question is as follows:

> [Using any] number from 0 to 100 where "0" means that you think there is absolutely no chance and "100" means that you think the event is absolutely sure to happen . . . [w]hat do you think are the chances that you will live to be at least A?

A is the target age. A is 80, 85, 90, 95, or 100 if the age of the respondent was less than 70, 70–74, 75–79, 80–84, or 85–89, respectively. The question was not asked of those aged 90 or over or of proxy respondents.

AHEAD queries about a wide range of health conditions. Many are asked of the respondent in the following form: "Has a doctor ever told you that you have . . . ?" We will use information on ten conditions such as cancer, heart attack/disease, and lung disease. The respondent is queried about limitations to activities of daily living (ADL). We will use as an indicator of poor health three or more ADL limitations.

AHEAD measures cognitive status in a battery of questions which aim to test a number of domains of cognition (Herzog and Wallace 1997). Learning and memory are assessed by immediate and delayed recall from a list of ten words that were read to the subject. Reasoning, orientation, and attention are assessed from Serial 7's, counting backward by one, and the naming of public figures, dates, and objects.[2] In prior work we have found that unrealistic stated subjective survival probabilities are associated with low cognitive performance (Hurd, McFadden, and Gan 1998). Therefore we aggregated the cognitive measures in AHEAD and formed a categorical variable to indicate low cognitive performance.

AHEAD also has a battery of questions that are extracted from the Center for Epidemiologic Studies (CESD) scale, which aims to assess depressed mood. We form an indicator of depressed mood based on these questions.

5.3 Results

The baseline AHEAD sample was 8,222, of which 813 died between waves 1 and 2, and 7,364 survived; the vital status of 45 is unknown. Excluding those forty-five, the two-year mortality rate was 0.099.[3] This mortality rate cannot be compared with any lifetable rate for two reasons:

---

2. "Serial 7's" asks the subject to subtract 7 from 100, and then to continue subtracting 7 from each successive difference for a total of five subtractions.

3. The mortality rate including the 45 cases among the living was 0.0988. Including them among the dead, the mortality rate was 0.104. In the rest of the paper we will include them among the living for convenience, but their treatment is not consequential compared with the lack of data on the institutionalized population.

Table 5.1   **Two-Year Mortality Rates (weighted)**

	Male		Female	
	N	Mortality Rate	N	Mortality Rate
69–74	1,170	0.064	1,626	0.058
75–79	820	0.126	1,264	0.080
80–84	574	0.164	953	0.104
85–89	268	0.216	468	0.169
90+	82	0.402	221	0.262
All	2,914	0.125	4,532	0.095

Source: Authors' calculations from AHEAD waves 1 and 2.

First, the AHEAD baseline is the community-based population, so that it excludes residents of long-term care facilities who have substantially higher mortality rates than the community-based population. Lifetables include residents of long-term care facilities and of other institutions.[4] Second, the AHEAD sample includes spouses of AHEAD age-eligible respondents, but the spouses may themselves not be age eligible. The age-ineligible spouses do not make up any population whose mortality rate can be compared with a lifetable.

The mortality rate of the AHEAD age-eligible sample ($N = 7,446$) was 0.107; the lifetable rate interpolated to 1993 was 0.155. The difference comes from the high mortality rates among the institutionalized.

Table 5.1 shows weighted mortality rates for the age-eligible part of the AHEAD population by age and sex, and the number of observations. A few respondents were aged sixty-nine at their initial interviews but we include them in the seventy to seventy-four age band. The weights account for the oversamples at baseline. The figures show sharply increasing mortality rates with age and a considerable difference between men and women. At older ages the number of subjects diminishes rapidly due to mortality, cohort effects, and the fact that the institutionalized are not in the AHEAD baseline.

Table 5.2 presents mean wealth and income by age and marital status. Wealth is the total of housing, financial, and business and other real estate wealth, but it does not include any pension wealth. Income includes all financial income such as pension income, but no flow from owner-occupied housing. Just as in other cross-sectional data sets, wealth and income fall with age, and both are higher among couples than among singles. The table makes clear that we cannot study the relationship between mortality and economic status without effectively controlling for age.

---

4. Because AHEAD will follow the baseline respondents into institutions, it will eventually be representative of the entire cohort of 1923 or earlier.

Table 5.2	Mean Wealth and Income, Weighted (thousands)				
	Age				
	70–74	75–79	80–84	85–89	90+
Wealth					
Singles	141.6	113.0	91.4	86.6	77.2
Couples	269.3	243.1	204.7	187.9	86.1
Income					
Singles	17.0	14.9	13.1	13.4	11.2
Couples	31.8	30.8	29.6	25.8	15.0

Source: Authors' calculations from AHEAD wave 1.

Note: For couples, "age" is the respondent's age, "Wealth" is the wealth of the couple, and "Income" is the income of the couple. Thus each couple enters the table twice.

5.3.1 Wealth, Income, and Education

Table 5.3 shows mean and median wealth in wave 1 by vital status in wave 2. At baseline among single males aged seventy to seventy-four who survived to wave 2, average wealth was about $216.5 thousand. Wealth was just $67.2 thousand among those who died. This is, of course, a substantial difference and indicates considerable differential mortality by wealth holdings. The difference among single females is smaller but still substantial. Among married males there is only a small difference, whereas married female survivors had almost twice the wealth on average as deceased married females. The medians also indicate considerable differential mortality by wealth.

There is diminished differential mortality by wealth among those aged seventy-five to seventy-nine. Given the amount of observation error on wealth, we judge there to be little difference in wealth holdings by mortality outcome among those married at baseline, either male or female. There is some difference among singles. The differences are smaller still among the eighty- to eighty-four-year-olds, and there are no consistent differences among the eighty-five-to eighty-nine-year-olds. The medians show somewhat more differential mortality but not as much as at the youngest age interval.

Among those aged ninety or over, sample sizes are small. For example, only thirty-nine single males and twenty married females were in the age interval at baseline. The group with the largest number of observations (single females) shows no differential mortality.

These data are summarized in figure 5.1, which shows the wealth of decedents relative to the wealth of survivors.[5] For example, single female decedents aged seventy to seventy-four had about 40 percent of the wealth of survivors. The figure shows a general trend to smaller differences in

5. Not shown when the category has fewer than 100 observations.

Table 5.3   **Wealth at Baseline (thousands)**

	All	Survived			Died		
	N	N	Mean	Median	N	Mean	Median
Ages 70–74							
Single							
Male	250	228	216.5	69.8	22	67.2	20.4
Female	828	776	128.7	51.7	52	52.9	25.6
Married							
Male	906	854	282.6	150.8	52	268.3	115.6
Female	777	737	260.3	140.6	40	138.6	100.8
Ages 75–79							
Single							
Male	204	176	176.7	68.3	28	129.9	96.0
Female	802	737	100.8	44.0	65	75.8	29.5
Married							
Male	606	531	255.3	125.2	75	225.8	103.0
Female	445	410	232.5	117.0	35	214.8	80.0
Ages 80–84							
Single							
Male	160	126	111.0	52.0	34	106.0	48.0
Female	704	624	91.4	42.4	80	60.5	25.8
Married							
Male	407	350	212.5	110.7	57	191.4	69.6
Female	244	225	201.2	113.3	19	144.6	95.5
Ages 85–89							
Single							
Male	106	84	111.9	35.8	22	75.8	11.0
Female	393	324	82.7	39.0	69	80.0	20.0
Married							
Male	161	125	178.3	74.3	36	135.0	63.2
Female	73	64	225.3	79.0	9	260.2	72.0
Ages 90+							
Single							
Male	39	23	205.2	25.9	16	65.7	26.2
Female	199	143	59.0	11.0	56	84.8	26.1
Married							
Male	43	26	97.7	66.5	17	81.9	35.0
Female	20	18	83.4	78.5	2	29.4	47.3

Source: Authors' calculations from AHEAD waves 1 and 2.

wealth at greater ages. We conclude that overall there is evidence of differential mortality by wealth: On average, those who died had about 70 percent of the wealth of those who survived. However, the difference decreases with age.

Table 5.4 has comparable results but for average education. Thus, among males aged seventy to seventy-four the average level of education

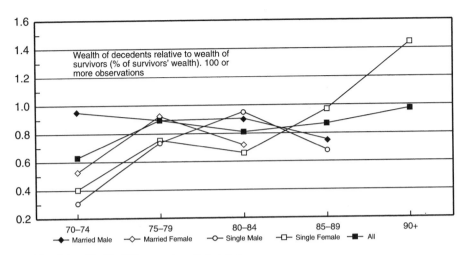

Fig. 5.1   Wealth differences by vital status

was 11.5 years among survivors and 10.4 among the deceased. In the first age band the differential is considerable and it is the same for each sex. At ages seventy-five to seventy-nine the differential decreases for men but remains about the same for women, and by ages eighty to eighty-four there is no differential among men. It is notable that in the highest age interval, the educational level of women is higher than that of men even though for these cohorts the educational level of a complete population of men would have been considerably higher. An explanation is found in the differential mortality at younger ages: Women consistently have a higher mortality gradient by education than men, causing the better-educated women to survive at a higher rate than the better-educated men.

Tables 5.5 and 5.6 show mortality rates by wealth and income quartiles, respectively. The quartiles are defined separately by marital status, but the quartile boundaries are the same over the entire age range. Because of the correlations between age and economic status, and between age and mortality, overall mortality varies strongly by wealth or income quartile as shown in the last line of each table. However, this relationship is much less clear when age is controlled for. In the first age band there is a consistent decline across the quartiles, but in the other age bands there is little consistent pattern even though mortality is generally the largest in the lowest wealth quartile. Mortality by income has a more consistent pattern and for some age intervals the effects are very strong. For example, among eighty to eighty-four-year-olds the mortality rate in the lowest income quartile is about 56 percent greater than in the highest. As with wealth, however, the differential seems to diminish with age.

These figures, particularly for wealth, suggest that differential mortality

Table 5.4 **Years of Education**

	70–74		75–79		80–84		85–89		90+	
	Male	Female	Male	Female	Male	Female	Male	Female	Male	Female
Survived	11.5	11.5	11.3	10.9	10.4	10.4	10.0	10.7	8.6	9.2
Died	10.4	10.4	11.1	10.0	10.4	10.2	8.5	10.2	8.1	9.1
N	1,170	1,626	820	1,264	574	953	268	468	82	221

Source: Authors' calculations from AHEAD waves 1 and 2.

Table 5.5   Two-Year Mortality Rates: Wealth Quartiles

	Wealth Quartile			
	Lowest	2nd	3rd	Highest
70–74	0.09	0.06	0.06	0.04
75–79	0.12	0.09	0.10	0.09
80–84	0.15	0.13	0.10	0.11
85–89	0.23	0.18	0.16	0.16
90+	0.30	0.29	0.27	0.37
All	0.14	0.11	0.10	0.08

Source: Authors' calculations from AHEAD waves 1 and 2.

Table 5.6   Two-Year Mortality Rates: Income Quartiles

	Income Quartile			
	Lowest	2nd	3rd	Highest
70–74	0.10	0.05	0.06	0.05
75–79	0.10	0.12	0.08	0.09
80–84	0.14	0.14	0.12	0.09
85–89	0.25	0.17	0.13	0.16
90+	0.31	0.32	0.27	0.28
All	0.14	0.11	0.09	0.08

Source: Authors' calculations from AHEAD waves 1 and 2.

may decrease with age. To test that idea we estimated analysis-of-variance models in which the observations are mortality rates classified by age intervals and income and wealth quartiles. The models had complete interactions between age intervals and income quartiles and between age intervals and wealth quartiles. We tested for significance of the interactions. We could reject the null hypothesis that the interactions for couples and separately for singles are all zero at the 5 percent level, but not at the 1 percent level. Because the age interactions are not particularly strong and in the interest of simplifying the analysis, our basic model will have age effects, and income and wealth quartiles but not interactions. We will leave the exploration of the age interaction for future research.

Table 5.7 has mortality rates by education level for males. As the table shows, in the AHEAD data mortality is higher for men with nine to eleven years of education than for males of zero to eight years of education, and this is true holding age constant. We have no good reason for this result, except possibly that those with zero to eight years of education have been highly selected by the time they reach the AHEAD ages. Holding age constant, we see some pattern of differential mortality in the younger age bands, but it is less apparent at older ages.

Table 5.7   **Two-Year Mortality Rates: Education (males)**

		Years of Education		
Age	0–8	9–11	12	12+
70–74	0.07	0.11	0.06	0.04
75–79	0.12	0.19	0.08	0.13
80–84	0.15	0.26	0.20	0.11
85–89	0.25	0.28	0.10	0.15
90+	0.43	0.48	0.42	0.37
All	0.14	0.18	0.09	0.09

Source: Authors' calculations from AHEAD waves 1 and 2.

Table 5.8   **Two-Year Mortality Rates: Education (females)**

		Years of Education		
Age	0–8	9–11	12	12+
70–74	0.09	0.06	0.05	0.04
75–79	0.11	0.08	0.07	0.06
80–84	0.10	0.11	0.12	0.10
85–89	0.20	0.20	0.14	0.16
90+	0.25	0.16	0.31	0.28
All	0.13	0.10	0.08	0.08

Source: Authors' calculations from AHEAD waves 1 and 2.

Among females in their seventies there is a strong and consistent relationship between mortality and education, but at older ages there is little if any (table 5.8).

Overall we conclude that there is differential mortality by educational attainment at the younger ages in the AHEAD population, but the effects diminish with age. Particularly among females, who comprise most of the observations in the population aged eighty or over, there is little evidence for a mortality gradient by education.

5.3.2   Subjective Probabilities of Survival

The subjective probability of survival has been studied extensively in data from the HRS (Hurd and McGarry 1995, forthcoming). In cross-section it aggregates well to lifetable levels and it varies appropriately with known risk factors. Furthermore, in panel it is a significant predictor of actual mortality even after accounting for SES and a number of disease conditions. In AHEAD baseline it aggregates well to lifetable values among those aged seventy to seventy-nine, but in the older age groups the subjective survival probabilities overstate survival compared with lifetable rates (Hurd, McFadden, and Gan 1998). One cause of the excess survival prob-

Table 5.9   Subjective Survival Probabilities: Wealth Quartiles (weighted)

	Wealth Quartile			
	Lowest	2nd	3rd	Highest
70–74	0.500	0.470	0.509	0.534
75–79	0.382	0.369	0.385	0.403
80–84	0.310	0.310	0.326	0.306
85–89	0.287	0.256	0.317	0.320
All	0.403	0.385	0.422	0.443

Source: Authors' calculations from AHEAD wave 1.

Notes: Target ages for survival are 85 for the 70–74 age group; 90 for the 75–79 age group; 95 for the 80–84 age group; and 100 for the 85–89 age group. Survival probabilities are not asked of persons aged 90 or above.

ability is that a fairly small number of subjects give a probability of 1.0 of surviving to the target age. The propensity to give a probability of 1.0 is related to low cognitive status, and often an individual will give a probability of 1.0 to a number of unrelated subjective probability questions. Such regularities provide evidence of error in some of the responses. Nonetheless, we will take the responses as they were given by the AHEAD subjects. We imagine, however, that the predictive power of the subjective survival probabilities could be increased were some of the reporting error removed by application of a model of the error.

Table 5.9 shows the average subjective survival probability by age band and wealth quartile.[6] It is important to group by age in this manner because all the respondents in each age band were given the same target age. As would be expected the average survival probability declines with age, but unlike actual mortality there is little systematic variation in the survival probability as a function of wealth. For example, among those aged seventy to seventy-four the average subjective survival probability is about the same in the lowest and the 3rd quartiles. Only in the highest quartile is it greater. Yet the actual two-year survival rate was 5 percentage points higher in the 4th quartile than in the 1st quartile: Such a large difference in two-year survival should accumulate to a much greater difference in subjective survival to the target age.

As shown in tables 5.10 and 5.11, there is little variation in the survival probabilities as a function of either income quartiles or education bands, respectively.

A possible reason for the lack of any pattern by wealth, income, or education is the rather high rate of nonresponse to the survival probabilities.[7] A substantial number of interviews were by proxy, often because of

6. Both the wealth and income quartiles are calculated separately by marital status.
7. This low response rate in AHEAD is in contrast to the very high response rate in HRS.

Table 5.10   **Subjective Survival Probabilities: Income Quartiles (weighted)**

	Income Quartile			
	Lowest	2nd	3rd	Highest
70–74	0.483	0.488	0.492	0.545
75–79	0.348	0.376	0.387	0.415
80–84	0.324	0.331	0.281	0.319
85–89	0.277	0.289	0.333	0.278
All	0.382	0.404	0.410	0.451

Note: See table 5.9 for source and notes.

Table 5.11   **Subjective Survival Probabilities: Education (weighted)**

	Years of Education			
	0–8	9–11	12	>12
70–74	0.494	0.508	0.491	0.532
75–79	0.341	0.388	0.384	0.417
80–84	0.308	0.338	0.274	0.340
85–89	0.354	0.241	0.308	0.258
All	0.382	0.411	0.413	0.442

Note: See table 5.9 for source and notes.

the frailty of the targeted respondent. In this case it made no sense to ask a proxy about the subject's subjective survival probability. In addition, a rather large number of respondents replied "Don't know" (DK) to the query. Table 5.12 has the counts of nonresponse as a function of wealth quartile. Overall, about 25 percent of singles and 21 percent of married persons were nonrespondents (not shown). It is clear that the rate of nonresponse is greatest among those in the lowest quartiles. For example, among seventy- to seventy-four-year-olds, the rate of nonresponse was about 31 percent in the lowest quartile and 11 percent in the highest. Furthermore, because the propensity to give a proxy interview and the likelihood of a DK response are related to health status, it is probable that the responding sample is systematically selected toward those with higher survival probabilities. Therefore, the averages in the lowest quartiles are higher than the true quartile averages whereas the averages in the highest quartiles are closer to the true averages, acting to reduce any upward trend in the subjective survival probabilities as a function of wealth.

We ask whether the pattern of nonresponse could conceivably be responsible for the lack of pattern in the subjective survival probabilities, even though there is a clear pattern in actual mortality. We illustrate that it could be responsible by assigning a subjective survival probability of

Table 5.12   Subjective Survival Probabilities: Number of Nonresponses (all)

	Wealth Quartile			
	Lowest	2nd	3rd	Highest
70–74				
Don't know	107	51	52	45
Refused	16	10	11	3
Proxy	62	47	54	39
Other	1	1	1	0
75–79				
Don't know	76	57	45	40
Refused	17	13	10	15
Proxy	67	48	38	31
Other	0	0	0	1
80–84				
Don't know	75	44	46	23
Refused	22	28	12	5
Proxy	75	44	36	24
Other	1	0	0	1
85–89				
Don't know	44	18	14	17
Refused	10	7	5	5
Proxy	55	18	23	15
Other	0	0	0	0
90+	120	77	62	42
Total missing	748	463	409	306

Source: Authors' calculations from AHEAD wave 1.

zero to the nonresponders. Figure 5.2 shows the variation in the subjective survival probabilities under that assignment. The probabilities increase in wealth in each age band. These results show that differential nonresponse has a quantitatively important effect on the level and variation in the subjective survival probabilities. In future work we will explore methods for imputing missing values, but for the rest of this paper we will, as appropriate, use categorical variables to account for nonresponse.

Table 5.13 shows the estimated regressions of the subjective survival probabilities on the wealth and income quartiles, education bands, and other explanatory variables. We control for age and for the varying interval between the interview and the target age by including as a right-hand variable the lifetable survival rate to the target age from the age of the respondent. If respondents reported their subjective survival probability to be the same as the lifetable rate, the coefficient on this variable would be 1.0. The estimated coefficient shows that the age gradient in the subjective survival probability is less than the age gradient in the lifetable rate. This is partly due to the overestimation of subjective survival probabilities among the oldest compared with the lifetable values.

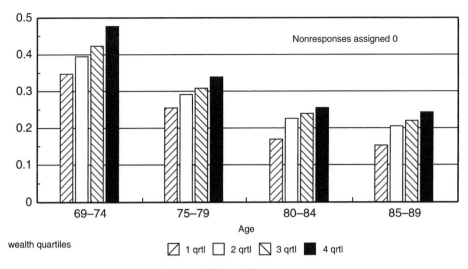

Fig. 5.2   Subjective survival probabilities (all)

The three sets of SES variables show no systematic pattern, which is the basic finding from the cross-tabulations in tables 5.9, 5.10, and 5.11. Relative to the lifetable, males overstate their survival chances by 0.07. This tendency toward over-optimism is also found in the HRS population (Hurd and McGarry 1995).

The last two columns of table 5.13 contain regressions that include controls for health condition. Most of the health conditions are asked of the respondent in the following form: "Has a doctor ever told you that you have . . . ?" The exceptions are "low cognitive score," which is a categorical variable indicating a low score on the sum of three items that were administered in the survey itself; and "Depression" (CESD8), which is based on eight items from the CESD (Wallace and Herzog 1995). A categorical variable for depression indicates a score of 5 or more on the CESD. Eight of the thirteen health variables are significant at the 0.05 level, and they are associated with a reduction in the subjective survival probabilities of 9–25 percent of the average probability. For example, having had heart disease of a heart attack prior to wave 1 is associated with a reduction in the subjective survival probability of 0.062 from a base of 0.415, or about 15 percent. Based on these results we would expect the subjective survival probabilities to predict actual mortality because of their association with the health conditions that, themselves, are associated with mortality.

5.3.3   Change in the Subjective Survival Probabilities

As individuals age the subjective survival probabilities should increase among survivors holding the target age constant. Between waves 1 and 2

Table 5.13   **Determinants of Subjective Survival Probabilities (average probability = 0.415)**

	$R^2 = 0.06$		$R^2 = 0.10$	
	Coefficient	t-statistic	Coefficient	t-statistic
Intercept	0.206	11.819	0.330	14.855
Wealth quartiles				
Lowest	—	—	—	—
2nd	−0.028	−2.029	−0.045	−3.247
3rd	−0.009	−0.617	−0.030	−2.062
Highest	−0.007	−0.465	−0.030	−1.921
Income quartiles				
Lowest	—	—	—	—
2nd	0.020	1.447	0.013	0.988
3rd	0.011	0.765	0.000	0.022
Highest	0.033	2.006	0.023	1.382
Years of education				
0–8	—	—	—	—
9–11	−0.001	−0.090	−0.006	−0.417
12	−0.019	−1.369	−0.029	−2.049
>12	0.012	0.828	0.004	0.259
Lifetime survival to target age	0.516	17.796	0.499	17.097
Male	0.072	4.330	0.070	4.253
Married	−0.006	−0.475	−0.020	−1.630
Married male	0.014	0.659	0.017	0.832
Health conditions				
Heart disease/attack			−0.062	−6.214
Cancer			−0.049	−3.748
Stroke			0.000	0.022
High blood pressure			−0.037	−4.037
Diabetes			−0.036	−2.612
Lung disease			−0.079	−5.665
Arthritis			−0.037	−3.444
Incontinence			−0.020	−1.705
Hip fracture			−0.044	−1.894
Fall requiring treatment			0.022	1.227
Low cognitive score			0.018	1.569
ADL limitation (>2)			−0.060	−3.040
Depression (CESD8 >4)			−0.103	−6.676
Missing cognition			0.019	0.571

Source: Authors' calculations from AHEAD wave 1.

Notes: Based on OLS estimation. ADL = activities of daily living; CESD8 = depression subtest of the Center for Epidemiologic Studies (CESD). Subjective survival probabilities are not asked of persons aged 90 or above. $N = 5,440$.

the average increase was 0.064 (16 percent) among singles and 0.051 (15 percent) among couples. Tables 5.14 and 5.15 show the levels and changes by age band and by sex. The tables show that the subjective survival probabilities are overstated relative to lifetables at older ages, particularly among men. For example, among men aged eighty-five to eighty-nine the

Table 5.14   **Change in Subjective Survival Probabilities and Lifetable Rates, Wave 1 to 2 (males)**

	Subjective Survival to Target Age			Lifetable Survival to Target Age		
	Wave 1	Wave 2	Percent Change	Wave 1	Wave 2	Percent Change
70–74	0.508	0.548	7.9	0.389	0.423	8.7
75–79	0.382	0.470	23.0	0.226	0.259	14.6
80–84	0.332	0.396	19.3	0.098	0.121	23.5
85–89	0.314	0.345	9.9	0.034	0.048	41.2

Source: Authors' calculations from AHEAD waves 1 and 2.

Notes: Target ages for survival are 85 for the 70–74 age group; 90 for the 75–79 age group; 95 for the 80–84 age group; and 100 for the 85–89 age group. Survival probabilities are not asked of persons aged 90 or above.

Table 5.15   **Change in Subjective Survival Probabilities and Lifetable Rates, Wave 1 to 2 (females)**

	Subjective Survival to Target Age			Lifetable Survival to Target Age		
	Wave 1	Wave 2	Percent Change	Wave 1	Wave 2	Percent Change
70–74	0.510	0.558	9.4	0.575	0.605	5.2
75–79	0.388	0.469	20.9	0.399	0.432	8.3
80–84	0.303	0.399	31.7	0.200	0.228	14.0
85–89	0.299	0.376	25.8	0.074	0.091	23.0

Note: See table 5.14 for source and notes.

average subjective survival probability to age 100 is 0.314, whereas the average lifetable value is 0.034. In terms of relative risk, the increases in the subjective survival probabilities from wave to wave are reasonably close to the increases in the lifetable probabilities except in the oldest age intervals. Although it is difficult to know what the appropriate standard of comparison is, it is notable that in all age bands the subjective survival probabilities increase between the waves. This increase was not found in HRS: Among survivors, the average subjective survival probability decreased slightly (Hurd and McGarry forthcoming).

Besides increases in the subjective survival probabilities that are due to the AHEAD subjects' surviving for two years, the probabilities should change in response to new information that alters survival chances. Such information would be onset of a health condition that is associated with an increased risk of death. Table 5.16 shows the incidence of new conditions between waves 1 and 2 for all respondents. Thus, for example, among singles who had not had cancer prior to the baseline interview, 5.1 percent had a cancer between the waves. Among all singles, including those with

Table 5.16   Incidence of Conditions between AHEAD Waves 1 and 2

	Singles (N = 3,410)		Married (N = 3,496)	
	N at risk	Rate	N at risk	Rate
Onset between waves 1 and 2				
Cancer	2,940	5.14	3,009	5.08
Cancer (including repeat cancer)	3,410	5.45	3,496	5.78
Stroke	3,095	4.78	3,214	4.54
Stroke (including repeat stroke)	3,410	5.81	3,496	5.49
Heart attack or disease	2,335	10.00	2,402	9.00
Heart attack or disease (including repeat attack)	3,410	13.96	3,496	12.04
High blood pressure[a]	1,430	12.03	1,693	9.27
Diabetes[a]	2,621	3.17	2,787	2.54
Lung disease	3,024	2.91	3,113	2.67
Arthritis[a]	2,113	17.13	2,460	13.74
Incontinence[a]	2,355	14.06	2,660	12.11
Hip fracture	3,190	2.70	3,379	1.10
Hip fracture (including repeat fracture)	3,410	3.05	3,496	1.37
Fall requiring treatment	3,099	12.62	3,278	9.37
Fall requiring treatment (including repeat fall)	3,410	14.81	3,496	10.76
Low cognitive score[b]	1,927	29.58	2,408	24.29
ADL limitations > 2	2,969	10.44	3,215	6.56
Depression (CESD8)[c]	2,667	6.11	2,847	4.95
Living in a nursing home wave 2	3,410	8.18	3,496	3.66
Spouse died	—	—	3,496	7.87

Source: Authors' calculations from AHEAD waves 1 and 2.

Notes: Sample includes all persons with a wave 1 and a wave 2 interview (including proxy and exit proxy interviews for the deceased).

[a] Condition not asked in exit proxy. Incidence may be underestimate, because it includes as at-risk those who died.

[b] Score of 15 or less on AHEAD cognitive battery questions.

[c] CESD8 score greater than 4; self-respondents only, N = 3,105 for singles and N = 3,096 for married.

a history of cancer prior to baseline, 5.5 percent had a new or initial cancer between the waves. Although it is not the focus of this paper, the table shows that having a prior history of cancer, stroke, heart attack/disease, hip fracture, or fall increases the risk of a new, similar event. Having a low cognitive score, which is associated with increased risk of dementia, has the greatest rate of onset.

About 8.2 percent of singles who were living in the community at wave 1 were in a nursing home at wave 2.

There is little difference in the rates of onset between singles and couples except for limitations on the activities of daily living (ADL limitations) and nursing home entry. The measure of ADL limitations is an indicator for ADL limitations greater than two, and singles had an incidence rate of

Table 5.17   Change in Subjective Survival Probabilities (average change = 0.057)

	Coefficient	t-statistic
Intercept	0.068	6.777
Married	−0.007	−0.483
Male	0.022	1.154
Married male	−0.030	−1.273
Incidence of health conditions		
Heart disease/attack	−0.000	−0.021
Cancer	−0.063	−2.328
Stroke	−0.025	−0.799
High blood pressure	−0.053	−2.249
Diabetes	−0.083	−2.478
Lung disease	−0.066	−1.840
Arthritis	0.016	0.965
Incontinence	−0.020	−1.133
Hip fracture	0.007	0.136
Fall requiring treatment	0.010	0.486
Low cognitive score	0.004	0.256
ADL limitations > 2	0.067	2.238
Depression	−0.061	−2.504
Spouse died	0.054	2.001
Entered nursing home	−0.017	−0.311

Source: Authors' calculations from AHEAD waves 1 and 2.

Notes: Change in the subjective survival probability is wave 2 report minus wave 1 report. Incidence of heart attack, cancer, and stroke includes new incidents among those with a prior history. Survival probabilities not asked of persons aged 90 or above. $N = 4,061$. $R^2 = 0.005$.

10.4 percent compared with couples of 6.6 percent. The difference likely comes from the fact that (on average) singles are older than couples, and from the ability of couples to help each other, disguising some mild cases of ADL limitations. As in the case of ADL limitations, the rate of entry into a nursing home is greater among singles because of age differences and because a spouse can provide help that will keep the other spouse in the community.

Table 5.17 shows the estimated regression of the change in the subjective survival probabilities between waves 1 and 2 on the incidence of health conditions and other events.[8] To the extent that the onset of a new condition provides new information about survival chances, onset should reduce the subjective survival probabilities. A number of the conditions have negative coefficients indicating that onset reduces the subjective survival probabilities, and cancer, high blood pressure, diabetes, and depression have negative effects that are significant at the 5 percent level. The depression indicator is somewhat different from the other health condition indicators in that it probably depends on the same or similar aspects of health as

8. For heart attack, cancer, and stroke, those with a history of the condition at baseline and who had a new incident between waves 1 and 2 are included as incident cases.

the subjective survival probabilities.[9] The death of a spouse increased the subjective survival probabilities. In the HRS, the death of a spouse *decreased* subjective survival probabilities (Hurd and McGarry forthcoming). An explanation for the difference may be that at the ages of the AHEAD respondents the death of a spouse is preceded by a period of care that reduces the optimism of the caregiver.

The onset of ADL limitations of 3 or more increased subjective survival probabilities. Because there is no obvious reason for this result, we performed some estimations with more detail. First, the increase is found in detailed regressions for singles and couples separately. Second, we defined some additional categories for change in ADL limitations and estimated their effects. The categories were (1) no baseline ADL limitation and one or more ADL limitations in wave 2; (2) one or more ADL limitations in baseline and an increase in limitations by wave 2; and (3) one or more ADL limitations in baseline and no increase by wave 2. For category (1), which is onset of any ADL limitation, the effect is to reduce the subjective survival probability by a small amount (-0.014, not significant). For category (2), the effect is to increase the subjective survival probability by 0.054 (p-value of 0.045), and for category (3) it is to increase the subjective survival probability by 0.040 (p-value of 0.109). Thus the increase in the subjective survival probability accompanying the onset of three or more ADL limitations is due to those who had existing baseline ADL limitations reporting higher probabilities in wave 2. We have no explanation for this increase.

5.3.4 Subjective Survival Probabilities and Mortality

As discussed earlier, the rate of response about subjective survival probabilities was rather low in AHEAD, and actual mortality between waves 1 and 2 was above average among the nonresponders. As shown in the last row of table 5.18, the overall mortality rate among the 7,446 age-eligible subjects in wave 1 was 10.6 percent. The other rows show mortality rates among those who did not answer the question about subjective survival probabilities. These nonrespondents are divided according to reason for nonresponse. The first row shows the mortality rate among those who were aged ninety or over at wave 1: By survey design, they were not asked the question about subjective survival, and their two-year mortality rate was about 0.30. Those who answered DK (don't know) had approximately average mortality rates, whereas those who refused to answer (RF) had somewhat elevated mortality rates. A large group (685) were interviewed by proxy in wave 1, and they had a substantially higher mortality rate than average. A main reason for interview by proxy was that the subject was

---

9. The depression indicator takes the value 1 if the sum of the eight items on the CESD8 is greater than 4.

Table 5.18   **Two-Year Mortality Rates among Nonrespondents to Subjective Survival Question**

	Mortality Rate	N
Reason for nonresponse		
90+	0.300	303
DK	0.109	765
RF	0.124	194
Other	0.042	24
Proxy	0.244	685
Responders and nonresponders	0.106	7,446

Source: Authors' calculations from AHEAD waves 1 and 2.

Table 5.19   **Two-Year Mortality Rates**

Subjective Survival Probability	Mortality Rate	N
0	0.13	1,254
1–10	0.10	608
11–20	0.07	218
21–30	0.05	327
31–49	0.06	148
50	0.05	1,331
51–70	0.04	224
71–80	0.05	486
81–90	0.04	222
91–99	0.07	41
100	0.05	616

Source: Authors' calculations from AHEAD waves 1 and 2.

too frail or cognitively impaired to be interviewed. This frailty is reflected in the mortality rate.

Table 5.19 has mortality rates by subjective survival probability in wave 1. The table shows that the subjective survival probabilities have considerable explanatory power for mortality, particularly in the low range. Thus, for example, the mortality rate among those who gave a zero probability of survival was about 0.13 compared with about 0.05 among those who gave a 0.50 probability of survival. The mortality rates are basically flat in the interval from 0.21 to 0.90. This is similar to the relationship found between the subjective survival probabilities and mortality in the HRS (Hurd and McGarry forthcoming). The increase in mortality at the two highest probability intervals indicates observation error that is likely related to misunderstanding or cognitive malfunctioning.

More detailed cross-tabulations of the correlates of mortality are not practical, so we turn to data-descriptive Probit estimation as a way to reduce the dimensionality of the predictors. Table 5.20 has the results from

Table 5.20 Determinants of Two-Year Mortality

	Effect	Asymptotic t	Effect	Asymptotic t	Effect	Asymptotic t
Intercept	-0.268	22.450	-0.304	22.353	-0.412	23.361
Lifetable mortality	0.566	13.014	0.645	9.979	0.577	8.486
Wealth quartiles						
Lowest	—	—	—	—	—	—
2nd	-0.014	1.351	-0.009	0.868	0.004	0.349
3rd	-0.017	1.533	-0.013	1.158	0.008	0.670
Highest	-0.026	2.031	-0.022	1.659	-0.001	0.079
Income quartiles						
Lowest	—	—	—	—	—	—
2nd	-0.014	1.367	-0.009	0.834	-0.003	0.238
3rd	-0.027	2.313	-0.022	1.873	-0.014	1.106
Highest	-0.023	1.698	-0.014	1.070	-0.003	0.203
Education level						
0-8	—	—	—	—	—	—
9-11	0.014	1.313	0.025	2.244	0.034	2.962
12	-0.005	0.468	0.003	0.235	0.020	1.753
>12	-0.017	1.405	0.000	0.006	0.017	1.356
Male	0.022	1.761	0.025	1.928	0.027	2.063
Married	-0.023	2.060	-0.028	2.451	-0.014	1.172
Married male	-0.007	0.422	-0.011	0.656	-0.017	0.978

Subjective survival				
Stated minus lifetable	-0.079	5.693	-0.053	3.693
Missing: proxy	0.114	10.118	0.085	6.782
Missing: refused	0.028	1.262	0.013	0.528
Missing: don't know	0.013	1.031	0.013	0.978
Missing: age 90+	-0.014	0.633	-0.009	0.389
Health conditions				
Heart disease/attack			0.028	3.357
Cancer			0.047	4.511
Stroke			0.045	3.695
High blood pressure			0.017	2.132
Diabetes			0.035	3.231
Lung disease			0.071	6.581
Arthritis			-0.014	1.578
Incontinence			-0.003	0.330
Hip fracture			0.038	2.413
Fall requiring treatment			0.000	0.034
Low cognitive score			0.047	5.109
ADL limitation (>2)			0.070	6.025
Depression (0,1)			0.036	3.010
Missing cognition			0.033	1.492

Source: Authors' calculations from AHEAD waves 1 and 2.

Notes: Based on probit estimation. $N = 7,367$. Average mortality $= 0.107$.

Probit estimation of the determinants of mortality. The left-hand variable takes the value of 1 if a subject died between the waves and zero otherwise. We control for age and sex by including as a right-hand variable the two-year mortality rate by age and sex from an interpolated 1993 lifetable. Thus, the other right-hand variables will show the deviation in mortality rates from the lifetable rate. The Probit coefficients have been translated into probability effects via the linear approximation

$$\frac{\partial P}{\partial x} = \beta\phi,$$

where β is the Probit coefficient on x and ϕ is the normal density evaluated at the average mortality rate of singles.[10]

The table has three sets of results depending on which variables are included. In each set the first column has the effects and the second the statistic for testing the null hypotheses that the effect is zero. Approximately, a statistic of 2.0 indicates significance at the 5 percent level.

The first entry in the table is the coefficient on two-year, age- and sex-specific mortality rates from a 1993 interpolated lifetable. The coefficient is less than 1.0, reflecting the fact that in AHEAD mortality does not increase with age as rapidly as the lifetable mortality. The difference in mortality is partly due to the increasing fraction of the population that is institutionalized at greater ages. In that this part of the population is missing from AHEAD, mortality rates in AHEAD will be progressively lower than lifetable mortality rates, which reflect the entire population. An additional factor could be that AHEAD is a more accurate measure of current mortality than the lifetables that we use.[11]

In the first column of table 5.20 mortality does systematically decrease in wealth in approximately the same way as in the cross-tabulations in table 5.5, but the coefficient on just one of the wealth quartiles is significant at the 5 percent level. Mortality is generally lower in the higher-income quartiles. The effect of education is partly obscured by the higher mortality rate in the second education band compared with the first, but moving from the second to the fourth education band reduces mortality by 0.039 (p-value of 0.054).

The mortality rate of men was about 0.022 greater than would be predicted from the lifetable.[12] Married respondents had mortality rates that

10. We will use the word "effects" when we refer to the probability coefficients. We recognize that while they describe systematic relationships in the data they do not necessarily measure causal relationships. It would require considerably more investigation to ascribe causality.

11. To test whether our single lifetable mortality rate was adequately controlling for age we also added five age intervals (not shown). None was significant and all were small. We conclude that there is no requirement for age indicators when the age- and sex-specific lifetable mortality rates are used.

12. Separate estimation of the mortality probit by sex shows that the coefficient on "lifetable" is different for male and female.

were about 0.023 lower than singles: This is a substantial reduction amounting to about 21 percent of average mortality. There was no differential effect of marital status for men compared with women. That is, marriage does not provide additional mortality protection for men relative to women.[13]

The next two columns show the effects when the subjective survival probability is added along with a set of variables to account for missing observations on the subjective survival probability. We entered the subjective survival probability as a deviation from the lifetable survival rate to the target age. We did this because of the varying time interval between the age of the subject and the target age. This formulation also automatically scales for the fact that the effect on two-year mortality of a survival probability to an age eleven to fifteen years in the future will vary with baseline age.

When the subjective survival probability is added, both the wealth and income effects are reduced and they are no longer statistically significant. The effect of education as measured by the difference between the second and fourth bands remains substantial and the difference is significant. The subjective survival probability is itself a powerful predictor of mortality: Varying the subjective survival probability from zero to 1 would reduce two-year mortality risk by 0.079, or 74 percent. The indicator variable for proxy interview predicts much higher mortality.

The last two columns have Probit results when the baseline health conditions are included. Of the thirteen health conditions, ten are significant at the 5 percent level, and each acts to increase mortality risk with the effects varying from 16 to 66 percent. Adding the health variables reduces the effect of the subjective survival probability by 33 percent, but it is still substantial. The effect of a proxy interview is reduced, as would be expected because proxy interviews are often due to poor health. Those with low cognitive score at baseline had elevated mortality rates.[14]

In additional estimations which we do not report here, we estimated separate mortality Probit models for males and for females. Our objective was to learn whether there were substantial differences in the effects of SES or health conditions on mortality. In general there were few differences: As in the pooled results, no income or wealth quartile had a sizable effect, nor was any significant. However, the education gradient between the second and fourth age bands, which we found in the pooled estimation, was found only in the results for men. The effect of marital status was somewhat greater for men than for women, reducing the mortality rate by 0.032 compared with 0.015. In terms of relative risk, the reduction in risk

---

13. See Lillard and Waite (1994) for the opposite finding.

14. We interacted low cognitive status with the subjective survival probability. The interaction did have a positive sign, indicating that among those with low cognitive status the subjective survival probability is less predictive of mortality, but the effect was small and not significant (not shown).

for men was 26 percent and for women it was 16 percent. The effects of health conditions were about the same for men and women.

5.4 Conclusion

We found that, as in other data, mortality is related to SES. The relationship is strong at younger ages in AHEAD and appears to weaken at older ages. Any explanation at this point would be rather speculative, but the finding is consistent with the view that the primary cause of the gradient is unobserved individual characteristics that cause bad health and therefore early death, and that cause lower earnings and therefore lower wealth and less education. Were the causality to run primarily from economic resources to health and mortality, we should see a persistent difference in mortality outcomes in very old age between those with substantial resources and those with few. We tentatively conclude that we do not see this, although we acknowledge this should be confirmed by further analysis. If the differential is due to unobserved individual differences, the mortality gradient operating at younger ages will have truncated the distribution, so that in extreme old age the variation in individual characteristics would be greatly reduced. Therefore, classifying people by SES would not produce any substantial differences in mortality.

In cross-section, the subjective survival probability is related to baseline health conditions, and there is some consistency in the relative importance of the health conditions on the subjective survival probability and in their importance in predicting actual mortality. For example, of the five largest health effects on the subjective survival probability, three are among the five largest predictors of mortality (cancer, lung disease, and ADL limitations > 2). In panel, the subjective survival probability increases among survivors, and the effects of new health conditions on the panel change in the subjective survival probabilities are similar to the cross-sectional effects of baseline health conditions. For example, of the five largest effects of the onset of health conditions on changes in the subjective survival probability, three are among the five largest cross-sectional effects (cancer, lung disease, and depression).

The subjective survival probability predicts actual mortality as in the HRS, which should increase our confidence that it can be used to construct individualized lifetables for models of life-cycle saving behavior as proposed by Hurd, McFadden, and Gan (1998). Whether such lifetables will have substantial explanatory power for saving remains to be determined as more waves of AHEAD become available.

The relationship between SES and mortality that is found in cross-tabulations (as in table 5.5) disappears when health status is controlled for (as in table 5.20). This result suggests that any differential access to health care services related to SES is small. Were that not the case, in a population with homogeneous baseline health (or with effective controls for baseline health status) those with higher SES would be more likely to receive appropriate treatment for the onset of a severe condition and, therefore, to survive. We do not find such a relationship. There could still be a role for SES, however, through modifications in the probability of the onset of health conditions, which, in turn, would affect mortality risk. To assess that path will require an additional dynamic model of health status.

References

Feinstein, J. 1992. The relationship between socioeconomic status and health: A review of the literature. *The Millbank Quarterly* 71 (2): 279–322.

Herzog, R., and R. Wallace. 1997. Measures of cognitive functioning in the AHEAD study. *The Journals of Gerontology.* Series B, *Psychological Sciences and Social Sciences,* vol. 52B (special issue): 37–48.

Hoynes, H., M. Hurd, and H. Chand. 1998. Household wealth of the elderly under alternative imputation procedures. In *Inquiries in the economics of aging,* ed. D. Wise, 229–57. Chicago: University of Chicago Press.

Hurd, M. 1987. Savings of the elderly and desired bequests. *American Economic Review* 77: 298–312.

Hurd, M., D. McFadden, and L. Gan. 1998. Subjective survival curves and life cycle behavior. In *Inquiries in the economics of aging,* ed. D. Wise, 259–305. Chicago: University of Chicago Press.

Hurd, M., and K. McGarry. 1995. Evaluation of the subjective probabilities of survival in the health and retirement survey. *Journal of Human Resources* 30: S268–S292.

———. forthcoming. The predictive validity of the subjective probabilities of survival in the Health and Retirement Survey. Paper presented at the HRS2 Early Results Workshop, Ann Arbor, Mich., and revised.

Hurd, M., and D. Wise. 1989. The wealth and poverty of widows: Assets before and after the husband's death. In *The economics of aging,* ed. D. Wise, 177–99. Chicago: University of Chicago Press.

Jianakoplos, N., P. Menchik, and O. Irvine. 1989. Using panel data to assess the bias in cross-sectional inferences of life-cycle changes in the level and composition of household wealth. In *The measurement of saving, investment, and wealth,* ed. R. Lipsey and H. S. Tice, 553–640. Studies in Income and Wealth, vol. 52. Chicago: University of Chicago Press.

Kitagawa, E., and P. Hauser. 1973. Differential mortality in the United States: A study in socioeconomic epidemiology. Cambridge: Harvard University Press.

Lillard, L., and L. Waite. 1994. Till death do us part: Marital disruption and mortality. *American Journal of Sociology* 100 (5): 1131–56.

Shorrocks, A. 1975. The age-wealth relationship: A cross-section and cohort analysis. *Review of Economics and Statistics* 57: 155–63.

Soldo, B., M. Hurd, W. Rodgers, and R. Wallace. 1997. Asset and Health Dynamics among the Oldest Old: An overview of the AHEAD study. *The Journals of Gerontology.* Series B, *Psychological Sciences and Social Sciences,* vol. 52B (special issue): 1–20.

Wallace, R., and R. Herzog. 1995. Overview of the health measures in the Health and Retirement Survey. *Journal of Human Resources* 30 (Suppl.): S84–S107.

Comment   Finis Welch

This paper is essentially a work-in-progress that to this point has shown no surprises. Among the elderly, those who believe they are unhealthy seem to be so, and those who have a serious condition that might be expected to increase mortality appear to be at greater risk than those without such conditions. Furthermore, as is true of all the comparisons I have seen, health and wealth seem to be positively correlated. I really have only two substantive comments and they are directed more toward work on data of this sort than to this paper specifically.

First, in using the Asset and Health Dynamics of the Oldest Old (AHEAD) survey, age and marital status cannot be treated blithely. This has several facets. Because the AHEAD survey is community based and excludes the institutionalized population, as age increases, members of the survey become progressively more healthy in comparison to the overall population of same-age and -sex individuals. Thus, one should be careful in making statements such as: "The mortality gradient, whether a function of wealth, income, or education, apparently decreases with age." Next, the age-ineligible members of AHEAD, by definition, are younger spouses of age-eligible members of the survey. As such, they are more likely than others of the same age to be healthy, and perhaps wealthy as well. Finally, marital status per se is associated with health.

The young and single, especially if never married, are less healthy. The old and formerly married, whose spouses have been deceased for a considerable period, as "survivors" may be more healthy than those whose spouses have survived. This is, of course, pure speculation, but the point is that in this sample, age and marital status—especially contemporary marital status without regard to marital history—should be handled with care.

Second, studies of mortality determinants among the elderly are likely to yield counter-intuitive results that are easily misunderstood. Consider a treatment, such as smoking, that increases mortality at relatively young ages. Since people are heterogeneous, the treatment will affect some more than others. As the effects of the treatment accrue, the most susceptible succumb and the strong survive. When observing mortality only at advanced ages, after the most susceptible have been lost to the sample, we should not be surprised to find that the treatment seems to have little or even perverse effect.

We have all heard stories about those who claimed to have lived lives from which few survived. Would we want to judge the effects of such behavior only by observing the subsequent mortality of the—perhaps few—hardy survivors?

Finis Welch is the Abell Professor of Liberal Arts and distinguished professor of economics at Texas A&M University, and Professor Emeritus at the University of California, Los Angeles.

III

Health Care

6

Trends in Medicare Spending Near the End of Life

Jeffrey Geppert and Mark McClellan

Recent decades have witnessed dramatic improvements in health at older ages, including reductions in both mortality and morbidity. Although real growth in health care costs has accompanied improvements in health for the past fifty years, improvements in health give hope that avoided medical utilization due to better health may lower health care costs, or at least significantly reduce the rate of growth. In this paper, we determine the importance of changes in Medicare costs that resulted from declines in age-specific mortality between 1988 and 1995, and describe the impact of the mortality improvement on Medicare expenditure trends.

A number of experts have suggested that improvements in health may work to reduce significantly the burden of health care on the economy (see Vaupel 1997, Pardes 1999, and Singer and Manton 1998). Some improvements in health are likely to be the result of the innovations that avoid costly illnesses or reduce their cost of treatment (e.g., new medical therapies and pharmaceuticals that replace expensive surgical procedures). Medical innovations may also have an indirect impact by increasing labor productivity, reducing the relative magnitude of the health care cost burden. Other studies have documented improvements in health due to non-medical factors such as better information, behavioral improvements, and economic developments that reduce disease morbidity (see Kennedy 1994). All else equal, all of these sources of improvements in health status

Jeffrey Geppert is a senior research analyst at the National Bureau of Economic Research. Mark McClellan is associate professor of economics and of medicine at Stanford University and a research associate of the National Bureau of Economic Research.

We thank Philip Ellis, Victor Fuchs, and Alan Garber for helpful discussions, and the National Institute on Aging for financial support. The opinions expressed in this paper do not represent the views of the U.S. Department of the Treasury.

would be expected to reduce the intensity of health care use, leading to lower overall health care spending.

In this paper, we present quantitative evidence on the likely importance of improvements in health for reducing future health care costs, focusing on changes in mortality. Perhaps the most widely cited paper on medical spending near death is Lubitz and Riley (1993), which describes trends in the share of Medicare program payments spent on persons aged sixty-five and older in the last year of life from 1976 to 1988. The principal finding of Lubitz and Riley is the large share of Medicare expenditures in the last year of life—around 28 percent of total expenditures. A second finding is that Medicare expenditures at the end of life decline with age.

Supporters of the view that health improvements should reduce health care costs have emphasized these findings. If individuals are living longer over time, then the higher costs of death are deferred. In addition, because costs of dying are lower at older ages, death may be less costly when it eventually occurs. Against these sources of saving are, first, the fact that medical costs rise with age among survivors, and second, the fact that health care costs have generally risen over time. Also, Medicare spending might rise because of increased longevity, although the effect has been estimated as not very large (see Lubitz 1995).

Although Lubitz and Riley's (1993) results have not previously been applied to the problem of understanding the implications of improving health for Medicare spending growth, they are directly relevant to considering the likely impact of improving survival on spending. They found that the share of Medicare spending that occurred in the last year of life had changed little during their 1976–88 study period, despite the improvements in life expectancy. This constancy despite substantial mortality improvements suggests that other factors may have been more important in determining overall spending levels. For example, many studies have documented greater use of various intensive medical procedures on Medicare beneficiaries during this time period. Alternatively, the introduction or expansion of Medicare benefits, like home health and hospice, may have influenced utilization and costs for both survivors and decedents. In any case, the constancy of the share spent on decedents suggests that other factors dominated the "health effect."

We extend the Lubitz and Riley (1993) work on Medicare spending near the end of life from 1988 to 1995, to provide direct evidence on the expenditure consequences of improved survival in Medicare during a longer and more recent period. Our goal is to present empirical evidence from the past decade on the relative importance of changes in expenditures associated with improvements in mortality, compared to changes in expenditures *given* survival status, and to examine how that empirical evidence differs by gender and age.

6.1   Data and Methods

As in the original Lubitz and Riley (1993) article, our data come from a longitudinal 5 percent random sample of Medicare beneficiaries. Rather than the Continuous Medicare History Sample, we calculate program payments from detailed micro-level Medicare claims data. The detailed claims permit us to explore the use and timing of specific services, and the diagnoses associated with them, in far more detail. Date of death was drawn from the Health Care Financing Administration (HCFA; 2000) Medicare Provider Analysis and Review File (MEDPAR), which in turn gets validated date-of-death information from Social Security records. Information on Medicare program payments and types of service come from MEDPAR and from HCFA's (2000) the Physician/Supplier Standard Analytic File (SAF), Home Health SAF and Hospice SAF, and Outpatient Hospital SAF.

Our sample includes only Medicare beneficiaries sixty-five years of age or older. Medicare beneficiaries enrolled in health maintenance organizations (HMO's) were excluded from the calculation of average program payments by type of service because some types of Medicare data are incomplete for HMO members. For other calculations, we included these HMO members, because monthly Medicare payments to their health plans are known. We report data from 1988, 1989, 1992, and 1995. The number of persons in each sample averaged 1.6 million beneficiaries.

As in Lubitz and Riley (1993), we assigned annual Medicare payments either to decedents (beneficiaries in the last year of life) or to survivors (all others). Because our data include dates of service for all service types, we assigned program payments to decedents or survivors on that basis (by date of discharge for inpatient and skilled nursing facility care). For example, a beneficiary who died in 1992 would contribute all 1992 program payments to decedent spending in 1992. A beneficiary who died on 1 April 1993 would contribute 1992 program payments incurred from 1 January 1992 to 30 March 1992 and 0.33 of a person-year to survivors, and program payments incurred after 1 April 1992 and 0.67 of a person-year to decedents. Beneficiaries who did not die in 1992 or 1993 contribute 100 percent of 1992 program payments and a full person-year to survivors.

To calculate the share of Medicare program payments to decedents, we divide the sum of program payments allocated to decedents using the method above by total Medicare payments (in constant dollars). We repeat the method by type of service, allocating acute inpatient, physician/supplier, hospital outpatient, and nonacute care (skilled nursing facility, home health agency, and hospice) to decedent and survivor spending to calculate the service share. Finally, we perform the allocation of dollars and person-years separately by age group. To calculate the average program payments for decedents (and survivors) by age group, we divide the sum of payments allocated to descendent (survivor) spending by the sum of decedent (survivor) person-year weights. The results reported in the tables are in constant dollars. To perform the decomposition described below, the age-specific average program payments for survivors and decedents are first inflated to 1995 dollars using the overall CPI.

We summarize the quantitative contribution of changes in mortality and changes in intensity to medical spending through a first-order decomposition of the total change in per capita expenditures over the 1988–95 period, $d(\exp)$:

$$d(\exp) = d[\Sigma_j(\text{share of population with health status type})_j$$
$$* (\exp \mid \text{type})_j],$$

where j denotes a particular health status group. The decomposition is generally applicable; here, we focus on decedents and survivors within particular demographic cells k:

$$d(\exp) = d[\Sigma_k \Pr(\text{decedent})_k * (\exp \mid \text{decedent})_k$$
$$+ \Pr(\text{survivor})_k * (\exp \mid \text{survivor})_k]$$
$$= \Sigma_k [d\Pr(\text{decedent})_k * (\exp \mid \text{decedent})_k$$
$$+ d\Pr(\text{survivor})_k * (\exp \mid \text{survivor})_k$$
$$+ \Pr(\text{decedent})_k * d(\exp \mid \text{decedent})_k$$
$$+ \Pr(\text{survivor})_k * d(\exp \mid \text{survivor})_k]$$
$$= [\text{mortality effect} + \text{utilization effect}]$$

The first component of the change is the "mortality effect," or the change in per capita spending that results only from the change in the rate at which the elderly die at each age, holding program payments (and demographics) constant. The second component is the "utilization effect," or the change in per capita spending that results only from the change in program payments given survival status (i.e., decedent or survivor), holding mortality (and demographics) constant. This decomposition of per capita growth does not reflect the growth in total Medicare spending due to the increased number of elderly, which we label the "demographic effect." The demographic effect captures the consequences for program expenditures of changes in the number of elderly in each age and gender segment of the population.

The utilization effect is the result of changes in utilization of particular services, and also of changes in the prices of those services. Because Medicare regulates service prices and has held price increases below the rate of inflation, growth in Medicare expenditures generally results from the provision of more or more-intensive covered services, and from changes in billing practices (e.g., upcoding).

6.2   Results

Figure 6.1 summarizes real expenditure growth rates by survival status, including a comparison to the earlier period studied by Lubitz and Riley (1993), and an even earlier period based on work by Piro and Lutins (1974). Over the past thirty years, the average annual percentage change in Medicare program payments has been high (3–7 percent per year) and relatively constant between survivors and decedents. In the earliest time period, between 1967 and 1976, real expenditure growth rates were slightly higher for decedents than survivors. In the time period between 1976 and 1988, real expenditure growth rates were the same for decedents and survivors and constant across ages. In more recent years, the growth rate for survivors has exceeded the growth rate for decedents, especially at older ages. The growth rate and pattern is largely the same for males and females from 1988 to 1995, with the overall growth rate for males slightly less than for females. The acceleration in spending growth for survivors at older ages is slightly greater for females than for males.

Figure 6.2 summarizes real acute and nonacute spending growth rates

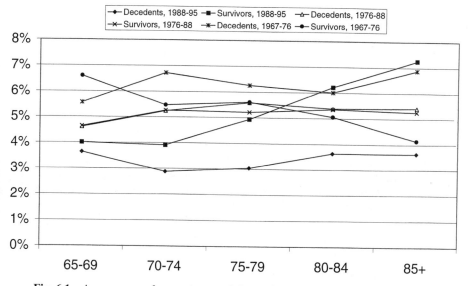

Fig. 6.1   **Average annual percentage real change in Medicare payments per person-year, according to survival status and age, 1967–76, 1976–88, and 1988–95**

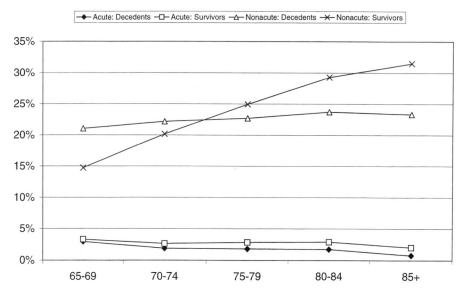

Fig. 6.2   Average annual percentage real change in Medicare payments per person-year, according to survival status and age, 1988–95

for the 1988–95 period. *Nonacute care* is defined to include skilled nursing facility (nonacute hospital) stays, home health care, and hospice care. These services are generally of lower intensity and are supportive in nature. *Acute care* includes services that are likely to be for acute illnesses, including acute hospitalizations, outpatient visits, and physician services. Many of these services are probably related to ongoing care or treatment for complications of chronic conditions. Nonetheless, in contrast to the nonacute services, these treatments consist primarily of medical interventions intended to alter the course of an illness, and not of supportive care. Such interventions are also provided in nonacute settings, but a much larger proportion of nonacute service use consists of supportive care for beneficiaries with chronic impairments. The figure shows that acute-care spending, which has historically been the bulk of Medicare expenditures, has increased at virtually identical rates for survivors and decedents, around 2–3 percent per year. Growth for nonacute services has been far more rapid since 1988, averaging well over 15 percent per year for both survivors and decedents. In contrast to a minimal relationship to age for decedents, the rate of nonacute spending growth for survivors was higher with increasing age, presumably reflecting the higher rates of chronic illness and disability among older survivors. As we describe in more detail below, nonacute spending growth has accounted for most of the spending growth in the past decade for decedents, and especially for survivors.

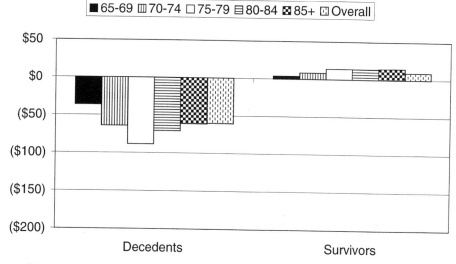

Fig. 6.3   **Per-person change in expenditures: 1988 payments · Change in Mortality, 1988–95**

Figure 6.3 shows the per-person change in Medicare spending resulting from mortality declines from 1988 to 1995, holding payments and demographics at 1988 levels. This figure isolates the contribution of changes in age-specific mortality rates to spending growth over the period. The left side of the figure (decedents) shows the per capita cost reduction from averting the higher costs of dying. The right side of the figure (survivors) shows the per capita cost increases from the greater number of survivors. Because we are focusing on current-year Medicare costs, we do not show the higher costs of survivors in future years in this figure. The net expenditure impact on current-year costs, the difference between the decedent and survivor effects, depends on both the change in mortality and the difference in expenditures between survivors and decedents in the demographic group. The expenditure impact of mortality rate declines was greatest for the seventy-five to seventy-nine age group (which has intermediate mortality rates and spending differences), resulting in a $74 per person decline in payments. The overall decline in per-person payments was $51. Thus, mortality improvements did influence spending growth, but the magnitude of the effect was modest.

Figure 6.4 shows that the expenditure impact of mortality-rate declines was larger for males, and more variable across age groups, with an overall decline in per-person payments of $88 (including a $147 per person decline for the seventy-five to seventy-nine age group). The per capita cost increases from the greater number of male survivors was also higher for the seventy-five to seventy-nine age group, but still small in magnitude. Figure

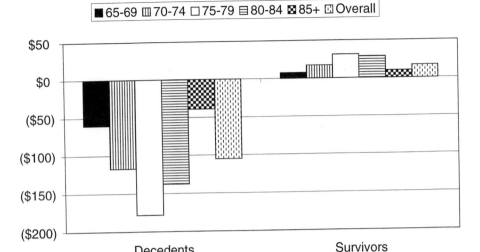

Fig. 6.4 **Per-male change in expenditures: 1988 Payments · Change in Mortality, 1988–95**

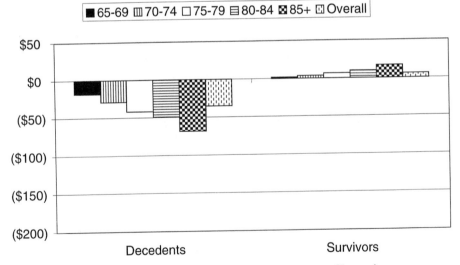

Fig. 6.5 **Per-female change in expenditures: 1988 Payments · Change in Mortality, 1988–95**

6.5 shows that, for females, the expenditure impact of mortality rate declines was considerably smaller, less than $30 per person. In contrast to males, the impact was greatest for the oldest females, those aged eighty-five and up, with a per-person decline in payments of $52. These differences were primarily the result of a weaker relationship between age and

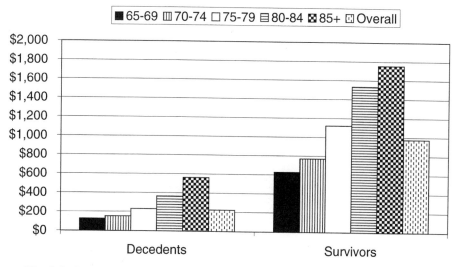

**Fig. 6.6   Per-person change in expenditures: 1988–95 Change in Payments ·
1988 Mortality**

the difference in expenditures between decedents and survivors than for
males; thus, the larger absolute mortality gains at older ages were relatively
more important.

Figure 6.6 shows the per-person change in Medicare spending resulting
from changes in expenditures per beneficiary, holding age-specific mortality rates (and demographics) at 1988 levels. This figure isolates the contribution to spending growth of changes in expenditures within survival
groups. It is obvious from the figure that these changes dwarf the reductions in expenditures from lower mortality over time. Not only does the
growth in per capita expenditures due to higher spending on decedents far
exceed the savings from reduced mortality, but the effect of spending
growth for survivors on per capita expenditures was significantly greater
than that for decedents. Even though the absolute spending increases were
lower, survivors comprise the bulk of Medicare spending because they
comprise the vast majority of Medicare beneficiaries. In contrast to the
mortality effects described above, the magnitude of the utilization effect
increases with age for both survivors and decedents. Figures 6.7 and 6.8
show that similar patterns hold for both males and females, with a slightly
larger utilization effect for females at older ages.

Table 6.1 summarizes the decomposition of expenditure growth described in the preceding figures. The *mortality effect* is the share of per-
person expenditure growth explained by the reduction in age-specific mortality, and the *utilization effect* is the share explained by the increase in
expenditures given survival status. These are both first-order approxima-
tions, but as the *interaction effect* shows, the approximation is close. The

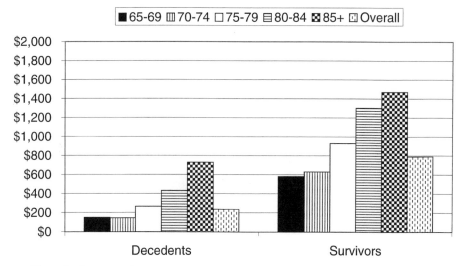

Fig. 6.7   Per-male change in expenditures: 1988–95 Change in Payments · 1988 Mortality

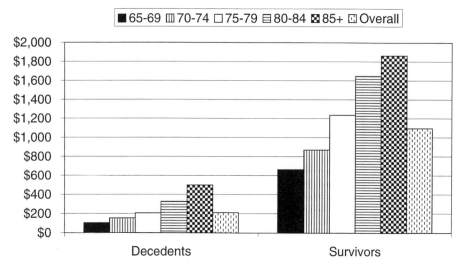

Fig. 6.8   Per-female change in expenditures: 1988–95 Change in Payments · 1988 Mortality

mortality effect is a small contributor to overall expenditure growth: Compared to observed expenditure growth, the analysis suggests that Medicare expenditures per beneficiary would have grown by about 4 percent more over the 1988–95 period if no mortality improvement had occurred. The mortality effect is larger for males than females. For males, Medicare ex-

Table 6.1   **Percent Explained by the Mortality Effect versus the Utilization Effect**

Gender and Age Groups	Per Person ($)	Demographic Effect (%)	Mortality Effect (%)	Utilization Effect (%)	Interaction Effect (%)
Overall	1,135	10.2	−4.5	105.5	−1.0
Males					
Overall	922	10.6	−9.6	111.4	−1.8
65–69	665	1.5	−7.9	110.2	−2.2
70–74	660	14.2	−15.1	117.2	−2.1
75–79	1,022	13.4	−14.4	116.9	−2.5
80–84	1,604	21.0	−6.8	108.1	−1.3
85+	2,163	21.2	−1.4	101.7	−0.3
Females					
Overall	1,269	9.9	−2.3	102.9	−0.6
65–69	746	0.0	−2.2	102.9	−0.7
70–74	990	12.4	−2.6	103.3	−0.7
75–79	1,397	9.8	−2.5	103.2	−0.6
80–84	1,924	16.8	−2.1	102.6	−0.6
85+	2,303	22.7	−2.2	102.6	−0.3

penditures per beneficiary would have grown by about 9.6 percent more if no mortality improvements had occurred. The percentage is even larger for middle-range elderly males (aged seventy to seventy-four and seventy-four to seventy-nine) nearly 15 percent. For females, expenditures per beneficiary would have grown only 2.3 percent more, and that percentage remains the same over all female age groups. This suggests that for one demographic group, namely males aged seventy to seventy-four and seventy-four to seventy-nine, the mortality effect did have some impact on expenditure growth, although the utilization effect was still eight times greater. Overall, the mortality effect had only a modest impact on per-beneficiary expenditure growth because the utilization effect was large in comparison, more than twenty times greater.

Table 6.2 describes the contributing factors to the large utilization effect in more detail. The table shows that utilization increases for survivors accounted for around 73 percent of utilization growth—virtually identical to their share of base-year spending, again indicating that utilization effects are large for survivors as well as decedents. Table 6.2 also shows that nonacute spending for both survivors and decedents accounted for just over half of the utilization effect. This may seem like a relatively small share given the enormous differences in growth rates, but it is a reflection of the fact that nonacute spending represented only a small share of Medicare costs at the beginning of the study period. This is a marked change from the earlier history of Medicare spending growth. For the 1976–88 analysis by Lubitz and Riley, nonacute spending growth likely accounted for virtually all of the utilization effect. Moreover, the importance of nonacute care

Table 6.2   **Contributing Factors to Utilization Effect**

Gender and Age Groups	Acute-Care Utilization		Nonacute-Care Utilization	
	Decedents (%)	Survivors (%)	Decedents (%)	Survivors (%)
Overall	12.39	36.03	14.72	36.86
	Males			
Overall	16.17	38.56	16.98	28.29
65–69	18.68	53.12	9.09	19.09
70–74	16.11	43.13	13.90	26.80
75–79	16.95	38.83	16.76	27.51
80–84	14.60	27.84	21.62	36.04
85+	12.16	16.52	31.63	39.60
	Females			
Overall	10.10	34.27	13.33	42.28
65–69	10.84	54.00	7.49	27.69
70–74	11.70	42.36	9.79	36.12
75–79	10.15	32.41	12.58	44.81
80–84	9.56	27.99	14.25	48.21
85+	8.34	16.92	21.92	52.78

in the utilization effect was highly age and sex dependent: For elderly males, nonacute care accounted for 45 percent of the utilization effect; for sixty-five-to sixty-nine-year-old males, nonacute care accounted for less than one-third of the total utilization effect; for sixty-five-to sixty-nine-year-old females, a little over one-third; and for beneficiaries aged eighty-five and older, it accounted for over two-thirds of the effect. For all ages, nonacute care was a somewhat more important contributor to the utilization effect for females than for males.

6.3   Discussion

Our analysis of recent trends in Medicare spending near the end of life has three major conclusions. First, the rate of spending growth was similar for survivors and decedents—actually slightly larger for the oldest female survivors than for other demographic groups, as a result of relatively more rapid growth in spending for nonacute services. Thus, spending growth for survivors continues to account for most of the growth in Medicare costs. This seems to reflect a modest but important long-term trend. For Medicare's first decade, the rate of spending growth was slightly higher for decedents than survivors; and between the late 1970s and late 1980s, the growth rate was similar for the two groups.

Second, in recent years growth in spending for nonacute services has accounted for half of overall spending growth. Thus, spending growth for decedents was not primarily the result of increasing heroic, intensive measures near the end of life. In addition, although greater coverage of nonacute alternatives might be expected to affect end-of-life costs disproportionately, growth rates for nonacute services were even greater for older survivors than decedents. Large utilization effects for both acute and nonacute services occurred in both groups.

Third, although improvements in mortality have helped limit Medicare spending growth over time, this effect has been swamped by the much larger increases in expenditures given survival status for decedents and survivors alike. Without the survival improvements, our estimates suggest that total Medicare spending per beneficiary would have grown only 4 percent more than it did. Improvements in mortality were relatively more important in limiting spending growth for males than for females, and for mid-elderly males especially, but still much smaller than the larger increases in expenditures given survival status. Thus, we conclude that increasing utilization for both survivors and decedents has been a far more important determinant of Medicare spending over time than have improvements in mortality. If anything, the slightly more rapid recent growth in spending in some survivor groups—due to the increasing importance of nonacute care—suggests that survival improvements have probably become even more marginal contributors to explaining trends in spending.

This is not to say that the growth in Medicare spending has been wasteful. Life expectancy for an average elderly Medicare beneficiary increased by 4.9 months between 1988 and 1995, at a total cost to Medicare of $1,135—that is, around $2,780 per additional life-year. If an additional life-year were valued at only $25,000, the increased Medicare spending would be worthwhile if it accounted for only 11 percent of the observed improvement in mortality. Moreover, as we noted above, much of the spending growth occurred in chronic, supportive-care services that would be expected to improve quality of life as well as its length. Thus, although improvements in health have probably offset a miniscule share of the growth in medical spending over the past decade, it does not imply that such spending growth is excessive. However, it does imply that, unless the future is fundamentally different, improving mortality may not have a very noticeable impact on medical spending growth.

References

Health Care Finance Administration (HCFA). 2000. Data users' reference guide. Baltimore, Md.: HCFA.

Kennedy, Donald. 1994. Health care costs and technologies. The *Western Journal of Medicine* 161:424–5.

Lubitz, James, James Beebe, and Colin Baker. 1995. Longevity and medicare expenditures. *New England Journal of Medicine* 332:999–1003.

Lubitz, James, and Gerald Riley. 1993. Trends in medicare payments in the last year of life. *New England Journal of Medicine* 338:1092–6.

Pardes, Herbert, Kenneth G. Manton, Eric S. Lander, H. Dennis Tolley, Arthur D. Ullian, and Hans Palmer. 1999. Effects of medical research on health care and the economy. *Science* 283:36–7.

Piro, Paula, and Theodore Lutins. 1974. Utilization and reimbursements under Medicare for persons who died in 1967 and 1968. Department of Health, Education, and Welfare Publication no. 74-11702.

Singer, Burton, and Kenneth Manton. 1998. The effects of health changes on projections of health service needs for the elderly population of the United States. *Proceedings of the National Academy of Sciences* 95:15618–22.

Vaupel, James. 1997. The remarkable improvements in survival at older ages. *Philosophical Transactions of the Royal Society of London Series B: Biological Sciences* 352:1799–1804.

Comment   David M. Cutler

Geppert and McClellan present an interesting analysis of the roles of mortality change and intensity change in explaining the growth of Medicare costs. End-of-life spending is a substantial component of Medicare costs; those in the last year of life use six times more Medicare services than those not in the last year of life. Furthermore, people who die at later ages consume fewer Medicare services at the end of life than those who die at younger ages. The combination of these two factors means that as mortality rates fall and deaths occur at later ages, Medicare spending should fall.

Geppert and McClellan argue that this view is right but quantitatively small. Much more important is the fact that costs have increased for everyone—those near and farther away from death. This "intrinsic cost growth" has driven the Medicare system in the past, they argue, and will continue to do so in the future.

Geppert and McClellan reach a conclusion similar to that of my own work (Cutler and Meara chap. 7 in this volume, and Cutler and Sheiner 1999). In all three papers, technological change is the beast in the system: rapid growth of technology, high Medicare costs; slow growth of technology, lower costs. I am more or less in agreement with all that Geppert and McClellan say.

My one hesitation is that Geppert and McClellan look only at mortality, not at overall health. In addition to living longer, people are healthier. Since healthier people spend less than sicker people, the improvement in health is another form of cost saving. For example, those with five or more

David M. Cutler is professor of economics at Harvard University and a research associate of the National Bureau of Economic Research.

Table 6C.1   **Forecasts of Medicare Spending**

	1992	2010	2030	2050
Age and sex only	1.00	1.03	1.01	1.09
Age, sex, and improved health	1.00	0.97	0.90	0.91
Age, sex, improved health, and intrinsic cost growth	1.00	1.59	3.59	6.12

Source: Cutler and Sheiner (1999).

activities of daily living (ADL) impairments (inability to perform basic tasks such as bathing, cleaning, etc.) spend perhaps $7,000 per year in Medicare, whereas those with no disability might spend $1,000 to $2,000. As disability rates fall, average spending will fall as well.

To evaluate the magnitude of this, Manton, Corder, and Stallard (1997) show that disability rates among the elderly are falling by 1 to 1.5 percent per year. Over the decade which Geppert and McClellan examine this would reduce average disability rates by 10 to 15 percent. The implied reduction in spending is about 5 to 10 percent. This is of moderate size.

Indeed, looking forward, improvements in health may play a more important role in forecasting medical costs than they did in the past. Table 6C.1 shows forecasts of medical spending on the elderly between 1992 and 2050, taken from Cutler and Sheiner (1999). The first row uses standard projections for Medicare projections. Medicare costs vary by age and sex, but not by health status. For clarity, age- and sex-specific costs are assumed to be constant over time, so only changes in the age and sex distribution of the population affects spending. The increased share of the older population is projected to raise spending by 9 percent over the next half-century.

The next row shows the effect of improved health—both reduced morbidity and reduced mortality. Compared to the projection without accounting for better health, the difference in 2050 is 18 percent (from a 9 percent increase to a 9 percent decrease). The change is substantial.

The third row shows the impact of intrinsic cost growth at the same rate relative to gross domestic product as the past half-century. If costs continue to rise at this rate, per-person spending will increase by 500 percent in the next half-century. Clearly, these intrinsic increases dominate the Medicare future. Demographics are much less important.

However, the link between demographics and intrinsic growth may be more subtle. On the one hand, health changes may be driven by increased spending, so that spending increases in the future might have even larger effects on the health of the elderly. On the other hand, demographic change may affect the rate of intrinsic cost growth. As people become healthier, will spending growth rise, as more-healthy people receive intensive treatments? Or will spending growth fall as we learn how to prevent disease more cheaply? These are the important questions that research needs to address. Geppert and McClellan's paper, along with other work on this topic, has provided an important start.

References

Cutler, David, and Louise Sheiner. 1999. Demographics and Medical Care Spending: Standard and Non-Standard Effects. In *Demographics and Fiscal Policy,* eds., A. Auerbach and R. Lee, Cambridge: Cambridge University Press.
Manton, Kenneth, Larry Corder, and Eric Stallard. 1997. Chronic Disability Trends in Elderly United States Populations: 1982–1994. *Proceedings of the National Academy of Sciences,* 94:2593–2598.

The Concentration of
Medical Spending
An Update

David M. Cutler and Ellen Meara

7.1 Introduction

Health care for the elderly in America is at the center of public debate. In the last two decades, the number of Medicare beneficiaries has increased by 50 percent, and Medicare spending per beneficiary has doubled in real terms.[1] Although rapid growth in medical spending affects all age groups, Cutler and Meara (1998) document that spending growth occurred most rapidly among the elderly from the 1950s through the 1980s, and that within the population over age sixty-five, spending grew fastest among the oldest old.[2]

These findings are difficult to understand, however, in light of changes in the health of the elderly. Manton and coauthors show that disability rates are falling among the elderly by about 1.5 percent per year (Manton, Corder, and Stallard 1997). Since the disabled spend much more than the nondisabled on medical care, it seems that in relative (if not absolute) terms spending on the elderly should be falling over time.

The combination of large increases in per-person spending and the reduction in disability leads to the paradoxical situation where policy ana-

David M. Cutler is professor of economics at Harvard University and a research associate of the National Bureau of Economic Research. Ellen Meara is assistant professor of health economics at Harvard Medical School and a faculty research fellow of the National Bureau of Economic Research.

We are grateful to Monica Singhal for excellent research assistance, to Joe Newhouse for comments, and to the National Institute on Aging for research support.

1. Based on total Medicare expenditures and total enrollees in 1975 and 1995. See Health United States (1998, p. 367).

2. Relative spending by age group was fairly flat in 1953. By 1987, spending on the average eighty-five-year-old was more than five times as high as spending on those aged thirty-five to forty-four.

lysts call simultaneously for reforms to control Medicare cost growth (to bring spending growth for the elderly in line with other age groups) and for Medicare to cover currently uncovered services such as prescription drugs (to promote further health improvements).

The goals of this paper are to document how trends in spending by age have changed among elderly Medicare beneficiaries in the last decade and to reconcile the decline in disability rates with rapid increases in spending among the elderly. The first goal follows from our earlier paper (Cutler and Meara 1998), in which we analyzed medical spending by age from the mid-1950s through 1987. Since the medical world changed dramatically after 1987, we consider what has happened to age-specific spending since then. In the post-1987 period, we cannot look at spending for the elderly in comparison to the nonelderly, but we can look at spending for the younger and older elderly. The second goal is an attempt to reconcile increased spending with sharply declining disability. In particular, we relate medical spending by age to six factors: demographics, disability, time until death, intensity of treatment, prices, and changes in the nature of care.

We reach two central conclusions. First, we find that the trend of disproportionate spending growth among the oldest old has continued during the decade between 1985 and 1995. Between 1985 and 1995, spending for the younger elderly (ages sixty-five to sixty-nine) rose by 2 percent annually in real, per-person terms, while spending for the older elderly (ages eighty-five and up) rose by 4 percent. This is similar to the differential increase in spending by age over the 1953–87 period.

Second, we show that the reason for the large increase in spending on the oldest elderly in comparison to the younger elderly is the rapid increase in use of postacute services—home health care and skilled nursing care in particular—among the oldest old. People aged eighty-five and older used on average $241 in postacute services in 1985 and $1,887 in 1995, a 20 percent annual increase. The younger elderly, in contrast, increased their use of postacute services from $49 to $257, a 15 percent annual increase. Use of acute-care services, in contrast, grew relatively evenly by age, 1.2 percent annually for the younger elderly and 0.7 percent annually for the older elderly.

The increase in postacute service use is the explanation for the discrepancy between rising medical spending and falling disability. Lower disability by itself contributes to lower spending than we would otherwise observe. However, the increase in use of nontraditional services more than offsets the effects of improved health. The increase in postacute service use is also a major difference between the pre- and post-1987 trends. In our earlier work (Cutler and Meara 1998), we found that rising expenditures on the older population were a result of increased intensity of acute-care services for that age group. In the post-1987 period, intensity changes in acute-care treatments do not account for a substantial discrepancy by age.

The increase in postacute service use may reflect several factors: true increased service use for people who were not receiving care in the past; "gaming" of the Medicare system, whereby providers now use out-of-hospital services instead of in-hospital services; or outright fraud. We are unable to discriminate among these explanations, although we suspect each is important.

The paper proceeds as follows. Section 7.2 describes our data. Section 7.3 begins the analysis by comparing past and current trends in medical spending by age. Section 7.4 analyzes how changes in demographics, disability, and death contribute to spending over time. Section 7.5 examines acute-care spending. Section 7.6 examines postacute-care spending, and section 7.7 concludes.

7.2   Data

The National Long-Term Care Surveys (NLTCS) were conducted in 1982, 1984, 1989, and 1994 to determine the prevalence of disability among the Medicare population. A sample of about 35,000 individuals was drawn from Medicare administrative records and surveyed in 1982. In addition to standard demographic information, the survey collected detailed information on each individual's instrumental activities of daily living (IADLs, such as managing money, keeping house, etc.) and activities of daily living (ADLs, such as dressing, bathing, etc.). In subsequent surveys, a subsample of those initially interviewed were rescreened to determine disability status and additional individuals "aged" into the NLTCS. In total, the NLTCS public use data set provides information on 35,848 individuals. The survey data for these individuals have been linked to all Medicare claims data from 1982 through 1995.

We use the NLTCS from the years 1984, 1989, and 1994, matched to Medicare records for 1984–85, 1989–90, and 1994–95.[3] We pooled the Medicare data in two-year increments to increase the precision of our estimates.[4] All numbers reported in the tables are in 1995 dollars adjusted using the Consumer Price Index Urban (CPI-U) deflator.

One drawback of the NLTCS for our purpose is that we have no link to other types of medical spending beyond Medicare. Approximately one-third of Medicaid's budget pays for nursing home services for elderly recipients. Because such services are disproportionately skewed toward the older elderly population, however, we suspect that the omission of Medicaid-covered long-term care understates the growth in spending by the oldest

---

3. All calculations use the Center for Demographic Studies "screener cross-sectional weights" to make tabulations representative of the Medicare population in those years.

4. We inflated expenditure data from 1984, 1989, and 1994 by the one-year nominal growth rate in per capita expenditures from 1984 to 1985, 1989 to 1990, and 1994 to 1995, respectively.

old. Further, nonhospital prescription drugs are not paid for by Medicare, and thus are unrecorded in the survey. We do not know how the omission of this category of care affects our results.

7.3   Past and Current Trends in Medical Spending by Age

During the period from the 1950s through the 1980s, the distribution of medical spending changed dramatically in the United States. Figure 7.1 and table 7.1 reproduce the trend in medical spending documented in Cutler and Meara (1998). The figure shows per capita medical spending relative to per capita spending for thirty-five-to forty-four-year-olds. In 1953, spending was fairly constant across age groups. Middle-aged and elderly individuals spent the same amount on medical care. From the 1950s to the 1980s, medical spending grew dramatically within all age groups, but by 1987, the oldest old (aged eighty-five and up) were spending over five times as much as the thirty-five to forty-four age group.

Panels *A* and *B* of figure 7.2 examine this trend for the NLTCS data between 1985 and 1995 for the population over the age of sixty-five. Over the last decade, spending among the youngest Medicare beneficiaries, those aged sixty-five to sixty-nine, grew by 2.0 percent annually, from $2,062 to $2,519. Among older age groups, particularly those over eighty-five, per-person spending grew at a staggering rate between 1990 and 1995. While the oldest old spent $3,730 in 1985, they were spending $5,709 by 1995, a 4.3 percent annual increase. To see this trend another way, panel *B* of

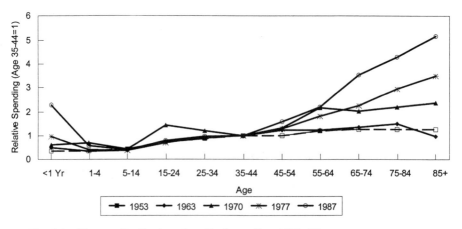

Fig. 7.1   The age distribution of medical spending, 1953–87

Source: Cutler and Meara (1998).

Notes: 1953 age groups include 0–5, 6–17, 18–24, 25–34, 35–54, 55–64, and 65 and up. Relative spending for 5–24-year-olds was constructed assuming a uniform age distribution. Dashed lines in 1953 connect all age groups that were combined when calculating relative spending.

Table 7.1   **Medical Spending by Age and Type of Care**

	65–69	70–74	75–79	80–84	85+
All medical spending (NMES)					
1963	1,102	1,178	1,417	964	819
1977	3,205	3,561	4,274	4,607	5,220
1987	4,999	5,451	5,594	7,522	7,580
Total Medicare spending (NLTCS)					
1985	2,062	2,479	2,918	3,505	3,730
1995	2,519	3,205	4,102	4,400	5,709
	(2.0%)	(2.6%)	(3.4%)	(2.3%)	(4.3%)
Acute-care Medicare spending					
1985	2,002	2,397	2,782	3,276	3,482
1995	2,255	2,782	3,370	3,389	3,734
	(1.2%)	(1.5%)	(1.9%)	(0.3%)	(0.7%)
Postacute-care Medicare spending					
1985	49	64	126	199	241
1995	227	375	693	975	1,887
	(15.3%)	(17.7%)	(17.0%)	(15.9%)	(20.6%)

Source: Cutler and Meara (1998) and authors' tabulations based on NLTCS data from 1984, 1989, and 1994, matched to Medicare records for 1984–85, 1989–90, and 1994–95.

Notes: Numbers in 1995 dollars adjusted using CPI-U deflator. Numbers in parentheses are the annual growth rates from the previous year. NMES is the National Medical Expenditure Survey. NLTCS is the National Long-Term Care Survey.

figure 7.2 normalizes spending in each age group and year relative to spending by those aged sixty-five to sixty-nine in that year. In 1985, the oldest old were spending about 80 percent more than this reference group. By 1995, the oldest old were spending over twice as much per year as sixty-five-to sixty-nine-year-olds.

The trend toward greater spending increases with age is generally true for most of the age groups, with the exception of the eighty- to eighty-four-year-old population. These findings represent a continuation of the trend documented from the early 1960s to the 1980s—medical spending is growing rapidly for all elderly, but particularly among the oldest age groups.

7.4   Demographics, Disability, and Time until Death

An important component of changes in medical spending is changes in disability status. Two measures of disability have been highlighted in the literature (see Cutler and Sheiner 2001): functional status and time until death. Functional status is typically measured with ADL or IADL impairments. People who are functionally impaired spend more on medical care

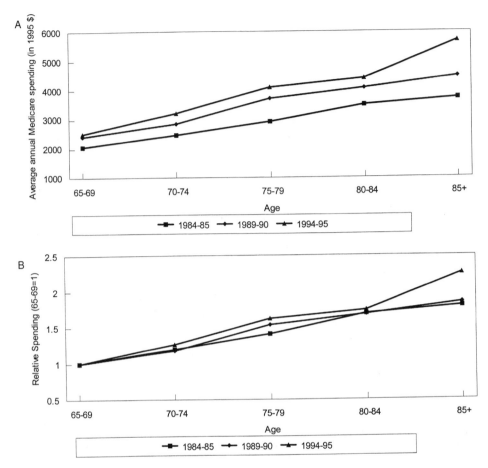

Fig. 7.2   Medicare spending per person: (*A*) total, (*B*) relative
Sources: Authors' tabulations based on National Long-Term Care Survey (NLTCS) data from 1984, 1989, and 1994, matched to Medicare records for 1984–85, 1989–90, and 1994–95.

than those who are not impaired. Research also shows that those near death spend much more on medical care than those farther away from death (Lubitz and Riley 1993). About one-third of Medicare spending is during the last year of life.

Table 7.2 examines how the patterns of age, disability, and death rates influence medical spending. The table shows four models of annual individual Medicare spending in 1989 and 1990 (in other words, each observation represents one person-year of spending). Individual spending is shown as a function of basic demographics (age, sex, race, and marital status), disability status, and time until death. Column (1) relates Medicare spending to age, sex, race, and marital status alone (the coefficients on

Table 7.2   **Explaining Medicare Reimbursement, 1989–90**

Independent Variable	(1)	(2)	(3)	(4)
Demographics				
Ages 70–74	369	251	289	201
	(151)	(148)	(149)	(147)
Ages 75–79	1,203	897	970	744
	(190)	(190)	(185)	(187)
Ages 80–84	1,559	878	1,154	646
	(177)	(183)	(174)	(187)
Ages 85+	1,990	398	1,120	−34
	(197)	(233)	(201)	(232)
Female	−696	−777	−436	−526
	(127)	(125)	(121)	(119)
Disability				
IADL limitations only	—	1,448	—	1,218
		(267)		(259)
1–2 ADL limitations	—	2,235	—	1,905
		(238)		(231)
3–4 ADL limitations	—	3,820	—	3,189
		(383)		(379)
5+ ADL limitations	—	6,735	—	5,412
		(617)		(593)
Institutionalized	—	3,594	—	2,464
		(392)		(371)
Time until death				
Died in first quarter	—	—	10,464	9,513
			(725)	(729)
Died in second quarter	—	—	7,242	6,402
			(954)	(967)
Died in third quarter	—	—	10,971	10,200
			(1,910)	(2,896)
Died in fourth quarter	—	—	12,460	11,824
			(1,200)	(1,202)
R^2	.0106	.0375	.0698	.0862

Sources: Authors' tabulations based on NLTCS data from 1989, matched to Medicare records for 1989–90.

Notes: There are 31,693 observations in each regression. Regressions include controls for race and marital status (see text). Dependent variable is individual annual spending. ADLs are activities of daily living. IADLs are instrumental activities of daily living.

race and marital status are not reported). Consistent with earlier work, Medicare spending is highest for the oldest old. Those over age eighty-five spend almost $2,000 more than those under seventy. Women spend $700 less than men on average; this is also true holding constant functional status and time until death.

Column (2) adds measures of functional status to the regression. The differences in spending by age are much less dramatic when we control for disability status in column (2). Only those aged seventy-five to eighty-four spend more than sixty-five-to sixty-nine-year-olds. Essentially all of the additional spending of those aged eighty-five and older is a result of greater disability.

Column (3) replaces the disability variables with measures of time until death. We include dummies for the quarter of death for those individuals who die in a given year. The result is similar in that in column (2). Time until death also explains a large part of the age effect. Advanced age is associated with only half as big a change when controlling for time until death.

Column (4) includes both functional status and time until death in the regression. Disability and time until death appear to have independent effects on Medicare spending. Together, these two variables explain essentially all of the age effect. The results in table 7.2 confirm those found in Cutler and Sheiner (2001) using the Medicare Current Beneficiary Survey. Age in itself is not associated with increased levels of Medicare spending; it is the decline in health status associated with both advanced ages and the period near death that leads to higher levels of medical spending.

As mortality rates among the elderly decline, fewer people are in the last year of life. Furthermore, disability among the elderly is falling. Table 7.3,

Table 7.3   Changes in Disease Incidence

Condition	Age- and Sex-Adjusted Rate		
	1984–85	1989–90	1994–95
All hospitalization	.306	.239	.218
Cardiovascular disease			
Acute myocardial infarction (AMI)	.012	.010	.010
Stroke	.006	.004	.003
Other ischemic heart disease	.022	.021	.020
Congestive heart failure	.017	.017	.016
Other cerebrovascular	.019	.016	.016
Cancer	.029	.021	.018
Respiratory disease			
Chronic obstructive pulmonary disease	.008	.005	.009
Emphysema	.0007	.0004	.0006
Kidney failure	.0020	.0015	.0018
Musculoskeletal injury			
Hip fracture	.010	.009	.009
Other fracture	.0086	.0065	.0051
Mental illness			
Depression	.0004	.0003	2.90e-05
Schizophrenia	.00018	.00014	.0004
Alzheimer's disease	.0022	.0018	.0018
N	42,986	32,294	33,786

Sources: Authors' tabulations based on NLTCS data for 1984, 1989, and 1994, matched to Medicare records for 1984–85, 1989–90, and 1994–95.

Notes: Disease rates are based on the 1990 age-sex distribution. An individual is defined as having a condition when hospitalized with the condition at any time during the year.

for example, shows rates of hospitalization for common illnesses. Overall hospitalization rates fell from 31 to 22 percent in the decade studied. There were declines in rates of hospitalization for virtually all diseases shown.

Table 7.4 shows rates of disability and mortality between 1984 and 1995. Overall disability rates fell by about one to four percentage point for those aged sixty-five to seventy-nine. For those over age eighty, however, rates of disability fell dramatically, by about 7 percentage points. Rates of severe disability were much more constant over this period, falling only slightly. The declines were greater, however, at older ages. These trends are striking in light of the pattern of declining mortality. The share of people who will die in a given year has declined on average within all age groups over sixty-five. As others have suggested (Manton, Corder, and Stallard 1997), not only are Americans living longer, but they are living with fewer functional limitations.

The combination of longer life and reduced disability suggests that medical spending for the elderly should be falling, particularly at advanced ages. In table 7.5 and figure 7.3, we combine changes in disability and death rates with our estimates of how disability and death impact medical spending to simulate how spending would have changed based solely on changes in disability and death rates. We use the regression coefficients from the fourth model in table 7.1 (excluding race and marital status) to make this prediction.[5] Predicted spending falls slightly, from $3,324 to $3,212 over the decade shown in table 7.5, and the decline is somewhat greater for the older elderly than for the younger elderly (figure 7.3).

It is apparent that figure 7.3 and panel *B* of figure 7.2 are in conflict. The changes in disability and death predict that relative spending for the oldest age groups should fall compared with those age sixty-five to sixty-nine, or at worst stay the same. In fact, medical spending increased twice as rapidly for the oldest elderly in comparison to the younger elderly.

The remainder of the paper aims to explain why spending by age is increasing when the underlying health of the population is improving.

7.5   Acute-Care Spending

To examine why age patterns in spending have changed, we divide medical spending into two parts: acute-care spending and postacute-care spending. *Acute care* is defined as spending for inpatient and outpatient care in general hospitals and physicians' offices. Postacute-care spending includes spending on skilled nursing facilities, hospice care, home health, and comprehensive outpatient rehabilitation facilities. This distinction is imperfect. Some rehabilitative care may show up in our measures of acute-care spending, since the Medicare claims data do not allow one to distin-

5. Our estimates hold constant the 1989–90 age and sex distribution.

Table 7.4   **Disability Rates by Age and Year (%)**

Age Group	Any Disability			Severe Disability			Share of People Dying that Year		
	1984	1989	1994	1984	1989	1994	1984	1989	1994
65–69	10.4	9.2	9.5	3.9	4.0	3.7	2.4	2.1	2.5
70–74	15.4	14.1	12.0	6.1	5.5	4.9	3.4	3.2	2.6
75–79	23.7	22.3	19.7	10.1	9.9	9.2	5.1	5.2	4.5
80–84	37.6	35.5	30.6	18.3	18.9	15.8	8.2	7.4	7.6
85+	63.7	60.4	57.1	39.3	39.5	38.0	14.2	13.1	14.2

Sources: See table 7.3.

Note: Severe disability is defined as either 3 or more ADL limitations, or institutionalization.

Table 7.5   **Predicted Spending Based on Disability and Death**

Year	Predicted Spending ($)	Ratio
1984–85	3,324	
1989–90	3,333	1.00
1994–95	3,212	0.97

Sources: See tables 7.2 and 7.3.

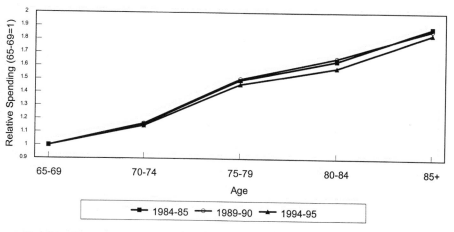

Fig. 7.3   Projected spending based on disability and death
Source: See fig. 7.2.

guish perfectly between rehabilitative care and acute care, but the distinction is generally a meaningful one.

The vast majority of spending on acute care is for inpatient hospital care. Inpatient care is reimbursed prospectively based on one of more than 400 diagnosis-related groups (DRGs). Each patient is assigned a DRG based on the predominant diagnosis of admission; DRGs are then given relative weights in accordance with the intensity of treatment typically provided for that diagnosis. Payments are formed as the product of the DRG weight and a price, as follows:

(1)   Reimbursement = DRG weight * Price

Over time, either weights or prices may change. For example, weights for surgical DRGs are generally higher than for medical DRGs, so that, as more people receive surgery over time, the average DRG weight will increase (Cutler and McClellan 1998). Changes in intensity of treatment have historically been significant. Cutler and Meara (1998) document that changes in technology for treatment of major illnesses such as cancers and heart disease coincide with large increases in spending for the elderly.

Medicare also updates the price paid for services over time. The increase in the update factor was designed to keep pace with the growth of input costs for hospitals, although actual update factors have increased less rapidly, in response to other changes in the health system (Cutler 1998).

We examine the intensity of treatment by focusing on major diseases of old age where hospital admission is a good indicator of illness. The diseases include acute myocardial infarction (AMI, or heart attack), stroke, other ischemic heart disease, congestive heart failure, other acute cerebrovascular disease, cancer, chronic obstructive pulmonary disease, hip fracture, other fracture, Alzheimer's disease, and kidney failure. For each individual we construct an intensity measure equal to the sum of DRG weights for all hospital visits in a year.

Table 7.6 shows the average intensity measure across respondents, and for respondents with each of the diseases listed above. The average intensity measure per Medicare beneficiary has actually declined over time, as hospitalization rates have fallen. Conditional on being admitted to the hospital, however, the intensity of treatment has risen over time by about 21 percent. Intensity is rising over time even within a diagnosis. To examine three well-defined acute diagnoses, we constructed several ninety-day intensity measures. We summed all DRG weights for services provided within ninety days of an admission for AMI, stroke, or hip fracture. The last three columns of table 7.6 demonstrate that the intensity of services for these three diagnoses has risen in the last decade. The rise in intensity of services overall implies about a $1,000 increase in spending. However, the rise in intensity cannot explain the roughly $5,000 per person increase in spending for individuals who were hospitalized in a year.

The other component in equation (1) that could lead to increased medical spending is the price paid for medical services. As noted above, however, the update factor has not increased rapidly. Indeed, in real terms between 1985 and 1994, the update factor fell by 7 percent. These cuts in the update factor were in response to gaming in the prospective payment system. Immediately following the implementation of prospective payment in 1984, the average diagnosis became much more serious relative to before prospective payment. The increase in serious diagnoses (or "diagnosis creep") reflected provider attempts to increase payment. Medicare officials responded by cutting the increase in the update factor. Further cuts in the update factor were a component of deficit reduction legislation in 1990 and 1993. Price increases, therefore, play no role in the rise of Medicare spending.

The net effect on acute-care spending is reflected in figure 7.4, panels *A* and *B*. Acute-care spending rose slightly in all age groups, but the rise was smaller among the older elderly than among the younger elderly. Among the sixty-five to sixty-nine age group, spending rose from $2,000 to about $2,300, a 1.2 percent annual increase (table 7.1). Elderly over age eighty-

Table 7.6   Changes in Intensity of Treatment

Condition	Annual DRG Weight for Individuals Admitted to Hospital for Condition			90-Day Episode DRG Weight for Individuals Admitted to Hospital for Condition		
	1984–85	1989–90	1994–95	1984–85	1989–90	1994–95
All respondents	0.580	0.542	0.507			
All hospitalized respondents	1.89	2.25	2.29			
Cardiovascular disease						
Acute myocardial infarction (AMI)	2.80	3.53	3.81	2.29	3.22	3.09
Stroke	2.56	3.59	3.07	2.25	1.82	2.33
Other ischemic heart disease	2.87	3.42	3.62			
Congestive heart failure	2.99	3.14	3.34			
Other cerebrovascular	2.17	2.50	2.40			
Cancer	2.99	3.32	2.87			
Respiratory disease						
Chronic obstructive pulmonary disease	2.70	2.76	2.86			
Musculoskeletal injury						
Hip fracture	3.03	3.38	3.27	2.70	3.01	2.76
Other fracture	1.64	1.83	2.02			
Alzheimer's disease	2.37	2.16	2.67			
Kidney failure	3.92	4.25	4.48			
N (total)	30,011	26,237	28,292			
N (hospitalized)	9,468	6,663	6,713			

Sources: See table 7.3.

Notes: DRGs are diagnosis-related groups. DRG weights are those prevailing in 1989. Ninety-day intensity measures constructed for AMI, stroke, and hip fracture only.

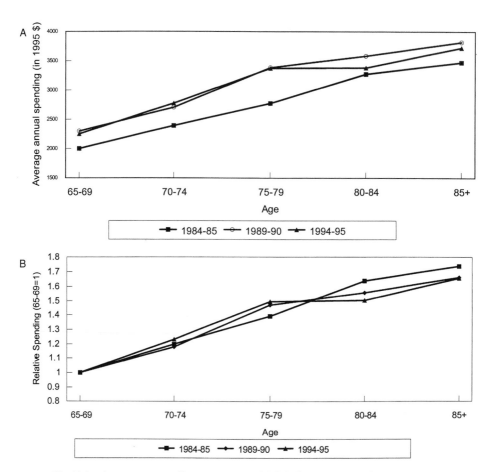

Fig. 7.4   Acute-care spending per person: (*A*) Medicare, (*B*) relative
Source: See fig. 7.2.
Note: Acute care includes inpatient and outpatient services delivered in general hospitals, doctors' offices, and other acute-care sites.

five witnessed a 0.7 percent annual increase, from $3,500 to $3,700. Relative spending on acute care actually fell modestly for the oldest age groups.

Taken together, the information on acute-care spending suggests that increases in the intensity of treatment offset disability changes slightly, but changes in prices do not. The overall annual change in medical spending for the elderly explained by increased use of acute-care services is only 1 percent (compared to a 3 percent average increase for the elderly population), and the increase is greater for the younger elderly than for the older elderly. Other explanations are clearly more important in explaining the growth in medical costs for the elderly population as a whole, particularly for the oldest elderly.

7.6 Postacute-Care Spending

To complete the picture of changing Medicare spending, we examine the fastest growing portion of Medicare costs, postacute-care services. As noted above, postacute-care spending includes home health, hospice care, comprehensive outpatient rehabilitation care, and skilled nursing care.

Figure 7.5, panels *A* and *B,* demonstrates the striking growth in real spending on these services. Growth in real, per-person postacute services ranged from 15 percent per year for the youngest elderly to 21 percent per year for the oldest elderly (table 7.1). The numbers are staggering. In 1995,

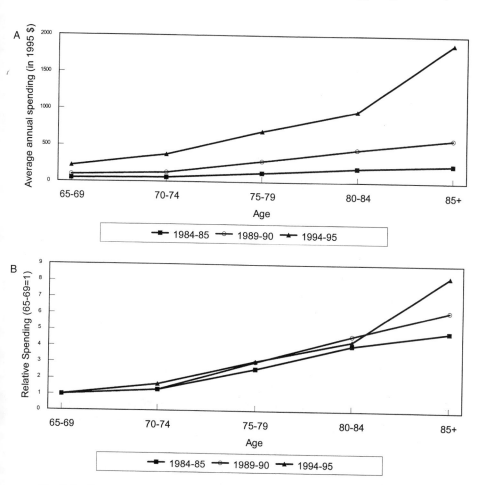

Fig. 7.5   Postacute-care spending: (*A*) average, (*B*) relative
Source: See fig. 7.2.
Note: Postacute care includes skilled nursing, home health, hospice care, and comprehensive outpatient rehabilitation facilities.

Table 7.7   Postacute-Care Spending for Hip Fracture and Stroke Patients ($)

Condition	1984–85	1989–90	1994–95
Hip fracture	1,567	3,207	5,220
Stroke	1,488	3,151	4,311

Sources: See table 7.3.

Notes: Postacute care includes skilled nursing, home health, hospice care, and comprehensive outpatient rehabilitation facilities. Spending is average annual spending for individuals admitted with hip fracture or stroke.

the oldest elderly averaged nearly $2,000 per person on postacute services, up from $240 in 1985. As displayed in figure 7.5, panel (b), this contributes significantly to higher relative spending among the population over age eighty-five. Relative postacute spending for the oldest elderly compared to the younger elderly rose from a factor of five to a factor of more than eight.

To understand what these services involve, consider the canonical case of an elderly person with a stroke or hip fracture. Such a person needs some acute-care services (for example, a hip replacement), and then a period of recovery involving physical and occupational therapy and perhaps help with routine services the person is not able to perform on his or her own.

Table 7.7 shows the steady rise in average annual postacute-care spending for individuals admitted to the hospital with a hip fracture or stroke. Hip fracture patients spent about $1,600 in 1984–85. By 1994–95, however, they spent about $5,200, an increase of more than 200 percent. Cost increases were similar for people with strokes. What is interesting about these conditions is that by most measures, people with hip fractures or strokes are getting healthier over time (Cutler and Richardson 1997). Thus, the increase in postacute service use is unlikely to be only a response to sicker elderly.

Increases in postacute service use might reflect one of three factors. The first is "gaming," or changes in the site of care. Care that follows an injury such as a hip fracture provides a good example of this. Inpatient care is reimbursed prospectively, so hospitals receive the same payment regardless of whether they provide rehabilitative care in the inpatient setting. Postacute care is reimbursed on a cost basis, however, when services are used. Thus, if hospitals unbundled postacute care from the inpatient setting, they can collect additional revenues at no extra cost.

In some cases, this unbundling occurs in the hospital itself. Hospitals can set up a wing for rehabilitation or skilled nursing care. These services many simply involve wheeling the hip fracture patient down the hall, delivering the same services as were delivered before but collecting higher reimbursement. In other cases, the home health agency or skilled nursing facility will be a separate provider. This increase in *spending* may be associated with a reduction in *costs*. Outpatient settings are generally cheaper than inpatient settings, so that total costs may fall even as reimbursement is rising.

A second explanation is that increased postacute spending reflects additional use of services. The rules on when the elderly could use postacute services were relaxed substantially in the late 1980s, just before the explosion in service use. At least some of the additional service use may be a result of individuals' having access to services they previously either went without or had a family member provide informally.

The final explanation is that increased postacute service use represents fraud in the program. Since postacute services are provided in a person's home, by small agencies that are not easily monitored, the potential for fraud is vast. Recent congressional testimony highlighted frequent instances of fraud in the home health program. The testimony cited one estimate suggesting that as many 40 percent of home health claims should have been denied.[6] This number is sobering, given that home health has risen from 1 percent of Medicare spending in 1970 to more than 13 percent in 1995.

We have no way to differentiate among these theories with our data, since the inpatient data do not indicate completely what services are provided. Disentangling the alternative sources of cost growth in postacute care is a major research topic.

A related topic is the health consequences of the shift in health care delivery toward more postacute-care settings. It may be socially beneficial, if costly, for people to receive care outside a hospital setting. Postacute providers may have more skill in their jobs than nurses in an inpatient setting have. Patients also prefer being at home over being in a hospital. This too is an important topic for future research.

7.7 Conclusion

Over the last decade, medical spending for the oldest old has continued to increase more rapidly than for the youngest old. However, unlike the spending growth in the early 1980s, this growth has little to do with increased intensity of treatment. Over the 1990s, much of the spending growth relates to increased use of postacute-care services. Some of the increased spending on postacute care likely reflects gaming of Medicare through such practices as unbundling care to maximize reimbursement; some may reflect increased service use; and some may be outright fraud.

Our results have not addressed the question of what this increased medical spending is buying. This question is central in evaluating the growth of medical costs for the elderly and nonelderly population. Medical spend-

6. See HCFA's website, [http://www.hcfa.gov/testmony/1998/980318.htm].

ing is valuable if it purchases services worth more than their cost and problematic if the services are worth less than their cost. Additional research on the importance of Medicare in improved health would complement the findings here about the sources of Medicare cost-increases.

References

Cutler, David. 1998. Cost shifting or cost cutting?: The incidence of reductions in Medicare payments. In *Tax policy and the economy, Vol.* 12, ed. James Poterba. Cambridge, Mass.: MIT Press.
Cutler, David, and Mark McClellan. 1998. What is technological change? In *Inquiries in the economics of aging,* ed. David Wise. Chicago: University of Chicago Press.
Cutler, David, and Ellen Meara. 1998. The medical costs of the young and old: A forty-year perspective. In *Frontiers in aging,* ed. David Wise. Chicago: University of Chicago Press.
Cutler, David, and Elizabeth Richardson. 1997. Measuring the health of the United States population. *Brookings Papers on Economic Activity, Microeconomics,* 217–72. Washington, D.C.: Brookings Institution.
Cutler, David, and Louise Sheiner. 2001. Demographics and medical care spending: Standard and non-standard effects. In *Demographics and fiscal policy,* ed. Alan Auerbach and Ronald Lee, 253–91. Cambridge: Cambridge University Press.
Lubitz, James D., and Gerald F. Riley. 1993. Trends in Medicare payments in the last year of life. *New England Journal of Medicine* 328:1092–96.
Manton, Kenneth, Larry Corder, and Eric Stallard. 1997. Chronic disability trends in elderly United States populations: 1982–1994. *Proceedings of the National Academy of Sciences* 94:2593–98.

Comment   Joseph P. Newhouse

This paper bears on both the short- and long-term futures of Medicare. By pointing to the postacute area it touches on a short-term issue, and by placing the role of disability and end-of-life care in perspective it touches on a long-term issue. In my remarks I wish to focus on the short-term issue because it seems more serious than is commonly recognized. Much of the debate of the past year or so has focused on how Medicare can be financed after the baby boomers begin to turn sixty-five in 2010. I wish to argue,

Joseph P. Newhouse is the John D. MacArthur Professor of Health Policy and Management at Harvard University and is on the faculties of the Kennedy School of Government, the Harvard Medical School, the Harvard School of Public Health, and the Harvard University Faculty of Arts and Sciences, and is a research associate of the National Bureau of Economic Research.

however, that there is a serious problem in the here and now, namely that Medicare's administered pricing systems are breaking down. Before turning to that point, however, I note that any overall appraisal of the importance of the decline in disability, and to a lesser degree the increase in life expectancy, should account for costs in the Medicaid program, especially those attributable to chronic long-term care.

Viewed from a very great distance, the history of how Medicare has reimbursed institutional providers might run as follows. Beginning in 1966, Medicare reimbursed the lesser of charges or patient care costs up to some specified limits. Costs rose, and critics pointed out that cost reimbursement was a low-powered payment method that permitted substantial inefficiencies. As a result, in fiscal 1984 the federal government enacted the prospective payment system (PPS) for inpatient hospital services, a higher-powered payment method. The government acted to change reimbursement for hospital services in part because such services represented the largest single expenditure of Medicare, around a third, and because a method for prospective payment was readily at hand, namely the diagnosis-related group (DRG) system. The DRG system, which aggregated the thousands of diagnosis codes into around 500 groups and paid each group a lump sum, had been under development for about a decade and a variant of it had been used to reimburse hospitals in New Jersey.[1] In part because prospective methods were not available for other institutional providers, the remainder of the reimbursement system remained cost based and entry rules were permissive.

Hospitals thus had an incentive to unbundle inpatient services and to shift as much overhead as regulations would permit to services other than inpatient services. As a result of unbundling, the last day in the hospital building was more frequently spent in the skilled nursing facility (SNF) or the rehabilitation unit than on the general medical or surgical service after 1984. Earlier discharge also resulted in more home health visits. Marginal revenue for the last day on the SNF or the rehabilitation unit or for a home health visit was positive, whereas (except for outlier cases) it was zero on the medical and surgical service.

Reimbursement for entrants was also permissive, leading to substantial entry. The number of home health agencies, SNFs, and rehabilitation facilities grew at annual rates of 9, 6, and 4 percent, respectively, in the 1990–97 period (Medicare Payment Advisory Commission 1998). The number of hospitals, by contrast, was falling during this period.

As a result of unbundling and entry, the use of SNF and home health services skyrocketed. The rate of increase was especially marked after

1. Although often referred to as a lump sum, in fact, around 5 percent of the dollars were placed in an outlier pool and paid on the basis of (approximately) marginal cost. Moreover, several of the DRGs depended on the procedure performed. The PPS was thus considerably less high powered than often asserted. See McClellan (1997).

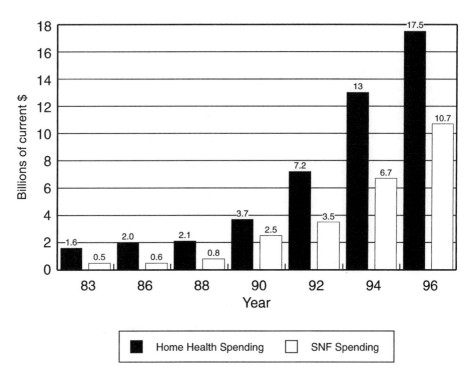

Fig. 7C.1   Spending on home health and skilled nursing facility services
Source: Author's tabulations based on Medicare Payment Advisory Commission (1998) data.

1988, when a court decision nullified the regulatory methods the Health Care Financing Administration had been using to hold down usage of SNF and home health services following the implementation of the PPS. About half of the home health use, however, comes from visits that do not follow a hospital stay, so causes other than unbundling were also important in the growth of home health services.

Figure 7C.1 shows the dramatic growth of SNF and home health spending, which grew 38 and 30 percent per year, respectively, between 1988 and 1996. Most of the spending growth reflected increases in services; during this period home health visits per beneficiary grew 25 percent per year and SNF days per beneficiary grew 18 percent per year (computed from data in Medicare Payment Advisory Commission 1998). As a result of this growth, postacute services, which include home health, SNF, rehabilitation hospitals and units, and long-term hospitals (with the first two being the largest), grew from less than 5 percent of Medicare Part A spending in 1988 to more than 25 percent of Part A spending in 1996. This is a percentage of a large pie, since Part A of Medicare is the second largest domestic program in the federal budget, exceeded only by Social Security.

Furthermore, the pie itself was growing at a rapid rate; Part A spending in real terms grew 8.5 percent per year between 1988 and 1996.[2] By 1996 the payment system for these services seemed to have reached the end of its useful life.

As a result, Congress in 1997 enacted the Balanced Budget Act, which decreed that separate prospective payment systems should be developed for the remaining institutional providers. In particular, home health, SNF, rehabilitation facilities, long-term hospitals, and outpatient departments of hospitals were all to have their own prospective payment systems. The general view seemed to be that the PPS had been a good thing for inpatient services, and that in any event spending on these other services seemed out of control, so prospective systems should be developed for these other services as well.

I want to argue that implementing such systems will be exceedingly difficult and that, more generally, the administered pricing system of traditional Medicare is breaking down. (The administered pricing system Medicare uses for health maintenance organizations (HMOs) also has serious problems, but I have discussed those issues elsewhere; see Newhouse, Beeuwkes Buntin, and Chapman 1997; Newhouse 1998; Wilensky and Newhouse 1999.) Traditional Medicare is by far the largest part of the Medicare program, accounting for more than 85 percent of the dollars. Because most observers believe traditional Medicare will continue to have a large share of enrollees well into the future, and because Medicare is such a large share of the federal budget—around an eighth and growing—this breakdown is a serious policy problem.[3]

There are at least four kinds of difficulties with implementing PPSs for these other institutional providers. The first two are related; I shall call them the *silo problem* and the *problem of substitution*. In effect, separate PPSs mandate a budget cap for each provider type. However, we have just seen that there has been rapid and to some extent unpredictable growth in these services from year to year. Although a budget cap may bring federal spending under control, the possibility of making a substantial error when setting the cap ex ante means that some beneficiaries may not receive needed services, and those beneficiaries may not be the ones that were intended to be without those services. Separate budget caps for various providers—different silos—only exacerbate the problem if some kind of technological change or change in the epidemiology of disease means that care should shift from one type of provider to another.

The problem of substitution arises because the patient can obtain many postacute services in several places. A stroke patient, for example, could

---

2. This calculation uses the GDP deflator to convert nominal spending to real terms.
3. Even if Medicare moves to a defined contribution or premium support approach, traditional Medicare seems likely to dominate in small towns and rural areas because of natural monopolies from having only one hospital or type of specialist nearby.

possibly obtain the necessary physical therapy in a freestanding rehabilitation hospital or a rehabilitation unit (part of a hospital), in a freestanding SNF or an SNF that is part of a hospital, in an outpatient department, at home, or in an outpatient rehabilitation facility. (Of course, not all these providers may be available in any given local market.) One would like the reimbursement system to be consistent with the optimal choice of facility.

Medicare can pay very different amounts per patient in different venues. This occurs partly because different types of cases go to different facilities. For example, patients who are to receive more intensive rehabilitation disproportionately go to the rehabilitation facility, whereas those receiving less intensive rehabilitation go to the SNF. As a result, costs per patient are higher at the rehabilitation facility. Under a cost-based system this difference did not much matter with regard to where the patient was treated; but if facilities are to be paid a set price that is a function of the national average cost of those admitted to that type of facility, it obviously does matter. There are regulations constraining admissions to rehabilitation facilities; otherwise the equilibrium with a much higher per-patient price for rehabilitation facilities than for SNFs would presumably find every patient in a rehabilitation facility.

Indeed, the basis of payment is not even the same for rehabilitation facilities and SNFs. Those admitted to the rehabilitation facility or unit, for example, are paid on a per-case (per-admission) basis, whereas those admitted to the SNF are paid on a per diem basis. If these differences were maintained in a prospective system, the incentive would be to admit the short-stayers to the rehabilitation facility and the long stayers to the SNF.

The third problem is that 18 percent of those who use postacute services use more than one service. This means that if payment is per case for each type of provider, some method will have to be found to allocate a given payment among many providers. A method has been developed in the PPS for doing this in the case of hospitalized patients who are transferred from one hospital to another, but the rate of such transfers is much less for acute hospital care, about one-twentieth as great as among postacute providers. As a result, errors in the allocation of the DRG payment among acute care hospitals are less serious.

A fourth problem is stinting or underservice. In general, economists do not believe that systems in which marginal revenue is zero will work well unless consumers are well informed and can monitor that they are receiving an entire bundle of services for which they contracted (Pauly 1980). There are well-known informational disadvantages of consumers in the medical marketplace in general, not to mention to rate of dementia among the Medicare population, so that consumer monitoring of the adequacy of the bundle seems like a weak reed to rely upon. Indeed, exactly what constitutes medically appropriate postacute care—what should be in any bundle of services for which Medicare is paying—is not nearly as clear as for acute hospital care. This is especially true for home care, where even monitoring what is delivered can be a problem. As a result, having a system with nothing paid for additional services, which is what many have in mind when they speak of prospective payment, would seem to invite underservice.

Because of the problem of substitution and multiple provider use, some have proposed one stand-alone prospective postacute system. This, however, would seem enormously vulnerable to moral hazard; 77 percent of Medicare beneficiaries discharged from the hospital currently use no postacute services. It would not seem difficult, however, to justify a few home health visits to check on possible side effects of prescribed medication if there were a large payment for any use of home health services, as opposed to the per-visit payment that exists now.

My own view is that it makes sense to bundle payment for postacute services with the payment for hospital services, but include a much more generous outlier provision than is the case for hospital services. The outlier provision would be budget neutral, as is the case for the existing hospital outlier program; the intent would be to have most services with some marginal revenue. As long as the marginal revenue did not substantially exceed marginal cost; one should not observe overservicing. The issue of developing prospective payment systems would still remain for the outlier part of the system, but errors would be less critical than if all payment for postacute services were running through the PPS.

There is an issue about who should receive this bundled payment. Postacute care providers have traditionally vehemently opposed giving such a payment to the hospital on the grounds that they would "medicalize" social services; but now that many large and medium-size hospitals own postacute providers this objection seems to have less force. A possible legal objection is that giving the entire payment to the hospital, along with the responsibility for the cost of the episode, would infringe upon the patient's freedom of choice of postacute provider. This could in principle be handled by new legislation; the issue is whether the home health agency with which the hospital contracts is seen more like the laboratory with which it contracts (where few seem concerned about freedom of choice) or the physician group with which it contracts with (where beneficiaries are generally allowed choice). An alternative to paying the hospital an amount that covers postacute in addition to acute services is to pay a third party and let that party contract for postacute services. Bundling, of course, does not resolve the issue of how to price the roughly half of home health services that are not preceded by a hospital stay.

Finally, there is an issue about whether Medicare in the aggregate has overpaid because of unbundling or gaming. Undoubtedly there is some overpayment, but the degree of overpayment is tempered by the update factor for hospital inpatient services, which is to some degree a function of the amount of unbundling. In particular, the Medicare Payment Advisory Commission (and the Prospective Payment Assessment Commission before it) explicitly includes a site-of-service adjustment in making its recommendation to Congress on the magnitude of the update factor for inpatient services. This site-of-service adjustment is intended to adjust for the amount of unbundling. Since that practice began three years ago, the magnitude of the site-of-service adjustment has been substantial. Ultimately the question of overpayment turns in part on how many postacute services in how many facilities should be delivered. That question, however, is well beyond the scope of this paper and may well be beyond the current state of the art.

In sum, Medicare is now trying to harden the budget constraint that postacute providers face. Doing so, however, poses large implementation problems, and finding a method that does not itself cause substantial distortions is very difficult. Although the issues of financing Medicare in the long run have grabbed the headlines, the short-run pricing issues seem equally serious.

References

McClellan, Mark. 1997. Hospital reimbursement incentives: An empirical analysis. *Journal of Economics and Management Strategy* 6 (1): 91–128.

Medicare Payment Advisory Commission. 1998. Health care spending and the Medicare program: A data book. Washington, D.C.: The Commission.

Newhouse, Joseph P. 1998. Risk adjustment: Where are we now? *Inquiry* 35 (Summer 1998) 122–131.

Newhouse, Joseph P., Melinda Beeuwkes Buntin, and John D. Chapman. 1997. Risk adjustment and Medicare: Taking a closer look. *Health Affairs* 16 (5): 26–43.

Pauly, Mark. 1980. *Doctors and their workshops.* Chicago: University of Chicago Press.

Wilensky, Gail R., and Joseph P. Newhouse. 1999. Medicare: What's right? What's wrong? What's next? *Health Affairs* 18 (1): 92–106.

8

The Sources of Cost Difference in Health Insurance Plans
A Decomposition Analysis

Matthew Eichner, Mark McClellan, and David A. Wise

Almost two-thirds of Americans under age sixty-five are covered by employer insurance plans. Like Medicare costs, employer medical costs have also risen quickly in recent years, and in many respects, even more dramatic reforms in have occurred in firm health insurance plans than in the Medicare program. Yet research on the consequences of these reforms, including many types of managed care reforms, has been limited. Unlike with Medicare, the provisions of employer plans vary a great deal from firm to firm, and so do the costs of medical care, suggesting that differences in plan provisions may have a substantial effect on health care expenditures. Thus analysis of employer plans provides a unique opportunity to understand the relationship between plan provisions and expenditures for health care.

The mechanisms that might be effective in controlling cost, however, will depend importantly on the source of cost differences. For example, if cost differences are accounted for in large part by a small number of plan enrollees who are treated for specific high-cost illnesses, efforts to control cost must necessarily focus on the treatment of these illness. If cost differences are due to the use of different procedures for treating seriously ill

Matthew Eichner was professor of economics at Columbia University Graduate School of Business when this work was completed. He is a research fellow of the National Bureau of Economic Research. Mark McClellan is associate professor of economics and of medicine at Stanford University and a research associate of the National Bureau of Economic Research. David A. Wise is the John F. Stambaugh Professor of Political Economy at the John F. Kennedy School of Government, Harvard University, and the director for health and retirement programs at the National Bureau of Economic Research.

We are grateful to the National Institute on Aging for research support through a grant to the National Bureau of Economic Research. We also thank Joe Newhouse for his comments on the paper.

patients, then it is important to know what the procedures are. In contrast, if cost differences result from more modest differences in the expenditures incurred by a large number of enrollees, then effective cost control mechanisms would have to be directed toward the medical utilization of more-typical enrollees, perhaps those who use only outpatient services.

In this paper we focus not on the incentive effects of plan provisions—whether demand-side price incentive or supply-side managed care limits on care—but on the sources of cost differences across plans. Our hope is that understanding the reasons for cost differences across plans will direct more focused attention to analysis of the ways that costs can be controlled. Indeed, this work is intended as an important first step in that direction.

We are engaged in a long-term project to analyze the determinants of cost differences across firms. In particular, we look forward to estimation that can be used to predict the effect on medical expenditures of specific changes in medical insurance plan provisions. The project is based on insurance claims records from a large number of employers. The vast amount of information in insurance claims records is both a blessing and a curse. A key advantage of claims data is the detail they provide. The detail also poses a challenge, however: how best to summarize and convey the information contained in the millions of claims filed each year under a typical employer-provided plan.

Our goal in this paper is to present a method that allows us conveniently to summarize information contained in the claims data. In particular, we want to describe the sources of cost differences across plans. We consider eight plans that vary in average expenditure for those filing claims, from a low expenditure of $1,645 to a high of $2,484. We then propose a method to decompose these differences into their component parts. The goal is to quantify the contribution of each of component to total cost variation across firms. We believe that this method allows us to point directly to the sources of cost difference and thus will help us to focus subsequent analysis where it is most likely to make a difference. Thus this general analysis of cost variation across plans will provide the basis for further studies of the incentive effects of plan provisions on costs.

Identifying the effect of plan provisions on health care costs is complicated for several reasons. Differences in plan costs may arise from many sources other than plan incentive effects, including geographic location and the demographic attributes of plan members. Much more difficult to account for are unobserved differences in the types of individuals selecting health plans: Individuals who expect to use more health care, who are more risk averse, or who have greater "taste" for health care are more likely to choose more generous coverage when an employer offers a menu of plans. This is the issue to which Eichner (1997) has devoted a great deal of attention, and it is the issue to which we will return once the sources of cost differences are better understood.

We believe that ours is the first effort at a detailed decomposition of the sources of cost differences across health plans. We consider both the rate of treatment and the treatment cost, given treatment, for thirty diagnostic groups. We first consider how much of the rate and the cost for each treatment can be attributed to the demographic mix of plan members. The total demographic effect is decomposed into the effect of demographic mix on the rate of diagnoses, and the effect on treatment cost given diagnosis. Then the cost differences that remain, after the demographic adjustment, are decomposed further into rate and treatment effects.

Previous descriptive studies have documented cost differences associated with firm location and employee demographic characteristics, based largely on aggregate cost differences. Yet it is unknown whether cost variation across plans is due to more intensive treatment of a few of high-cost enrollees or to marginally more intensive treatment for the majority of plan enrollees. We believe that understanding where the intensity, and hence cost, of treatment differs will be a basis for further analysis of the effects of plan provisions on costs.

Detailed descriptive analyses may also provide evidence on how cost differences due to selection effects arise within plans. Understanding both the incentives of plan provisions and the effects of self-selection into plans may be enhanced by detailed analyses of what kinds of patients and medical treatments contribute to cost differences. For example, a larger proportion of patients with heart disease or other chronic illness in one of two or more plans from which employees may choose may well reflect selection effects. On the other hand, higher costs due to more "elastic" conditions such as mental illness or back pain may well reflect plan provision (incentive) effects. Similarly, higher costs due to more intensive treatment given the occurrence of an illness may well represent plan incentive effects because these affect patients, providers, or both. Describing the sources of cost differences at this level of detail not only provides some evidence on whether cost differences are due to selection or incentives, but also provides a detailed foundation for more explicit causal studies of how plan provisions affect expenditures. For example, studies of changes in incidence or intensity of particular health problems resulting from reforms in health plan structure are likely to provide detailed insights into how particular plan provisions affect expenditures.

We address many, but not all, of these questions by analyzing cost differences in insurance plans offered by eight firms. We first describe the claims data that are used for the analysis and present summary information on medical expenditures in the selected firms. We then describe the decomposition method that is used to determine the sources of cost differences among these eight firms. Calculations based on this method are then presented, primarily using graphical representations. The last section is a summary and discussion.

8.1   The Data and Summary Description

8.1.1   The Data

The analysis is based on a unique data set obtained from MedStat. The data provide comprehensive information on medical utilization for enrollees in a variety of employer-provided health insurance regimes. The data include all inpatient and outpatient health insurance claims filed by employees and their dependents in forty-five firms that self-insure (i.e., these firms may pay an insurance carrier to process claims, but not to assume risk). All risk is borne by the employer, who essentially pays the annual medical bills of its employees and their dependents. The firms include a variety of industries, health care costs, plan provisions, and workforce characteristics.

The data content is standardized by MedStat, providing essentially identical data for each firm. Each claim includes a patient identifier, a provider identifier, the date of the medical service, the claim amount, the copayment and deductible amounts paid by the patient, the place of service—hospital, physician office, intermediate care facility, etc.—and International Classification of Disease, Ninth Revision (ICD-9) and Current Procedural Terminology (CPT) codes identifying the principal diagnoses and procedures performed. The patient's age, sex, and relationship to the employee, and employment status—hourly or salaried, active or retired—are also reported.

The primary goal of this paper is to illustrate the decomposition procedure. The analysis is based on expenditures in eight plans in seven large firms. These firms were selected for this initial study in part because they offer only one plan to each employee (one of the firms has two plans, but each plan serves a different employee group). To simplify interpretation of the results, we wish to confine the analysis here to differences across plans that can be attributed not to self-selection of plans by employees who are offered a menu of plans from which to choose, which is typical of most firm insurance regimes, but to the incentive effects of plan provisions. Selecting one-plan firms assures that (by and large) the cost differences observed are not confounded by the self-selection of employees into plans. The analysis is based on annual expenditure, where data for three years are used to calculate rates and treatment costs by plan.

8.1.2   Summary Description

Each person who reports medical spending in a year is assigned to a predominant diagnosis group. This is the group to which the largest share of an enrollee's expenditures can be allocated. There are thirty such groups listed in table 8.1. These include outpatient and residual (which includes

Table 8.1   Summary: Mean Cost by Diagnosis

Diagnosis	Mean Rate of Diagnosis	Mean Cost, Given Diagnosis ($)	Mean Expenditure per Enrollee	Percent of Total Expenditure
Lung cancer	0.00027	34,736	9.36	0.0044
Colorectal cancer	0.00031	27,819	8.71	0.0041
Acute myocardial infarction	0.00117	26,651	31.29	0.0147
Chronic obstructive pulmonary disease	0.00056	25,179	14.17	0.0067
Stroke (occlusive and hemorrhagic)	0.00077	24,901	19.19	0.0090
Congenital disease or disorder	0.00034	23,131	7.78	0.0037
Neonatal care	0.00091	22,917	20.83	0.0098
Heart failure	0.00072	22,826	16.40	0.0077
Arthritis	0.00087	22,788	19.82	0.0093
Prostate cancer	0.00029	20,000	5.87	0.0028
Ischemic heart disease, chest pain	0.00558	18,270	102.02	0.0480
Residual diagnoses	0.02225	17,656	392.93	0.1847
Breast cancer	0.00032	17,594	5.67	0.0027
Psychotic/major affective psychosis	0.00413	16,759	69.28	0.0326
Back/spine disorders	0.00257	15,509	39.92	0.0188
Neurotic disease or disorder	0.00144	15,050	21.73	0.0102
Injury/trauma	0.00401	13,964	55.94	0.0263
Diabetes	0.00081	13,228	10.70	0.0050
Gallbladder disease	0.00213	11,442	24.34	0.0114
(continued)				

Table 8.1 (continued)

Diagnosis	Mean Rate of Diagnosis	Mean Cost, Given Diagnosis ($)	Mean Expenditure per Enrollee	Percent of Total Expenditure
Substance abuse	0.00262	10,944	28.70	0.0135
Respiratory infection	0.00299	9,872	29.48	0.0139
Benign female pelvic, etc.	0.00469	9,383	44.02	0.0207
Appendicitis	0.00104	8,123	8.49	0.0040
Benign prostate hypertrophy/urinary obstruction	0.00145	7,972	11.57	0.0054
Asthma	0.00126	7,792	9.84	0.0046
Abnormal pregnancy	0.00393	7,406	29.09	0.0137
Abnormal childbirth	0.00653	6,234	40.73	0.0191
Normal childbirth, mother	0.00279	5,350	14.94	0.0070
Normal childbirth, child	0.00475	3,152	14.97	0.0070
Outpatient	0.91847	1,110	1,019.55	0.4793
All	1.00000		2,127.33	1.0000

Source: Authors' tabulations based on MedStat data.

Note: Residual diagnoses are those not assigned to any of the other identified groups.

expenditures not assigned to any of the identified groups). Persons who are assigned to the lung cancer group, for example, having incurred substantial expenditure for the treatment of lung cancer, are likely to have incurred expenditures related to other diagnosis groups as well.

The diagnosis groups are listed in table 8.1 by the average cost of treatment—over all of the eight plans—given that diagnosis group. The average treatment cost ranges from $34,736 for lung cancer to $1,110 for the outpatient predominant diagnosis group. The average diagnosis rate is shown in the first column of the table. Almost 92 percent of enrollees are in the outpatient group. The diagnosis rate for the other groups is typically well under 1 in 100 and often as low as 1 in 1,000. Approximately 2 percent of enrollees are in the residual group. The diagnosis rate times the treatment cost given diagnosis give the average cost per enrollee, shown in the third column of the table. Finally, the proportion of total expenditures accounted for by each diagnosis group is shown in the last column. About 48 percent of cost is accounted for by the 92 percent of employees in the outpatient group and about 18 percent is accounted for by the approximately 2 percent who are in the residual category. The remaining 34 percent is accounted for by the 6 percent of persons in the other diagnostic groups. We will see that differences across firms in both diagnosis rates and treatment cost given diagnosis account for large differences in average expenditure. Indeed, both may contribute to higher or lower costs in the same firm, or one may increase and the other decrease cost in the same firm.

The key elements of cost difference are the diagnosis rate and treatment cost given diagnosis. The diagnosis rates in each plan are shown in table 8.2; the treatment costs are shown in table 8.3. Consider substance abuse, for example: The diagnosis rate varies from a low of 5 in 10,000 enrollees to a high of 6 in 1,000. The treatment cost varies from a high of $17,377 to a low of $7,117.

Beginning with the data in these two tables (including the raw data that underlie the means) we want to decompose the differences in average cost across plans that range from an overall low of $1,645 to a high of $2,484, a difference of more than 50 percent. There are three reasons for cost differences: (1) differences in the demographic attributes—age and gender—of enrollees, (2) differences in the illnesses that are treated—the diagnosis rate, and (3) differences in the cost of treating illnesses. Our goal is to attribute observed cost differences to these three sources. A particular complication is that treatment cost differences across plans may differ substantially by diagnosis, and we would like to know which diagnoses account for differences in treatment cost. A firm with low treatment cost for one diagnosis may have high treatment cost for another diagnosis; thus it is important to consider the interaction between diagnosis and treatment cost.

Table 8.2   Rate by Diagnosis and Plan

	Plan 15	Plan 26	Plan 12	Plan 25	Plan 18	Plan 2a	Plan 21	Plan 2b
Lung cancer	0.00037	0.00013	0.00009	0.00014	0.00016	0.00034	0.00016	0.00051
Colorectal cancer	0.00041	0.00010	0.00015	0.00019	0.00025	0.00041	0.00020	0.00050
Acute myocardial infarction	0.00103	0.00084	0.00049	0.00059	0.00087	0.00135	0.00080	0.00200
Chronic obstructive pulmonary disease	0.00022	0.00024	0.00017	0.00011	0.00039	0.00058	0.00035	0.00111
Stroke (occlusive and hemorrhagic)	0.00070	0.00033	0.00023	0.00030	0.00056	0.00080	0.00048	0.00147
Congenital disease or disorder	0.00022	0.00038	0.00047	0.00023	0.00031	0.00028	0.00028	0.00034
Neonatal care	0.00111	0.00072	0.00192	0.00065	0.00097	0.00057	0.00081	0.00054
Heart failure	0.00041	0.00025	0.00025	0.00024	0.00051	0.00054	0.00036	0.00150
Arthritis	0.00122	0.00083	0.00028	0.00060	0.00087	0.00123	0.00046	0.00126
Prostate cancer	0.00030	0.00020	0.00007	0.00034	0.00024	0.00054	0.00024	0.00039
Ischemic heart disease, chest pain	0.00465	0.00315	0.00252	0.00297	0.00398	0.00614	0.00295	0.01010
Residual diagnoses	0.01808	0.01639	0.02003	0.01451	0.01826	0.02017	0.01667	0.03169
Breast cancer	0.00055	0.00016	0.00017	0.00024	0.00022	0.00051	0.00020	0.00048
Psychotic/major affective psychosis	0.00240	0.00104	0.00302	0.00213	0.00327	0.00254	0.00338	0.00713

Back/spine disorders	0.00382	0.00197	0.00240	0.00210	0.00231	0.00179	0.00208	0.00185
Neurotic disease or disorder	0.00202	0.00114	0.00083	0.00132	0.00087	0.00145	0.00117	0.00137
Injury/trauma	0.00519	0.00335	0.00323	0.00330	0.00332	0.00390	0.00441	0.00399
Diabetes	0.00154	0.00050	0.00048	0.00051	0.00027	0.00059	0.00045	0.00078
Gallbladder disease	0.00267	0.00160	0.00186	0.00234	0.00150	0.00166	0.00163	0.00325
Substance abuse	0.00621	0.00126	0.00099	0.00050	0.00113	0.00212	0.00082	0.00052
Respiratory infection	0.00411	0.00240	0.00175	0.00228	0.00150	0.00381	0.00232	0.00247
Benign female pelvic, etc.	0.00520	0.00489	0.00370	0.00472	0.00395	0.00448	0.00468	0.00461
Appendicitis	0.00099	0.00119	0.00072	0.00087	0.00111	0.00143	0.00124	0.00100
Benign prostate hypertrophy/urinary obstruction	0.00227	0.00100	0.00146	0.00097	0.00105	0.00113	0.00111	0.00159
Asthma	0.00183	0.00101	0.00060	0.00098	0.00053	0.00155	0.00103	0.00092
Abnormal pregnancy	0.00243	0.00538	0.00168	0.00294	0.00432	0.00853	0.00318	0.00432
Abnormal childbirth	0.00397	0.00806	0.00251	0.00524	0.00815	0.01408	0.00613	0.00941
Normal childbirth, mother	0.00164	0.00316	0.00238	0.00185	0.00297	0.00640	0.00164	0.00332
Normal childbirth, child	0.00054	0.00853	0.00045	0.00023	0.01064	0.01613	0.00923	0.00004
Outpatient	0.89655	0.92725	0.93896	0.93897	0.93317	0.90112	0.93412	0.92892

Note: See table 8.1 for source and note.

Table 8.3   Cost by Diagnosis and Plan

	Plan 15	Plan 26	Plan 12	Plan 25	Plan 18	Plan 2a	Plan 21	Plan 2b
Lung cancer	22,811	51,401	36,164	35,193	38,320	31,841	34,712	34,209
Colorectal cancer	24,576	28,769	33,665	25,479	24,847	25,359	22,566	29,821
Acute myocardial infarction	26,572	30,417	30,825	31,205	24,331	27,610	31,244	25,388
Chronic obstructive pulmonary disease	11,355	43,222	18,236	33,461	29,452	21,320	44,338	22,318
Stroke (occlusive and hemorrhagic)	25,468	24,623	36,725	35,269	23,475	25,844	29,249	23,183
Congenital disease or disorder	18,123	17,152	25,688	22,122	20,862	25,945	26,587	21,877
Neonatal care	13,544	25,369	29,121	33,228	14,083	16,873	32,230	17,474
Heart failure	22,848	26,413	23,686	26,731	22,892	25,866	38,023	20,620
Arthritis	18,519	23,485	22,720	25,130	21,505	23,450	26,065	22,625
Prostate cancer	15,646	16,693	21,843	18,360	18,972	20,155	20,292	20,720
Ischemic heart disease, chest pain	15,981	17,984	16,908	25,762	17,707	21,073	26,401	16,699
Residual diagnoses	16,846	16,888	14,788	21,046	17,413	19,925	20,193	17,486
Breast cancer	17,875	19,052	27,399	14,944	13,997	15,489	32,427	15,288
Psychotic/major affective psychosis	16,513	17,825	17,559	26,429	17,627	19,508	24,956	13,837
Back/spine disorders	14,056	16,823	16,329	15,666	15,327	17,056	17,424	14,487

Neurotic disease or disorder	9,791	14,648	14,566	21,646	17,012	20,141	24,849	10,939
Injury/trauma	11,044	12,468	12,594	16,056	13,465	13,570	15,476	14,529
Diabetes	12,690	8,793	11,970	31,533	16,054	15,273	17,609	11,715
Gallbladder disease	9,353	10,884	12,167	12,194	9,843	12,333	13,282	11,606
Substance abuse	7,117	9,261	11,777	11,745	9,400	12,881	17,377	10,238
Respiratory infection	9,660	8,595	7,473	14,659	8,789	12,454	10,524	10,805
Benign female pelvic, etc.	8,031	8,729	10,218	10,446	8,822	9,904	9,799	9,073
Appendicitis	6,627	7,912	8,146	7,362	7,327	9,839	7,978	8,429
Benign prostate hypertrophy/urinary obstruction	6,310	7,138	6,939	8,312	8,335	10,066	6,868	7,911
Asthma	4,966	8,571	6,639	7,868	7,628	8,321	7,811	8,304
Abnormal pregnancy	6,475	7,679	7,575	8,767	7,120	7,749	7,406	6,907
Abnormal childbirth	5,421	6,275	6,388	6,708	5,887	6,557	6,345	6,020
Normal childbirth, mother	4,752	5,184	5,262	5,300	5,058	6,638	5,024	5,403
Normal childbirth, child	6,010	2,666	2,826	2,797	8,727	5,256	3,760	4,240
Outpatient	851	1,013	952	1,106	1,224	1,138	1,188	1,091
All	1,645	1,729	1,860	1,941	1,994	2,097	2,138	2,484

Note: See table 8.1 for source and note.

8.2 The Decomposition of Cost Differences

We begin with the eight plans described above. As explained, the members of each plan are divided into thirty predominant diagnosis categories, defined by the diagnosis group in which the largest share of a member's expenditure—in a given year—occurred. The data can be thought of as arranged in two 30×5 matrices, as shown in tables 8.2 and 8.3. The first matrix reports the proportion of enrollees in each plan who are in each of the diagnosis groups. The elements of this matrix are "rates" δ_{ki}, the proportion of enrollees in plan i who are in diagnosis group k. The second matrix reports the average cost of treating patients in each of the diagnosis groups. The elements of this matrix are costs d_{ki}, the cost of treating persons in plan i who are in diagnosis group k.

We want to know why the costs in one plan differ from the average cost. That is, we want to decompose the cost differences. Consider diagnosis k: What accounts for the difference in expenditure for treating patients in this diagnosis in Plan i, compared to the average expenditure for diagnosis k patients. The diagnosis could be pregnancy, cancer, or outpatient care, for example. The cost depends on two factors: (1) the proportion of enrollees treated for diagnosis k (the rate), and (2) the cost of their treatment given that diagnosis. Both the rate and the cost will depend on the demographic mix (age and gender) of persons in Plan i as compared to the average mix across all plans. Suppose that both the rate and the cost are adjusted for demographic mix, as explained below. Call the adjusted elements $\tilde{\delta}_{ki}$ and $\tilde{d}_{ki}$. Then the deviation from the average rate, and the deviation from the average cost, due to demographic mix, can be denoted by $\Delta\delta_{ki} = \tilde{\delta}_{ki} - \bar{\delta}$ and $\Delta d_{ki} = \tilde{d}_{ki} - \bar{d}_k$, respectively.

Table 8.4 illustrates the adjustment for substance abuse. The first row shows the unadjusted diagnosis rate by plan. The next row shows the rate adjusted for the demographic mix of each plan. While the unadjusted rates vary from 50 to 621 in 10,000, the rates adjusted for demographic mix range only from 250 to 278 per 10,000 enrollees. The rate deviations due to demographic mix are shown in the third row and are quite small compared to the unadjusted rate differences. Thus, for the group with substance abuse as a predominate diagnosis, not much of the rate difference can be attributed to differences in demographic mix across firms. Unadjusted treatment costs are shown in the fourth row and the costs adjusted for demographic mix in the fifth row. The deviation for average treatment cost that can be attributed to demographic mix ranges from −$71.33 to $574.51, which is very small compared to the unadjusted differences in treatment cost across plans.

We can write the total deviation of the rate and cost elements of Plan i from the average across plans as the sum of two parts, one due to demographic mix and the other due to other factors:

Table 8.4   Unadjusted and Adjusted Rates and Costs for Substance Abuse

	Plan 15	Plan 26	Plan 12	Plan 25	Plan 18	Plan 2a	Plan 21	Plan 2b	Average
Rate unadjusted for demographic mix	0.00052	0.00082	0.00212	0.00113	0.00050	0.00099	0.00126	0.00621	0.00262
Rate adjusted for demographic mix	0.00266	0.00274	0.00278	0.00259	0.00255	0.00250	0.00271	0.00258	
$\Delta\delta_{ki} = \tilde\delta_{ki} - \bar\delta_k$	0.00004	0.00012	0.00016	−0.00003	−0.00007	−0.00013	0.00009	−0.00004	
Cost unadjusted for demographic mix	7,117	9,261	11,777	11,745	9,400	12,881	17,377	10,238	10,944
Cost adjusted for demographic mix	11,519	11,169	10,994	11,057	11,091	11,153	11,337	10,873	
$\Delta d_{ki} = \tilde d_{ki} - \bar d_k$	574.51	224.65	50.36	113.35	146.69	209.16	392.61	−71.33	

Source: See table 8.1.

(1)
$$\delta_{ki} = \left(\delta_{ki} - \tilde{\delta}_{ki}\right) + \left(\tilde{\delta}_{ki} - \bar{\delta}_{k}\right) + \bar{\delta}_{k}$$

$$= \tilde{\Delta}\delta_{ki} + \Delta\delta_{ki} + \bar{\delta}_{k} \quad \text{and}$$

$$d_{ki} = \left(d_{ki} - \tilde{d}_{ki}\right) + \left(\tilde{d}_{ki} - \bar{d}_{k}\right) + \bar{d}_{k}$$

$$= \tilde{\Delta}d_{ki} + \Delta d_{ki} + \bar{d}_{k}$$

Now we can decompose the expenditure on diagnosis k in firm i (that is, the proportion of enrollees in diagnosis group k times the treatment cost given that diagnosis) as

(2) $M_{ki} = \delta_{ki} * d_{ki}$

$$= \left(\bar{\delta}_{k} * \bar{d}_{k} + \Delta\delta_{ki} * \bar{d}_{k} + \Delta d_{ki} * \bar{\delta}_{k} + \Delta\delta_{ki} * \Delta d_{ki}\right)$$

$$+ \left(\bar{\delta}_{k} * \bar{d}_{k} + \tilde{\Delta}\delta_{ki} * \bar{d}_{k} + \tilde{\Delta}d_{ki} * \bar{\delta}_{k} + \tilde{\Delta}\delta_{ki} * \tilde{\Delta}d_{ki}\right)$$

$$+ \left(\tilde{\Delta}\delta_{ki} * \Delta d_{ki} + \tilde{\Delta}d_{ki} * \Delta\delta_{ki}\right) - \bar{\delta}_{k} * \bar{d}_{k}.$$

The first term in parentheses decomposes the cost difference—between firm i and the average cost—due to demographic mix. The second term in parentheses decomposes the difference due to other factors, after controlling for demographic differences. That is, this line indicates how the cost in firm i differs from the average assuming the demographic mix in firm i to be identical to the average demographic mix. The third term in parentheses recognizes the interaction between the deviation due to demographic mix and the deviation in adjusted costs. (The first term in the third line is the adjusted rate deviation times the cost deviation due to demographic mix. The second term is the adjusted cost deviation times the rate deviation due to demographic mix.) The components of the first two terms are easily interpreted. The third term, which in practice is very small, is less intuitive.

   The decomposition in either of the first two brackets is illustrated graphically in figure 8.1. Consider the second term, which decomposes cost differences that remain after controlling for demographic mix. The square defined by heavy lines represents the average cost—across all firms—of treating persons in diagnosis group k. The deviation of the cost in Plan i from the average over all plans is represented by the three components of the outer box: (1) the ith plan deviation in the rate of diagnosis k holding the expenditure at the base level, which is represented by the top slice; (2) the ith plan deviation in treatment cost holding the rate at the base level, which is represented by the right slice; and (3) the product of the rate deviation times the expenditure deviation for Plan i, the interaction term, which is represented by the small square to the northeast. These terms

DIAGNOSIS k TREATMENT COST IN FIRM i

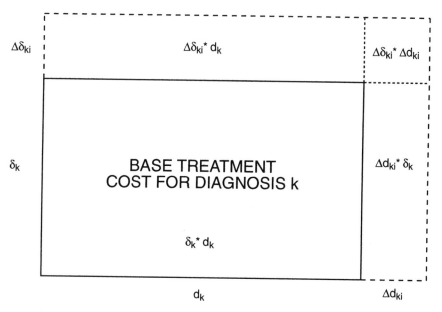

Fig. 8.1   Schematic decomposition of cost

essentially represent a total derivative describing how the cost in Plan i differs from the average cost. Both the effect of demographic mix and the effects of other factors can be decomposed in the same way.

The mean cost in firm i is obtained by summing over all diagnosis groups and is given by

$$(3) \quad \overline{M}_i = \sum_{i=1}^{30} \delta_{ki} * d_{ki}$$

$$= \left(\sum_{i=1}^{30} \overline{\delta}_k * \overline{d}_k + \sum_{i=1}^{30} \Delta \delta_{ki} * \overline{d}_k + \sum_{i=1}^{30} \Delta d_{ki} * \overline{\delta}_k + \sum_{i=1}^{30} \Delta \delta_{ki} * \Delta d_{ki} \right)$$

$$+ \left(\sum_{i=1}^{30} \overline{\delta}_k * \overline{d}_k + \sum_{i=1}^{30} \widetilde{\Delta \delta}_{ki} * \overline{d}_k + \sum_{i=1}^{30} \widetilde{\Delta d}_{ki} * \overline{\delta}_k + \sum_{i=1}^{30} \widetilde{\Delta \delta}_{ki} * \widetilde{\Delta d}_{ki} \right)$$

$$+ \left(\sum_{i=1}^{30} \widetilde{\Delta \delta}_{ki} * \Delta d_{ki} + \sum_{i=1}^{30} \widetilde{\Delta d}_{ki} * \Delta \delta_{ki} \right) - \sum_{i=1}^{30} \overline{\delta}_k * \overline{d}_k .$$

These terms simply add up over all diagnoses the terms represented in the figure for one of the diagnoses. In addition to the BASE component, we refer to the terms in the three parts of this decomposition as mix effects with these names:

$$
(4) \quad \overline{M}_i =
\begin{bmatrix}
\text{Demographic} \\
\text{Adjustment} = \\
\text{BASE} + \text{Rate Mix} \\
+ \text{Cost Mix} \\
+ \text{Rate} * \text{Cost Mix}
\end{bmatrix}
+
\begin{bmatrix}
\text{Demographic} \\
\text{Adjusted} \\
\text{Differences} = \\
\text{BASE} + \text{Rate Mix} \\
+ \text{Cost Mix} \\
+ \text{Rate} * \text{Cost Mix}
\end{bmatrix}
+
\begin{bmatrix}
\text{Interaction} = \\
\text{DemoRate} * \\
\text{OtherCost Mix} \\
+ \text{DemoCost} * \\
\text{OtherRate Mix} \\
- \text{BASE}
\end{bmatrix}.
$$

Consider the demographic adjustment. The BASE is just the average cost over all plans—in this case, $2,127.33. The rate mix is the deviation from the average that can be attributed the effect of demographic mix on the rate at which diagnoses are treated. The cost mix is the deviation that can be attributed to the effect of demographic mix on treatment cost given diagnosis. Rate $*$ cost mix is the interaction between the two. This term will be positive if the rate adjustment and the cost adjustment tend to be positively correlated. The terms in the second bracket have the same interpretation, but pertain to differences in rates and costs that remain after taking out the deviations from the average that can be attributed to demographic differences across firms.

The decomposition of the difference between medical expenditures in Plan i and the average over all plans we call $\Delta \overline{M}_i$ and is given by the equation above, less the BASE terms.

8.3   Results for the Eight Plans

8.3.1   Differences across Plans

The decomposition results for the eight plans are explained in some detail here. The presentation is primarily graphical, but we begin with table 8.5, which presents the complete decomposition succinctly. The eight plans are ordered from left to right by mean expenditure per enrollee, which is shown in the last row of the table. The average cost over all plans ($2,127) is shown in the second to last row. The difference between the plan mean and the overall average is decomposed into the elements shown in the rows above. The difference is divided into three main components, which correspond to the sources identified in the equation for $\overline{M}_i$ above: demographic adjustment, demographic adjusted difference, and the interaction between the first two. Each of the first two main components is decomposed into three mix effects: rate, cost, and interaction. The third main component is composed of only two terms. The sum of the sources of cost

Table 8.5   Summary of Decomposition Results

Source		Plan 15	Plan 26	Plan 12	Plan 25	Plan 18	Plan 2a	Plan 21	Plan 2b
Demographic adjustment									
Rate	Term 1	65	-80	-168	-41	-24	130	-69	104
Cost	Term 2	86	-101	-208	-50	-21	151	-67	101 ln
Interaction	Term 3	1	3	16	1	0	7	1	2
Total		152	-179	-360	-90	-44	289	-135	207
Demographic adjusted									
Rate	Term 4	-197	-206	95	-285	-191	-281	-157	341
Cost	Term 5	-432	-1	10	296	119	-1	375	-160
Interaction	Term 6	7	-9	1	-102	-20	-29	-54	-31
Total		-622	-216	106	-91	-91	-311	163	150
Interaction									
First	Term 7	-1	4	-5	6	0	-11	2	6
Second	Term 8	-11	-7	-8	-12	1	3	-20	-6
Total		-12	-3	-13	-5	2	-8	-18	-1
Base		2,127	2,127	2,127	2,127	2,127	2,127	2,127	2,127
Mean		1,645	1,729	1,860	1,941	1,994	2,097	2,138	2,484

Source: Authors' tabulations based on MedStat data.

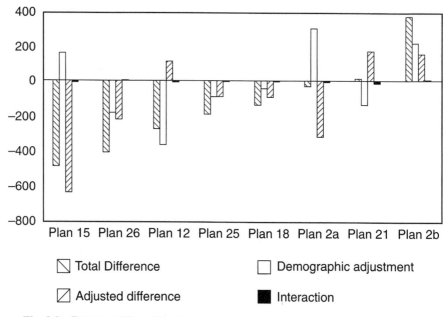

Fig. 8.2   Decomposition of total cost
Source: Authors' tabulations based on MedStat data

difference is equal to the difference between the plan cost and the overall average across all plans. Equivalently, the sum of the sources of cost difference plus the overall mean equals the plan mean.

The decomposition is more easily seen graphically and we explain the details of the decomposition with the aid of several figures. The first bar for each plan in figure 8.2 shows the difference between each of the plan costs and the overall average cost. The range is from −$482 to $356, a difference of $838. This cost can be decomposed into the three main components. The first is the cost difference that is accounted for by differences in plan member demographic characteristics. The second component is the remaining cost difference after adjustment for demographic differences. The third is a very small interaction component. Plan 2a, for example, is disadvantaged, in the sense of having higher costs, by the demographic mix of its members. If for each demographic group expenditures in Plan 2a were equal to the average expenditure, expenditures in Plan 2a would be higher than the average by $130 because Plan 2a members are more highly concentrated (than the average over all plans) in demographic groups that tend to use more medical care. On the other hand, adjusted for demographic mix, expenditures in Plan 2a are unusually low—$151 below the average. Plan 2b is disadvantaged both by demographic mix and by higher costs adjusting for demographic mix. The third interaction term is very small and can essentially be ignored.

Both the demographic adjustment and the adjusted expenditure differences can be further decomposed into three components. The decomposition of the demographic adjustment is shown in figure 8.3. The first bar reproduces the total demographic adjustment from figure 8.2. The second bar shows the effect of demographic mix on the rate at which diagnoses are treated (holding the treatment cost constant). A bar extending upward indicates that the demographic mix increases the diagnosis rate in higher-cost diagnosis groups. (That is, the rate would be higher if the diagnosis rate for each demographic group in the plan were the same as the overall average.) The third bar shows the effect of demographic mix on treatment cost (holding the rate constant). Again, a bar extending upward indicates that the demographic mix increases the cost of treatment. (That is, the treatment cost would be higher if the cost of treating each diagnosis for a given demographic group in the plan were the same as the overall average treatment cost for that demographic group.) The fourth bar represents the very small interaction effect between these two components. As might be anticipated, the second and third bars move in parallel: Groups that are more likely to be in high-cost diagnosis groups are also more costly to treat

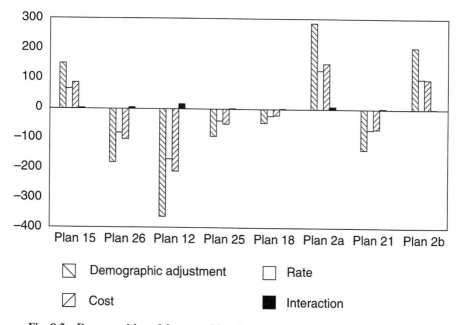

Fig. 8.3   Decomposition of demographic adjustment
Source: Authors' tabulations based on MedStat data

given that they are in the group. Thus the strong correlation between the two components.

Perhaps the most important differences are shown in figure 8.4, panel A, which describes the decomposition of the difference in cost that remains after the demographic adjustment. That is, suppose that all rates and treatment costs have been adjusted for demographic mix, and then ask what accounts for the remaining difference. With reference to the diagram again, there are three sources of difference between the expenditure in a plan and the average expenditure over all plans: (1) the difference in diagnosis rate, holding the treatment cost at the average, (2) the difference in treatment cost, holding the diagnosis rate at the average, and (3) the interaction of the first two. The first bar reproduces the difference in expenditure adjusted for demographic mix. Note that unadjusted average plan expenditures vary by $838 (from −$482 to $356) as shown in figure 8.2. Even after adjusting for demographic mix differences among plans, however, the range is still very large, from −$642 in Plan 15 to $163 in Plan 21, a difference of $805.

The next three bars show how the difference holding demographic mix constant is decomposed into the three sources. The second bar shows the difference that can be attributed to the diagnosis rate mix. A bar extending upward, as for plan 2b for example, indicates that the rate mix is concentrated in higher cost diagnoses. The difference attributable to rate mix ranges from a low of −$285 in Plan 25 to a high of $341 in Plan 2b, difference of $626. The next bar indicates the difference that can be attributed to differences in treatment cost. Again, a bar extending upward indicates that treatment cost, given diagnosis, is higher than the average. After adjusting for demographic mix, the range in cost that can be attributed to treatment cost differences alone is still very large—from a low of −$432 in Plan 15 to a high of $375 in Plan 21, a difference of $807.

The last bar shows the interaction between diagnosis rate deviations from the average rate and treatment cost deviations from the average. A bar extending downward indicates a negative correlation between the two. This component is typically negative, although there are two very small positive values (Plan 15 and Plan 12). Consider Plan 25, for example. The diagnosis rate mix favors diagnoses having low average treatment cost. However, in this firm treatment costs tend to be higher than the average. Looking across the plans, the negative interaction component indicates that lower diagnosis rates are associated with higher treatment costs. The firm, on average, treats fewer enrollees for high-cost diagnoses, but treatment cost for those who are treated are higher than the average treatment cost.

Unlike the demographic mix, which operates to change the rate mix and the cost mix in the same direction, the demographically adjusted rate and cost mix seem to follow no particular pattern across firms. (The

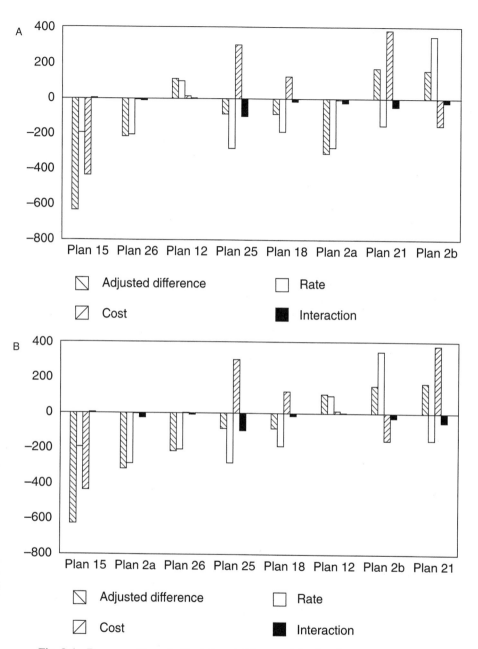

Fig. 8.4 Decomposition of adjusted cost difference (*A*) after demographic adjustment, and (*B*) after total adjusted cost difference
Source: Authors' tabulations based on MedStat data

within-firm interaction between rate and cost tends to be negative, as emphasized above.) Panel *B* of figure 8.4 presents the same data as panel *A*, but in this figure the plans are ordered by the total adjusted cost difference. It is easy to see in this figure that there seems to be no particular relationship between the component attributable to the rate mix and the portion attributable to the cost mix. While for the three plans with the lowest adjusted cost no component is positive (with the exception of the small interaction term for Plan 2a), for the other plans the rate and cost mix components seem to follow no particular pattern. Plans 2a and 2b are in the same firm and adjusted costs differ by $461. (The unadjusted cost difference is $387.) The difference is primarily accounted for the rate mix, which accounts for a difference of $622. The Plan 2a rate mix is concentrated in low-cost diagnoses and the Plan 2b rate mix is concentrated in high-cost diagnoses. This difference attributable to rate mix is partially offset by the cost difference: Costs are in fact $159 lower in Plan 2b than in Plan 2a.

For completeness, the very small differences that can be attributed to the interaction between the demographic adjustment and the adjusted cost differences is shown in figure 8.5. The last bar, for example, typically extends downward. This indicates that for most plans there is a small negative relationship between the demographic adjustment to treatment cost for a diagnosis and the adjusted rate deviation for that diagnosis.

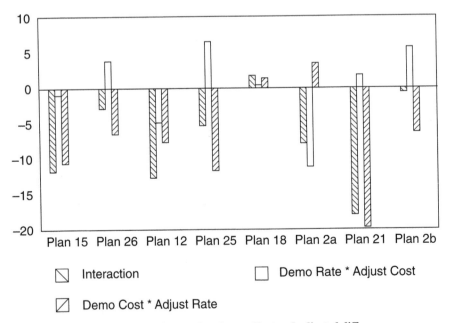

Fig. 8.5   Decomposition of interaction demo adjust and adjusted difference
Source: Authors' tabulations based on MedStat data

The tabulation below summarizes the results thus far. It shows first the range in unadjusted expenditures, then the range in demographic mix adjustments, the range in adjusted expenditures, and finally the range in adjusted treatment costs.

Range in differences by source

Source	Range ($)
Unadjusted expenditures	838
Demographic mix: Total	649
Demographic adjusted expenditures: Total	772
Rate mix	626
Treatment cost mix	807

Perhaps the most noticeable feature of these results is that the range in demographic adjusted expenditures accounted for by the treatment cost mix ($807) is almost as wide as the unadjusted range in expenditures ($838). That is, even though the effects of demographic mix are large, with the difference between the lowest and highest adjustments equal to $649, remaining differences in treatment cost are still very large. Differences in cost due to the different mixes of illness that are treated also accounts for large differences in cost ($626), once demographic mix is controlled for.

Once the decomposition has been set out in this way, more detailed comparisons can be made. For example, suppose we want to know for which diagnoses the treatment cost differences are the largest. Figure 8.6, panel *A*, compares the differences between treatment costs by diagnosis in the highest and lowest treatment cost plans (demographically adjusted). Plan 21 has the highest treatment cost and Plan 15 the lowest. The important feature of this figure is that in all but two diagnoses—which are ordered by average treatment cost—the cost is higher in the high-cost Plan 21 than in the low-cost Plan 2a. The differences are likely to be related to the mean cost of treatment. Thus panel *B* of figure 8.6 shows the cost difference normalized by the mean treatment cost (across all plans) for each diagnosis. Panel *C* of that figure shows the difference between the maximum and minimum treatment cost (over all eight plans), divided by the mean treatment cost. Is seems clear that the difference normalized in this way does not depend systematically on the average treatment cost. (This finding is closely related to evidence reported below on the proportion of variation in expenditures accounted for by each diagnosis.)

In contrast, figure 8.7 shows no evident pattern in the treatment rates in Plan 21 and Plan 15. Similar decomposition calculations based on plans from multiplan firms suggest that the rate as well as the treatment cost may vary systematically by plan, with the treatment cost negatively related

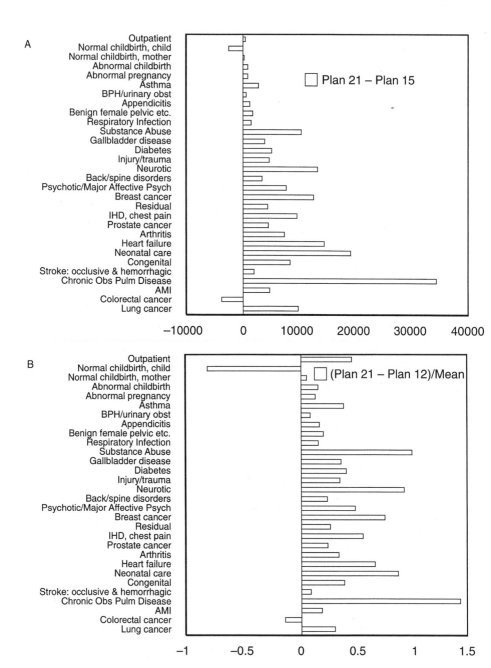

Fig. 8.6 (*A*) Adjusted cost difference, (*B*) adjusted cost difference versus mean, and (*C*) adjusted cost range versus mean
Source: Authors' tabulations based on MedStat data

C

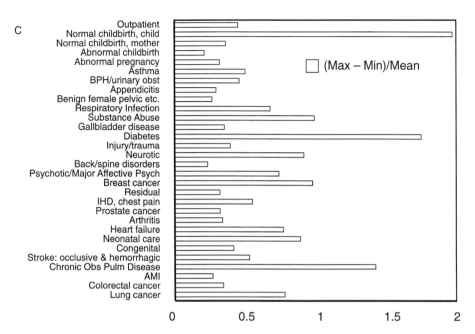

Fig. 8.6   (cont.)

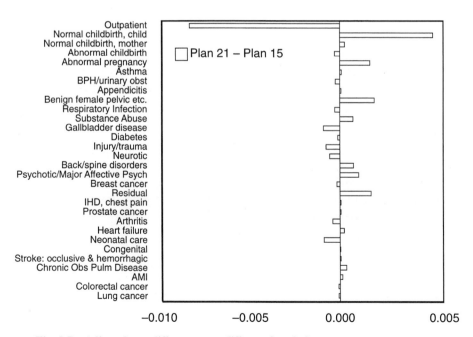

Fig. 8.7   Adjusted rate difference, two different firms' plans
Source: Authors' tabulations based on MedStat data

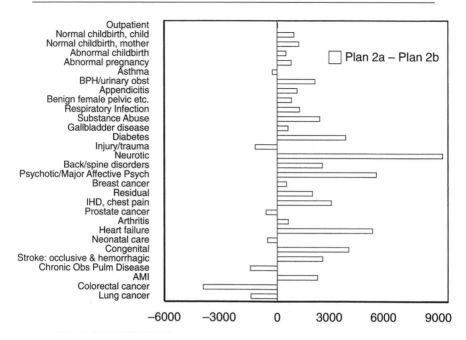

Fig. 8.8   Adjusted cost difference

Source: Authors' tabulations based on MedStat data

to the diagnosis rate. This negative correlation may well be due to plan self-selection effects, with persons more likely to incur high cost.

Figures 8.8 and 8.9 show the cost and rate differences, respectively, by diagnosis for the two plans—2a and 2b—that are in the same firm. Demographically adjusted costs are $159 higher in Plan 2a than in Plan 2b. It can be seen in figure 8.8 that the cost is greater in all but seven of the thirty diagnosis groups. On the other hand, the rate mix in Plan 2a is more concentrated in low-cost diagnoses than it is in Plan 2b. Indeed, the rate in the three lowest cost diagnoses is higher in Plan 2a, but lower in all but two of the remaining diagnoses. Thus these data suggest that the differences in plan provisions yield higher treatment costs in Plan 2a but fewer treatments for high-cost diagnoses. On balance, the lower treatment rate outweighs the higher costs.

8.3.2   Decomposing Total Variation

The description above, summarized in particular in the tabulation on page 257, decomposes into its component parts the difference between the expenditure in a given firm and the average expenditure across all the firms. It is clear, for example, that both the rate of treatment and the treatment cost given treatment, as well as demographic differences, contribute

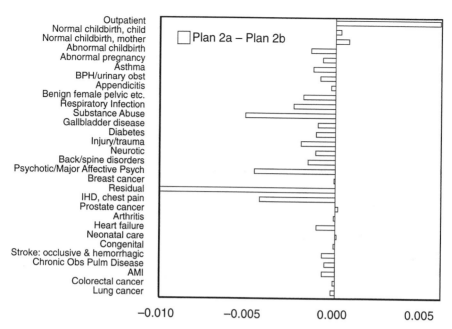

Fig. 8.9   Adjusted rate difference, two plans within one firm
Source: Authors' tabulations based on MedStat data

importantly to differences in expenditures. Another way to think about what accounts for the difference in expenditures across firms is to decompose the variance in expenditures. Unlike the decomposition described above, however, there is no mathematically exact way of doing this. However, we can provide an approximate decomposition of variation based on the extent to which each of these components differs from the overall average.

The procedure can be explained with reference to figure 8.1. For each diagnosis, the difference between the expenditure in a given firm and the average over all firms can be divided into the three components of the difference: rate, treatment cost, and interaction. With reference to the diagram, recall that d_k and δ_k are overall cost and rate averages, respectively, for disease k, and that Δd_{ki} and $\Delta \delta_{ki}$ are the firm-specific deviations from these averages. We use the absolute value of these deviations to describe potentially explainable variation across firms. First we calculate the sum of the absolute values of the three firm-specific rectangles for all diseases, which is given by

$$\sum_i \sum_k |\Delta d_{ki} * \delta_k| + |\Delta \delta_{ki} * d_k| + |\Delta d_{ki} * \Delta \delta_{ki}|.$$

The relative contribution of a particular disease to total variation is quantified by dividing the terms attributable to disease k by this measure of total variation, and is given by

$$\frac{\sum_i \left| \Delta d_{ki} * \delta_k \right| + \left| \Delta \delta_{ki} * d_k \right| + \left| \Delta d_{ki} * \Delta \delta_{ki} \right|}{\sum_i \sum_k \left| \Delta d_{ki} * \delta_k \right| + \left| \Delta \delta_{ki} * d_k \right| + \left| \Delta d_{ki} * \Delta \delta_{ki} \right|} .$$

Analogously, the contribution of cost variation (versus the contribution of variation in treatment rates, or the interaction terms) to this measure of total variation is given by

$$\frac{\sum_i \sum_k \left| \Delta d_{ki} * \delta_k \right|}{\sum_i \sum_k \left| \Delta d_{ki} * \delta_k \right| + \left| \Delta \delta_{ki} * d_k \right| + \left| \Delta d_{ki} * \Delta \delta_{ki} \right|} ,$$

and similarly for the contribution of variation in treatment rates and the contribution of the interaction terms.

Figure 8.10 shows the proportion of the variation accounted for by each of the diagnoses, after controlling for demographic differences across firms. Outpatient treatment and the residual treatments account for the largest proportions. These diagnosis groups also account for a large fraction of expenditures on average, as shown in figure 8.11, and it is not surprising that they should also account for a large fraction of the variation of cost across firms. Thus figure 8.12 shows the *ratio* of the proportion of

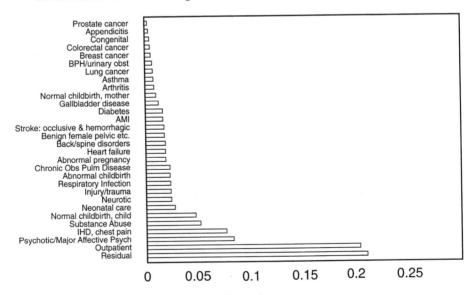

Fig. 8.10   Percentage of variation by diagnosis
Source: Authors' tabulations based on MedStat data

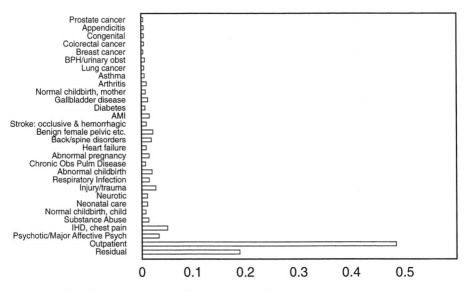

Fig. 8.11 Percentage of expenditure by diagnosis
Source: Authors' tabulations based on MedStat data

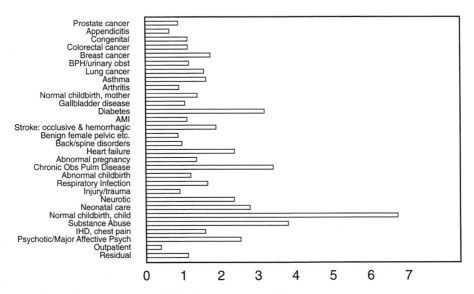

Fig. 8.12 Percentage variation/percentage expenditure
Source: Authors' tabulations based on MedStat data

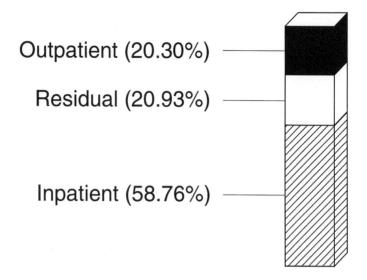

Fig. 8.13   Percentage of variation from outpatient, residual, and inpatient care
Source: Authors' tabulations based on MedStat data

variation explained to the proportion of expenditure, for each diagnosis. Relative to expenditure, outpatient care accounts for the smallest proportion of variation. Normal childbirth accounts for the highest proportion.

Perhaps more informative is the comparison between inpatient and all outpatient care, shown in figure 8.13. Although outpatient care accounts for almost 50 percent of expenditures on average, it accounts for only about 20 percent of the variation in cost across firms. Inpatient care accounts for about 34 percent of expenditures on average, but almost 59 percent of the variation in expenditures. Thus, one can conclude that inpatient care, which tends to include the most intensive medical treatments, varies substantially from firm to firm. (The residual group accounts for about 20 percent of expenditure and about 20 percent of variation in expenditure across firms.) With reference to figure 8.1, figure 8.14 shows that the most important component of variation is the diagnosis rate, which accounts for about 52 percent of variation across firms. Cost differences account for about 40 percent, and the interaction between the two for about 8 percent.

8.4   Summary and Discussion

To gain a better understanding of the sources of cost differences in health care expenditures across firms, we have developed a method to decompose expenditure differences across firms into their component parts.

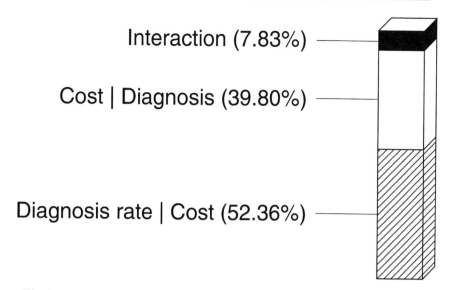

Interaction (7.83%)

Cost | Diagnosis (39.80%)

Diagnosis rate | Cost (52.36%)

Fig. 8.14   Percentage of variation from diagnosis rate, cost differences, and the interaction of the two
Source: Authors' tabulations based on MedStat data

While an important goal is to illustrate the method, the substantive results also seem striking. We have documented large differences in health care spending across the eight firms included in our analysis. Our decomposition, of course, does not say why the differences exist, but it does indicate which differences must be explained, if differences in health care costs are to be understood. The results show large differences across plans in both treatment cost and in the rate of treatment for various diagnoses even after the demographic mix effects have been removed. Thus the findings suggest that differences in treatment intensity as well as diagnosis mix may be affected by differences in plan provisions. Both differences could be attributed to plan incentives. Recall that this analysis is based on one-plan firms, so that selection effects within firms are not confounded with incentive effects, as is typically the case when employees are offered a menu of plans from which to choose. Although these results do not adjust for regional differences in health care cost, they are consistent with cost differences attributed in part to regional differences in treatment practice and the price of health care. We know, however, that differences in treatment cost like those shown in figure 8.6 exist between firms in the same geographic locations. Indeed, there is a large difference between the costs in Plans 2a and 2b, which are in the same geographic locations. In this case the cost difference can be attributed primarily to difference in diagnosis rate mix.

We have also provided an approximate decomposition in the variation of expenditures across firms. Although outpatient care accounts for almost

50 percent of expenditures on average, it accounts for only about 20 percent of the variation in cost across firms. Inpatient care accounts for about 34 percent of expenditures on average, but almost 59 percent of the variation in expenditures. Thus one can conclude that high-cost inpatient treatments vary substantially from firm to firm. Understanding the exact sources of this variation may provide insights into reducing the cost of intensive treatments. (The residual group accounts for about 20 percent of expenditure and about 20 percent of variation in expenditure across firms.) The most important component of variation is the diagnosis rate, which accounts for about 52 percent of variation across firms. Cost differences account for about 40 percent, with the remainder accounted for by the interaction between the two.

Some of these descriptive findings on the relationship between demographic characteristics, disease treatment rates, and expenditures associated with particular diseases can be translated almost directly into implications for policy and further research. For example, we can quantify the average effects of each of these factors on private health care spending, and identify the high-variation groups that account for the bulk of differences in expenditures across employers. By using these methods with panel data, we can similarly quantify the main sources of changes in health care expenditures and the high-variation components of expenditure growth across firms. When combined with a breakdown of trends in the major components of health care cost, the decomposition will permit assessment of the determinants of future medical cost increases, under the current system. The findings can also be used to assess the effects of trends in the demographic composition of firm workforces. Finally, we can assess the effects of changes in insurance coverage, like opening Medicare to persons aged fifty-five to sixty-four. We believe that the method of decomposing cost differences among firms, as well as the method of apportioning variation, can now be fruitfully extended to analysis of the much larger number of plans in our file of firm claims data.

Reference

Eichner, Matthew J. 1997. Incentives, price expectations, and medical expenditures: An analysis of claims under employer-provided health insurance. Columbia University, Graduate School of Business. Mimeograph.

Comment   Joseph P. Newhouse

This paper uses data from eight firms to decompose variation in medical spending across the firms. The firms' spending per person for medical care services varies from low to high by a factor of roughly 50 percent, and the main task of the paper is to understand what could account for such variation. In particular, the paper seeks to decompose spending differences among the firms into differences in the age-sex mix of persons enrolled (demographics), the incidence of diagnoses, and the cost of a given diagnosis. None of the firms permits choice of health insurance plan, which should minimize the role of selection in causing between-firm variation in spending.

The finding of variation in medical care spending, of course, is hardly unique to this study. Similar variation exists even at the state level. In 1991 the three lowest-spending states, Utah, Idaho, and Mississippi, spent $1,904, $2,037, and $2,162 per resident respectively, whereas the three highest-spending states, Massachusetts, Connecticut, and New York spent $3,333, $3,298, and $3,255 respectively (Basu 1996; the District of Columbia spent even more: $4,693). As a percentage of the national average of $2,648, Massachusetts spent 126 percent and Utah 72 percent.

Although no one has examined spending at the county level for the entire population, spending by Medicare enrollees varies substantially across counties. After adjusting for factor price and demographic variation across counties, variation in spending across counties is similar in magnitude to variation in spending across the eight firms (figure 8C.1).[1] However, because prices are set administratively in the Medicare system and because the values in figure 8C.1 approximately adjust for the geographic variation in price, almost all of the across-county variation comes from variation in the quantity of services delivered.

There is also substantial variation across areas in rates of diagnoses and procedures. For example, heart disease and cancer rates are known to vary geographically. Deaths from heart disease per 100,000 in 1995 were 216 in California and 350 in New York (U.S. Bureau of the Census 1998). The

Joseph P. Newhouse is the John D. MacArthur Professor of Health Policy and Management at Harvard University and is on the faculties of the Kennedy School of Government, the Harvard Medical School, the Harvard School of Public Health, and the Harvard University Faculty of Arts and Sciences, and is a research associate of the National Bureau of Economic Research.

1. These data are actual payments made by Medicare for health maintenance organization enrollees, and are 95 percent of spending in traditional Medicare by county, adjusted for variation in age, sex, institutional status, welfare status, and employment status across counties, averaged over five years, and adjusted for inflation. Seventy percent of the amount is adjusted for variation in Medicare's hospital wage index to reflect factor price variation. The range of variation unadjusted for factor price variation but adjusted for the other factors listed above is from $221 (Arthur County, Nebraska) to $767 (Richmond County, New York).

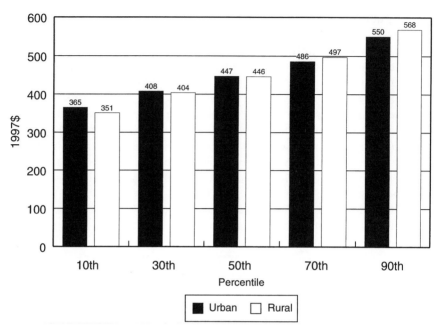

Fig. 8C.1   Standardized Medicare payments, by percentile, urban and rural counties, 1997
Source: Prospective Payment Assessment Commission (1997, 37)

cancer death rates in the two states were 162 and 213 respectively; it was 250 in Pennsylvania. Chassin et al. (1986) examined variation in the rates at which common procedures were performed in the Medicare population across ten states or large substate areas (e.g., coastal California, eastern Massachusetts). Typically the area with the highest rate carried out the procedure at about four times the rate of the lowest area, with the distribution of rates across the areas reasonably uniform. Furthermore, there was no strong correlation across procedures; areas that performed one procedure at high rates did not necessarily perform another procedure at high rates.

In short, there is enormous variation in both disease and spending geographically, and one would expect at least as much variation at the firm level. The data in Eichner, McClellan, and Wise, therefore, are consistent with what we know about variation in medical spending from other sources.

Typically, much of the variation in spending is attributed to differences in practice patterns among physicians, which in turn is related to medical uncertainty (Phelps 1992, 2000). Some variation is explained by plan provisions, but not a great deal. In the RAND Health Insurance Experiment, for example, which had substantial differences in mean spending across plans, the between-plan variation accounted for only 1 percent of the total variance in spending across individuals (Newhouse and the Insurance Experiment Group 1993). To the degree that there are coverage differences among the plans (e.g., one plan covering eyeglasses and another not), of course, there would be additional variation.

In decomposing the variation, the authors here show that the variation in spending across the eight firms is attributable partly to demographics, partly to variation in the incidence of diagnoses, and partly to variation in the costliness of diagnoses. Firms that have substantial positive deviations in one dimension may or may not have positive deviations in other dimensions, and vice versa. I now turn to some comments.

It is hard to know what to make of the size of the demographic deviations without knowing how well these eight firms represent the universe of all firms. It is not surprising, however, that demographics explain variation in spending. Firms differ in the age and sex mix of their workforces, and age and sex predict medical spending. Hence, some differences in spending across firms will inevitably be explained by age and sex. One might, therefore, attempt to focus on the variation in spending after adjustment for age and sex.

Here one runs into the problem that, although inpatient diagnoses tend to be coded reliably, outpatient diagnoses do not. Inpatient coding is thought to be reasonably complete and accurate because Medicare and some private-payer payment turn on the accuracy of inpatient diagnosis coding. (The diagnosis codes determine the Medicare diagnosis-related group and, in turn, payment.) In the case of outpatient diagnoses, however, payment does not turn on the coding for almost all payers. As a result, the coding of outpatient diagnoses can be seriously incomplete and/or inaccurate.

Table 8C.1 presents some data from Medicare on this point. These data

Table 8C.1   **Consistency of Part B Diagnosis Coding**

Diagnosis	Likelihood of a Part B Claim in 1995 Given a Claim in 1994 (%)
Hypertension	59
Coronary artery disease	53
Chronic obstructive pulmonary disease	62
Congestive heart failure	61
Stroke	51
Dementia	59
Rheumatoid arthritis	55
High-cost diabetes	58
Renal failure	56
Quadriplegia/paraplegia	52
Dialysis	59

Source: Medicare Payment Advisory Commission (1998, 17).

show the likelihood of a physician (Part B) claim in 1995 with the diagnosis conditional on there being a 1994 claim with the diagnosis; only those Medicare beneficiaries alive in 1994 and 1995 are included in the sample. For all eleven diagnoses examined, the likelihood of a claim is only moderately over 50 percent. Because one would have expected virtually all persons with these diagnoses to have made a physician visit in 1995, there would appear to be three possibilities: The 1994 diagnosis was in error; the 1995 diagnosis was in error; or the physician failed to write down a diagnosis in 1995. Because these problems occur upstream of MedStat, the firm Eichner, McClellan, and Wise use to collect and standardize the data, they suggest that some of the variation shown for outpatient diagnoses, which account for nearly half the spending, could be attributable to variation in coding practices. Moreover, if there is any non-randomness in coding errors, some of the variation in mean spending conditional on a diagnosis could also be noise.

Although employees at the firms had no choice of insurance plan, there could nonetheless be some selection effects in the data. The most worrisome diagnoses are perhaps mental health and substance abuse. Here the problem could occur if certain occupations or firms were more likely to attract individuals with such diagnoses, even independently of coverage provisions. Generous coverage provisions relative to other firms in the local labor market might motivate some job choice and add to the variation. Other diagnoses may also differ across firms for noneconomic reasons. Some occupations or industries may also be associated with certain cancers or with trauma, for example. In other words, some of the observed variation across the firms could well be epidemiologic as well as economic.

A possibly fruitful alternative decomposition would be into unit price and the real quantity of services. If this is done, it might prove interesting to compare the variation in the quantity of services with the variation in the quantity of Medicare services across the counties of residence of the workers in these firms. To the degree that employee use and Medicare use covary, one would emphasize physician practice patterns as an explanation of the variation.

References

Basu, Joy. 1996. Border crossing adjustment and personal health care spending by state. *Health Care Financing Review* 18 (1): 215–36.
Chassin, Mark, Robert H. Brook, Rolla Edward Park, Joan Keesey, Arleen Fink, Jacquilene Kosecoff, Katherine Kahn, Nancy Merrick, and David H. Solomon. 1986. Variations in the use of medical and surgical services by the Medicare population. *New England Journal of Medicine* 314 (5): 285–90.
Medicare Payment Advisory Commission. 1998. *Report to the Congress,* vol. 2. Washington, D.C.: The Commission.

Newhouse, Joseph P. 1993. *Free for all? Lessons from the RAND Health Insurance Experiment.* Cambridge, Mass.: Harvard University Press.

Phelps, Charles E. 1992. Diffusion of information in medical care. *Journal of Economic Perspectives* 6 (3): 23–42.

————. 2000. Information diffusion and best practice adoption. In *Handbook of health economics,* ed. Anthony J. Culyer and Joseph P. Newhouse, 223–64. Amsterdam: Elsevier.

Prospective Payment Assessment Commission. 1997. Medicare and the American health care system: Report to the Congress. Washington, D.C.: The Commission.

United States Bureau of the Census. 1998. *Statistical abstract. 1998.* Washington: GPO.

IV

Social Security Provisions
and Retirement

9
Incentive Effects of Social Security under an Uncertain Disability Option

Axel Börsch-Supan

9.1 Introduction

In most industrialized countries, old-age labor force participation has declined dramatically during the last decades. Together with population aging, this puts the social security systems of the industrialized countries under a double threat: Retirees receive pensions for a longer time while there are less workers per retiree to shoulder the financial burden of the pension system. The decline of old-age labor force participation has therefore turned attention to the incentive effects of social security systems: Is a significant part of the threat homemade because pension systems provide overly strong incentives to retire early? This "pull" view—that labor supply has declined because early retirement provisions pull old workers out of employment—is in contrast to the "push" view—that a secularly declining demand for labor has created unemployment, one form of which is to push older workers into early retirement.

The pull view is prominently put forward in a recent volume edited by Gruber and Wise (1999). The authors from eleven countries argue that the declining old-age labor force is strongly correlated with the incentives created by generous early retirement provisions. Formal econometric analyses (e.g., Stock and Wise 1990 for the United States; Meghir and Whitehouse 1997 for the United Kingdom; Börsch-Supan 1992, 2000 for

Axel Börsch-Supan is professor of economics and director of the Institute of Economics and Statistics at the University of Mannheim, and a research associate of the National Bureau of Economic Research.

Financial support was provided by the Deutsche Forschungsgemeinschaft through the Sonderforschungsbereich 504 and by the National Institute on Aging through the National Bureau of Economic Research. Comments by Anne Case and David Cutler and, in particular, by Daniel McFadden were greatly appreciated.

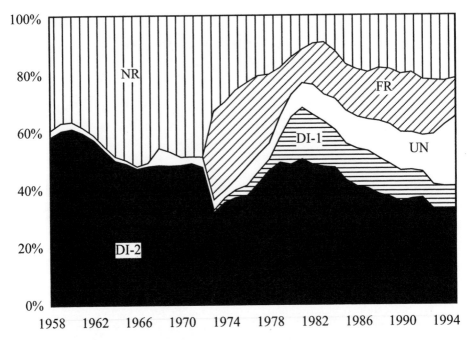

Fig. 9.1 Pathways to retirement
Notes: The figure shows the share of pathways by year. The shaded areas are NR (normal retirement); FR (flexible retirement [only after the 1972 reform]); UN (early retirement because of unemployment); DI-1 (early retirement because of onset of disability after age sixty [only after the 1972 reform]); DI-2 (early retirement because of onset of disability before age sixty).
Source: Verband deutscher Rentenversicherungsträger (1997)

Germany) find strongly significant coefficients of variables measuring the incentive effects of pension rules (e.g., the option value to postpone retirement).

Incentive effects of pension rules are usually estimated under the assumption that the institutional environment provides a single optimal pathway for retirement. This optimal pathway then defines present values of retirement income at any retirement age, or an option value of postponing retirement at any prospective retirement age. However, most countries provide competing pathways that include several early retirement options in addition to normal retirement, typically at age sixty-five.

Jacobs et al. (1991) have stressed the variety of these pathway options across Europe. Figure 9.1 shows how important these different exit routes or pathways are in Germany. It is particularly impressive that early retirement due to a disability before age sixty (denoted by DI-2) was the most common pathway in most of the years 1958–94, while "normal" retirement (denoted by NR) has a share of less than 20 percent since the mid-1970s.

Early retirement due to unemployment (denoted by UN) increased steeply in the early 1990s and accounted for roughly another 20 percent of labor market exits. Complicating this picture even more, the exit routes depicted in figure 9.1 are frequently preceded by preretirement schemes. These schemes are industry- or company-specific and are popular not only in Germany but also in many other European countries.

When measuring incentive effects, one encounters two distinct problems associated with this multitude of exit routes. First, early retirement options such as the special provisions for disabled and unemployed workers can effectively be strategic variables for the employer and the employee. Employers may have an incentive to let the social security system pay for the costs of restructuring the workforce, whereas employees may have an incentive to enjoy leisure early at the expense of the contributors to the social security system. As a result, constructs of incentive effects that rely on indicators for the availability of a certain pathway are endogenous. A prime example of such an indicator is the reported health status, often measured as the extent of disability in percent of full work ability. This is frequently the legal prerequisite for early retirement and can be manipulated at least to some extent, as has been controversially discussed by Bound (1989) and Parsons (1991). The complicated interaction between health and the eligibility for disability benefits has been documented by a working group led by John Rust (Benitez et al. 1998) as a prerequisite for a structural estimation of incentive effects due to disability benefits, improving on the large U.S. literature on this topic.

A second technical problem associated with the multitude of exit routes is that the choice of a specific pathway to retirement is made when it is not clear whether certain options are actually relevant for the individual contemplating early retirement. Again, disability is the prime example: Even if the reported health status has not been manipulated, econometricians face the problem that the outcome of the screening process for eligibility is far from certain ex ante. If econometricians specify the option set too generously, they exaggerate the incentives at work and thus underestimate the coefficient of the incentive variable. In turn, incentive effects may be overestimated—and thus the pull view of early retirement—if the option set is too restrictive.

This paper shows that ignoring the uncertainty and endogeneity of the relevant institutional setting (i.e., the available pathways) can severely bias the estimates of incentive effects. The paper focuses on the disability option that provides particularly strong incentives. It proposes several estimates to bound the "true" incentive effects of social security on early retirement in the face of uncertainty, and it uses an approximate two-stage procedure to tackle the endogeneity problem.

Section 9.2 provides the institutional background of the German pension system and the early retirement incentives it creates. Section 9.3 introduces the data, a sample of German workers aged fifty-five to seventy drawn from the German Socio-Economic Panel, and describes patterns of retirement, disability and health in the sample. Section 9.4 presents estimation results for several specifications aimed at correcting for uncertainty and endogeneity of the disability benefit eligibility. Section 9.5 concludes and draws policy recommendations.

9.2   Incentives Created by the German Public Pension System

The German public pension system is particularly well suited to a microeconometric study of incentive effects on labor force participation because it is almost universal and we do not need to account for a variety of firm pension plans that create their own incentive effects but are usually not well captured in survey data (Börsch-Supan and Schnabel 1998). The homogeneity arises for two reasons. First, the German public pension system is mandatory for every worker except for the self-employed and those with very small labor incomes. Because almost all German workers have been dependently employed at least at some point in their working careers, almost every worker has a claim on a public pension. Second, the system has a very high replacement rate, generating net retirement incomes that are currently about 70 percent of preretirement net earnings for a worker with a forty-five-year earnings history and average lifetime earnings. This is substantially higher than the corresponding U.S. net replacement rate of about 53 percent. In addition, the system provides relatively generous survivor benefits that constitute a substantial proportion of the total pension liability. As a result, social security income represents about 80 percent of household income for households headed by persons aged sixty-five and over; the remainder is divided about equally among firm pensions, asset income, and private transfers.

A detailed description of the German public pension system is given by Börsch-Supan and Schnabel (1999). In the sequel, we only summarize the features that create incentives to retire early. Until 1972, retirement was mandatory at age sixty-five. Early retirement was possible and frequent through the disability pathway (see fig. 9.1). With the landmark 1972 pension reform, several early retirement options were introduced. Figure 9.1 shows that early retirement almost instantaneously substituted for a considerable portion of disability benefits—a fairly strong indication that disability status was not related only to health. The pension system established in 1972 now provides *old-age pensions* for workers aged sixty and older, and, for workers below age sixty, *disability benefits,* which are converted to old-age pensions at age sixty-five at the latest.

The main feature of the *old-age pensions* is flexible retirement from age sixty-three for workers with long service histories. In addition, retirement at age sixty is possible for women, unemployed workers, and workers who cannot be employed appropriately for health or labor market reasons. It is noteworthy that these features were introduced by the 1972 reform as social achievements *before* unemployment began to rise in the mid-1970s. Only later was it realized that they helped to keep the unemployment rate down. Twenty years after the introduction of the various early retirement options, the 1992 pension reform is attempting to close some of those options. However, the effects are irrelevant for the current sample because they will be visible only after the year 2004.

Old-age pension benefits are computed on a lifetime contribution basis. They are the product of four elements: (1) the employee's relative wage position, averaged over the entire earnings history, (2) the number of years of service life, (3) several adjustment factors, and (4) the average pension level. The first three factors make up the "personal pension base," which is calculated when one is entering retirement. Old-age pensions are proportional to length of service life, a specific feature of the German pension system. The fourth factor determines the income distribution between workers and pensioners in general and is adjusted annually to net wages. Thus, productivity gains are transferred each year to all pensioners, not only to new entrants. Due to a generous exemption, social security benefits are tax free unless income from other sources is high.

Early retirement incentives are created by the (lack of) adjustment factors. Before the 1992 pension reform, there was no explicit adjustment of benefits when a worker retired earlier than age sixty-five, except for a bonus when retirement was postponed from ages sixty-five or sixty-six by one year. Nevertheless, because benefits are proportional to the years of service, a worker with fewer years of service would get lower benefits even before the bonus. With a constant income profile and forty years of service, each year of earlier retirement decreased pension benefits by 2.5 percent. This is substantially less than the actuarial adjustment, which increases from about 5.5 percent for postponing retirement one year at age sixty to 8 percent for postponing retirement one year at age sixty-five. The 1992 pension reform will gradually change this by introducing retirement age–specific adjustment factors to the benefit formula. However, they will remain about 2 percent below those required for actuarial fairness. Figure 9.2 displays actuarial adjustments as well as those under the current (i.e., relevant for our working sample) and future institutional settings.

Disability pensions before reaching age sixty are particularly generous. First, the service life used in a similar computation as for old-age pensions is extended by the time between the onset of the disability and age sixty, albeit at a reduced earnings base at two-thirds of the last earnings. Second, disability benefits are not actuarially adjusted, even after the 1992 reform, but are computed as if the worker had retired at age sixty. Disability pensions after age sixty are computed like old-age pensions, but without actuarial adjustments.

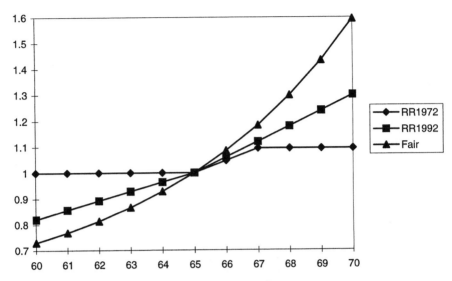

Fig. 9.2   Adjustment of retirement benefits to retirement age

Source: Börsch-Supan and Schnabel 1998.

Notes: RR1972 denotes the adjustment factors introduced by the 1972 pension reform. RR1992 symbolizes the adjustments that will be phased in by the 1992 pension reform. "Fair" refers to actuarially fair adjustment factors.

The key statistic needed to measure the early retirement incentives exerted by the actuarially unfair adjustment factors is the change in social security wealth. If social security wealth declines because the increase in the annual pension is not large enough to offset the shorter time of pension receipt, workers have a financial incentive to retire earlier. We define social security wealth as the expected present discounted value of benefits minus applicable contributions. Seen from the perspective of a worker who is S years old and plans to retire at age R, social security wealth (SSW) is

$$\text{SSW}_S(R) = \left(\sum_{t=R}^{\infty} \text{YRET}_t(R) \cdot a_t \cdot \delta^{t-S} \right) - \left(\sum_{t=S}^{R-1} c \cdot \text{YLAB}_t \cdot a_t \cdot \delta^{t-S} \right),$$

with

SSW	present discounted value of retirement benefits (= social security wealth),
S	planning age,
R	retirement age,
YLAB_t	labor income at age t,
$\text{YPEN}_t(R)$	pension income at age t for retirement at age R,
c_t	contribution rate to pension system at age t,

a_t probability to survive at least until age t given survival until age S, and

δ discount factor $= 1/(1 + r)$.

The accrual rate of social security wealth between age $t - 1$ and t is

$$\text{ACCR}_s(t) = \frac{[SSW_S(t) - SSW_S(t - 1)]}{SSW_S(t - 1)}.$$

A negative accrual can be interpreted as a tax on further labor force participation. It is particularly handy to express this as an implicit tax rate: the ratio of the (negative) social security wealth accrual to the net wages (YLAB^{NET}) that workers would earn if they would postpone retirement by one year

$$\text{TAXR}_s(t) = \frac{- [SSW_S(t) - SSW_S(t - 1)]}{\text{YLAB}_t^{\text{NET}}}.$$

Figure 9.3 shows that the early retirement incentives created by the old-age pension formula in Germany are strong. We will see below that the incentives created by disability benefits are even stronger. The accrual function (panel A) has three distinctive kink points. The first kink occurs at age sixty, the earliest retirement age into the public pension system with-

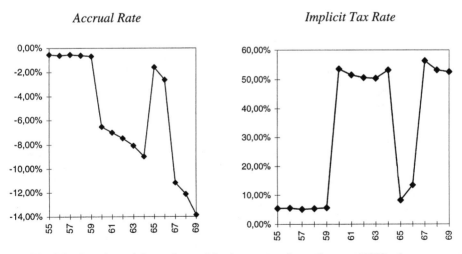

Accrual Rate   *Implicit Tax Rate*

Fig. 9.3   Loss in social security wealth when postponing retirement (1972 rules, old-age pensions only): (A) accrual rate, (B) implicit tax rate
Source: Börsch-Supan and Schnabel 1998
Note: See text for definition of accrual rate $ACCR_s(t)$ and implicit tax rate $TAXR_s(t)$ for $S = 55$ and $t = 55 \ldots 69$.

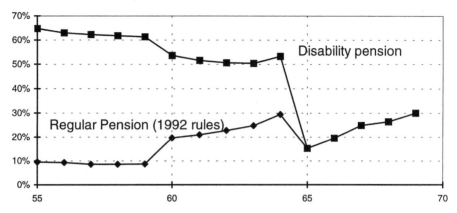

Fig. 9.4   Implicit tax on postponing retirement, disability case
Source: Börsch-Supan and Schnabel 1998.
Note: See text for definition of implicit tax rate TAXR$_s(t)$.

out disability status. Two other kinks are generated by the bonus for postponing retirement at ages sixty-five and sixty-six, interrupting the steady increase in negative pension wealth accrual.

The lack of actuarial fairness of the old-age pension system creates a negative accrual of pension wealth during the early retirement window at a rate reaching −9 percent when retirement is postponed from age sixty-four to sixty-five. In 1995, this was a loss of about 22,000 deutsche mark (US$10,500 at purchasing power parity) for the average worker. Expressed as a percentage of annual labor income, the loss corresponds to a "tax" that exceeds 50 percent.

The 1992 pension reform will moderate but not abolish this incentive effect. After 2004, when the 1992 reform will have been fully phased in, the negative accrual rate will reach −5 percent, corresponding to an implicit tax rate of almost 30 percent when retirement is postponed by one year at age sixty-four.

Disability benefits create even stronger labor supply disincentives. The resulting implicit tax rates for postponing retirement are very large (see figure 9.4). They are likely to create strong incentives to manipulate disability eligibility: If there is a chance to claim disability, not taking it corresponds to a 60 percent implicit tax on earnings.

9.3   Data and Descriptive Statistics

How do these incentives affect actual retirement behavior? We use the 1984–96 waves of the German Socio-Economic Panel (GSOEP) to tackle this question. The GSOEP is an annual panel study of some 6,000 households and some 15,000 individuals. Its design corresponds closely to that of the U.S. Panel Study of Income Dynamics (PSID). Response rates and panel mortality are also comparable to those for the PSID. The GSOEP data provide a detailed account of income and employment status. The data are used extensively in Germany, and the increasing interest in the United States prompted the construction of an English-language user file available from Richard Burkhauser and his associates at Syracuse University. Burkhauser (1991) reports on the usefulness of the German panel data and provides English-language code books for the internationally accessible GSOEP version. Since 1990, the West German panel has been augmented by an East German sample.

For this paper, however, I use only West German workers because preretirement is frequent in East Germany and I lack the necessary company-specific information to describe the incentives appropriately. My working sample consists of all West Germans who are aged fifty-five to seventy years and have at least one spell of employment in this window in order to reconstruct an earning history. This working sample includes 1,610 individuals. We construct an unbalanced panel of these individuals with 8,577 observations and an average observation time of 5.3 years. A few sample persons are right-truncated with respect to retirement (i.e., they are employed throughout the entire window period) but most individuals retire before the age of seventy. Of the 1987 individuals, 666 have no transitions, 643 have a single transition from employment to retirement, and 301 individuals have more complex histories with at least one reverse transition. Thirty-five percent are female, and the most common retirement age is sixty.

I define a worker to be retired when the self-reported employment status is "out of labor force." This includes unemployed workers and workers on preretirement who may not receive public pensions but may receive other support ranging from unemployment benefits to severance pay. Figure 9.5 depicts the percentage of retired persons in my working sample and shows three distinct jumps: the largest at age sixty, and two smaller ones at ages sixty-three and sixty-five, corresponding to the earliest ages at which eligibility to various pension types begins (see section 9.2). Very few individuals are working after age sixty-five. These patterns in the working sample strongly correspond to administrative records (e.g., Verband deutscher Rentenversicherungsträger [VdR] 1997). Even before official old-age retirement begins, about 15 percent of the workers have retired. This percentage in our working sample is somewhat lower than in the administrative records, depicted in figure 9.1, indicating that the working sample underrepresents problem cases who retire very early. This reflects the middle-class bias typical for the GSOEP.

The jump at age sixty is due to three institutional features. Women with a work history of at least fifteen years may retire at age sixty; any unemployed worker may retire at age sixty if certain mild requirements are satis-

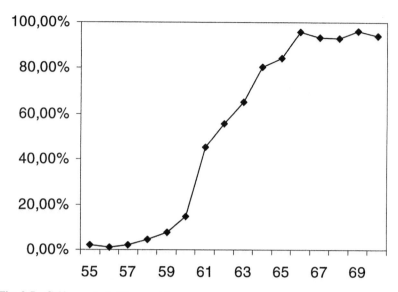

Fig. 9.5   Self-reported retirement by age
Source: German Socio-Economic Panel (GSOEP) 1984–96 and author's calculations.

fied; and, most importantly, workers who are able to claim "old-age disability" may also retire already at age sixty. This old-age disability between ages sixty-one and sixty-five has weaker health and job status requirements than "normal disability" before age sixty.

Disability is officially measured as percent of earnings capability. If this falls below 50 percent, workers after age sixty can claim a disability pension that corresponds to a normal pension, without actuarial adjustments. Indeed, the average degree of disability in the sample increases steadily until age sixty-two, when it reaches 20 percent. After age sixty-three, it increases much more slowly (see fig. 9.6).

Since it seems implausible that this sudden change is caused by a change in health status, this pattern suggests an institutional reason. It is easy to find. From age sixty-three on, all male workers can receive a normal pension, provided they have thirty-five years of work (which most male workers have). In fact, a striking finding is the weak correlation between the degree of disability and self-reported health. Figure 9.7 shows that self-reported health changes very little, and although a regression of the degree of disability on self-reported health features a significant positive correlation between bad health and disability, its R^2 is only about 3 percent. Partly, this weak correlation is due to the fact that disability status is granted not only for health-related but also for employment-related reasons. Even healthy workers are classified as disabled if there are no jobs available for their specific skills. Leniency in those regulations has changed frequently and unpredictably. They were subject not only to government

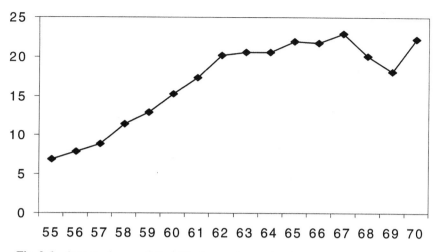

Fig. 9.6   **Average degree of disability by age (percentage)**
Source: GSOEP 1984–96 and author's calculations

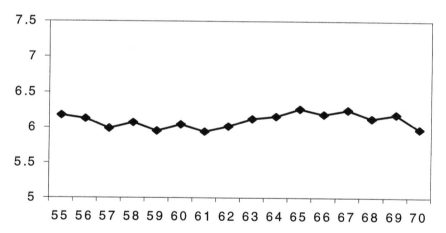

Fig. 9.7   **Average self-reported health on a 0–10 scale**
Source: GSOEP 1984–96 and author's calculations

policy (e.g., in order to manipulate the unemployment rate) but also to law cases (which at some point ruled, for example, that earnings tests for disabled workers were illegal).

9.4   Alternative Estimates of Incentive Effects to Retire Early

The evidence in the previous section suggests that disability is an important mechanism for early retirement. However, even in the lenient German system, disability is not granted automatically. Only 16 percent in my working sample report a disability status of 50 percent or more. In addition, the discussion at the end of the preceding section has shown that when one is planning ahead for the choice of retirement age, it is far from clear whether this exit pathway can be taken. Incentives for early retirement thus have a strong element of uncertainty, which must be built into measures of incentive effects.

I capture the economic incentives provided by the pension system using the option value to postpone retirement (Stock and Wise 1990). This value captures for each retirement age the trade-off between retiring now (resulting in a stream of retirement benefits that depends on this retirement age) and keeping all options open for some later retirement date (with associated streams of first labor, then retirement incomes for all possible later retirement ages). Consequently, the option value for a specific age is defined as the difference between the maximum attainable consumption utility if the worker postpones retirement to some later year minus the utility of consumption that the worker can afford if he or she would retire now. The definition corresponds closely to the construction of social security wealth in the preceding section.

Let $V_t(R)$ denote the expected discounted future utility at age t if the worker retires at age R. Let $R^*(t)$ denote the optimal retirement age if the worker postpones retirement past age t, i.e., $\max[V_t(R)]$ for $r > t$. With this notation, the option value is

$$\text{OPTVAL}(t) = V_t[R^*(t)] - V_t(t).$$

Since a worker is likely to retire as soon as the utility of the option to postpone retirement becomes smaller than the utility of retiring now, retirement probabilities should depend negatively on the option value.

I specify the expected utility as follows:

$$V_t(R) = \sum_{s=t}^{R-1} u(\text{YLAB}_s) \cdot a_s \cdot \delta^{s-t} + \alpha \sum_{s=R}^{\infty} u[\text{YRET}_s(R)] a_s \cdot \delta^{s-t}$$

with

YLAB_s labor income at age s, $s = t \ldots R - 1$,
$\text{YRET}_s(R)$ expected retirement income at age s, $s > R$,
R retirement age,
α marginal utility of leisure, to be estimated,
a probability to survive at least until age s, and
δ discount factor, set at 3 percent.

To capture the utility from leisure, utility during retirement is weighted by $\alpha > 1$, where $1/\alpha$ is the marginal disutility of work. We use an estimate of $\alpha = 3.13$ that was obtained by grid search (see Börsch-Supan 2000). A dollar that must be earned by work is therefore valued at only about a third of a dollar that is given as a public transfer through the retirement system. This value is somewhat higher than estimates for the United States (Stock and Wise 1990) but not implausible for Germany with an arguably higher preference for leisure. I apply a very simple utility function by identifying consumption with income. Preliminary estimates with an isoelastic utility function, $u(Y) = Y^\gamma$, yield a γ coefficient that is not significantly different from 1. Finally, the discount factor δ is assumed to be 3 percent. Other discount factors in the range between 1 and 6 percent yield qualitatively similar results.

Uncertainty enters the option value through future income. For labor income, I assume it to be constant after age fifty-five. This is typical for German workers who have seniority rules that flatten out about this age. However, retirement income depends on retirement age and the rules applicable to the individual at that age. As stressed before, it is uncertain which rules will actually apply.

The common procedure in the literature is to use the retirement income according to the rules that have ex post been applied to the sample individual. This procedure is correct for fixed personal characteristics. For example, as pointed out in section 9.2, German public pension rules have a more generous retirement age for women than for men. Hence, male persons are assigned pension rules for males, and females likewise.

Similarly, the literature has typically assigned disabled individuals a pension according to the rules for disabled workers. However, as opposed to such fixed characteristics as gender, this procedure ignores both uncertainty and potential endogeneity. First, the option value approach is an ex ante (not an ex post) view of the utility of a certain retirement age. The ex ante uncertainty cannot be resolved by the econometrician by using its ex post value. Rather, one needs to use the expected value applicable at the time of decision making. Specifically, the ability to claim disability status is not certain at age fifty-five, the beginning of my decision window. The retirement income YRET in the above equation should therefore be a probability-weighted sum of the relevant pathways, in this simple case "disability" and "normal retirement."

Moreover, as stressed before, eligibility can be manipulated to some extent, and there are strong incentives to do so. Thus the probability of taking this pathway is potentially endogenous. I therefore must use an instrumental variable (IV) approach to compute fitted probabilities of the pathways "disability" and "normal retirement." This leads to four variants of the option value to postpone retirement:

- *The tough variant.* All individuals are assigned retirement incomes according to normal retirement rules.
- *The generous variant.* All individuals are assigned retirement incomes as if they could claim disability benefits.

- *The endogenous variant.* Disabled persons are assigned disability pensions, nondisabled persons normal pensions.
- *The probabilistic variant.* Individuals are assigned an expected value, where disability pensions are weighted by a probability p, and normal pensions by $(1 - p)$. Taking the endogeneity of p into account, I use three IV approaches:
  a. I use the population frequency of being disabled (15.97 percent),
  b. I regress the probability of having a degree of disability of 50 percent or higher on a cubic polynomial in age and use this fitted value as probability p, and
  c. I regress the probability of having a degree of disability of 50 percent or higher on a cubic polynomial in age, a set of branch and education dummies, plus gender and marital status, and use this fitted value as probability p.

I then insert the resulting option value into a discrete choice model with "retired" as the dependent variable, and add the usual suspects as other explanatory variables: an array of socioeconomic variables such as gender, marital status, and wealth (indicator variables of several financial and real wealth categories), and a self-assessed health measure. Obviously, I cannot use the legal disability status as a measure of health because this is potentially endogenous.

Inserting the option value in a regression-type model is much less computationally involved and more practical than the estimation procedure employed by Stock and Wise (1990), which in turn much more closely approximates the underlying dynamic programming structure (Rust and Phelan 1997; see Lumsdaine, Stock, and Wise 1992). The regression approach generates robust estimates of the average effects of the option value on retirement, although it is inferior in predicting individual choices when incentives vary widely across individuals.

I begin by using a simple logit model. Table 9.1 presents a summary, table 9.2 the full range of results.

In the "generous" specification of expected retirement income—"everybody is eligible for disability benefits"—the sign of the option value coefficient is counterintuitive. All other specifications have the expected negative sign: An increase in the option value to postpone retirement decreases the probability of being retired. The probabilistic variants are very close to each other and are bracketed by the "generous" and the "tough" variants. The first-stage R^2s in the last two specifications are 8 and 15 percent, respectively. The "endogenous" specification, however, is far outside this bracket, considerably larger and with an (apparent) very high precision as indicated by the t-statistic. The endogeneity bias produces a threefold higher estimate of the option value coefficient than the probability-weighted specifications.

Table 9.1   **Option Value Coefficients for Six Variants of Expected
                      Retirement Income**

	Estimated Coefficient of Option Value	*t*-statistic
Model 1 (generous variant)	0.0053	4.63
	(0.00115)	
Model 2 (tough variant)	−0.0046	−4.72
	(0.00098)	
Model 3 (endogenous variant)	−0.0096	−12.02
	(0.00080)	
Model 4a (p = sample frequency)	−0.0034	−2.79
	(0.00122)	
Model 4b (p = age polynomial)	−0.0038	−3.28
	(0.00116)	
Model 4c (p = full regression)	−0.0032	−2.84
	(0.00114)	

Source: Author's calculations based on GSOEP working panel of men, 1984–96.
Notes: Standard errors in parentheses. See text for explanation of variants.

Table 9.2 presents the full results. A positive coefficient indicates that the corresponding explanatory variable increases the probability of retirement. In addition to the option value, health, and an array of socioeconomic variables, we include a full set of age dummies to nonparametrically capture all other unmeasured effects on the retirement decision that are systematically related to age, such as social customs. The reference category is age sixty-five.

Prediction success rates are high and vary from 88.7 to 89.3. This fit compares favorably to the baseline probability of 67.9 percent of retirees in our working sample. Except for the difference among the option value coefficients, all other coefficient estimates are fairly close to each across the six specifications.

The other economic incentives for retirement, namely the wealth variables, are only partially significant. The GSOEP data do not contain levels of wealth and provide only indicators of whether certain portfolio components—firm pension, life insurance, stock and bonds, and real estate—are present. There are many missing values, here coded as "not present." In general, presence of financial and real wealth decreases the retirement probability. This is not especially plausible for the presence of a firm pension. However, significant firm pensions are rare in Germany and usually indicate more highly valued jobs in which retirement may occur later for reasons not related to the firm pension per se.

The pattern of age dummies reflects the obvious: Older workers are more likely retired than younger ones. It is important to measure the option value with the age dummies included in order to purge its estimated

Table 9.2   **Logit Model of the Retirement Decision (parameters)**

Variable	Model 1 (generous variant)	Model 2 (tough variant)	Model 3 (endogenous variant)	Probabilistic Variants		
				Model 4a (p = sample frequency)	Model 4b (p = age polynomial)	Model 4c (p = full regression)
Option value	0.0053 (4.63)	−0.0046 (−4.72)	−0.0096 (−12.02)	−0.0034 (−2.79)	−0.0038 (−3.28)	−0.0032 (−2.84)
Health	−0.1781 (−9.83)	−0.1803 (−9.96)	−0.1512 (−8.23)	−0.1813 (−10.02)	−0.1810 (−10.01)	−0.1804 (−9.98)
Female	0.0995 (1.10)	0.0434 (0.46)	0.0277 (0.33)	0.1553 (1.72)	0.1416 (1.58)	0.1711 (1.94)
Married	−0.0404 (−0.41)	−0.0394 (−0.40)	−0.0461 (−0.47)	−0.0358 (−0.36)	−0.0376 (−0.38)	−0.0437 (−0.44)
Education	−0.6230 (−4.73)	−0.6166 (−4.60)	−0.5811 (−4.23)	−0.6303 (−4.74)	−0.6295 (−4.72)	−0.6199 (−4.65)
Civil servant	0.4733 (3.29)	0.4988 (3.38)	0.4860 (3.22)	0.4691 (3.23)	0.4719 (3.24)	0.4493 (3.11)
Firm pension	−2.7015 (−10.15)	−2.7712 (−10.31)	−2.7925 (−10.33)	−2.7551 (−10.29)	−2.7604 (−10.31)	−2.7516 (−10.29)
Life insurance	−0.0997 (−1.27)	−0.1104 (−1.40)	−0.1496 (−1.88)	−0.1166 (−1.48)	−0.1154 (−1.47)	−0.1178 (−1.50)
Stocks/bonds	0.0280 (0.30)	0.0089 (0.09)	0.0135 (0.14)	−0.0018 (−0.02)	−0.0007 (−0.01)	−0.0014 (−0.02)
Real estate	−0.8257 (−7.55)	−0.8019 (−7.33)	−0.8212 (−7.43)	−0.7984 (−7.31)	−0.7993 (−7.32)	−0.7961 (−7.29)
Owner occupation	0.3148 (3.76)	0.3214 (3.84)	0.3423 (4.04)	0.3126 (3.74)	0.3138 (3.75)	0.3102 (3.71)

	(1)	(2)	(3)	(4)	(5)	(6)
Age ≤ 59	-5.2324	-4.6547	-4.3121	-4.9478	-4.8577	-4.9335
	(-29.33)	(-21.32)	(-22.86)	(-23.17)	(-22.30)	(-23.00)
Age = 60	-3.4990	-3.2143	-3.0945	-3.3805	-3.3655	-3.4124
	(-17.93)	(-15.51)	(-15.60)	(-16.45)	(-16.52)	(-16.90)
Age = 61	-1.8945	-1.6760	-1.5080	-1.8075	-1.8030	-1.8392
	(-10.67)	(-8.99)	(-8.33)	(-9.76)	(-9.84)	(-10.11)
Age = 62	-1.4035	-1.2739	-1.1792	-1.3567	-1.3548	-1.3793
	(-7.79)	(-6.93)	(-6.51)	(-7.38)	(-7.42)	(-7.57)
Age = 63	-1.0178	-1.1048	-1.1363	-1.1024	-1.1059	-1.1015
	(-5.48)	(-5.98)	(-6.15)	(-5.96)	(-5.98)	(-5.96)
Age = 64	-0.2414	-0.3323	-0.3682	-0.3248	-0.3287	-0.3238
	(-1.20)	(-1.66)	(-1.84)	(-1.62)	(-1.64)	(-1.62)
Age = 66	1.4228	1.3819	1.3616	1.3876	1.3860	1.3875
	(4.36)	(4.24)	(4.18)	(4.26)	(4.25)	(4.26)
Age = 67	0.9167	0.7985	0.7402	0.8107	0.8063	0.8116
	(3.15)	(2.75)	(2.55)	(2.79)	(2.77)	(2.79)
Age ≥ 68	1.0680	1.0241	1.0025	1.0325	1.0308	1.0326
	(4.27)	(4.10)	(4.01)	(4.13)	(4.12)	(4.13)
Constant	3.1187	2.9654	2.7042	2.9713	2.9662	2.9718
	(14.27)	(13.67)	(12.41)	(13.67)	(13.65)	(13.67)
Log-likelihood	-2,338.1	-2,336.1	-2,271.1	-2,343.6	-2,342.1	-2,343.5
N	8,577	8,577	8,577	8,577	8,577	8,577

Source: See table 9.1.

Notes: Dependent variable is dummy variable "retired." Log-likelihood value at zero is 5,954.1. Numbers in parentheses are t-statistics.

coefficient from all other noneconomic effects. The omission of age dummies roughly triples the estimated coefficient of the option value. Quite noticeable is the lack of spikes in the pattern of age dummies. In this sense, retirement behavior is correctly described by the option value, the main economic incentive for retirement.

Most other sociodemographic variables are not significant. The important differences between social security regulations for women and men (women can retire at age sixty if they have at least fifteen years of retirement insurance history, whereas men need thirty-five years to retire at age sixty-three, unless they claim disability) appears to be fully captured by the option value. Marital status and education is also insignificant. I did not do full justice to the retirement subsystem for civil servants. They are actually treated as if they were part of the standard social security system, which is not really the case. Civil servants are required to work longer than other employees, with a fairly rigid retirement age at sixty-five, although claims to disability are frequent, as is early retirement due to the downsizing of the civil service sector. I find an expected negative coefficient, indicating later retirement for civil servants.

One may be suspicious that a simple logit model biases results because it ignores the panel nature of the working sample. I therefore employ a panel Probit model that permits a combination of random effects and serial correlation. This model follows Börsch-Supan (2000), where all necessary econometric details are presented. It is estimated by numerical simulation methods (see Börsch-Supan and Hajivassiliou 1993). The model can be interpreted as a semi-nonparametric hazard model for multiple-spell data, permitting unobserved heterogeneity and state dependence. It is nonparametric in the sense that the model does not impose a functional form on the duration in a given state. Fairly flexible hazard rate models of retirement have been estimated by Sueyoshi (1989) and Meghir and Whitehouse (1997), although not in combination with an option value describing the incentives to retire. Parametric hazard rate models for German data have been estimated by Schmidt (1995) and Börsch-Supan and Schmidt (1996).

I estimate three models, using the probabilistic version of the option value based on the full regression (specification 4c in tables 9.1 and 9.2). Model 1 has independently and identically distributed (i.i.d.) errors and corresponds to the logit model of the last three columns of table 2. Note that Probit coefficient estimates are smaller by the square root of $\pi/6$ (which is 0.7797) than their logit counterparts. Model 2 corrects for unobserved heterogeneity by a random effect whose standard deviation is reported at the bottom of table 9. 3. Finally, Model 3 adds an autoregressive error component to Model 2. Estimation results are presented in table 9.3.

Although even the simple i.i.d. model fits the data well (the pseudo-R^2— one minus the ratio of the likelihood at the estimated parameters over the

Table 9.3   **Multiperiod Probit Model of the Retirement Decision**

Variable	Model 1 (i.i.d.)		Model 2 (RAN)		Model 3 (RAN + AR1)	
	Parameter	t-statistic	Parameter	t-statistic	Parameter	t-statistic
Option value	−0.0028	−3.38	−0.0110	−6.04	−0.0115	−6.81
Health	−0.1349	−9.97	−0.1029	−3.68	−0.0865	−3.26
Female	0.0745	1.11	−0.0678	−0.31	−0.1195	−0.59
Married	−0.0177	−0.23	−0.0153	−0.07	−0.0449	−0.36
Education	−0.4115	−3.96	−0.6257	−2.00	−0.6020	−1.88
Civil servant	0.3536	3.16	1.0587	3.04	1.0337	2.95
Firm pension	−2.0030	−10.93	−2.3893	−8.14	−2.2043	−7.95
Life insurance	−0.0969	−1.62	−0.2577	−2.00	−0.2123	−1.72
Stocks/bonds	−0.0028	−0.04	−0.1340	−0.86	−0.1286	−0.89
Real estate	−0.6298	−7.42	−0.9597	−5.04	−0.8639	−4.76
Owner occupation	0.2175	3.42	−0.1036	−0.55	−0.1138	−0.64
Age ≤ 59	−3.8816	−24.81	−7.6382	−21.01	−7.2894	−24.02
Age = 60	−2.8372	−18.24	−5.6820	−18.00	−5.4844	−20.32
Age = 61	−1.5157	−10.58	−3.1143	−12.13	−2.9953	−12.70
Age = 62	−1.1331	−7.85	−2.2996	−9.46	−2.2247	−9.79
Age = 63	−0.8955	−6.10	−2.0115	−8.44	−1.9826	−9.05

(*continued*)

Table 9.3 (continued)

Variable	Model 1 (i.i.d.)		Model 2 (RAN)		Model 3 (RAN + AR1)	
	Parameter	t-statistic	Parameter	t-statistic	Parameter	t-statistic
Age = 64	−0.2588	−1.66	−0.4417	−1.84	−0.4516	−2.06
Age = 66	0.9843	4.46	1.9338	5.68	1.8089	5.82
Age = 67	0.5858	2.83	1.3707	4.16	1.3116	4.29
Age ≥ 68	0.7606	4.24	1.8981	6.35	1.8450	6.36
Constant	2.3834	14.46	3.9641	10.87	3.7499	13.94
RAN			2.8358	19.85	2.8356	13.58
AR1					0.6093	10.66
Log-likelihood	−2,350.03		−1,808.39		−1,778.35	
Individuals	8,577		1,610		1,610	
Maximum periods	1		13		13	
N	8,577		8,577		8,577	

Source: See table 9.1.

Notes: Dependent variable is the dummy variable "retired." Log-likelihood value at zero parameter values is 5,954.1. All estimates based on twenty replications in simulated maximum likelihood estimator.

likelihood at zero—is 60.5 percent), introducing random effects increases the log-likelihood significantly: The pseudo-R^2 increases to 69.7 percent. The additional inclusion of an autoregressive component is also statistically significant: The pseudo-R^2 now rises to 70.1 percent). The prediction success is about 89 percent for all three models, the same as for the logit models.

My most important results relate to the coefficients of the option value. Taking account of the intertemporal correlations in the panel appears to be very important. The numerical value of the option value coefficient is severely underestimated in the i.i.d. model. With random effects (capturing individual specific unobserved variables) and an autoregressive error (capturing the declining influence of such shocks as illness), the coefficient estimate of the option value quadruples and is estimated much more precisely. This also holds for the endogenous specification, although to a lesser extent (see Börsch-Supan, 2000).

There is little change in the other explanatory variables across disturbance specifications, with one important exception: the estimated coefficients of the health variable, which is coded 0 for "very poor" to 10 for "excellent." As expected, the coefficients are negative. Less-healthy workers retire earlier. In the i.i.d. model, health is more significant than the option value. However, as soon as unobserved population heterogeneity is accounted for, this changes, and the estimated coefficient becomes somewhat smaller. This shows the importance to account for intertemporal linkages. In the absence of random effects, health appears to capture unmeasured population heterogeneity that is taken out by the random effects to the extent that it is time invariant.

9.5 Conclusions

The main point of the paper was to account for uncertainty and potential endogeneity of the expected retirement income in models measuring the incentive effects of public pension rules on early retirement. We were able to bracket the coefficient estimates in an option value model by the two extremes (all are eligible for disability benefits; nobody is eligible for disability benefits). However, using the endogenous specification (all those are ex ante eligible for disability benefits who have ex post disability status) yields a badly upwardly-biased coefficient (i.e., it badly exaggerates the incentive effects of pension provisions). I employ an IV approach to correct for this endogeneity, using employment and human capital characteristics as instruments in a first-stage regression that generates a fitted probability for the pathway "disabled."

I then proceeded to a more complicated stochastic model that accounts for random effects (capturing individual-specific unobserved variables) and an autoregressive error (capturing the declining influence of such shocks as illness). Such a model can be interpreted as some convenient functional form to account for individual-specific deviations from the fitted expected retirement income as well, although the model is not structural because expected retirement income enters the option value in a complicated nonlinear fashion, due to the maximization over present discounted values. Our fullest specification yields a coefficient estimate of the option value that is quadrupled relative to the i.i.d. case. Moreover, it is estimated much more precisely than by the i.i.d. model.

I thus have corrected for two effects vis-à-vis conventional models. First, I corrected for the exaggerated option value coefficient due to uncertainty and endogeneity of expected retirement income. Second, I corrected for the underestimated option value coefficient in a model that disregards the panel nature of the data. By chance, the two effects roughly compensate each other in my working sample of German workers aged fifty-five to seventy.

What do the estimated magnitudes of the option value coefficients mean in practice? Using the full model in table 9.3, one can simulate a shift from the currently less than actuarially fair system of adjustment factors (see fig. 9.2) to an actuarially fair system. This change would shift the cumulative retirement distribution function down from what it is currently, as depicted in figure 9. 5. The effect is most dramatic for very early retirement, where the discrepancy between disability and normal retirement incentives are the largest (see fig. 9.4). The policy change would cause retirement at ages fifty-nine and below to drop from 28.6 percent to about 16.5 percent.

References

Benitez-Silva, H., M. Buchinsky, H. Chan, J. Rust, and S. Sheidvasser. 1998. An empirical analysis of the Social Security disability application, appeal, and awards process. Yale University, Department of Economics, mimeograph.

Börsch-Supan, A. 1992. Population aging, social security design, and early retirement. *Journal of Institutional and Theoretical Economics* 148:533–57.

———. 2000. Incentive effects of social security on labor force participation: Evidence in Germany and across Europe. *Journal of Public Economics* 78:25–49.

Börsch-Supan, A., and V. Hajivassiliou. 1993. Smooth unbiased multivariate probability simulators for limited dependent variable models. *Journal of Econometrics* 58:347–68.

Börsch-Supan, A., and P. Schmidt. 1996. Early retirement in East and West Germany. In *Employment policy in transition: The lessons of German integration for the labor market,* ed. R. T. Riphahn, D. Snower, and K. F. Zimmermann, 83–102. Berlin: Springer.

Börsch-Supan, A., and R. Schnabel. 1998. Social security and declining labor force participation in Germany. *American Economic Review* 88 (2): 173–78.

———. 1999. Social security and retirement in Germany. In *International social security comparisons,* ed. J. Gruber and D. A. Wise, 135–80. Chicago: University of Chicago Press.

Bound, J. 1989. The health and earnings of rejected disability insurance applicants. *American Economic Review* 79:482–503.

Burkhauser, R. 1991. An introduction to the German Socio-Economic Panel for English speaking researchers. Syracuse University, Maxwell School of Public Policy, working paper.

Jacobs, K., M. Kohli, and K. Rein. 1991. Germany: The diversity of pathways. In *Time for retirement: Comparative studies of early exit from the labor force,* ed. M. Kohli, M. Rein, A.-M. Guillemard, and H. van Gunsteren, 36–66. Cambridge: Cambridge University Press.

Lumsdaine, R. L., J. H. Stock, and D. A. Wise. 1992. Three models of retirement: Computational complexity versus predictive validity. In *Topics in the economics of aging,* ed. D. A. Wise, 16–60. Chicago: University of Chicago Press.

Meghir, C., and E. Whitehouse. 1997. Labour market transitions and retirement of men in the UK. *Journal of Econometrics* 79:327–54.

Parsons, D. 1991. The health and earnings of rejected disability insurance applicants: Comment. *American Economic Review* 81:1419–26.

Rust, J. 1990. Behavior of male workers at the end of the life cycle: An empirical analysis of states and controls. In *Issues in the economics of aging,* ed. D. A. Wise, 317–82. Chicago: University of Chicago Press.

Rust, J., and C. Phelan. 1997. How Social Security and Medicare affect retirement behavior in a world of incomplete markets. *Econometrica* 65 (4): 781–831.

Schmidt, P. 1995. *Die Wahl des Rentenalters: Theoretische und empirische Analyse des Rentenzugangsverhaltens in West- und Ostdeutschland* (The choice of retirement age: A theoretical and empirical analysis of the entry into retirement in West and East Germany).

Stock, J. H., and D. A. Wise. 1990. The pension inducement to retire: An option value analysis. In *Issues in the economics of aging,* ed. D. A. Wise, 205–30. Chicago: University of Chicago Press.

Sueyoshi, G. T. 1989. Social Security and the determinants of full and partial retirement: A competing risk analysis. NBER Working Paper no. 3113. Cambridge, Mass.: National Bureau of Economic Research.

Verband deutscher Rentenversicherungsträger (VdR). 1997. *Die Rentenversicherung in Zeitreihen* (The public pension system in time series). Frankfurt am Main: VdR.

Comment   Daniel McFadden

Working within the NBER framework for analysis of retirement behavior established by David Wise and various coauthors (see Hausman and Wise 1985, Stock and Wise 1990, and Lumsdaine, Stock, and Wise 1994), Börsch-Supan's paper addresses the problems presented when there are

Daniel McFadden is the E. Morris Cox Professor of Economics and director of the econometrics laboratory at the University of California, Berkeley, a 2000 Nobel Laureate in Economics, and a research associate of the National Bureau of Economic Research.

multiple paths to retirement. The setting is the German social security system, where early retirement options based on disability are an important alternative to normal retirement. This is an outstanding paper that identifies an important errors-in-variables issue in estimating option value models for retirement behavior when ex ante option values are latent. Börsch-Supan demonstrates a practical, statistically satisfactory method for dealing with this problem, and uses it to show that appropriate handling can make a big difference in the inferences one draws about the effectiveness of economic incentives in modifying retirement behavior.

The retirement decision is modeled as a series of binomial choices that depend in each year on the option value of remaining in the labor force. I have found it useful to start from a slight reformulation of the current paper's NBER model of the consumer's life-cycle planning problem. Suppose consumers are risk neutral with perfect intertemporal substitution of consumption, and discount the future at the market rate, so that their objective function from a planning age s is

$$(1) \qquad \sum_{t=s}^{\infty} C_t \cdot \pi(t \mid s) \cdot \delta^{t-s} \ - \ \sum_{t=s}^{R-1} L_t \cdot \pi(t \mid s) \cdot \delta^{t-s} \,,$$

where C_t is consumption at age t, L_t is the consumption opportunity cost of foregone leisure when working at age t, R is the retirement age, $\pi(t|s)$ is the probability of survival at age t conditioned on survival at age s, and δ is the market discount rate.[1] The expected value of this objective function will be maximized subject to the life-cycle budget constraint

$$(2) \qquad \sum_{t=s}^{\infty} C_t \cdot \pi(t \mid s) \cdot \delta^{t-s} \ = \ W_s \ + \ \sum_{t=s}^{R-1} \text{YLAB}_t \cdot (1 \ - \ c_t) \cdot \pi(t \mid s) \cdot \delta^{t-s}$$

$$+ \ \sum_{t=R}^{\infty} \text{YRET}_t(R) \cdot \pi(t \mid s) \cdot \delta^{t-s}$$

$$= \ \text{PW}_s(R) \ + \ \text{SSW}_s(R) \,,$$

where YLAB_t is labor income at age t if working, net of taxes other than social security tax, $\text{YRET}_t(R)$ is labor income at age t if retired at age R,

---

1. In the Stock-Wise formulation, the utility of consumption is weighted differently in work and retirement years. When hours are set institutionally for workers, rather than being chosen by optimization, this setup follows naturally from a Cobb-Douglas utility function of consumption and leisure. My reformulation follows from a utility function that is additive in consumption and a function of leisure. In the Stock-Wise formulation, intertemporal substitution of consumption through borrowing and lending is ignored, and current disposable income is fully consumed. This is a substantial simplification that, as an empirical matter, is not a bad approximation. On the other hand, private saving decisions are potentially quite important at the retirement timing margin. In my reformulation, private saving is permitted, but because of perfect intertemporal substitution of consumption, is essentially irrelevant to the retirement decision.

W_s is the value of assets (including the actuarial value of private pensions) at age s, c_t is the social security tax rate,

$$PW_s(R) = W_s + \sum_{t=s}^{R-1} YLAB_t \cdot \pi(t \mid s) \cdot \delta^{t-s}$$

is private wealth (the sum of current assets and the expected present value of future labor income), and

$$SSW_s(R) = -\sum_{t=s}^{R-1} c_t \cdot YLAB_t \cdot \pi(t \mid s) \cdot \delta^{t-s}$$

$$+ \sum_{t=R}^{\infty} YRET_t(R) \cdot \pi(t \mid s) \cdot \delta^{t-s}$$

is the expected net present value of social security benefits. Define

$$(3) \qquad PL_s(R) = \sum_{t=s}^{R-1} L_t \cdot \pi(t \mid s) \cdot \delta^{t-s},$$

the expected present value of the consumption opportunity cost of foregone leisure. Substituting the constraint into the objective function yields the result that R will be chosen to maximize the expected value of

$$(4) \qquad PW_s(R) + SSW_s(R) - PL_s(R).$$

The option value of postponing retirement at planning age s is

$$(5) \quad G_s = \max_R\{PW_s(R) + SSW_s(R) - PL_s(R)\}$$

$$- \{PW_s(s) + SSW_s(s) - PL_s(s)\}$$

$$= \max_R\{PW_s(R) - W_s + SSW_s(R) - SSW_s(s) - PL_s(R)\}$$

$$= \max_R\left\{\sum_{t=s}^{R-1} [YLAB_t - L_t] \cdot \pi(t \mid s) \cdot \delta^{t-s} + SSW_s(R) - SSW_s(s)\right\}.$$

Retirement occurs at the age R^* where G_s first turns negative. Let $H_s = \{SSW_s(R^*) - SSW_s(s)\}$; then H_s can be interpreted as the contribution of social security wealth to option value. Ordinarily one would expect $[YLAB_t - L_t]$ to be a monotonically declining function of age t over the relevant age range, as worker productivity reflected in $YLAB_t$ stabilizes or falls and the burden of working reflected in L_t rises. If this expression goes from positive to negative at an age R_N, then this is a "natural" retirement age in the absence of a social security system. If $H_s < 0$ for $s \le R_N$, the social security system creates an incentive to retire earlier than the natural age. A necessary condition for the consumer planning at age s to retire immediately is the one-year-ahead comparison

$$\text{PW}_s(s + 1) + \text{SSW}_s(s + 1) - \text{PL}_s(s + 1)$$

$$< \text{PW}_s(s) + \text{SSW}_s(s) - \text{PL}_s(s),$$

or

$$\text{YINC}_s \cdot [1 - \text{TAXR}_s(s + 1) < L_s,$$

where the implicit tax rate is

$$\text{TAXR}_s(s + 1) = \frac{[\text{SSW}_s(s) - \text{SSW}_s(s + 1)]}{\text{YINC}_s}.$$

A reduction in social security wealth when retirement is postponed, due to incomplete actuarial adjustment for delayed benefits, imposes an implicit tax rate on income that is a disincentive to continued work. This may be enough to trigger early retirement. It is the possibility of opportunities in the future, encoded in the option value, that prevents this condition's being necessary and sufficient; the option value may make postponing attractive even if a one-year delay is not. However, a sufficient condition for the consumer to postpone retirement is that this inequality be reversed.

To convert equation (5) to an econometric model, one could plausibly assume that the L_t are randomly distributed across individuals, with means that are functions of observed demographics. If, for example, the L_t contain additive independent Extreme Value I errors, then the binomial decision to retire now will be given by a mixed logit model, with mixing over any remaining random elements in the option values. This differs in some details from the models fitted in the paper, particularly the weighting of retirement versus wage income to account for the value of leisure, but it is essentially the same in its general approach. In particular, the mixing would permit consideration of unobserved effects that extend over a sequence of years, including individual random effects and serially correlated effects, and would provide one practical alternative to the multinomial probit analysis in the paper; see McFadden and Train (2000). The reformulated option value model makes it clear why the spectacular implicit tax rates in the German social security system, shown in Börsch-Supan's figures 9.3 and 9.4, provide a powerful incentive for early retirement.

Before turning to the issue of multiple retirement paths induced by the disability options in the German social security system, it is useful to make some general comments on the NBER formulation of the consumer's problem and the reformulation just given. First, the assumptions that the consumer is risk neutral, that consumption is perfectly substitutable between periods, and that the rate of substitution is the market discount rate times the one-year-ahead survival probability are all very special, and not necessarily realistic. Add the further assumptions that the uncertain future, conditioned on survival, can be expressed in terms of certainty equivalents, that current wealth and future income streams can be annuitized effectively into a consumption stream with the same present value, and that the consumer places no additional strategic value on new information that will be garnered if retirement is postponed. Then the retirement decision will be driven by the option value equation (5). The NBER formulation that flows from these assumptions is an analytically simple and empirically relevant approximation that provides a powerful tool for analyzing retirement behavior. It avoids the problems of a dynamic stochastic programming formulation of the life-cycle planning problem, which produces an analytic dog's breakfast. However, the assumptions listed above indicate that it has a cost in that it may miss critical interactions of saving behavior, consumption profiles, and retirement timing that can arise if intertemporal substitution is imperfect and risk aversion is significant. Furthermore, simple certainty-equivalence and independence assumptions may miss economically important interactions; for example, if uncertain retirement income is correlated with mortality risk because frail individuals are less productive and shorter lived, or because frail individuals are more likely to attain retirement paths based on disability or opt for retirement payout options that are front-loaded, then the relevant certainty-equivalent retirement income should be conditioned on individual frailty. These are already issues in the standard NBER retirement analysis, and even more so when disability-dependent retirement paths and attendant uncertain retirement income are introduced.

I turn finally to the substance of Börsch-Supan's paper, the innovative examination of the impact of multiple retirement paths induced by disability retirement possibilities in the German social security system. The relevant number for the consumer's decision is the ex ante option value of delaying retirement, taking into account the probabilities of various retirement path/retirement income alternatives. As the paper explains, if a consumer qualifies for a disability pension now or in the future, the option of early retirement may open, and the actuarial treatment of these pensions may operate to the consumer's benefit. This creates an incentive for the employee to game the system by feigning more incapacitating disabilities, possibly with the connivance of the employer if the productivity of the worker is below the legal or contractual wage level. As detective novels point out, murder is a matter of motive and opportunity. It appears that many German employees have the motive to qualify as excessively disabled; the question is how much opportunity the system provides, through lax or ambiguous standards for qualification. Börsch-Supan observes a natural experiment in which disability-qualified retirements dropped sharply following a 1972 reform that offered flexible retirement as an alternative. This could certainly have been the result of improper disability qualification before 1972; but a more benign alternative is that after 1972 the flexible retirement option was financially or administratively more attractive to individuals who might otherwise have legitimately qualified for a disability-based pension. If disability qualification is endogenous, influenced by worker productivity and commitments to work, the problem that this introduces for the economic analyst is that instead of having one-way causation from retirement income to the retirement decision, one has simultaneous determination of retirement and postretirement income.

The possibility of disability-based retirement introduces uncertainty into the option value calculation at several points. From the standpoint of the consumer, option values are uncertain because pension payments in future years will depend on whether the consumer would at those times qualify under a disability option. The paper does not spell it out, but there may also be uncertainty associated with application for a disability-qualified pension: What happens to the individual if an application is qualified at a different disability level than anticipated, or if the application is refused? Are there any downstream consequences to applying for a disability-based pension and not qualifying, such as more careful review of a subsequent application? An important econometric implication of uncertainty is that ex post observed retirement income is not the same as the ex ante certainty equivalent upon which option value–based retirement decisions are made. This can be cast as an errors-in-variables problem, with the nonlinearity of the retirement probability model precluding the simplest corrections for this problem.

The paper provides a practical solution to the errors-in-variables problem, carrying out careful reconstruction of an ex ante probabilistically weighted option value, with probabilities that are themselves estimated taking into account the reduced-form probability of being disabled. The paper also considers, for purposes of comparison, two extreme ex ante alternatives: the "tough" variant, in which no disability-based pensions are considered, and the "generous" variant, in which only disability-based pensions are considered. A final "endogenous" variant is close to an ex post representation of the option value, using the eventual classification of the individual as disabled to impute a retirement path.

It may be useful to comment on the relationship between these constructions and purely statistical methods of dealing with the nonlinear errors-in-variables problems. Abstracting from the model details, the binomial indicator r_s for retirement at age s, given no earlier retirement, has expectation $p(r_s|G_s^*)$, where G_s^* is the latent ex ante option value. The observed ex post option value G_s (which may be multidimensional) and G_s^* have a joint density $f(G_s, G_s^*|x_s)$ conditioned on exogenous variables x_s. The probability of r_s given x_s and G_s is then

$$P(r_s|G_s, x_s) = \frac{\int p(r_s|G_s^*) \cdot f(G_s, G_s^*|x_s) \cdot dG_s^*}{\int f(G_s, G_s^*|x_s) \cdot dG_s^*}.$$

If a functional form is specified for p and a parametric density for f, then the probability P can be formed analytically or numerically, and ordinary maximum likelihood estimation can be carried out using P. Alternately, one can assume that P is contained in a specified parametric family; under quite general conditions, there will exist f and p functions that are consistent with P. The approach of the paper follows the second alternative. This is just as legitimate as the first method, particularly given the lack of reliable a priori information on the forms of p and f. However, it becomes an interesting question whether the family of $\{f, p\}$ pairs that generate specified P functions are economically plausible.

The key findings of the paper are that the endogenous (or ex post) variant of the option value gives what appears to be a misleadingly large coefficient on the option value, and that the "generous" and "tough" variants introduce substantial bias. Three alternative methods are tested for construction of the probabilities in the probability-weighted option value; they all give similar results. The paper also finds significant individual random effects that appear in the sequence of decisions on retirement, and finds that ignoring these effects in applying the option value analysis leads to substantial underestimates of the coefficient on option value. The mechanism driving this result is that when individual random effects are strong, it is less likely that option values will by chance be large positive, and less likely that a decision to retire will be taken despite what appears to be a positive option value. The implication is that—unlike many discrete panel data applications in which quasi-maximum likelihood estimation ignoring serial correlation is consistent—this situation, in which the ex ante option value depends on the joint distribution of the disturbances, requires full consideration of the panel error structure to achieve consistency. While these comments suggest that there are opportunities for interesting research, I strongly endorse Börsch-Supan's main conclusion that it is important and practical to reconstruct an accurate probability-weighted option value when multiple retirement paths or pension qualifications introduce uncertainty.

References

Börsch-Supan, A., and R. Schnabel. 1998. Social Security and retirement in Germany. In *International Social Security Comparisons,* ed. J. Gruber and D. Wise, Chicago: University of Chicago Press.

Gruber, J., and D. Wise. Eds. 1999. *Social Security and retirement around the world.* Chicago: University of Chicago Press.

Hausman, J., and D. Wise. 1985. Social Security, health status, and retirement. In *Pensions, Labor, and Individual Choice,* ed. D. Wise, Chicago: University of Chicago Press.

Lumsdaine, R., J. Stock, and D. Wise. 1994. Pension plan provisions and retirement: Men and women, Medicare, and models. In *Studies in the Economics of Aging,* ed. D. Wise, Chicago: University of Chicago Press.

McFadden, D., and K. Train. 2000. Mixed MNL models for discrete response. *Journal of Applied Econometrics* 15:447–70.

Stock, J., and D. Wise. 1990a. Pensions, the option value of work, and retirement. *Econometrica* 58:1151–80.

———. 1990b. The pension inducement to retire: An option value analysis. In *Issues in the Economics of Aging,* ed. D. Wise, Chicago: University of Chicago Press.

10
Social Security Incentives for Retirement

Courtney Coile and Jonathan Gruber

One of the most striking labor force phenomena of the second half of the twentieth century has been the rapid decline in the labor force participation rate of older men. In 1950, for example, 81 percent of sixty-two-year-old men were in the labor force; by 1995, this figure had fallen to 51 percent, although it has rebounded slightly in the past few years (Quinn 1999). Declines have been seen for all groups of older men, as illustrated by figure 10.1. For women, these declines with age have been offset by an overall rising trend in labor force participation, as shown in figure 10.2.[1]

Much has been written about the proximate causes of this important trend among older men, and in particular about the role of the Social Security program. A large number of articles have documented pronounced spikes in retirement at ages sixty-two and sixty-five, which correspond to the early and normal retirement ages for Social Security, respectively. While there are some other explanations for a spike at age sixty-five, such as entitlement to health insurance under the Medicare program or rounding error in surveys, there is little reason to see a spike at sixty-two other than the Social Security program. Indeed, as Burtless and Moffitt (1984) document, this spike at age sixty-two emerged only after the early retirement eligibility age for men was introduced in 1961.

Courtney Coile is assistant professor of economics at Wellesley College and a faculty research fellow at the National Bureau of Economic Research. Jonathan Gruber is professor of economics at the Massachusetts Institute of Technology and a research associate and director of the program on children at the National Bureau of Economic Research.

This work builds on earlier joint research with Peter Diamond, and we are grateful to him for his continuing guidance throughout this project. We are also grateful to Dean Karlan for excellent research assistance, and to the National Institute on Aging for financial support.

1. Both figures are from Diamond and Gruber (1998).

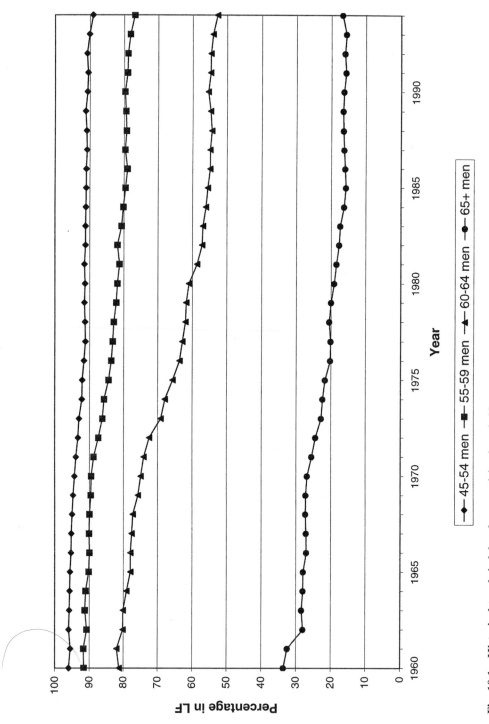

Fig. 10.1 Historical trends in labor force participation of older men
Source: Data from Bureau of Labor Statistics website (http://www.bls.gov)

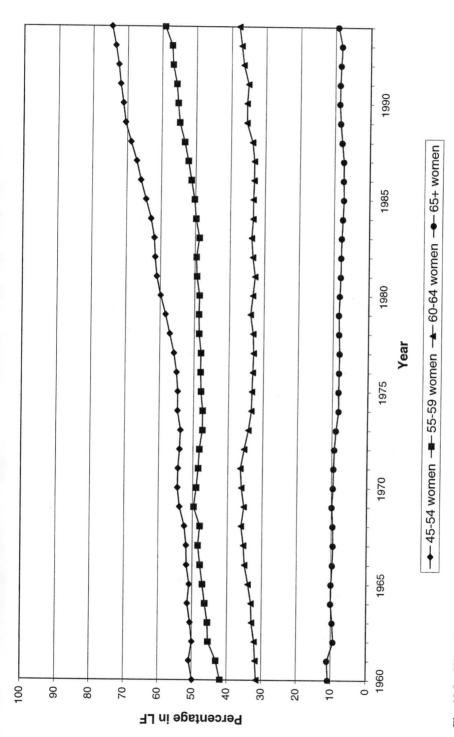

Fig. 10.2 Historical trends in labor force participation of older women
Source: See fig. 10.1.

The presence of these strong patterns in retirement data suggests that Social Security is playing a critical role in determining retirement decisions. But in order to model the impact of Social Security reform on retirement behavior, it is critical to understand what this role is. The evidence of spikes at age sixty-two, for example, is consistent with at least three alternative hypotheses. The first is that there is an actuarial unfairness built into the system penalizing work past age sixty-two, so that there is a tax effect that leads workers to leave at that age. The second is that workers are liquidity constrained; they would like to retire before age sixty-two, but cannot because they are unable to borrow against their Social Security benefits and have no other sources of retirement support. In this case, there will be a large exit at age sixty-two as benefits first become available. The third explanation is that workers are information constrained or myopic; they either do not understand or do not appreciate the actuarial incentives for additional work past age sixty-two, so they retire as soon as benefits become available.

The existing evidence would appear to refute the first explanation. Diamond and Gruber (1998) calculate for a typical individual the implicit tax on continued work at each age from the Social Security system and find that there is actually a small subsidy to continued work at age sixty-two. There is some supportive evidence for the second view; Kahn (1988) finds a pronounced spike in the retirement hazard at age sixty-two for those with low wealth, but that the much larger spike is at age sixty-five for those with higher wealth. There is little work on the third view, other than a recent careful exposition of the model by Diamond and Koszegi (1999).

This paper provides a more thorough investigation of the first effect, the tax effect, along four dimensions. First, we assess whether the tax rate Diamond and Gruber compute using a synthetic individual with annual earnings at the median of his cohort is similar to the tax rate of the real median person. We might expect a difference, as the shape of the earnings history is a significant determinant of Social Security incentives through the dropout-years provision, and this is not appropriately reflected with a synthetic earnings history. Second, we assess the *distribution* of retirement incentives across the population. Even if there is no significant disincentive for the typical worker, disincentives for a large subset of workers could still be associated with a spike in the aggregate retirement data. Third, we assess the importance of considering incentives for retirement in the next year versus incentives for retirement over all possible years, drawing on the insights of the option value model of Stock and Wise (1990a,b). Finally, we incorporate the role of private pensions, an important determinant of retirement for a large share of workers.

Our strategy is to apply the model of Diamond and Gruber to a set of real individuals, the older persons surveyed by the Health and Retirement Survey (HRS). This is a very rich survey with information on individual

Social Security earnings histories, private pension plan details, and demographics. These data allow us to compute carefully the incentives for retirement from Social Security and pensions, both for the median individual and across the distribution.

Our paper proceeds as follows. We begin, in section 10.1, with background on the relevant institutional features of the Social Security system and the previous literature in this area. In section 10.2 we describe our data and empirical strategy. Section 10.3 presents our basic results for the accrual of Social Security wealth with additional work and the associated tax/subsidy relative to potential earnings, both on average and across the distribution. Section 10.4 then highlights the fundamental weakness of simple one-year accrual measures of this type: Many Social Security wealth trajectories are nonmonotonic, suggesting that the appropriate measure must look across all years to find the optimal retirement date. We then present calculations for what we label "peak value," an incentive measure that provides a middle ground between accrual and the utility-based option value metric of Stock and Wise (1990a,b) by comparing retirement wealth at the current retirement date to retirement wealth at its global maximum. In this section, we also extend the results to incorporate private pensions. Section 10.5 concludes by discussing the implications of our findings and the directions for future research.

10.1 Background

10.1.1 Institutional Features of Social Security

The Social Security system is financed by a payroll tax that is levied equally on workers and firms. The total payroll tax paid by each party is 7.65 percentage points; 5.3 percentage points are devoted to the Old-Age and Survivors Insurance (OASI) program, with 0.9 percentage points funding the Disability Insurance (DI) system and 1.45 percentage points funding Medicare's Hospital Insurance (HI) program.[2] The payroll tax that funds OASI and DI is levied on earnings up to the taxable maximum, $72,600 in 1999; the HI tax is uncapped.

Individuals qualify for an OASI pension by working for forty quarters in covered employment, which now encompasses most sectors of the economy. Benefits are determined in several steps. The first step is computation of the worker's averaged indexed monthly earnings (AIME), which is one-twelfth the average of the worker's annual earnings in covered employment, indexed by a national wage index. A key feature of this process is

---

2. The total OASI + DI contribution rate has been 6.20 percent since 1990, although the division between the two parts has varied slightly from year to year; the OASI portion is 5.35 percent in 1999 and will be 5.30 percent starting in 2000.

that additional higher earnings years can replace earlier lower earnings years, since only the highest thirty-five years of earnings are used in the calculation (the "dropout year" provision).[3]

The next step of the benefits calculation is to convert the AIME into the primary insurance amount (PIA). This is done by applying a three-piece linear progressive schedule to an individual's average earnings, whereby ninety cents of the first dollar of earnings is converted to benefits, while only fifteen cents of the last dollar of earnings (up to the taxable maximum) is so converted. As a result, the rate at which Social Security replaces past earnings (the replacement rate) falls with the level of lifetime earnings. Although up to 85 percent of Social Security benefits are subject to tax for retirees with sufficiently high incomes (couples with non-Social Security income above $32,000 in 1999), all of earnings are taxed (including the employee portion of the payroll tax), raising the effective replacement rate of the program.

The final step is to adjust the PIA based on the age at which benefits are first claimed. For workers commencing benefit receipt at the normal retirement age (NRA; currently sixty-five, but legislated to increase slowly to age sixty-seven), the monthly benefit is the PIA. For workers claiming before the NRA, benefits are decreased by an actuarial reduction factor of five-ninths of one percent per month; thus, a worker claiming on his sixty-second birthday receives 80 percent of the PIA.[4] Individuals can also delay the receipt of benefits beyond the NRA and receive a delayed retirement credit (DRC). For workers reaching age sixty-five in 1999, an additional 5.5 percent is paid for each year of delay; this amount will steadily increase until it reaches 8 percent per year in 2008.

While a worker may claim as early as age sixty-two, receipt of Social Security benefits is conditioned on the earnings test until the worker reaches age seventy. A worker aged sixty-two to sixty-five may earn up to $9,600 in 1999 without the loss of any benefits; then benefits are reduced $1 for each $2 of earnings above this amount. For workers aged sixty-five to sixty-nine, the earnings test floor is $15,500 and benefits are reduced at a rate of $1 for each $3 in earnings. Months of benefits lost through the earnings test are treated as delayed receipt, entitling the worker to a DRC on the lost benefits when he or she does claim benefits. Despite this, the earnings test appears to have a pronounced effect on retirement decisions,

---

3. In particular, although earnings through age fifty-nine are converted to real dollars for averaging, earnings after age sixty are treated nominally. There is a two-year lag in availability of the wage index, calling for a base in the year in which the worker turns sixty in order to compute benefits for workers retiring at their sixty-second birthdays. Although it would be possible to make adjustments as data become available, this is not done. This gap would become important if we had large and varying inflation rates.

4. The reduction factor will be only five-twelfths of 1 percent for months beyond thirty-six months before the NRA, which will become relevant once the delay in NRA becomes effective.

with evidence of extreme piling-up of the earnings distribution among elderly workers at the earnings test limit (Friedberg 1998).

One of the most important features of Social Security is that it also provides benefits to dependents of covered workers. Spouses of Social Security beneficiaries receive a dependent spouse benefit equal to 50 percent of the worker's PIA, which is available once the worker has claimed benefits and the spouse has reached age sixty-two; however, the spouse receives only the larger of this and his or her own entitlement as a worker.[5] Dependent children are also each eligible for 50 percent of the PIA, but the total family benefit cannot exceed a maximum, which is roughly 175 percent of the PIA. Surviving spouses receive 100 percent of the PIA, beginning at age sixty, although there is an actuarial reduction for claiming benefits before age sixty-five or if the worker had an actuarial reduction. In practice, estimating a family's total benefits is complicated by the fact that both spouses may qualify for Social Security benefits as retired workers. Finally, benefit payments are adjusted for increases in the consumer price index (CPI) after the worker has reached age sixty-two; thus, Social Security provides a real annuity.

10.1.2 Previous Related Literature

There are two broad strands of the literature on Social Security that are related to this paper. The first strand attempts to document the labor force disincentives inherent in Social Security, or implicit Social Security "tax rates." Feldstein and Samwick (1992) model the tax rates on the marginal earnings decision for simulated workers of different ages, earnings, and marital status. They find that there are significant marginal tax rates on earnings for higher-income workers and secondary earners, and for younger workers as well.[6]

A subsequent paper by Diamond and Gruber (1998) focuses more directly on tax rates around the time of retirement. They build a simulation model similar to that used here and compute Social Security tax rates for simulated workers. As noted above, they find that for the median worker, there is little net incentive or disincentive for continued work at age sixty-two, although there is a sizeable positive tax rate at age sixty-five and beyond due to the unfair DRC still in place. They also find that tax rates are higher for single workers, because they do not benefit from dependent and survivors benefits, and that tax rates are initially lower for low earners (who benefit from the redistributive nature of benefits) but eventually higher (since they are penalized more by actuarial unfairness after age sixty-five).

---

5. Spousal benefits can begin earlier if there is a dependent child in the household; spousal benefits are also subject to actuarial reduction if receipt commences before the spouse's NRA.

6. Earlier work by Blinder, Gordon, and Wise (1980, 1981) and Burkhauser and Turner (1981) calculates tax rates under the pre-1977 Social Security rules.

While suggestive, both of these studies suffer from a key limitation: They do not consider the incentives facing real individuals. This is important because of the dropout year provision, which implies that the actual pattern of earnings, and not just the level of average or final earnings, matters for benefits determination. As we will show later, even for workers with the same average and final earnings, there is considerable heterogeneity in Social Security tax rates. By considering a real sample of individuals, we will be able to measure appropriately both the incentives for the median worker and the underlying heterogeneity in these incentives.

The second literature is that on the retirement effects of Social Security. A number of studies use aggregate information on the labor force behavior of workers at different ages, such as that documented in the introduction, to infer the role that is played by Social Security. Hurd (1990) and Ruhm (1995) emphasize the spike in the age pattern of retirement at age sixty-two; as Hurd (1990) states, "there are no other institutional or economic reasons for the peak" (597). Using precise quarterly data, Blau (1994) finds that almost one-fourth of the men remaining in the labor force at their sixty-fifth birthdays retire within the next three months; this hazard rate is more than 2.5 times as large as the rate in surrounding quarters. However, Lumsdaine and Wise (1994) document that this penalty alone cannot account for this excess retirement at age sixty-five, nor can the incentives embedded in private pension plans or the availability of retirement health insurance through the Medicare program. This does not rule out a role for Social Security; by setting up the focal point of a normal retirement age, the program may be the causal factor in explaining this spike.

The main body of the retirement-incentives literature attempts to model specifically the role that potential Social Security benefits play in determining retirement. The general strategy followed by this literature is to use microdata sets with information on potential Social Security benefit determinants (earnings histories) or ex post benefit levels to measure the incentives to retire across individuals in the data.[7] Then, retirement models are estimated as a function of these incentive measures. While the exact modeling technique differs substantially across papers,[8] the conclusions drawn are fairly similar: Social Security has large effects on retirement,

7. The data used are generally the Retirement History Survey (Boskin and Hurd 1978; Burtless 1986; Burtless and Moffitt 1984; Hurd and Boskin 1984; Fields and Mitchell 1984; Blau 1994), although some authors have relied on the National Longitudinal Survey of Older Men (Diamond and Hausman 1984), and recent work uses the Survey of Consumer Finances (Samwick 1998).

8. The earliest studies (Boskin and Hurd 1978; Fields and Mitchell 1984) used standard linear or nonlinear regression techniques. Later research (Burtless 1986; Burtless and Moffitt 1984) used nonlinear budget constraint estimation to capture the richness of Social Security's effects on the opportunity set. The most recent work (Diamond and Hausman 1984; Hausman and Wise 1985; Samwick 1998; Blau 1994) uses dynamic estimation of the retirement transition.

but the effects are small relative to the trends over time documented in figures 10.1 and 10.2. For example, Burtless (1986) found that the 20 percent benefit rise of the 1969–72 period raised the probability of retirement at sixty-two and sixty-five by about 2 percentage points. Over this period, however, the labor force participation of older men fell by more than 6 percent, so that Social Security can explain only about one-third of the change.[9]

This literature suffers from two important limitations. First, the key regressor, Social Security benefits, is a nonlinear function of past earnings, and retirement propensities are clearly correlated with past earnings levels. This problem is common to the social insurance literature in the United States.[10] For other social insurance programs, however, there is often variation along dimensions arguably exogenous to individual tastes, such as different legislative regimes across locations or within locations over time, that can be used to identify behavioral models. There is no comparable variation in Social Security, which is a nationally homogeneous program. Of course, this criticism does not necessarily imply that the estimates of this cross-sectional literature are flawed; as Hurd (1990) emphasizes, the nonlinearities in the Social Security benefits determination process are unlikely to be correlated with retirement propensities. However, there has been little serious effort to decompose the sources of variation in Social Security benefits in an effort to assess whether the determinants that drive retirement behavior are plausibly excluded from a retirement equation.[11]

This criticism is levied most compellingly by Krueger and Pischke (1992), who note that there is a unique "natural experiment" provided by the end of double-indexing for the "notch generation" that retired in the late 1970s and early 1980s. For this cohort, Social Security benefits were greatly reduced relative to what they would have expected based on the experience of the early to mid-1970s. Yet, the dramatic fall in labor force participation continued unabated in this era. This raises important questions about the identification of this cross-sectional literature.

The second problem with this literature is that it generally focuses on only one of the two key Social Security benefits variables, including Social Security benefits or wealth but ignoring the Social Security tax/subsidy

9. One exception is Hurd and Boskin (1984), who claim that the large benefits increases of the 1968–73 period can explain all of the change in labor force participation in those years.

10. See Meyer (1989) for a careful discussion of this issue in the context of Unemployment Insurance (UI).

11. At a minimum, one would want to include the level of lifetime earnings as a regressor, but most studies include only earnings in a recent year (i.e., Boskin and Hurd 1978; Burtless 1986). In addition, even using a somewhat longer time frame for measuring the earnings control (as do Diamond and Hausman 1984) does not solve the problem; one could imagine that certain features of the lifetime pattern of earnings are correlated with both benefit levels and retirement decisions, such as the ratio of earnings around age sixty-two to earnings at earlier ages (since individuals who have relatively high earnings at older ages may have better labor market opportunities around the age of retirement and may therefore work longer).

rate documented above. In theory, as discussed above, both of these factors play an important role in determining retirement behavior. Studies that include the tax/subsidy rate find it to have a significant role in explaining retirement (Fields and Mitchell 1984; Samwick 1998); indeed, even in Krueger and Pischke's (1992) paper the accrual rate is often right-signed and significant, even as the wealth effect is insignificant. More recently, Stock and Wise (1990a,b) note that the correct regressor for considering both Social Security and pension incentives for retirement is not the year-to-year accrual rate, but the return to working this year relative to retiring at some future optimal date.

Our findings are relevant to addressing both of these shortcomings. To the extent that we find substantial variation in the retirement incentives facing workers under the Social Security system, even after conditioning on correlates of the retirement decision such as earnings, it suggests that there are significant nonlinearities in the determination of Social Security incentives that can help identify retirement impacts. We will also compare the retirement incentives over the subsequent year with those over all future years, following the insights of Stock and Wise.

10.2   Data and Empirical Strategy

10.2.1   Data

Our data for this analysis comes from the Health and Retirement Study (HRS), a survey of individuals aged fifty-one to sixty-one in 1992 with reinterviews every two years. The first two waves of the survey (1992 and 1994) and preliminary data for the third and fourth waves (1996 and 1998) are available at this time. Spouses of respondents are also interviewed, so the total age range covered by the survey is much wider.

A key feature of the HRS is that it includes Social Security earnings histories back to 1951 for most respondents. This provides two advantages for our empirical work. First, it allows us appropriately to calculate benefit entitlements, which depend (through the dropout year provision) on the entire history of earnings.[12] Second, it allows us to construct a large sample of person-year observations by using the earnings histories to compute Social Security retirement incentives and labor force participation at each age. We use all person-year observations on men aged fifty-five to sixty-nine for our analysis, subject to the exclusions detailed below.

Our sample is selected conditional on working, so that we examine the incentives for retirement conditional on being in the labor force. Work is

---

12. Only earnings since 1950 are required to compute Social Security benefits for our sample's age range; the benefit rules specify that a shorter averaging period is used for persons born prior to 1929.

Table 10.1   **Sample for Analysis**

Category	Number of Obs		Obs Lost	
	Obs	Person-Year Obs	Obs	Person-Year Obs
Men in HRS aged 55–69, 1980–97	6,173	40,614	—	—
Drop if born before 1922	6,052	39,658	121	956
Drop if missing earnings history	4,305	29,110	1,747	10,548
Drop if not working	3,445	20,059	860	9,051
Drop if missing spouse's earnings history	3,231	18,903	214	1,156
Drop if reentered labor force	3,231	17,547	—	1,356

Note: Obs is the number of persons for which we have Health and Retirement Survey (HRS) data. Person-Year Obs is the number of person-year observations for which we have data. Each row in the first two columns shows the number of observations after the exclusion labeled in that row. Each row in the second two columns shows the number of observations lost through the exclusion labeled in that row.

defined in one of two ways. For those person-years before 1992, when we are using earnings histories, we define work as positive earnings in two consecutive years; if earnings are positive this year but zero the next, we consider the person to have retired this year. For person-years from 1992 onward, when we have the actual survey responses, we cannot use this earnings-based definition, since we have earnings at two year intervals only. For this era, we use information on self-reported retirement status and dates of retirement to construct annual retirement measures. Although these are somewhat different constructs, the retirement rates by age are similar across the two samples, so we combine them for precision purposes. We also consider individuals before their first retirement only; if a person who is categorized as retired reenters the labor force, the later observations are not used.

Our sample selection criteria are documented in table 10.1. There are 6,173 men who participate in one or more waves of the HRS. We exclude 121 men who were born before 1922 and thus are subject to different Social Security benefit rules. We lose an additional 1,747 men due to a lack of Social Security earnings history data.[13] We lose 860 men who ceased working prior to age fifty-five, and an additional 214 men due to a lack of information on their wives' Social Security earnings histories (necessary due to the family structure of benefits).[14] The 3,231 remaining observa-

13. Individuals were required to sign a permission form in order for their Social Security records to be attached; approximately 75 percent of the sample gave permission. Haider and Solon (1999) find that willingness to give permission varies only weakly with observable characteristics.
14. We keep observations for which the wife's Social Security earnings records are not available, but we can ascertain from the self-reported labor force histories that the wife worked less than half as many years as the husband.

tions are converted into 18,903 person-year observations by creating one observation for each year from 1980 through 1997 in which the individual is between the ages of fifty-five and sixty-nine and working. Finally, we lose 1,356 person-year observations where the individual is working after a previous retirement. The final sample size is 17,547 person-year observations.

10.2.2   Empirical Strategy

Our goal is to measure the retirement incentives inherent in Social Security and private pension systems. For the case of Social Security, we begin with the calculation of an individual's Social Security wealth. The basis for this calculation is a simulation model that we have developed to compute for any individual his or her Social Security entitlement for any age of retirement. This is based on a careful modeling of Social Security benefits rules, and our simulation model has been cross-checked against the Social Security Administration's ANYPIA model for accuracy.

The next step in our simulation is to take these monthly benefit entitlements and compute an expected net present discounted value of Social Security wealth. This requires projecting benefits out until workers reach age 120, and then taking a weighted sum that discounts future benefits by both the individual discount rate and the probability that the worker will live to a given future age. Our methodology for doing so is described in the appendix. For the worker himself, this is fairly straightforward; it is simply a sum of future benefits, discounted backward by time-preference rates and mortality rates. For dependent and survivor benefits it is more complicated, since we must account for the joint likelihood of survival of the worker and the dependent. In our base case, we use a real discount rate of 3 percent. To adjust for mortality prospects, we use the sex/age-specific U.S. lifetables from the 1995 OASDI Trustees Report (intermediate assumption case).[15] All figures are discounted back to age fifty-five by both time preference rates and mortality risk.

For the output of the simulations, we calculate several different concepts. The first is the level of Social Security wealth. The second is the accrual, or the dollar change in Social Security wealth from the previous year. We then compute the "after-tax accrual," which subtracts from this dollar change the payroll taxes paid by the worker and his employer (assuming full tax incidence on wages). Finally, since it is natural to think about these incentives relative to the returns from additional work, we also follow Diamond and Gruber (1998) in calculating the implicit tax/subsidy rate on additional work, which normalizes the negative of the accrual by the

---

15. In principle, individual-specific mortality prospects should be used to compute SSW and related retirement incentives. In future work, we plan to use the richer information in the HRS on health and even subjective mortality evaluation to do these richer calculations.

potential wage for that year; a positive accrual implies a negative tax rate and vice versa. Thus, if the tax rate is positive, it implies that the Social Security system causes a disincentive to additional work through foregone Social Security wealth. To measure the full tax wedge, we use the gross wage in the denominator; under the assumption that the employer portion of payroll taxes is reflected in wages, we increase reported wages by 6.2 percent.

For assessing the accrual rate and related concepts used later in the paper, we must project the worker's earnings over the next year (or all future years) if he continues to work. We considered a number of different projection methodologies, and found that the best predictive performance was from a model that simply grew earnings from the last observation by 1 percent real growth per year, so this is the assumption we use for our simulations.

For the purposes of the simulations below, we assume that workers claim Social Security benefits at the point of retirement, or when they become eligible if they retire before the point of eligibility. In fact, this is not necessarily true; retirement and claiming are two distinct events, and for certain values of mortality prospects and discount rates it is optimal to delay claiming until some time after retirement (due to the actuarial adjustment of benefits). Coile et al. (2001) investigate this issue in some detail, using simulation analysis to document the gains to delaying claiming and showing that a nontrivial share of individuals do delay claiming past age sixty-two. In this case, our calculations will overstate any subsidies to continued work, since part of this subsidy will come from delayed claiming that could be obtained without delaying retirement.

Also, it is important to highlight that our work is focused on the impact of Social Security on the labor force participation decision. A separate and interesting issue is the impact of Social Security on the marginal labor supply decision among those participating in the labor force, which was the focus of the Feldstein and Samwick (1992) analysis. This is more complicated for those around retirement age, since it involves incorporating the role of the earnings test, which we avoid with our analysis of participation. This, in turn, would involve modeling expectations about the earnings test, since individuals appear not to understand that this is only a benefits delay instead of a benefits cut. This is clearly a fruitful avenue for further research.

10.3   Social Security Accruals and Tax/Subsidies

10.3.1   Median Worker

We begin by considering the incentives facing the median worker at each age. These results are presented in table 10.2. Each row represents

Table 10.2   **Accrual and Tax Rate, Medians by Age**

Age	Obs	SSW	Benefit Accrual	After-Tax Accrual	Tax/Subsidy Rate	Diamond-Gruber Tax Rate
55	2,811	154,928	2,277	−933	0.047	−0.022
56	2,746	157,205	2,136	−1,136	0.052	0.046
57	2,444	159,341	1,958	−1,314	0.057	0.060
58	2,131	161,299	1,791	−1,517	0.061	0.069
59	1,822	163,090	1,687	−1,781	0.067	0.072
60	1,547	164,777	1,563	−1,848	0.073	0.071
61	1,252	166,340	1,643	−1,848	0.073	0.064
62	1,010	167,983	3,855	−48	0.002	−0.028
63	688	171,838	4,019	46	−0.001	−0.005
64	443	175,857	2,849	−843	0.027	0.031
65	313	178,706	−902	−4,831	0.145	0.188
66	159	177,804	−2,074	−5,833	0.176	0.225
67	91	175,730	−2,908	−6,418	0.249	0.269
68	57	172,822	−4,190	−6,989	0.334	0.439
69	33	168,632	−4,043	−7,138	0.252	0.455

Notes: Each row reflects the incentives workers face for continued work that year (e.g., the Age-55 row is the incentive to delay retirement until age 56). SSW is the net present discounted value of Social Security wealth at the beginning of the year. Benefit accrual is the change in SSW that results from working that year. After-tax accrual is the benefit accrual net of Social Security taxes paid during the year. Tax rate is the negative of the after-tax accrual divided by annual earnings. Diamond-Gruber tax rate replicates results from table 1 in Diamond and Gruber (1999).

the incentives facing a worker whose last year of work is labeled in the first column; that is, the "Age 55" row represents the incentives facing a worker who decides to retire on his fifty-sixth birthday.[16] We show for each age the Social Security wealth, the accrual, the after-tax accrual, and tax/subsidy rate. In the final column, we show the tax/subsidy rate from Diamond and Gruber (1999), for comparison; their results are for a married male, which is appropriate since 90 percent of our sample is married.

We find that the median Social Security wealth for workers who retire on their fifty-fifth birthdays is $154,928. Social Security wealth grows steadily through age sixty-five, then declines. This is shown most clearly

16. The SSW value is calculated from the data for age fifty-five, and is then constrained to follow the pattern of accruals from age fifty-six onward. We do this because the actual median SSW at each age does not correspond to the accrual pattern. If we use the SSW of the person with the median accrual, the pattern of SSW is nonsensical (with large shifts from year to year), since that person is different at every year. If we use the median SSW across the sample in each year (picking the median SSW in our sample, and not the SSW of the median accrual person), the SSW rises substantially over all years, due to sample selection. Another alternative is to project retirement incentives up to age sixty-nine for the sample working at age fifty-five; doing so, we find that the median SSW follows the same pattern as accruals, and that the accrual and tax variables are very similar to what we report here.

in the next column, which presents the benefit accruals at each age. From ages fifty-five to sixty-one, these accruals are positive due to the dropout year provision; the median worker is increasing his Social Security wealth by replacing lower earnings years in his earnings average. These accruals then get much larger between ages sixty-two and sixty-four, due to the actuarial adjustment. That is, the fact that accruals are larger after age sixty-two suggests that the actuarial adjustment is more than fair for the median worker; the gain to delaying receipt outweighs the fact that benefits are received for fewer years. At age sixty-five and thereafter, however, there are negative accruals for working additional years because the delayed retirement credit is not sufficiently large to compensate workers fairly.

The next column amends the benefit accrual by incorporating the fact that the worker and his employer must pay payroll taxes for additional work. This reverses the signs on the accruals at ages fifty-five to sixty-one, which are now negative, as the small benefit of AIME recomputation is outweighed by paying 12.4 percent of wages in tax. However, at ages sixty-two to sixty-four, the larger benefit accruals approximately offset the taxes incurred through additional work, so that the after-tax accrual for the median person is near zero. The after-tax accrual then turns sharply negative from age sixty-five onward.

The next column converts these after-tax accruals into tax/subsidy rates by dividing by the gross wage. There are positive taxes on work from ages fifty-five to sixty-one, but these taxes are significantly lower than the statutory 12.4 percent payroll tax rate, due to the benefit of additional earnings through the dropout year provision. The tax rate is near zero for the median worker at ages sixty-two and sixty-three and is 2.7 percent at age sixty-four. From age sixty-five onward, the tax rate is positive and very large. By age sixty-eight, the tax rate exceeds 30 percent, it drops back down again at age sixty-nine, but the samples at these ages in the HRS are very small.

These results are very similar to those in Diamond and Gruber, in spite of several important differences in methodology. First, Diamond and Gruber use a smooth age-earnings profile, which underestimates the value of the dropout year provision for people with real earnings trajectories with more variance. Second, Diamond and Gruber take an individual aged fifty-five and simulate his incentives to work at each future age, while the current calculations potentially incorporate some selection effects by using only those individuals still working at each age. The most notable differences between the two sets of results are at age fifty-five, where Diamond and Gruber find a subsidy to work (by construction, their individual replaces a zero year of earnings with his fifty-fifth year of work), and at age sixty-two, where Diamond and Gruber find a subsidy of 2.8 percent and we find a zero tax rate. The bottom line is very similar, however: Small taxes on work up through age sixty-one, tax rates near zero at ages sixty-two to sixty-four, and more sizeable taxes after age sixty-five. Thus, we reaffirm the important conclusion of previous studies that the Social Security system does not place a significant tax on work at age sixty-two for the median worker.

10.3.2   Heterogeneity

As emphasized earlier, the incentives facing the median worker may mask considerable heterogeneity across the population in retirement incentives. Substantial heterogeneity may in turn be associated with an increase in retirement rates at age sixty-two, even if the incentives are small for the median worker. If, for example, there are large tax rates on work for 50 percent of the population, then there may be a zero tax rate for the median worker, but still potentially a large amount of retirement at age sixty-two.

We explore the heterogeneity in incentives in table 10.3, which shows the distribution of after-tax accruals and of tax/subsidy rates by age. As is immediately apparent, there is a substantial amount of heterogeneity in the accruals and tax rates. For example, from age fifty-five to sixty-one, while the median tax rate is positive and nontrivial, roughly one-sixth of the sample actually has a subsidy to additional work. At age sixty-two, while there is a zero tax rate for the median worker, 10 percent of the sample faces a tax rate of 6.8 percent or higher, and the standard deviation of the tax rate is 17.8 percent. After age sixty-five, while virtually all of the sample faces positive tax rates, there remains substantial variation in the magnitude of the tax rate; at age sixty-five, the standard deviation is nearly twice as large as the median tax rate.

What explains this substantial heterogeneity in Social Security incentives? This is an important question both for understanding how Social Security incentives work and for considering the validity of empirical work which relies on Social Security incentives to identify retirement behavior. As highlighted by Krueger and Pischke's (1992) criticism of the previous literature, if the vast majority of the variation in these incentives comes from factors such as wages or marital status, which are themselves likely to be independently correlated with retirement decisions, we might worry that incentive measures are capturing these other aspects of retirement decisions. If, however, as suggested by Hurd's (1990) rebuttal to this line of criticism, there are significant nonlinearities and interactions otherwise (likely) uncorrelated with retirement that primarily identify the impact of these incentive measures, one might feel more confident about retirement estimates.

We next turn to regression modeling of Social Security accruals and tax/subsidy rates to address this question. We consider in turn various potential determinants of the variation in incentives:

Table 10.3   **Heterogeneity in Accrual and Tax Rate**

	After-Tax Accrual			Tax/Subsidy Rate			
Age	10th Percentile	90th Percentile	Standard Deviation	10th Percentile	90th Percentile	Standard Deviation	Percent with Tax < 0
55	−3,977	92	2,553	−0.003	0.090	0.059	0.175
56	−4,100	154	3,416	−0.006	0.093	0.073	0.176
57	−4,205	178	3,492	−0.008	0.098	0.081	0.152
58	−4,342	212	2,778	−0.010	0.103	0.069	0.144
59	−4,476	212	3,458	−0.012	0.109	0.076	0.135
60	−4,478	272	4,005	−0.014	0.116	0.073	0.140
61	−4,365	340	4,971	−0.017	0.113	0.076	0.150
62	−1,592	2,291	2,945	−0.139	0.068	0.178	0.493
63	−1,657	2,490	2,888	−0.156	0.089	0.172	0.515
64	−2,497	1,628	1,985	−0.110	0.117	0.161	0.336
65	−7,462	−882	4,196	0.044	0.556	0.268	0.058
66	−8,365	−1,591	3,073	0.093	0.771	0.290	0.050
67	−8,627	−1,321	11,069	0.117	1.000	0.386	0.055
68	−9,391	−2,010	3,397	0.117	1.000	0.351	0.053
69	−9,878	−278	3,630	0.117	1.000	0.360	0.061

Notes: This table shows the 10th and 90th percentiles and the standard deviations of the distribution of after-tax accruals and tax rates, as well as (in the last column) the percent of the sample with negative tax rates. For a description of the incentive variables, see notes to table 10.2.

- *Age.* As shown earlier, there is important variation in tax rates with age.
- *Earnings in the last year of work.* This is the denominator of the tax rate, and will also enter through the dropout year provision. This may, as a result, have both linear and nonlinear effects, so we try both a linear earnings term and an earnings quartic.
- *AIME.* Average lifetime earnings is the primary determinant of benefits. Once again, the effects will be nonlinear, through the redistributive function that determines the PIA.
- *Marital status and age difference with spouse.* Marital status will be an important determinant of tax rates through the dependent benefits structure. In addition, the larger the positive age difference between spouses (a larger number of years by which the husband is older), the larger the value of the dependent spouse and survivor benefits.
- *Earnings in lowest year.* In combination with earnings in the last year, earnings in the lowest year will determine the value of the dropout year provision. We also include the number of years in the thirty-five-year earnings history with earnings below current earnings.

The results of this exercise are shown in table 10.4. We find that the explanatory power on the accrual is much more substantial than on the tax/subsidy rate, which is not surprising since the tax/subsidy rate introduces additional variation simply by normalizing by the wage. Thus, we focus on the accrual in our discussion.

Our overall conclusion is that, although these factors have some ability

Table 10.4   Variance Decomposition, Accrual, and Tax/Subsidy Rate

	After-Tax Accrual		Tax/Subsidy Rate	
Variable	R^2 of Variable	Cumulative R^2	R^2 of Variable	Cumulative R^2
Age dummies	0.062	—	0.044	—
Earnings	0.087	0.155	0.000	0.045
Earnings quartic	0.092	0.158	0.000	0.045
AIME	0.156	0.230	0.012	0.059
AIME quartic	0.171	0.238	0.015	0.064
Earn * AIME quartic	0.198	0.266	0.039	0.081
Married, agediff	0.002	0.270	0.001	0.082
Spouse earn * AIME^4	0.169	0.280	0.033	0.110
Low earn year	0.074	0.284	0.010	0.110

Notes: The second and fourth columns of the table show the R^2 from regressions of the after-tax accrual or tax/subsidy rate on the variable in the first column; the third and fifth columns show the cumulative R^2 from including that variable and all previous variables in the regression. Low earn year includes earning in lowest year and number of years with earnings below current years. For a description of the incentive variables, see notes to table 10.2.

to explain accrual patterns, the overall explanatory power is small. Factors clearly (potentially) correlated with tastes for retirement such as age, current earnings, and lifetime earnings, even when the former is entered as a series of dummies and the latter as flexible cubic functions, explains less than 25 percent of the variation in accruals. Even if we include a full set of interactions of these cubic functions of earnings and AIME, we explain only 27 percent of the variation. Adding marital status, age difference with spouse, spouse's earnings, and the low earnings year explains only another 2 percent of variation. Thus there appears to be a substantial amount of variation in the accrual that is not explained by factors that would plausibly otherwise be correlated with retirement.

10.4   Peak Value Calculations

10.4.1   Motivation

The results thus far have focused on one-year accruals of Social Security wealth and the associated tax/subsidy rates on an additional year of work. As noted above, a key insight of Stock and Wise (1988) in the private pension context is that one-year forward measures of this type may be misleading if there are substantial incentives or disincentives for retirement in future years. This was a natural concern in the context of private pensions, which often have dramatic and explicit retirement incentives at certain ages, such as the plan's early and normal retirement ages. However, is this an important issue in the context of Social Security?

In fact, the critical importance of considering the entire future path of incentives is illustrated in figure 10.3. This figure shows the most common patterns of after-tax Social Security wealth evolution (including payroll taxes paid for additional work) across our sample. In each figure, we graph for a group of workers the pattern of Social Security wealth evolution over all future years; this is done for the full cross-sectional sample, comparable to table 10.2, in which each worker contributes an observation for up to fourteen years. Each observation is then the pattern of Social Security wealth from that year forward, based on that year's characteristics. Under each graph is a figure for the percentage of our full cross-sectional sample that is in each case, and the cumulative share across the cases. For example, as shown in Pattern 1, 1 percent of the sample has an Social Security wealth that is everywhere increasing, while Pattern 3 shows that 14 percent of the sample has an Social Security wealth that first rises, then falls. In each case, the length of each segment is defined by the median starting and ending ages of the segment, and the slope of the segment is determined by the median Social Security wealth at the beginning and end of the segment.

As these graphs illustrate, substantial nonmonotonicities of the type

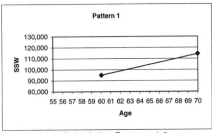

Percent=1.0, Cumulative Percent=1.0

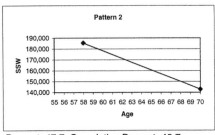

Percent=47.7, Cumulative Percent=48.7

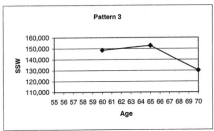

Percent=13.6, Cumulative Percent=62.3

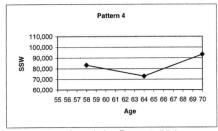

Percent=1.8, Cumulative Percent=64.1

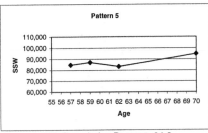

Percent=0.2, Cumulative Percent=64.3

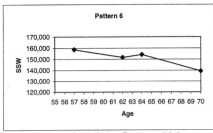

Percent=29.0, Cumulative Percent=93.3

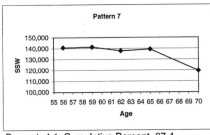

Percent=4.1, Cumulative Percent=97.4

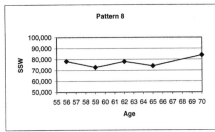

Percent=0.3, Cumulative Percent=97.8

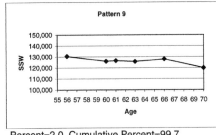

Percent=2.0, Cumulative Percent=99.7

Fig. 10.3   After-tax Social Security Wealth Patterns

seen for private pensions also exist for Social Security. For 38 percent of our sample, there is a local maximum that is not a global maximum. The most common data pattern (Pattern 2), which applies to 48 percent of the sample, is one in which after-tax Social Security wealth is always declining. However, the second most common pattern (Pattern 6), which applies to 29 percent of the sample, is one in which after-tax Social Security wealth declines from fifty-five to sixty-one, rises from sixty-two to sixty-four, then falls.

This is a striking finding, because it highlights an important weakness of the accrual measure. For any given year from age fifty-five to sixty-one, a typical worker will be lose money on net through the Social Security system by working. However, by working, that worker is also *buying an option* on the more than fair actuarial adjustment that exists from age sixty-two to sixty-four. Incorporating this option, as shown in Pattern 6, leads to the conclusion that there may overall be net subsidies to work before age sixty-two for many workers through the Social Security system.

10.4.2   Peak Value

To incorporate this feature into our incentive calculations, we move away from the accrual and tax/subsidy rates to a more forward looking measure of incentives, which we call "peak value." This is the value of continuing to work until the future year when Social Security wealth is maximized, or the difference between the expected present discounted value (PDV) of Social Security wealth at its highest possible value in the future and the expected PDV of Social Security wealth if one retires this year. This is thus like the typical accrual concept, except that the individual looks forward to the optimal year, rather than only to next year. If the individual is at an age beyond the Social Security wealth optimum, then the peak value is the difference between retirement this year and next year, which is exactly the accrual rate. Once again, it is natural to think about this type of concept relative to potential earnings, but here what is relevant is the entire stream of earnings until the optimal Social Security wealth is reached. That is, if the optimum is $5,000 higher than Social Security wealth today and is one year away, then this is a larger subsidy to continuing to work than if the optimum were higher by the same amount but is five years away. We therefore normalize this peak value by the expected PDV of wages over the period between this year and the year of maximal Social Security wealth. Thus, this concept captures the benefits of continuing to work toward the peak Social Security wealth year, relative to earnings over that period.

We show our peak value calculations in table 10.5. On a pretax basis, peak value is $22,426 at age fifty-five and falls steadily, becoming negative at age sixty-five. For the median worker, post-tax peak value is negative at all ages except for ages sixty-two to sixty-three. However, 30–40 percent of workers have positive after-tax peak values at ages fifty-five to sixty-

Table 10.5   **Peak Value, Medians by Age**

Age	Obs	SSW	Peak Value, Pretax	Peak Value, After-Tax	Percent with After-Tax PV > 0
55	2,811	154,928	22,426	−820	0.307
56	2,746	157,205	20,477	−1,018	0.292
57	2,444	159,341	18,339	−1,213	0.275
58	2,131	161,299	16,395	−1,399	0.282
59	1,822	163,090	15,228	−1,675	0.288
60	1,547	164,777	13,500	−1,701	0.326
61	1,252	166,340	12,245	−1,694	0.380
62	1,010	167,983	10,812	192	0.525
63	688	171,838	7,652	170	0.538
64	443	175,857	3,280	−758	0.359
65	313	178,706	−864	−4,808	0.077
66	159	177,804	−1,984	−5,799	0.069
67	91	175,730	−2,908	−6,418	0.066
68	57	172,822	−4,190	−6,989	0.053
69	33	168,632	−4,043	−7,138	0.061

Notes: PV is peak value, which is the change in SSW (Social Security wealth) that results from working until the age at which SSW is maximized (if peak has passed, PV is the after-tax accrual). Peak Value, Pretax excludes Social Security payroll taxes; Peak Value, After-Tax is net of taxes.

one. For these workers, the option value of a more than fair actuarial adjustment after age sixty-two outweighs payroll tax payments before age sixty-two. As a result, Social Security is actually providing a subsidy to additional work throughout all ages from fifty-five to sixty-four. This subsidy is rather small relative to earnings; the median after-tax peak value for those with positive value is about $3,000. After age sixty-five, there is a negative return to additional work for the vast majority of workers.

Thus, viewed from a year-to-year perspective, the Social Security system taxes work between ages fifty-five and sixty-one at a modest rate for more than 80 percent of workers; but, viewed from a more forward-looking perspective, there are actually modest subsidies at those ages for 30–40 percent of workers because workers are buying the option of delaying claiming at a more than actuarially fair rate. Of course, this conclusion is somewhat overstated, for two reasons. First, as noted above, exercising the option to delay claiming does not require additional work, but simply delayed claiming. Second, for an individual who was planning to retire and claim at sixty-two for other reasons, there is no option value from delayed claiming. Thus, whether peak value is the relevant concept for actual retirement decisions at this age is an empirical question, and one we plan to explore in further work. The fact remains, however, that this option exists and is not recognized by the accrual concept.

It is worth noting an apparent inconsistency between table 10.2 and

Table 10.6   **Accrual and Peak Value for Sample Observation**

Age	Benefit Accrual	After-Tax Accrual	Tax/Subsidy Rate	Peak Value, Pretax	Peak Value, After-Tax
55	2,120	−1,388	0.046	19,170	−1,388
56	2,093	−1,218	0.041	17,050	−1,218
57	2,029	−1,159	0.039	14,957	−1,159
58	1,730	−1,360	0.046	12,928	−1,360
59	1,018	−1,996	0.066	11,198	−1,996
60	674	−2,287	0.074	10,180	−2,287
61	781	−2,077	0.066	9,505	−2,077
62	2,863	110	−0.003	8,725	274
63	2,817	164	−0.005	5,862	164
64	1,747	−804	0.025	3,045	−804
65	999	−1,451	0.045	1,297	−1,451
66	298	−2,052	0.063	298	−2,052
67	−368	−2,621	0.080	−368	−2,621
68	−960	−3,116	0.094	−960	−3,116
69	−1,480	−3,540	0.112	−1,480	−3,540

Notes: Table shows the incentives for one sample observation. For a description of the incentive variables, see notes to tables 10.2 and 10.5.

table 10.5. As should be obvious, the peak value at any given age is just the sum of all future accruals to the year when Social Security wealth is maximized. Yet the sum of the benefit accruals from age fifty-five forward in table 10.2 is not equal to the age-fifty-five pretax peak value from table 10.5. The reason for this apparent inconsistency is simply composition effects; the median individuals at each age and across the two tables are different. There is no clear way to address this in the aggregate while still representing the median values for our incentive variables of interest.

Instead, we illustrate that this is not a problem at the individual level in table 10.6, where we show these concepts for a typical individual in our data, who was fifty-five years old in 1992 and who has roughly the median earnings of his age cohort in our data. For this individual, the sum of the benefit accruals from any given age forward to the peak of Social Security wealth (age sixty-six) does equal the pretax peak value at that age. That is, at age fifty-five, the peak value pretax is $19,170, which is the sum of the pre-tax accruals from age fifty-five through age sixty-six. Thus, for a typical individual in our data, we see that there is no inconsistency across these concepts; it arises only when we try to compare sample medians across the concepts.

10.4.3   Heterogeneity

As with after-tax accruals, there is a substantial amount of heterogeneity in after-tax peak values, as illustrated in table 10.7. At age sixty-two, for example, the median after-tax peak value is $192. However, at that age,

Table 10.7   **Heterogeneity in Peak Value**

| | Peak Value, After-Tax | | | |
Age	10th Percentile	90th Percentile	Standard Deviation	Percent with PV > 0
55	−3,936	3,441	8,027	0.307
56	−4,081	4,095	8,384	0.292
57	−4,171	4,808	8,019	0.275
58	−4,310	5,221	8,260	0.282
59	−4,443	5,587	8,803	0.288
60	−4,441	6,589	9,435	0.326
61	−4,338	6,690	9,400	0.380
62	−1,515	6,299	7,852	0.525
63	−1,484	4,628	7,527	0.538
64	−2,428	2,023	5,684	0.359
65	−7,462	−215	7,943	0.077
66	−8,365	−994	10,680	0.069
67	−8,627	−1,200	12,274	0.066
68	−9,391	−2,010	3,849	0.053
69	−9,878	−278	3,630	0.061

Notes: PV is peak value. For a description of the incentive variables, see notes to table 10.5.

48 percent of the sample has peak values that are less than zero, the 90th percentile value is $6,299, and the standard deviation is $7,852, nearly thirty times the median.

The variation in peak values is more readily explained by the other factors that might naturally be included in a retirement model, as is shown in table 10.8. For the after-tax peak value, the inclusion of flexible functions of age, earnings, and AIME can explain about half of the variation; adding marital status, spousal characteristics, and lowest earnings year can explain another 3 percent. Still, a substantial share of the variation in peak value remains unexplained, suggesting that there is useful identifying variation available for inclusion in a retirement model.

10.4.4   Incorporating Private Pensions

We can also incorporate private pension incentives into our analysis. The HRS collected detailed pension-determination information from employers for roughly 60 percent of the individuals with pensions in the sample.[17] They then used this information to create a pension benefits calculator that is comparable to the PIA simulation model we developed for Social Security. We use these calculated pension benefits at each retire-

---

17. Conversations with HRS staff indicate the HRS did not attempt to collect pension information for people in firms with fewer than 100 employees and that the nonresponse rate among employers they did contact was about 30 percent.

Table 10.8   **Variance Decomposition, Peak Value (full sample)**

	Peak Value, After-Tax	
Variable	R^2 of Variable	Cumulative R^2
Age dummies	0.014	—
Earnings	0.024	0.040
Earnings quartic	0.025	0.041
AIME	0.254	0.318
AIME quartic	0.297	0.350
Earn * AIME quartic	0.473	0.491
Married, agediff	0.006	0.497
Spouse earn * AIME^4	0.162	0.518
Low earn year	0.100	0.521

Notes: See notes to table 10.4 for description of table layout. Low earn year includes earnings in lowest year and number of years with earnings below current earnings. For a description of the incentive variables, see notes to table 10.5.

Table 10.9   **Peak Value Including Pensions, Medians by Age**

Age	Obs	SSW	Accrual After-Tax	Tax Rate	Peak Value, Pretax	Peak Value, After-Tax
55	2,811	183,138	−342	0.019	28,417	326
56	2,746	185,767	−381	0.018	25,843	197
57	2,444	188,380	−540	0.032	23,120	−61
58	2,131	190,675	−649	0.040	20,524	−18
59	1,822	192,781	−857	0.047	18,757	−90
60	1,547	194,637	−956	0.051	16,518	329
61	1,252	196,384	−1,003	0.053	14,341	1,143
62	1,010	198,149	672	−0.030	11,431	1,857
63	688	202,891	662	−0.025	7,949	863
64	443	208,312	−381	0.014	3,382	−172
65	313	212,733	−4,237	0.145	−774	−4,179
66	159	211,980	−5,384	0.189	−1,984	−5,369
67	91	210,024	−6,201	0.246	−3,538	−6,137
68	57	207,164	−6,916	0.344	−4,330	−6,916
69	33	203,236	−7,138	0.278	−4,452	−7,138

Notes: For a description of the incentive variables, see notes to tables 10.2 and 10.5. These results differ through the inclusion of pension incentives as well as Social Security program incentives.

ment age to create an analogous set of retirement incentive variables that include pensions.

The results of doing this for both of our incentive concepts (accrual and peak value) are presented in table 10.9. The patterns of incentives by age for the median worker are very similar to those shown in tables 10.2 and 10.5. This should not be surprising because only 40 percent of the individuals in our sample have pensions. Annual accruals are roughly $700 larger at ages fifty-five to sixty-four when pensions are included. The median tax/subsidy rate with pensions is roughly 2–3 percentage points lower at ages fifty-five to sixty-four than the median tax rate without pensions, and is similar at ages sixty-five to sixty-nine. With the inclusion of pension, the after-tax peak value is now often positive for the median person at ages fifty-five to sixty-four.

Table 10.10 shows the impact of including pensions on the distribution of the incentive measures. There is a substantial increase in the variation for all measures, particularly at ages fifty-five to sixty-one. For example, at age sixty, the ratio of the standard deviation to the median is close to 1 for the tax rate in the no-pensions case, but is higher than 3 in the with-pensions case. For the peak value measures, there are similarly large increases in heterogeneity, particularly at younger ages. Thus, adding pensions to the analysis does not dramatically change the incentives at the median, but does add substantial variation to the distribution of incentives.

10.5   Conclusions

The substantial time series decline in older male labor-force participation, as well as the striking correlation between the labor force departure rates of older workers and the early and normal retirement ages for Social Security, has motivated an enormous body of literature on how the Social Security program affects retirement. Yet there has been little recognition of a fundamental mystery in the relationship between Social Security incentives and retirement behavior: There is no evidence of a substantial disincentive to continued work at age sixty-two, despite the enormous increase in labor force exit at that age. This point was highlighted by Diamond and Gruber (1998), but this was based on a typical (simulated) individual.

In this paper, we have expanded on the earlier analysis in four ways. First, we have considered the impact of Social Security retirement incentives in real data, the HRS. We confirm in these data that there is, in fact, no tax on work at ages sixty-two to sixty-four at the median, further heightening the disconnect between observed retirement patterns and the pattern of Social Security retirement incentives. Second, however, we have shown that there is a substantial amount of heterogeneity in these incentives across our sample, and that (for example) there is a net tax on work at age sixty-two for about one-half of our sample. This would be more consistent with a spike in the hazard rate at that age, if it is those individuals being taxed who are responding by retiring. We also show that factors that otherwise might be expected naturally to impact retirement decisions can explain only a small share of the variation in accruals, suggesting that these are fruitful regressors for explaining retirement decisions.

Table 10.10   Heterogeneity in Peak Value and Accrual, Including Pensions

Age	Accrual, After-Tax			Tax Rate				Peak Value, After-Tax			
	10th Percentile	90th Percentile	Standard Deviation	10th Percentile	90th Percentile	Standard Deviation	Percent with Tax < 0	10th Percentile	90th Percentile	Standard Deviation	Percent with PV < 0
55	−3,700	6,213	12,980	−0.177	0.091	0.195	0.366	−3,511	73,702	63,294	0.454
56	−3,701	6,914	10,779	−0.191	0.093	0.181	0.381	−3,570	69,620	57,529	0.476
57	−3,954	6,506	11,202	−0.185	0.100	0.186	0.340	−3,739	58,252	50,959	0.505
58	−4,158	6,517	9,477	−0.182	0.109	0.194	0.334	−3,973	50,340	38,199	0.501
59	−4,436	6,054	11,703	−0.171	0.117	0.189	0.323	−4,251	41,994	34,032	0.504
60	−4,410	5,021	9,189	−0.147	0.117	0.177	0.312	−4,245	34,273	29,530	0.483
61	−4,373	5,339	9,833	−0.149	0.117	0.166	0.322	−4,210	30,574	27,320	0.446
62	−1,677	6,512	7,269	−0.283	0.081	0.216	0.615	−1,495	24,078	21,155	0.347
63	−2,085	5,669	7,410	−0.272	0.106	0.214	0.606	−1,815	17,647	19,821	0.362
64	−2,637	4,540	7,662	−0.188	0.123	0.211	0.447	−2,535	8,479	16,403	0.517
65	−7,762	657	9,306	−0.028	0.556	0.304	0.121	−7,702	1,949	14,390	0.853
66	−9,392	11	5,459	−0.003	0.771	0.308	0.101	−9,392	987	13,680	0.874
67	−9,039	358	11,588	−0.015	1.000	0.403	0.121	−9,039	1,590	14,935	0.857
68	−10,830	−485	11,266	0.067	1.000	0.396	0.053	−10,830	−485	11,267	0.947
69	−10,370	−278	4,407	0.109	1.000	0.358	0.061	−10,370	−278	4,407	0.939

Notes: PV is peak value. For a description of the incentive variables, see notes to tables 10.2 and 10.5. These results differ through the inclusion of pension incentives as well as Social Security program incentives.

Third, we have suggested that the focus on next-year measures such as accruals and tax/subsidy rates might be misleading, particularly at ages fifty-five to sixty-one, because they ignore the option value of reaching age sixty-two and taking advantage of a (for many workers) more than fair actuarial adjustment. Thus, we also have considered a peak-value concept that compares wealth accruals not between this year and the next, but instead between this year and the year in which Social Security wealth reaches its peak. We find that using peak values instead of accruals leads to very similar results at the median after age sixty-two, but to subsidies to work rather than to taxes at ages fifty-five to sixty-one for a large share of the sample. Finally, we incorporate private pensions into our analysis; we find that the addition of pensions increases the return to additional work modestly at the median and substantially increases heterogeneity in the measures.

Our findings have two important implications for future empirical work on Social Security and retirement. First, our results suggest that if researchers are careful to condition on the determinants of both retirement and Social Security incentive measures, there may be sufficient remaining variation to identify the impact of these measures on retirement decisions. Second, our results suggest that, even in a Social Security-only context, it is important to consider forward-looking measures of the type pioneered by Stock and Wise (1990a,b). In preliminary work on retirement decisions (Coile and Gruber 1999), we have found that these forward-looking measures are indeed an important determinant of retirement behavior, while there is a much weaker relationship between retirement and accruals.

Appendix

In this appendix, we provide the formula for the computation of Social Security wealth.

Notation

t = year of observation

R = year of retirement

T = last year either spouse could be alive (maximum age is 120)

$\text{pr}_{h,s|t}$ = probability husband is alive at time s conditional on being alive at time t

$\text{pr}_{w,s|t}$ = probability wife is alive at time s conditional on being alive at time t

d = real discount rate (.03 in base case)

$\text{age62}_{h,s}$ = indicator variable equal to 1 if husband is age sixty-two or over at time s

$age62_{w,s}$ = indicator variable equal to 1 if wife is age sixty-two or over at time s

$age60_{h,s}$ = indicator variable equal to 1 if husband is age sixty or over at time s

$age60_{w,s}$ = indicator variable equal to 1 if wife is age sixty or over at time s

$rwb_{h,s}$ = retired worker benefit of husband if husband retires at time s

$rwb_{w,62}$ = retired worker benefit of wife if wife retires at age sixty-two

$dsb_{h,62}$ = dependent spouse benefit of husband if wife retires at age sixty-two

$dsb_{w,s}$ = dependent spouse benefit of wife if husband retires at time s

$svb_{h,s}$ = survivor benefit of husband if wife dies at time s

$svb_{w,s}$ = survivor benefit of wife if husband dies at time s

s, k = simple counting variables

Formula

$$SSW_t(R) = \sum_{s=t}^{R-1}(1 + d)^{-(s-t)}\left[pr_{h,s|t} * pr_{w,s|t} * age62_{w,s} * rwb_{w,62} \right.$$

$$+ (1 - pr_{h,s|t}) * pr_{w,s|t} * age62_{w,s}$$

$$\left. * \max\left(rwb_{w,62}, \sum_{k=t}^{s-1} \frac{pr_{h,k|t} - pr_{h,(k+1)|t}}{pr_{h,t|t} - pr_{h,s|t}} svb_{w,k} \right) \right]$$

$$+ \sum_{s=R}^{T}(1 + d)^{-(s-t)}\left\langle pr_{h,s|t} * pr_{w,s|t} * \{age62_{h,s} * [rwb_{h,R} + age62_{w,s} \right.$$

$$* \max(0, dsb_{h,62} - rwb_{h,R})] + age62_{w,s} * [rwb_{w,62} + age62_{h,s}$$

$$* \max(0, dsb_{w,R} - rwb_{w,62})]\} + pr_{h,s|t} * (1 - pr_{w,s|t}) * age62_{h,s}$$

$$* \max\left(rwb_{h,R}, \sum_{k=t}^{s-1} \frac{pr_{w,k|t} - pr_{w,(k+t)|t}}{pr_{w,t|t} - pr_{w,s|t}} svb_{h,k} \right) + (1 - pr_{h,s|t}) * pr_{w,s|t}$$

$$\left. * age62_{w,s} * \max\left(rwb_{w,62}, \sum_{k=t}^{s-1} \frac{pr_{h,k|t} - pr_{h,(k+1)|t}}{pr_{h,t|t} - pr_{h,s|t}} svb_{w,k} \right) \right\rangle$$

An important assumption built into the calculation is that the spouse retires at age sixty-two.

The benefit variables (rwb, dsb, and svb) are adjusted appropriately for actuarial adjustment or delayed retirement credit. The adjustment depends on R, the birth year of each spouse (since Social Security rules differ by birth cohort), and age difference between the spouses. Where an individual first claims retired worker benefits and later tops them up to the level of the dependent spouse benefit, the appropriate actuarial adjustment is applied to each part of the total benefit.

Claiming is assumed to occur at first eligibility (the age of retirement or age sixty-two, whichever is later). For simplicity, survivor benefits are assumed to be claimed no earlier than age sixty-two, though individuals are allowed to claim them at age sixty, or earlier if there are dependent children.

The calculations including pensions are analogous, except that pension receipt commences as soon as the individual retires (not at age sixty-two).

References

Blau, David M. 1994. Labor force dynamics of older men. *Econometrica* 62 (1): 117–56.

Blinder, Alan S., Roger H. Gordon, and Donald E. Wise. 1981. Rhetoric and reality in Social Security—A rejoinder. *National Tax Journal* 34 (4): 473–78.

———. 1980. Reconsidering the work disincentive effects of Social Security. *National Tax Journal* 33 (4): 431–42.

Boskin, Michael J., and Michael D. Hurd. 1978. The effect of Social Security on early retirement. *Journal of Public Economics* 10 (3): 361–77.

Burkhauser, Richard V., and John Turner. 1981. Can twenty-five million Americans be wrong?—A response to Blinder, Gordon, and Wise. *National Tax Journal* 34 (4): 467–72.

Burtless, Gary. 1986. Social Security, unanticipated benefit increases, and the timing of retirement. *Review of Economic Studies* 53 (5): 781–805.

Burtless, Gary, and Robert Moffitt. 1984. The effect of Social Security benefits on the labor supply of the aged. In *Retirement and economic behavior,* ed. Henry J. Aaron and Gary T. Burtless, 135–75. Washington, D.C.: Brookings Institution.

Coile, Courtney, Peter Diamond, Jonathan Gruber, and Alain Jousten. (2001). Delays in claiming Social Security benefits. *Journal of Public Economics,* forthcoming.

Coile, Courtney, and Jonathan Gruber. 1999. Social Security and retirement. NBER Working Paper no. 7830. Cambridge, Mass.: National Bureau of Economic Research.

Diamond, Peter, and Jonathan Gruber. 1999. Social Security and retirement in the United States. In *Social Security and retirement around the world,* ed. Jonathan Gruber and David A. Wise, 437–73. Chicago: University of Chicago Press.

Diamond, Peter, and Jerry Hausman. 1984. Retirement and unemployment behavior of older men. In *Retirement and economic behavior,* ed. Henry J. Aaron and Gary T. Burtless, 97–135, Washington, D.C.: Brookings Institution.

Diamond, Peter, and Botond Koszegi. (1999). Quasi-hyperbolic discounting and retirement. MIT, Mimeograph.

Feldstein, Martin A., and Andrew A. Samwick. 1992. Social Security rules and marginal tax rates. *National Tax Journal* 45 (1): 1–22.

Fields, Gary S., and Olivia S. Mitchell. 1984. Economic determinants of the optimal retirement age: An empirical investigation. *Journal of Human Resources* 19 (2): 245–62.

Friedberg, Leora. (2000). The labor supply effects of the Social Security earnings test. *Review of Economics and Statistics* 82 (1): 48–63.

Haider, Steven, and Gary Solon. (1999). Nonrandom selection in the HRS Social

Security earnings sample. Unpublished paper, RAND and University of Michigan, Department of Economics.

Hausman, Jerry A., and David A. Wise. 1985. Social Security, health status, and retirement. In *Pensions, labor, and individual choice,* 159–91. ed. David A. Wise, Chicago: University of Chicago Press.

Hurd, Michael D. 1990. Research on the elderly: Economic status, retirement, and consumption and saving. *Journal of Economic Literature* 28 (2): 565–637.

Hurd, Michael D., and Michael J. Boskin. 1984. The effect of Social Security on retirement in the early 1970s. *Quarterly Journal of Economics* 99 (4): 767–90.

Kahn, James A. (1988). Social Security, liquidity, and early retirement. *Journal of Public Economics* 35 (1): 97–117.

Krueger, Alan B., and Jorn-Steffan Pischke. 1992. The effect of Social Security on labor supply: A cohort analysis of the notch generation. *Journal of Labor Economics* 10 (4): 412–37.

Lumsdaine, Robin, and David Wise. 1994. Aging and labor force participation: A review of trends and explanations. In *Aging in the United States and Japan: Economic Trends,* ed. Y. Noguchi and D. Wise, 7–41. Chicago: University of Chicago Press.

Meyer, Bruce D. 1989. A quasi-experimental approach to the effects of unemployment insurance. NBER Working Paper no. 3159. Cambridge, Mass.: National Bureau of Economic Research.

Quinn, Joseph. 1999. Retirement patterns and bridge jobs in the 1990s. Policy Brief for the Employee Benefit Research Institute. Washington, D.C.: EBRI.

Ruhm, Christopher. 1995. Secular changes in the work and retirement patterns of older men. *Journal of Human Resources* 30 (2): 362–85.

Samwick, Andrew A. 1998. New evidence on pensions, Social Security, and the timing of retirement. *Journal of Public Economics* 70 (2): 207–36.

Stock, James H., and David A. Wise. 1990a. Pensions, the option value of work, and retirement. *Econometrica* 58 (5): 1151–80.

———. 1990b. The pension inducement to retire: An option value analysis. In *Issues in the economics of aging,* ed. David A. Wise, 205–29. Chicago: University of Chicago Press.

Comment   Andrew A. Samwick

The Social Security program in the United States grew substantially in coverage and generosity during the postwar period. Motivated by the large, contemporaneous reductions in the labor force participation of older workers, a substantial literature emerged during the 1970s and 1980s on the effects of Social Security on the timing of retirement. Surveys of the literature can be found in Atkinson (1987) and Quinn, Burkhauser, and Myers (1990). Most studies estimate statistically significant relationships between the level of Social Security benefits and the likelihood of retirement at various ages. However, these estimated relationships typically im-

Andrew A. Samwick is a professor of economics at Dartmouth and a research associate of the National Bureau of Economic Research.

ply a small economic impact of altering Social Security benefits on the average age of retirement or probability of retirement.

This finding is rather surprising, and I believe that it is a consequence of examining retirement primarily in a cross-section. I doubt that it has convinced too many people that the differences in Social Security replacement rates between cohorts who turned sixty-five in 1950 and those who turned sixty-five in 1975 have nothing to do with the differences in the cohorts' respective retirement ages. The finding does tell us that, within a given cohort, workers who are observed to have different entitlements under Social Security are not observed to retire at dramatically different ages. Even without time-series implications, this is an interesting result that is worthy of continued study.

There are several possible explanations that can be explored as a response to this finding. The first is that investigators have made an inappropriate simplifying assumption regarding an important aspect of the retirement decision. For example, Gustman and Steinmeier (2000) and Coile (1999) have shown that retirement decisions of spouses should be modeled jointly, rather than independently, as is done in most of the literature. Another simplification is the separation of the household's intertemporal consumption problem from its retirement decisions. Although option value models have made important advances toward incorporating intertemporal tradeoffs in the labor market, they typically assume uniformity in the way households make those choices. Recent work on consumption has shown that household consumption choices are characterized by higher and more variable discount rates than are typically assumed in retirement analyses. I will return to this issue at the end of my comments.

A second explanation is that the primary determinant of cross-sectional retirement patterns is some other phenomenon, such as the incentives from employer-provided pensions. This is the motivation behind the original Stock and Wise (1990a, b) option value model and the many subsequent papers based on it. As documented in Kotlikoff and Wise (1987), defined benefit (DB) pension plans typically provide large financial incentives to delay or hasten retirement at various ages. These incentives vary substantially across plans. Further, DB plans also grew in coverage and generosity during the postwar period and, as shown in Luzadis and Mitchell (1991), the ages at which retirement incentives are strongest has been falling over time. The key ages for pensions are currently younger than the Social Security early retirement age.

A third explanation is the one pursued by the authors in this chapter. The thrust of their argument is that Social Security itself provides a variety of different incentives to workers with different earnings histories. In order to calculate these incentives, rich data on earnings histories are required. The failure to find an effect of Social Security on retirement may in fact be due to measurement problems. It would be tempting for a reader of the option value literature to date to conclude that Social Security incentives are not an important source of cross-sectional variation in retirement outcomes in the United States. The authors have done the literature on the incentive effects of retirement programs a great service in carefully measuring Social Security incentives. The main lesson the reader takes away from this chapter is that rumors of Social Security's irrelevance may have been greatly exaggerated.

Beginning with the seminal work of Stock and Wise (1990a, b), studies of the option value of retirement have utilized strong data on pensions and weak data on Social Security. These studies have also found that in comparison to incentives from pensions, Social Security incentives have little explanatory power for retirement decisions. Samwick (1998b) acknowledges the link between the poor quality of his Social Security data and the imprecision of the estimates of retirement incentive effects based on them. Note that Social Security calculations place a greater demand on the earnings data. Pension incentives depend only on the earnings history at the current employer and a forecast of future earnings with that same employer.[1] In addition to these earnings, Social Security incentives depend on earnings in years prior to those spent with the current employer, earnings at other jobs worked while with the current employer, and a forecast of earnings that may be received after the employee leaves the current employer but before claiming benefits.

The present chapter provides a basis for quantifying how important Social Security retirement incentives are when measured with as much attention to detail as the pension incentives in past option value studies. It is a tantalizing prelude to econometric analyses of retirement for male workers in Coile and Gruber (1999) and working couples in Coile (1999). My comments will therefore include some issues that are relevant to the authors' broader research agenda. In the present chapter, the authors make two arguments. The first is that careful calculation and rich data yield substantial heterogeneity in financial incentives to retire from Social Security. The second is that the authors' measure of "peak value" is a comprehensive and robust measure of incentives to hasten or delay retirement. My main remarks will assess the validity of these points and make suggestions for further research on the effect of financial incentives on retirement.

Heterogeneity in Social Security Retirement Incentives

The Health and Retirement Study (HRS) is ideally suited to examining the financial incentives inherent in the Social Security system. The initial HRS cross-section in 1992 is a nationally representative sample of households between the ages of fifty-one and sixty-one. Subsequent interview

---

1. However, as discussed below, pension calculations are far more susceptible to measurement error in the earnings histories.

waves are conducted every two years, and the authors have matched the household data to Social Security earnings histories. This allows them to calculate Social Security wealth at various ages and thereby estimate the financial incentives to retire at each age.

There are two characteristics of the data that must be demonstrated in order to suggest that they will be useful for further analyses of retirement behavior. The first is the heterogeneity in incentives, controlling for age. The results are presented in tables 10.2 and 10.3 for the one-year accrual of wealth and tables 10.5 and 10.7 for peak value. Median accruals are positive before age sixty-two, large and positive from age sixty-two to age sixty-four, and negative and declining at ages beyond sixty-five. Tables 10.3 and 10.7 suggest that there is variation in the magnitude of accruals by age around the medians, although I will argue below that this variation is small compared to the variation in incentives caused by pensions. Tables 10.4 and 10.8 give an indication that much of this variation in accruals is not simply the result of differences in the factors (e.g., age, earnings, and marital status) that help determine benefits but might also affect retirement directly.

The second characteristic is the nonmonotonic pattern of accruals as workers approach retirement. These patterns are shown in figure 10.3 for the authors' measure of After-Tax Social Security wealth. The results here are somewhat disappointing, in that nearly half, or 47.7 percent, have monotonically decreasing Social Security wealth as given by Pattern 2. Pattern 6 is the next most frequent pattern, with 29.0 percent of the sample. This pattern differs from Pattern 2 in that the negative accruals are interrupted by an interval of positive accruals. These positive accruals are fairly small and do not last very long, suggesting at least from the figure that they are not too important in dollar terms. Taken together, these two patterns—with little if any departure from a simple profile of declining Social Security wealth—account for more than three-fourths of the observations. As the authors note, in the absence of nonmonotonicities, it becomes more difficult to econometrically identify the effects of Social Security from other factors that may be increasing or decreasing with age.

It may be that the use of medians and piecewise-linear segments in figure 10.3 masks some important differences within the patterns. For example, there may be an important subset of workers who have very large positive accruals between ages sixty-two and sixty-five, despite the low median. It could also be that some of the workers in Pattern 2 look a lot like those in Patterns 3 and 7, and that some look like Patterns 4 and 10 (with flat segments instead of increases). The lack of variation indicated in this descriptive work and the "success" of the initial econometric estimations in Coile and Gruber (1999) and Coile (1999) present a bit of a puzzle. More explanation is warranted if the latter estimates are to be thought of as identified by Social Security wealth rather than as other factors that change monotonically for a given worker over time.

As a final note about the Social Security wealth calculations, it is worth emphasizing that the idea for calculating Social Security retirement incentives is not original to this chapter. The real novelty in this chapter is the data that are used, particularly the Social Security earnings histories. Because obtaining the earnings histories and working with them are not trivial processes, the authors could do a useful service in this chapter if they also calculated incentives using only the data on prior earnings available in the public use files of the HRS. Comparisons of the pattern of incentives with and without the earnings histories would help determine how useful the extra data are. What will users of the HRS miss if they do not use the detailed earnings histories?

Retirement Incentives from Pensions

The next interesting question to ask about the calculated Social Security incentives concerns their magnitude—are these numbers large or small? Since most of the recent research on the accrual of retirement wealth is based on option value models of pensions, a natural benchmark is the distribution of pension incentives. The authors make use of the Pension Provider Survey (PPS) that accompanied the first wave of the HRS. As implemented, the PPS includes detailed pension information on roughly 60 percent of the workers eligible for pensions.

The authors do not present analogous distributions of the incentives from pensions in the HRS.[2] However, they report distributions of peak value including pensions in tables 10.9 and 10.10. The effect of adding the pension data is substantial. Comparing median peak (pretax) values in tables 10.5 and 10.9, the inclusion of pensions adds about $6,000 at age fifty-five and $3,000 at age sixty. Tables 10.7 and 10.10 show that the most dramatic effects are (for this sample) at the higher retirement income levels. The standard deviation of peak after-tax value at age fifty-five increases from $8,027 to $63,294 when pensions are included, and the 90th percentile increases from $3,441 to $73,702. The inclusion of the pension data has a smaller effect at older ages, because most pensions have their early retirement ages (and therefore largest incentives) between the ages of fifty and sixty. Very few workers who have pensions are still working past age sixty-five.

To get an idea of the whole distribution of incentives, figure 10c.1 is a graphical representation of incentives from pensions, taken from Samwick (1998b). It shows the mean, 10th percentile, and 90th percentile of the one-year benefit accruals (see table 10.2, column 4) from the pensions in

2. See Gustman et al. (1999, 2000) for preliminary tabulations.

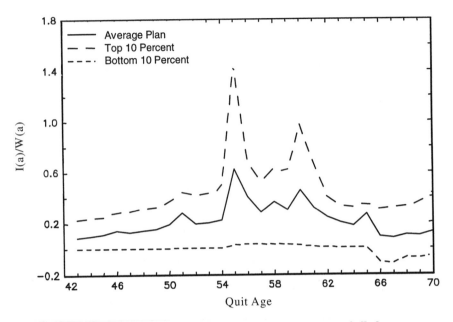

Fig. 10C.1   Pension accruals relative to wages, weighted average of all plans: Hired at age 31, average wage
Source: Samwick (1998b, fig. 2)

the PPS that accompanied the Survey of Consumer Finances (SCF) 1983. This distribution is for a worker with average earnings who started working for his current employer at age thirty-one. That worker's benefits under all pension plans in the sample are calculated and appropriately weighted to reflect the distribution of workers in those plans. The vertical axis shows the accrual as a share of current earnings. The graph shows that accruals due to pensions are many times larger than those from Social Security. The 90th percentiles at ages fifty-five and sixty are roughly 1.4 and 1.0 times earnings in those years. Even the mean accruals are close to 60 percent and 40 percent of current earnings at those ages.[3]

The main conclusion to be drawn from the pension results is that incentives from pensions will dwarf incentives from Social Security for workers who are covered by both. This is the general result found in Stock and Wise's (1990a) sample of salesmen covered by the same pension. This result strongly suggests that researchers should examine workers with pen-

---

3. It is not uncommon for pension plans to provide multiple spikes in a worker's accrual of pension wealth. Workers who start working for their employers at older ages typically have fewer and later (but larger) spikes in their accrual profiles.

sions separately from those without pensions. It would also be interesting to see how much the inclusion of pensions changes the optimal retirement date in the peak value formula (discussed below).

Regarding the specific calculations with pensions in this chapter, I have two primary concerns. The first is that, when the distributions with pensions are presented, only 60 percent of the pension-covered population is represented. And considering the way that observations get lost in moving from the HRS to the PPS, it seems clear that the subsample of pensions that are found will be disproportionately those from the government sector and large corporations. These employers typically are easier to locate, have better record keeping, and account for multiple respondents to the survey. This was certainly the case in the SCF 1983, which had about 70 percent of the observations with pensions in its PPS, and the authors note (see n. 17) that the same is true here. Thus, the subsample of the pension-covered population that is included in this PPS is more homogeneous than the excluded subsample, which includes many fewer observations per plan and hence more plans. Even the very large effects of pensions on the distribution shown in tables 10.9 and 10.10 are likely underestimates of the true contributions of pensions to heterogeneity in retirement incentives.

One possible remedy would be to control for this sample selection directly, perhaps by modeling it as a function of firm size, occupation, and industry. This would essentially re-weight the sample to increase the representation of the workers who are in the HRS and PPS with characteristics, such as working at a small firm, that are associated with being omitted from the PPS. In the absence of such a remedy, the variance decompositions of the sort presented in table 10.8 are likely to miss a lot of the variation in retirement incentives due to pensions.

My second concern is that pension calculations are extremely sensitive to the quality of the inputs, particularly age, tenure, and the details of the pension formulas themselves. The potential for coding errors is large, and although the Survey Research Center staff and other researchers have worked diligently to make the formulas error free, pension calculations must be checked for anomalous results in each application. It is a tedious but necessary process. For example, suppose that, either because the respondent reported a year of hire that was one year later than the actual starting year or the pension formula was miscoded in the PPS to have early retirement eligibility at an age one year too late. Consider a worker who paid a lot of attention to financial incentives and therefore stayed with the firm until the large spike in the accrual profile at early retirement, and then retired. We will observe this worker's retiring just before a large financial incentive to delay retirement, because we have gotten the timing of that accrual wrong by only one year. Note as well that the effect on a maximum likelihood estimation will be asymmetric—retiring one year after a large spike is not so different from retiring at the spike, but retiring one year before the large spike strongly suggests that financial incentives do not affect retirement.

The point is that fairly small errors in either the household or the pension survey can have potentially large effects on econometric analyses. Because the present chapter seeks only to present a distribution of incentives without estimating a behavioral effect, the problem is less severe. Some of the large accruals are probably off by a year or two in the calculations underlying tables 10.9 and 10.10; however, these sorts of errors may in large measure offset each other, unless tenure or age is systematically over- or underreported.

At this stage, I can only offer suggestions to minimize the exposure to these problems in subsequent work. An example is the way the authors have backcast pension formulas to the years prior to the initial survey (1992). Comparisons of pension formulas in the 1983 and 1989 SCF Pension Provider Surveys in Samwick (1993) and Gustman and Steinmeier (1998) show that pension formulas changed substantially during the 1980s. In particular, early retirement ages continued their downward trend, and the growing inequality in wages was also reflected in growing inequality in pension entitlements. Using the pension formula in 1992 to describe pension incentives during the 1980s is likely to expose the calculations to error. It is quite unlikely that the historical provisions of the plans are accurately represented in the summary plan description as of 1992. For example, do we see evidence of the temporary early retirement windows that were popular in the early 1980s and analyzed in Stock and Wise (1990b) in the current formulas?

Peak Value versus Option Value

The authors begin to make the case in this chapter, and follow it up in Coile and Gruber (1999), that their measure of peak value is a robust measure of retirement incentives. *Peak value* is defined as the maximum increment to the actuarial present value of future retirement benefits for any possible year of retirement. Like the option value on which it is based, it has the advantage of being forward-looking. It evaluates the financial gains to delaying retirement to the most advantageous year, not just the next year as in a typical retirement wealth accrual variable.[4] Peak value is also easily scaled by the present value of future wages until that date.

In fact, peak value is equivalent to the option value under a set of pa-

---

4. Peak value also shares with the option value the potential drawback that it is not a full dynamic programming model—it is calculated conditional on a given R^* and considers only the value of retiring in the best year. Lumsdaine, Stock, and Wise (1992) compare the option value model to a dynamic programming model that compares the value of retirement in the current year to the value of reevaluating all retirement possibilities next year. The distinction is shown not to be important in their work.

rameter restrictions. To see this, consider the original derivation of the option value from Stock and Wise (1990a). It begins with the indirect utility function

$$(1) \quad V_t(R) = \sum_{s=t}^{R-1} \beta^{s-t} \pi(s \mid t) E_t(y_s^\gamma) + \sum_{s=R}^{T} \beta^{s-t} \pi(s \mid t) E_t[k \cdot B_s(R)^\gamma].$$

In this expression, R denotes the date of retirement and t denotes the current date. The probability of living to year s conditional on being alive in year t is $\pi(s|t)$. The discount factor is denoted by β, and risk aversion (or intertemporal substitution) is measured by γ. The final parameter is k, which represents the additional value of receiving income during retirement rather than the working year. It is designed to capture the utility value of leisure and is expected to be greater than unity. In evaluating retirement possibilities, a worker would trade one dollar of income while working for k dollars during retirement. Income takes the form of earnings, y_s, during the remaining years of work or retirement benefits, $B_s(R)$, during retirement. Note that benefits are a function of the year in which retirement occurs.

Using this indirect utility function, the worker chooses the optimal date of retirement, R^*, as the one that maximizes $V_t(R)$. The option value of continued work is the excess of the indirect utility of retiring at R^* rather than the current date t. The option value is $V_t(R^*) - V_t(t)$, or

$$(2) \qquad OV_t(R^*) = \sum_{s=t}^{R^*-1} \beta^{s-t} \pi(s \mid t) E_t(y_s^\gamma)$$

$$+ \sum_{s=R^*}^{T} \beta^{s-t} \pi(s \mid t) E_t[k \cdot B_s(R^*)]$$

$$- \sum_{s=t}^{T} \beta^{s-t} \pi(s \mid t) E_t[k \cdot B_s(t)^\gamma].$$

The first two terms are $V_t(R^*)$, and the last term is $V_t(t)$. When retirement occurs at the current date, there are no terms reflecting the utility from additional years of labor income.

By comparison, the authors' peak value calculation is given by

$$(3) \qquad PKV_t(R^*) = \sum_{s=R^*}^{T} \beta^{s-t} \pi(s \mid t) E_t[B_s(R^*)]$$

$$- \sum_{s=t}^{T} \beta^{s-t} \pi(s \mid t) E_t[B_s(t)].$$

Peak value imposes three restrictions on the option value. The first restriction is that the first term in equation (2), pertaining to future earnings, is dropped. This restriction should be innocuous. Variance decompositions of the sort done in table 10.8 would show that earnings explain a larger fraction of option values than peak values, but this would not necessarily suggest that one measure is preferred to the other in a regression. The present value of earnings through the optimal retirement date can simply be included in the regression in addition to the option value or the peak value. For example, Samwick (1998b) finds that, controlling for the option value of retirement, earnings do not have a significant effect on retirement in most specifications. Additionally, this first term (with the subsequent two restrictions imposed) is the quantity that the authors use to scale peak value in the right-most columns of tables 10.5 through 10.8.

The second restriction is that k is equal to unity. In an option value calculation, this restriction implies that there is no disutility of working relative to being retired. In that context, such a restriction would be counterintuitive and is not supported by the estimates of about 1.6 from Stock and Wise (1990a, table 4). However, peak value compares income flows only during retirement, so this assumption is without loss of generality. Additionally, a value of k can be estimated in a simple regression as long as the first term from the option value calculation (the present value of future earnings) is included as a regressor along with peak value. The value of k would be the ratio of the coefficient on the peak value term to the coefficient on the earnings term.

The third restriction is that γ is equal to unity. Setting $\gamma = 1$ implies that workers are indifferent to whether income and retirement benefit payments vary across years. Values less than unity, such as the estimates of approximately 0.75 in Stock and Wise (1990a), are consistent with individuals who derive more utility from smooth income flows than from variable ones. In the option value calculation, the main variation in income across periods pertains to the retirement replacement rate. Since the peak value calculation pertains only to income received in retirement and both Social Security and DB pensions typically pay annuities, the choice of γ is much less critical in the peak value calculation. However, it would still be useful to experiment with different values of γ, applied to both peak value and the present value of earnings in a regression, in order to determine how sensitive empirical estimates are to the smoothness of income over time.

A more subtle difference between the two concepts is that the optimal retirement date, R^*, may change when the present value of future earnings is dropped from the option value to get peak value. Given the central role of the optimal retirement date, the authors should investigate the extent to which the two concepts yield different values of R^*. Doing so would require a more sophisticated procedure for forecasting future wages than simply assuming a 1 percent growth rate, as assumed here.

Parameter Selection and Heterogeneity

As discussed above, the main difference between the formulas for peak value and option value is whether the first term of the option value, representing the present value of future earnings until the optimal retirement date, is included in the calculation. Much of that difference can be eliminated in practice by simply including that first term as an additional explanatory variable in a reduced-form specification. Since future earnings are an appropriate variable in that regression anyway, the real issue with using peak value rather than the option value is whether the values of the parameters are estimated, as in Stock and Wise (1990a), or simply assumed, as in reduced-form approaches in Samwick (1998b) or Coile and Gruber (1999). This issue is relevant but perhaps not too important for the risk aversion and leisure parameters, γ and k.

The remaining parameter in both the option value and peak value calculations is the discount factor, β, in the formulas above. Mathematically, $\beta = 1/(1 + \delta)$, where δ is the discount rate or rate of time preference. The choice of discount rate is not a trivial matter in retirement analyses. Berkovec and Stern (1991) report that in their dynamic programming model, "the estimation algorithm would not converge" when they attempted to estimate the discount factor. They fixed it at 0.95. My own efforts to estimate option value models in Samwick (1998b) were similarly unsuccessful, as it was not possible to obtain reliable estimates for both the discount factor and the leisure parameter, k. As in this chapter, the value of β was set to correspond to a discount rate of 3 percent per year. Stock and Wise (1990a) estimate values for β of approximately 0.75 across several specifications.

Part of the explanation for Stock and Wises's estimate of such a high discount rate (nearly 33 percent per year) is that it is discounting utility rather than dollars. Another part of the explanation, however, is that discount rates may in fact be very large. The best evidence for this comes from wealth levels—even among households on the verge of retirement, median financial wealth corresponds to less than a year's worth of income. If discount rates were as low as 3 percent over the life cycle, then household wealth accumulation would be much larger than we observe for the median household (by perhaps a factor of 4 or 5, based on simulations in Samwick [1998a]). The median peak value of about $25,000 in table 10.5 would not be very large in comparison.

Other evidence on the magnitude of discount rates comes from the cross-sectional variation in wealth. Rates of time-preference as low as 3 percent are inconsistent with the observed sensitivities of household wealth to income uncertainty (Carroll and Samwick 1997) and to the retirement replacement rate (Samwick 1995). In both cases, the observed sensitivities are of the correct sign but are too low to be consistent with patient consumers. If households discounted the future at only 3 percent, then they would react more strongly to differences in income uncertainty and differences in the retirement replacement rate that imply very different possibilities for future resources.

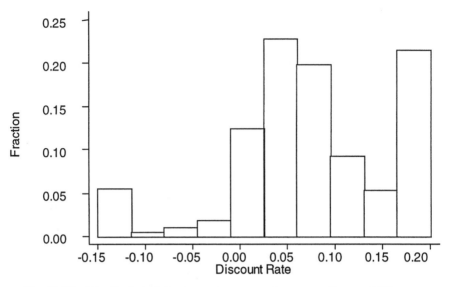

Fig. 10C.2   Distribution of discount rates, survey of consumer finances 1992
Source: Samwick (1998a, fig. 3)

Another characteristic of the distribution of wealth is its wide dispersion. Although many factors affect wealth accumulation, it seems hard to
believe that we could generate the observed distribution of wealth if all
households had the same 3 percent rate of time preference. Instead, we
should infer from the distribution of wealth that there are also distributions of underlying preference parameters, such as the discount rate. In a
first attempt to make such inference, Samwick (1998a) estimates using the
1992 SCF that the median discount rate (δ) is 7.63 percent, compared to
an assumed interest rate of 4 percent. A household's estimated discount
rate reflects the value that would be needed in a stochastic life-cycle model
of consumption to generate a predicted wealth-to-income ratio that
matches the household's observed wealth-to-income ratio.

More importantly, although factors such as the retirement replacement
rate and income uncertainty are accounted for in the estimation, much of
the heterogeneity in wealth holdings appears as heterogeneity in discount
rates. The 25th and 75th percentiles of the distribution are 2.93 percent
and 14.66 percent, respectively. The difference in behavior for households
with these two discount rates is enormous. The full distribution is shown
in figure 10C.2.[5] Samwick (1998a) also compares the estimated discount
rates across different responses to a question regarding the household's

5. Values higher than 20 percent and lower than −15 percent have been truncated at
those levels.

most important financial planning horizon. Households who responded "the next few months" had average discount rates of 10.43 percent, compared to an average of 5.91 percent for households who reported "ten years or more."

Evidence from wealth holding allows us to determine whether parameters used in studying the financial incentives to retire are reasonable. Although a uniform discount rate of 3 percent is fine for the descriptive, univariate analyses in this chapter, more attention must be paid to the choice of parameters in subsequent econometric models. The benchmark should be a higher median value that is consistent with the median household's low financial wealth accumulation over the life cycle. The heterogeneity in discount rates, implied by the heterogeneity of wealth holdings, should also be incorporated into the econometric specification as a topic for further research. This will necessitate a return to the structural estimation of parameters in the option value, as in the original work of Stock and Wise (1990a, b).

Conclusion

Overall, this chapter provides an interesting starting point for the growing literature that uses the rich data in the HRS to estimate the effect of financial incentives on the timing of retirement. The main contribution is to show that, when modeled with careful attention to detail, Social Security itself yields both heterogeneity and, to a lesser extent, nonmonotonicities in retirement incentives. These findings suggest a potentially larger role for Social Security in explaining cross-sectional retirement patterns than is currently believed.

The authors also make a strong case that, for the purpose of providing descriptive statistics on forward-looking measures of incentives, peak value is useful because it does not rely on parameters of an indirect utility function. Most of that advantage will not be present in econometric analyses, for two reasons. First, including the present value of earnings in the regression accounts for most of the difference between calculations of peak value and option value. Second, we actually do care about the parameters that are chosen and about gaining a deeper understanding of the appropriate model for retirement decisions. Further improvements should enable researchers to estimate the role of pensions more precisely, and to provide better links between retirement and saving behavior.

References

Atkinson, Anthony B. 1987. Income maintenance and social insurance. In *Handbook of public economics, Vol. 2,* ed. Alan J. Auerbach and Martin S. Feldstein. New York: North-Holland.

Berkovec, James, and Steven Stern. 1991. Job exit behavior of older men. *Econometrica* 59:189–210.

Carroll, Christopher D., and Andrew A. Samwick. 1997. The nature of precautionary wealth. *Journal of Monetary Economics* 40:41–72.

Coile, Courtney. 1999. Social Security, pensions, and the retirement decisions of couples. Manuscript, Massachusetts Institute of Technology, April.

Coile, Courtney, and Jonathan Gruber. 2000. Social Security and retirement. NBER Working Paper no. W7830. Cambridge, Mass.: National Bureau of Economic Research, August.

Gustman, Alan L., Olivia S. Mitchell, Andrew A. Samwick, and Thomas L. Steinmeier. 1999. Pension and Social Security wealth in the health and retirement study. In *Wealth, work, and health: Innovations in measurement in the social sciences,* ed. Robert Willis and James Smith, 150–208. Ann Arbor: University of Michigan Press.

———. 2000. Evaluating pension entitlements. In *Forecasting retirement needs and retirement wealth,* ed. P. Brett Hammond, Olivia Mitchell, and Anna Rappaport, 309–26. Philadelphia: University of Pennsylvania Press.

Gustman, Alan L., and Thomas L. Steinmeier. 1998. Changing pensions in cross-section and panel data: Analysis with employer provided plan descriptions. *National Tax Association Proceedings—1998,* 371–77.

———. 2000. Retirement in dual-career families: A structural model. *Journal of Labor Economics* 18:503–45.

Kotlikoff, Laurence J., and David A. Wise. 1987. The incentive effects of private pension plans. In *Issues in pension economics,* ed. Zvi Bodie, John B. Shoven, and David A. Wise, 283–339. Chicago: University of Chicago Press.

Lumsdaine, Robin L., and James H. Stock, and David A. Wise. 1992. Three models of retirement: Computational complexity versus predictive validity. In *Topics in the economics of aging,* ed. David A. Wise, 19–57. Chicago: University of Chicago Press.

Luzadis, Rebecca A., and Olivia S. Mitchell. 1991. Explaining pension dynamics. *Journal of Human Resources* 26:679–703.

Quinn, Joseph, Richard Burkhauser, and Daniel Myers. 1990. *Passing the torch: The influence of economic incentives on work and retirement.* Kalamazoo, Mich.: W. E. Upjohn Institute for Employment Research.

Samwick, Andrew A. 1993. The effect of tax reform act of 1986 on pension coverage: Evidence from pension provider surveys. Manuscript, National Bureau of Economic Research, July.

———. 1995. The limited offset between pension wealth and other private wealth: Implications of buffer-stock saving. Manuscript, Dartmouth College, December.

———. 1998a. Discount rate heterogeneity and Social Security reform. *Journal of Development Economics* 57:177–46.

———. 1998b. New evidence on pensions, Social Security, and the timing of retirement. *Journal of Public Economics* 70:207–36.

Stock, James H., and David A. Wise. 1990a. Pensions, the option value of work, and retirement. *Econometrica* 58:1151–80.

———. 1990b. The pension inducement to retire: An option value analysis. In *Issues in the economics of aging,* ed. David A. Wise, 205–24. Chicago: University of Chicago Press.

V

Bequests and Dissaving

Anticipated and Actual Bequests

Michael D. Hurd and James P. Smith

11.1 Introduction

Important advances have recently been made in documenting the process of wealth accumulation by households. Because of better data our knowledge is rapidly increasing about the facts surrounding the distribution of household wealth and, to a lesser extent, household saving behavior. However, this improved factual base has not yet been translated into a deeper understanding of the theoretical reasons people save. The candidates remain much the same (life-cycle timing, risk aversion, and bequests), but we appear to be no more certain about their relative importance. Advances in our understanding of bequest motives have been particularly difficult, in part due to the inherent difficulties in measuring the bequests that individuals anticipate making and the inheritances that they actually bequeath.

This paper will study the role of inheritances and bequests in shaping household decisions on wealth accumulation. We will learn about bequests by using new methods of measuring anticipated and actual bequests: We will examine actual bequests made by individuals upon their deaths, and compare them with their previously stated bequest intentions. Using panel data with two measurements of subjective bequest probabilities, we will

Michael D. Hurd is a senior economist at RAND and a research associate of the National Bureau of Economic Research. James P. Smith is a senior economist at RAND.

We gratefully acknowledge the expert programming assistance of David Rumpel and Iva Maclennan and the very constructive suggestions of David Laibson and participants at the NBER conference. Research support for this paper was provided by a grant from the National Institute on Aging to RAND.

explore the reasons individuals might revise their bequest expectations. These reasons may include, among other things, new information on health or economic conditions of household members. Our results are based on wealth, anticipated bequests, and actual bequests from two waves of the Health and Retirement Study (HRS), and the Asset and Health Dynamics among the Oldest Old (AHEAD) study.

Because the paper uses two new types of data, considerable space will be allocated to validation of them. In section 11.2 we outline a model of consumption and saving behavior that will guide our analysis and provide a framework for the validation. Section 11.3 describes the data sets that we will use. Section 11.4 examines the information from exit interviews given by proxy respondents for 774 AHEAD respondents who died after the baseline AHEAD survey. These exit interviews provide, among other things, data about the medical and nonmedical costs associated with illnesses of the respondents and the value and distribution of their estates. We compare average bequests with average wealth in the baseline interview, and we study how bequests covary with observable characteristics. These analyses are consistent with the proxy reports' being valid measures of actual bequests.

In section 11.5 we discuss the theoretical and empirical properties of our measure of bequest expectations. If bequest expectations are valid predictors of actual bequests, they should evolve in a predictable way in a population over time. The actual data conform to the predictions. Based on predictions from the theoretical model of consumption and saving behavior, we then analyze panel data on changes at the individual level in the subjective probability of leaving bequests. According to our results, individuals revise their expectations of bequests appropriately in response to new information. Having found the data on actual and anticipated bequests to be consistent with our expectations and theoretical predictions, we use them in section 11.6 to construct an index of saving intentions. Our results suggest that people plan to dissave before they die. Section 11.7 is the conclusion and summary.

11.2   Model of Consumption and Saving

Our thinking about how to organize the data will be shaped by the life-cycle model of consumption (LCH) as explicated in Yaari (1965) and Hurd (1989) for singles and in Hurd (1999) for couples. The model has these features and restrictions. The only uncertainty is the date of death. Resources are bequeathable wealth and a stream of annuity income such as Social Security, and annuity income cannot be borrowed against. Long-lived individuals may use up their bequeathable wealth and then live solely from annuity income, which would lead to a corner solution in the utility maximization. The model allows for a bequest motive for saving.

We outline the model for singles and discuss the implications for bequest behavior. The model for couples, although substantially more complicated, is in the same spirit, so we will give only some implications of it.

The single's problem is to maximize in the consumption path $\{c_t\}$ expected lifetime utility

$$\int_0^N u(c_t)e^{-\rho t}a_t\,dt \; + \; \int_0^N V(w_t)e^{-\rho t}m_t\,dt$$

The first term is expected discounted utility from consumption:

$u(\cdot)$ the utility flow from consumption;
ρ = the subjective time rate of discount;
a_t = the probability of being alive at t; and
N = the maximum age to which anyone can live ($a_N = 0$).

The second term is the expected discounted utility of bequests:

$V(\cdot)$ = utility from bequests, which may depend on the economic status
   of children as in an altruistic model or in a strategic bequest model;
w_t = bequeathable wealth at t; and
m_t = probability of dying at t.

The constraints on the maximization are

w_0 = initial bequeathable wealth that is given, and
$w_t \geq 0 \forall\ t$ is the nonnegativity constraint.

The equation of motion of wealth is

$$(1) \qquad\qquad \frac{dw_t}{dt} = rw_t - c_t + A_t,$$

in which

r = real interest rate (constant and known) and
A_t = flow of annuities at time t.

The solution is an equation of motion in marginal utility

$$(2) \qquad\qquad \frac{du_t}{dt} = u_t(h_t + \rho - r) - h_t V_t \qquad \text{for}\quad w_t > 0$$

$$c_t = A_t \qquad \text{for}\quad w_t = 0$$

and w_0 given. Here,

u_t = marginal utility of consumption at time t,
$h_t = m_t/a_t$ = mortality risk (mortality hazard), and
V_t = marginal utility of bequests at time t.

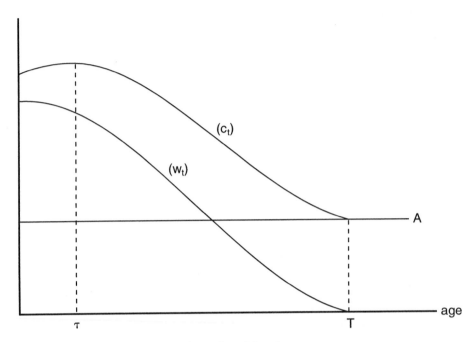

Fig. 11.1   Life-cycle consumption and wealth paths

A typical solution as would be found in data is shown in figure 11.1. At T, bequeathable wealth has been consumed, and consumption equals annuity income after T.

Suppose there is no bequest motive, which means that $V_t = 0$ in equation (2). If $\rho > r$, $(du_t/dt) > 0$ so that $(dc_t/dt) < 0$ provided $u(\cdot)$ is concave, and consumption will always decline with age. If $r > \rho$ and h_t is small, as would be the case at young ages, $(du_t/dt) < 0$ and consumption will increase with age. At older ages, however, h_t is approximately exponential so that at some age (τ in fig. 11.1), $h_t + \rho - r = 0$, and $(du_t/dt) = 0$ at $t = \tau$. For $t \geq \tau$, $(du_t/dt) > 0$ and $(dc_t/dt) < 0$.

A condition on global utility maximization requires that if consumption declines, wealth must also decline. Therefore a main implication of the LCH is that bequeathable wealth will decline at sufficiently advanced age. Expected actual bequests will be

$$\int_0^N w_t^* e^{-\rho t} m_t \, dt \, ,$$

where w_t^* is the optimal wealth path. Under the assumption that there is no bequest motive, such bequests will be accidental, but if individuals are highly risk averse, bequests could be a large fraction of bequeathable wealth.

If $t > \tau$ so that wealth is declining with age, an increase in life expectancy via an unexpected decrease in mortality risk at all ages will reduce bequests were there no behavioral response to the change in mortality risk: Individuals consume more of their bequeathable wealth before they die. If there is a behavioral response, however, bequests could increase: A decline in mortality risk will flatten the consumption path and reduce initial consumption, causing more wealth to be held against the increased risk of outliving resources. If wealth increases substantially, bequests could increase.

Whether bequests increase or decrease depends on the shape of the new optimal wealth path and the shape of the mortality curve $\{m_t\}$. In simulations based on an estimated model for singles, Hurd (1992) found that in baseline simulations, 20.7 percent of initial bequeathable wealth was (accidentally) bequeathed; with an increase in life expectancy of about three years, 16.5 percent was bequeathed when there was no behavioral response, but 23.0 percent was bequeathed when there was a behavioral response. The simulations were based on the constant relative risk aversion (CRRA) in which $u(c) = (c^{1-\gamma})/(1 - \gamma)$, with a rather low value of risk aversion ($\gamma = 1.12$), which implies a rather large behavioral response to changes in mortality risk. Large values of γ will reduce the behavioral response to a reduction in mortality risk, so that larger values of γ could lead to little change or even a reduction in bequests.

An increase in the annuity stream also has an ambiguous effect. If individuals are highly risk averse, consumption will change little in response to the increase. Therefore, wealth will decline more slowly and, in figure 11.1, T will increase and bequeathable wealth will be greater. If mortality risk is unchanged, bequests will be greater. However, in some circumstances, an increase in annuities could increase consumption enough that the path of bequeathable declines relative to the base situation. This is illustrated in figure 11.2. It can be shown analytically that this obtains under the CRRA utility function (Hurd 1999), and simulations showed that bequests decreased when annuity income was increased (Hurd 1993). From the point of view of public policy it is important to understand whether increases in Social Security benefits are partly bequeathed back to the younger generation, which would offset some of the increase in taxes required to fund the increase.

The effect of age on bequest probabilities is unambiguous in a stationary environment. If the anticipated wealth path from time t onward is declining, leaving a bequest greater than b is the same as dying before age A^* as shown in figure 11.3. If an individual survives until time $t + 1$, he will have followed the wealth path from t to $t + 1$ and he will still anticipate following the same wealth path in future periods. Now, however, the probability of surviving to age A^* is greater because, of course, the conditional probability of surviving to A^* increases from t to $t + 1$. Thus the probability of leaving a bequest greater than b should decline as individuals age.

We have been discussing the situation in which there is no bequest mo-

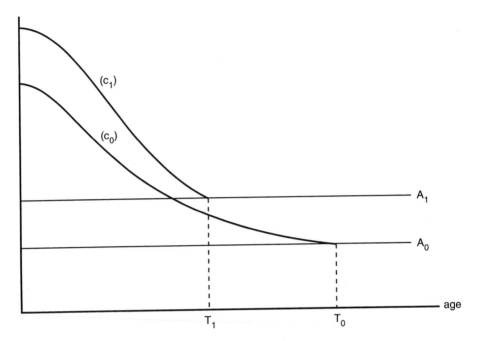

Fig. 11.2   The effect of annuity level on consumption

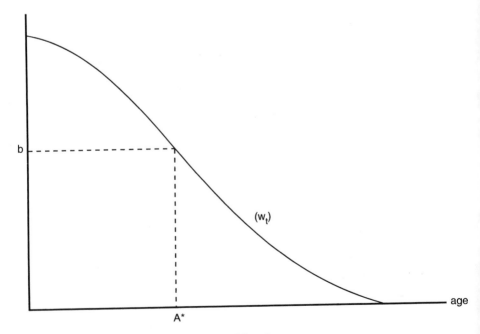

Fig. 11.3   The relationship between wealth and age

tive for saving. A bequest motive means that $V_t > 0$. At any given level of wealth we would expect V_t to depend on the characteristics of the target of the bequest. For example, if the children of an elderly person are well off, V_t will be small because the marginal utility of additional wealth to the children will be small. We would expect that if bequests are altruistic, V_t will depend on the characteristics of all the children of the parent.

A bequest motive flattens the consumption path and reduces initial consumption, causing more wealth to be held. If the probability of dying at any age is unchanged, expected bequests will increase.

Tests of a bequest motive are of two types. The first is based on a main prediction of the life-cycle model: In the absence of a bequest motive, bequeathable wealth should decline at sufficiently advanced ages. Such wealth decline has been found consistently in panel data sets (Hurd 1999). It should be noted, however, that although a wealth increase is not consistent with a life-cycle model that excludes a bequest motive, a wealth decline is consistent with a life-cycle model that includes a bequest motive.

The second type of test is based on variation in the rate of wealth change as a function of covariates that are assumed to be related to the strength of a bequest motive. Because most bequests are made to close relatives, it is reasonable to assume that the number and characteristics of relatives are related to the strength of a bequest motive. This thinking leads to a comparison of the rates of wealth change among those with children to those without children. A consistent finding is that there is little difference, with the implication that any bequest motive for saving is weak on average (Hurd 1987, 1989).

11.2.1   Life-Cycle Model of Consumption by Couples

The model for couples is similar to the model for singles: Couples have a utility function defined over consumption while both spouses are alive, and they get utility from contemplating "bequests." However, there are two types of bequests: wealth to a surviving spouse, and wealth to a third person at the death of the surviving spouse.[1] It is important to distinguish between these two types of bequests because a bequest to a surviving spouse increases only slightly the time horizon for decision making by the couple, whereas a bequest to children can lengthen the planning horizon to many generations. Furthermore, a spouse anticipating widowhood can affect the prior consumption decisions of the couple, but in most cases children cannot.

Analysis similar to that for singles will show that a bequest motive (desiring to bequeath to someone outside the household) will flatten the consumption path and reduce initial consumption, causing more wealth to be

---

1. In this model, all of the wealth of the couple is transferred to the surviving spouse at the death of one spouse. It is only at the death of the second spouse that wealth is inherited by children or others.

held. Thus, expected bequests will increase. Of course, the effects of changes in life expectancy and changes in the annuity stream are ambiguous, as they are in the case of singles.

The death of a spouse should alter the bequest probabilities of the surviving spouse for a number of reasons. The date at which the last spouse is expected to die is reduced, and in the absence of any behavioral reaction bequests should increase. The surviving spouse has high bequeathable wealth relative to needs: If the couple had contemplated a declining wealth path, the early death will cause bequests to increase. The annuity stream of the household is typically altered because both Social Security and pension benefits typically change at the death of a spouse. The surviving spouse will reoptimize given the new situation, causing the path of bequeathable wealth to differ from what it would have been had the death occurred later. The total effect on bequests is not obvious, and we will leave it to be determined empirically.

11.2.2 Summary of Implications

When there is no bequest motive, at sufficiently advanced old ages individuals will plan to dissave, and, therefore, the population will dissave provided on average the anticipations of individuals are realized. With increasing age wealth will decline and expected bequests will decline. However, an unexpected reduction in survival probabilities causes different effects from an expected reduction in survival chances that accompanies aging: The unexpected reduction should cause a behavioral response, which will make its effect on wealth change ambiguous. Therefore, we should find in panel a reduction in anticipated bequests as the population ages, but not necessarily a reduction in anticipated bequests as survival chances vary at the individual level.

In cross-section, greater wealth should be associated with higher anticipated bequests even where there is no bequest motive. In panel there should be no relationship between wealth change and anticipated bequests as long as the observed wealth change is due to anticipated dissaving.[2] An unanticipated wealth change, however, should change anticipated bequests.

In cross-section, variation in annuity income such as pensions and Social Security could affect anticipated bequests, but the sign of the effect depends on utility function parameters. In panel, anticipated changes in annuity income will not change the wealth path and thus should not affect anticipated bequests. Unanticipated changes in annuity income act in the same way as cross-section variation in annuity income, so the effect on anticipated bequests cannot be signed.

---

2. This statement assumes that there is no change in survival chances or that they are adequately controlled.

A bequest motive for saving requires only one substantive change to the preceding summary: Wealth can increase with age (but does not have to), even at advanced old age. The other analyses of the difference between anticipated and unanticipated changes in survival, wealth, and income remain the same.

We will use two types of panel data to test implications of this model of consumption and saving. The first type will be information about actual bequests, and the second will be about anticipated bequests.

11.3 Data

Our data come from the Asset and Health Dynamics among the Oldest Old (AHEAD) study and from the Health and Retirement Study (HRS). These studies are large panel surveys of individuals. They obtain extensive information about the domains of health, economic status, family relations, and labor market activity. AHEAD is representative of the population born in 1923 or earlier and their spouses (Soldo et al. 1997). At baseline in 1993 it obtained interviews from 8,222 persons who were approximately aged seventy or over. We will use information from the baseline interview and from wave 2, which was fielded in 1995. The HRS is representative of the population born in the years 1931 through 1941 and their spouses (Juster and Suzman 1995). At baseline in 1992 it interviewed 12,654 persons. We will use information from waves 2 and 3, which were fielded in 1994 and 1996.[3]

These surveys obtained extensive information about the economic situation of the households that were interviewed. Of particular importance for this paper are the data on income and assets. The surveys asked for a complete accounting of income and assets, and they used bracketing methods to reduce the rate of item nonresponse, resulting in economic data of high quality. The surveys used innovative questions about subjective probabilities to query individuals about their perceptions of their survival chances and of leaving bequests. Respondents were asked about their health in a number of ways. Here we use self-reports about health events such as heart attack, cancer, diabetes, arthritis, stroke, high blood pressure, and lung disease to find the incidence of these conditions between waves of AHEAD and HRS.

11.4 Actual Bequests

Actual bequests are inherently difficult to measure in the population and frequently escape detection in traditional household surveys. Household

---

3. We cannot use wave 1 because the questions about anticipated bequests were not asked in that wave.

surveys typically do not include any post-death interviews with relatives, which is probably the only feasible way to obtain information about bequests in the population. Therefore, most applied research on inheritances has relied instead on estate records (David and Menchik 1985). While valuable, estate data can provide only a limited picture. Many inheritances are below the estate tax thresholds and so do not appear in official estate records. Even when available, estate records provide very limited information about the deceased person or about the actual and potential heirs.[4]

The AHEAD survey measured bequests by conducting an exit interview following the death of a respondent. These exit interviews are given to proxies, often relatives of the deceased, and represent a condensed version of the normal AHEAD interview. In addition, detailed questions were asked about the nature and costs associated with any illnesses and other death-related expenses, and about the distribution and values of estates and inheritances. Exit interviews are available for 774 persons who were respondents in wave 1 but who died between wave 1 and wave 2.[5] In this section, we summarize data from these AHEAD exit interviews. Our analysis focuses on what happened to wealth as measured in wave 1, and how prior-wave household wealth corresponds to the values of estates.

11.4.1   The Cost of Illness Associated with Death

Decedents in the AHEAD age range may leave no bequests because of large expenses associated with their deaths. Many of the AHEAD respondents who died between the waves died as a result of frequent and severe illnesses. For example, according to the exit interviews, 82 percent of the decedents were hospitalized at least once between their wave 1 interviews and the time of death. Many of these hospitalizations involved multiple visits. Even if the hospitalization associated with the death of the respondent is excluded, more than 40 percent of respondents had three or more hospital visits during this time interval. The median number of nights spent in the hospital was thirteen days, but one in twenty respondents spent seventy days or more in a hospital. The intensity and expense of the medical care provided during these visits was dramatic. Half of those hospitalized received intensive care, and 30 percent were on life support.

The total costs of providing such care were substantial. As reported in the exit interviews, median total costs were about $25 thousand, and one in nine of the deceased had medical expenses in excess of $100,000. For the purposes of relating wave 1 wealth to bequests, however, out-of-pocket

4. For example, Mulligan (1995) reports that estate tax returns are filed for only 5–10 percent of those who died after the age of forty-five. At the time of the AHEAD survey, the threshold at which estate taxes start was $600,000 for an individual and as high as $1,200,000 for a married couple.

5. AHEAD staff estimate that they were able to conduct exit interviews with more than 90 percent of respondents who died between the first and second waves.

Table 11.1   **Distribution of Estates (thousands of dollars): AHEAD Decedents**

Percentile	Single	Married	All
5	0.0	0.0	0.0
10	0.0	0.0	0.0
20	0.0	2.0	0.0
30	2.0	20.0	10.0
40	20.0	35.0	30.8
50	33.3	50.0	50.0
60	50.0	100.0	54.4
70	77.0	150.0	100.0
80	125.1	150.0	150.0
90	180.0	200.0	188.5
95	250.0	400.0	322.7
98	600.0	600.0	600.0

Note: N = 774.

costs, not total costs, are relevant. The exit interviews aimed to measure all out-of-pocket expenses associated with these illnesses. Out-of-pocket costs were queried separately for hospital and nursing home visits, hospice, doctor and dental payments, drugs, in-home need care or special facilities or services, and other health care expenses. In each case, the lead-in question asks whether the care was fully or partially insured with follow-up questions about the sum of out-of-pocket cost involved.[6]

The proxy respondents report that 68 percent of AHEAD decedents had fully insured hospital costs and that another 30 percent had partially insured costs. Fifty-two percent of nursing home costs were fully insured while another 30 percent were partially paid for through insurance. Most doctor visits were also reimbursed (61 percent totally reimbursed and 38 percent partially covered), leaving drugs as the principal personal financial exposure. One-third of the AHEAD decedents had to pay their full drug costs and another 39 percent paid at least part of these expenses. The magnitude of these out-of-pocket expenses and their implication for the value of estates is discussed in the next section.

11.4.2   Estates

Table 11.1 shows the distribution of values of estates as reported by the proxy respondents. Because the interpretation of what is labeled inheritances depends on whether there remains a surviving spouse, these distributions are provided separately for married and nonmarried families. One in five of the deceased AHEAD respondents had estates of no value. Mir-

6. Following the normal procedures used in HRS and AHEAD, if respondents initially did not provide an exact dollar amount, they were allowed (encouraged) to answer using a sequence of bracketed categories. We used within-bracket values for exact-amount respondents to impute values within these brackets.

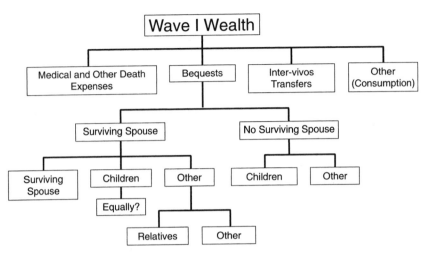

Fig. 11.4   The flow of wealth

roring the distribution of wealth among these households, the distribution of estate values are similarly quite dispersed and highly skewed. The mean estate value is $94,469, but the median is half as much, $50,000. Some respondents leave relatively large estates: Thirty percent are $100,000 or more and 7 percent are in excess of $200,000. Only 3 percent of the estates were valued at $600,000 or more, which is the lower limit for estates to be subject to the estate tax. Consequently, estate tax records are extremely incomplete and they give a very distorted picture of bequests and the attributes of households who bequeath. For example, the 774 AHEAD deceased respondents left bequests worth more than $73 million, but only one-fourth of that value would appear in estate tax files.

In addition to estate records, some analyses of bequests rely on information from wills that pass through probate. While the selectivity of such cases is not as extreme as those that use estate tax record data, probated wills also represent a selective sample. Only one-third of AHEAD decedents had probated wills and the average value of those estates was $130.4 thousand; yet those estates that were not probated averaged just $51.9 thousand. Therefore, analyses based on probated wills cannot describe average bequest behavior in the population.

Because the maximum time span between wave 1 and the death of the decedent was two years, the value of the estate should be closely related to household wealth as measured in wave 1. If it were not, at least on average, we would be skeptical of the validity of the reports on the estate in the exit interview. Of course, there could be expenditures between wave 1 and the death that would reduce the correspondence. Figure 11.4 has a schematic of the leakages that may occur. Some wealth may be used to pay for medical and other expenses associated with the death; some to give inter vivos transfers, perhaps to compensate for help received or to escape taxation; some to finance household consumption of the deceased and other family members. Only the remainder is available for the estate.

Table 11.2 compares estate values and wave 1 household wealth of the deceased AHEAD respondents. On average, wave 1 wealth was $130.2 thousand, and the estates averaged $94.5 thousand. However, in married households, the estate is quite close to nonhousing wealth, suggesting that when there is a surviving spouse, the house (presumably jointly owned) is often not included in the estate. When there is no surviving spouse, mean estate values are virtually identical to prior-wave total household wealth. We consider the close correspondence of wave 1 wealth to estate value as good evidence of the validity of the estate reports by the proxy respondents.

The second part of the table shows costs associated with the death of the AHEAD wave 1 respondent. Although substantial on an absolute scale, these costs are not particularly large relative to average wave 1 wealth. For all households, death costs are about 5 percent of wave 1 household wealth and about 10 percent of the estate. On average, death expenses by themselves did not lead to a significant depletion of household wealth; nor can these death expenses account for much of the difference between wave 1 wealth and estate values.

Another source of leakage is that during this time period, households may have been engaging in higher amounts of inter vivos transfers than usual to avoid estate taxation. The exit interviews inquired about the extent and amount of such transfers. There is a legitimate question about the ability of proxy interviews to answer accurately questions about these before-death transfers; nonetheless, the fraction of cases in which these transfers occurred was relatively small. Transfers to children were made in roughly 10 percent of all these households with a median transfer of about $900 (not shown), and few households appear to have given transfers that

Table 11.2   **Wealth, Estate Value, and Expenses Associated with Death (thousands of dollars): AHEAD Decedents**

	Single	Married	All
Wave 1 wealth	80.7	184.7	130.2
Wave 1 wealth excluding housing	42.4	104.8	72.1
Value of estate at death	80.6	109.8	94.5
Total out-of-pocket costs	9.3	9.4	9.4
Medical	3.7	4.6	4.2
Death expenses	4.4	4.1	4.3
Other	1.2	0.6	0.9

Note: N = 774.

were influenced by the tax-exempt limit of $10,000 per recipient. We conclude that although there is some inter vivos giving before death for the average household, it is minor relative to the size of the estate.

Table 11.2 suggests that estate values as reported by proxy respondents are reasonably accurate on average. We can informally validate them further by investigating whether estate values vary in an appropriate way with covariates known to be related to wealth. Because many households leave no estate at all, we estimate the effects of covariates in two stages. The first is a probit specification for the probability that an estate is positive, and the second is an ordinary least squares (OLS) estimation for the log value of the estate conditional on its being positive.

The results in table 11.3 are similar to estimates of the determinants of wealth. Higher education is associated with a greater probability of a positive estate and with a higher value of the estate. Similarly, income has an important positive impact both on the probability of leaving any estate and on the value of the estate, although the elasticity is less than unity. African American and Hispanic households have lower probabilities of leaving an estate, but do not appear to differ from white households in the amount of money that is left in an estate. Since household income is controlled for in both models, any remaining race- and ethnicity-specific behavioral differentials associated with bequest-leaving behavior appear to rest largely in whether a bequest is left at all.

Inheritances are smaller in families in which there is a surviving spouse, an indication that some fraction of family wealth is simply kept by the surviving spouse without passing through the estate or being labeled an inheritance. In the theory outlined in the previous section, we suggested that one way of evaluating whether a bequest motive existed was to examine whether bequests are related to the existence and number of close relatives. None of the family-structure variables (the number of living children, grandchildren, or great-grandchildren; the number of living siblings) has any significant relation to the size of the inheritance. This finding is consistent with what is found in studies based on wealth data: At older ages, changes in wealth as individuals age are unrelated to the number of children (Hurd 1987, 1989). The only significant effect is on the probability of having an estate: Increasing the number of children reduces the probability, which is not a result that would be predicated by a bequest motive for saving.

11.5   Anticipated Bequests

Information about the relative importance of bequests and the reasons for making them can be obtained either by studying the value of inheritances received by the current generation or by studying what that generation plans to bequeath. Studying anticipated bequests has many advan-

Table 11.3   **Determinants of Estate**

	Probability of a Positive Estate	Logarithm of Estate among Positive Estates
Education		
Less than high school	—	—
	—	—
High school	0.517	0.564
	(3.24)	(2.72)
College	0.365	0.995
	(1.35)	(3.08)
Black	−0.995	−0.009
	(5.87)	(0.02)
Hispanic	−1.268	−0.496
	(4.97)	(0.88)
Female	−0.225	−0.362
	(1.54)	(1.77)
Household income (log, thousands)	0.220	0.596
	(2.23)	(4.23)
Surviving spouse	0.231	−0.931
	(0.92)	(2.47)
Death expenses (thousands)	0.012	0.009
	(1.93)	(0.11)
Number of living children	−0.050	−0.063
	(1.52)	(1.13)
Number of grandchildren	−0.003	0.008
	(0.24)	(0.30)
Number of great-grandchildren	0.006	−0.018
	(0.42)	(0.60)
Number of living siblings	0.041	−0.022
	(1.38)	(0.57)
Parents dead	0.245	0.311
	(1.53)	(1.19)
Spouse's parents dead	−0.208	1.273
	(0.88)	(3.80)
Intercept	−1.574	4.487
	(1.64)	(3.28)
N	594	451

Notes: Absolute *t*-statistics in parentheses. Probability coefficients are from probit estimation.

tages because it relates directly to the motives for current saving decisions of households. However, it is difficult to infer bequest intentions from current household decisions about wealth accumulation, because other saving motives coexist and actual bequest realizations may take place far in the future. Many subsequent events may break the link between current intentions and future reality.

A promising new way of obtaining insight into the existence and

Table 11.4   **Average Subjective Probability of a Bequest (percent)**

Wealth Decile	Target Amount			
	$10,000		$100,000	
	AHEAD	HRS	AHEAD	HRS
10	90	92	75	78
9	83	87	56	66
8	77	85	44	57
7	71	81	34	49
6	65	78	18	41
5	56	72	10	30
4	40	67	7	22
3	30	56	5	14
2	13	46	2	11
1	4	25	1	7

Source: Smith (2001).

strength of bequest motives relies on the subjective probability of leaving a bequest, which was ascertained in HRS waves 2 and 3 and in AHEAD waves 1 and 2. Although there is some difference in the wording, as between HRS and AHEAD, the substance is illustrated by the question from AHEAD wave 2:

> Using a number between 0 and 100 what are the chances that you (or your husband/wife/partner) will leave an inheritance of at least $10,000?

The respondent had previously been instructed to interpret zero as absolutely no chance and 100 as absolutely certain. If the answer was 31 or higher, the question was repeated but with a target of $100,000. In the case of couples, each spouse was asked these questions independently so that within-family comparisons can be made.

We will use the subjective probability of leaving a bequest as our measure of anticipated bequests. In prior work, Smith (1999a) established some of the properties in cross-section of the subjective probabilities by relating them to wealth and other characteristics. As an example of his findings, table 11.4 has the average subjective bequest probabilities in AHEAD wave 1 and HRS wave 1 for each decile of wealth. The average subjective bequest probabilities are sharply lower when the target is $100,000 rather than $10,000, and the differences are not proportionate. For example, in the top decile the difference in probabilities is 15 percentage points (AHEAD), whereas the difference in the 5th decile is 46 percentage points. In the lowest decile the probabilities are both essentially zero.

At both target levels and in both surveys the average bequest probability increases monotonically and sharply with wealth. Although in the very top deciles there are no large differences between HRS and AHEAD, the differences are substantial in the lower part of the distribution. For example, the average over the bottom half of the wealth distribution is 29 percent for the target of $10,000 for AHEAD but 53 percent for HRS. For a target of $100,000 the averages are 5 percent and 17 percent, respectively. This is reasonable because the HRS cohort has more wealth than the AHEAD cohort, and many in the HRS cohort are still working—and at the ages at which their saving rates will be at a maximum. The implication of this difference between the AHEAD and HRS cohorts is that we can expect bequests to rise over time.

11.5.1 Predictive Validity of the Subjective Bequest Probabilities

Because observations on subjective bequest probabilities have not previously been available, they have not been subject to scrutiny about their properties and their predictive power. Therefore, it is reasonable to wonder about their validity. We will say that the subjective bequest probabilities are valid if they are accurate predictors of the probabilities of actual bequests. Once the cohort has died, the associated validity can be evaluated by comparing the subjective bequest probabilities with actual bequests; but because the AHEAD population is aged seventy or over, it will be many years before such a comparison is possible. However, we can derive a test based on the estates of the part of the population that died between the waves, and on the change in the subjective bequest probabilities of the part of the population that survived, providing a test that can be carried out with just two waves of the data.

In panel, the subjective probabilities of bequests will change in response to new information. Some individuals will have unanticipated health changes that will affect their survival chances; some will have unexpected wealth changes, such as capital gains or losses. These kinds of events should change the subjective bequest probabilities of the affected individuals. However, to the extent that these events occur at the average ex ante or anticipated rate, they do not constitute new information in the population and, therefore, should not lead to changes in the average subjective bequest probabilities. At the population level, unanticipated changes in the survival chances of the population or macro-events that systematically lead to windfall gains or losses will change average subjective bequest probabilities.

If we assume that there are no such macro-shocks, we can derive an equation of motion for the average subjective bequest probability. Suppose that the environment is stationary, so that individual anticipated wealth paths do not change as each survivor ages. The assumption of stationarity can be used to derive a test of the validity of the subjective probabilities of bequests. The test will be based on the relationship between the bequest probabilities at time t, actual bequests among those who die between t and $t + 1$, and bequest probabilities at time $t + 1$.

Let $P_t(B > b)$ be the probability at time t that bequests will be greater than b. Then

(3) $\quad\quad\quad P_t(B > b) = P_t(B > b | D_t)P_t(D_t)$

$$+ P_t(B > b | D > t)P_t(D > t)$$

where $P_t(D_t)$ is the probability of death at t, and $P_t(D > t)$ is the probability of death at a time greater than t.

Under stationarity,

$$P_t(B > b | D > t) = P_{t+1}(B > b)$$

because the anticipated wealth path is unchanging.

In a population of n individuals of age t, let $D_{it} = 1$ if the ith person dies at t and zero otherwise. Then $(1/n)\Sigma \, P_{it}(B_i > b | D_t)P_{it}(D_t)$ is the population average of the first term on the right-hand side of equation (3), and it can be estimated by $(1/n)\Sigma \, P_{it}(B_i > b | D_t)D_{it}$ because

$$E\left[\sum P_{it}(B_i > b | D_t)D_{it}\right] = \sum P_{it}(B_i > b | D_t)P_{it}(D_t).$$

We can write that

$$\sum P_{it}(B_i > b | D_t)D_{it} = \sum_{i \in d} P_{it}(B_i > b)$$

where d is the set of individuals who died between t and $t + 1$. We note that

$$P_t(B > b | D_t) = \begin{cases} 1 \text{ if } w_t > b \\ 0 \text{ otherwise} \end{cases},$$

provided the time interval between t and $t + 1$ is short. Therefore, in large samples

(4) $\quad \dfrac{1}{n}\sum P_{it}(B_i > b) \approx \dfrac{1}{n}\sum_{i \in d} I(w_{it} - b) + \dfrac{1}{n}\sum_{i \in s} P_{i,t+1}(B_i > b)$

where $I(x) = 1$ if $x > 0$ and 0 otherwise, and s is the set of persons who survived from t to $t + 1$. Thus, we can approximately estimate in the panel all of the elements of equation (4). The right-hand side is the sum of the fraction of those who died having baseline wealth greater than b weighted by the population mortality rate and of the average probability in wave 2 that bequests will be greater than b weighted by the population survival rate.

This relationship should hold approximately in the panel. It requires that the anticipated wealth path be unchanging among survivors, on the validity of the subjective bequest probabilities as stated by decedents in wave 1, and on the time consistency in the statements of the bequest prob-

Table 11.5   **Comparison of Wave 1 Bequest Probabilities with Actual Estates and Wave 2 Bequest Probabilities (percentages)**

	Target Amount	
	$10,000	$100,000
Wave 1		
Average subjective probability, survivors to wave 2	58.30	28.87
Average subjective probability, decedents before wave 2	47.83	19.60
Overall average	57.38	28.05
Wave 2		
Average subjective probability, survivors to wave 2	56.33	27.97
Percent of estates with wealth ≥ target, decedents before wave 2	73.68	36.00
Weighted average[a]	57.82	28.68
Difference, wave 1 − wave 2	−0.44	−0.63
Standard error	0.56	0.48
N	5,204	5,073

[a]Weights are survival rate (0.912) and mortality rate (0.088).

abilities by survivors in wave 2. In particular, it does not require that people consume according to the life-cycle model.

We can perform a test of the validity of the subjective bequest probabilities based on the estimated elements of equation (4). Table 11.5 shows the average wave 1 subjective bequest probabilities among those who survived to wave 2 and among those who died between the waves. We note that the deceased had lower bequest probabilities, reflecting their lower wealth holdings. The overall average is the left-hand side of equation (4). The table shows the right-hand side of equation (4) as the weighted average of bequest probabilities among survivors and the average percent of estates as large as the target. The difference between wave 1 and wave 2 is the difference between the left-hand and right-hand sides of equation (4). For both targets they are small, and comparisons with the standard errors of the difference show that we cannot reject the null hypothesis that the left-hand and right-hand sides of equation (4) are equal. We interpret this result as evidence for the validity of the subjective bequest probabilities.

11.5.2   Changes in the Subjective Probabilities of Leaving Bequests

During the two years between waves, new information should affect the subjective bequest probabilities. Among survivors, an important piece of information is simply that they survived. As discussed earlier, in steady-state under the assumption of planned dissaving there should be a decrease with age in the average subjective bequest probability: The survivors will die at a greater age when wealth is lower. Other types of new information would include health events that could affect both current expenditures on health care and future expenditures; unanticipated wealth change, such as

Table 11.6	Distribution of Bequest Probabilities (percent): AHEAD Waves 1 and 2					
	Wave 2					
Wave 1	0.00	0.01–0.49	0.50	0.51–0.99	1.00	All
	Probability bequest ≥ $10,000 (N = 4,748)					
0.00	21.6	2.0	1.7	1.3	4.1	30.7
0.01–0.49	2.0	1.3	0.8	0.9	1.0	6.0
0.50	1.7	1.1	1.5	1.1	2.3	7.6
0.51–0.99	1.2	0.9	1.9	3.9	4.2	12.2
1.00	4.4	1.3	3.2	7.1	27.5	43.5
All	30.9	6.6	9.1	14.3	39.1	100.0
	Probability bequest ≥ $100,000 (N = 4,623)					
0.00	52.1	3.3	2.2	1.6	2.3	61.4
0.01–0.49	2.4	1.5	0.9	0.8	0.4	6.0
0.50	2.0	0.8	1.4	1.3	1.2	6.7
0.51–0.99	1.1	0.9	1.1	2.4	1.9	7.4
1.00	2.9	1.0	1.6	2.5	10.5	18.5
All	60.6	7.5	7.2	8.5	16.2	100.1

capital gains from holdings of stocks and bonds; and events that would change the anticipated consumption path, such as a change in the utility from a bequest due to a change in the economic status of children.

Table 11.6 shows the joint distributions of the subjective probabilities of leaving bequests for those AHEAD respondents who were interviewed in the first and second waves of AHEAD. The distribution of responses in wave 1, which is shown in the right-most (All) column, has large percentages at zero and at 1.0. Between waves 1 and 2, the distribution shifted slightly toward lower probabilities of bequests; for example, 43.5 percent in wave 1 reported a probability of 1.0 but in wave 2 just 39.1 percent reported a probability of 1.0. The percentage at 0.5 or less shifted from 44.3 to 46.6. These are not large changes but they are consistent with a life-cycle model in which individuals anticipate dissaving and when there are no population-wide shocks that affect all or most expectations or that cause unexpected wealth change.

Even so, there are examples of large changes. About 4 percent reported probabilities of 0.0 in wave 1 and 1.0 in wave 2 for the target of $10,000, implying a transition probability from 0.0 to 1.0 of 13 percent. The probability of reporting 0.0 in wave 2 conditional on a report of 1.0 in wave 1 was about 10 percent. Such changes could, of course, be the result of large unexpected wealth changes or of measurement error. We will investigate later in this paper the correlates of these changes.

When the target is $100,000 we find a modest reduction in the bequest probabilities between the waves. For example, the percentage reporting a probability of 1.0 declined from 18.5 to 16.2. Compared with the distribu-

Table 11.7   Distribution of Bequest Probabilities (percent): HRS Waves 2 and 3

Wave 2	Wave 3					
	0.00	0.01–0.49	0.50	0.51–0.99	1.00	All
Probability bequest ≥ $10,000 (N = 9,084)						
0.00	10.9	1.6	1.4	1.1	3.2	18.1
0.01–0.49	2.1	1.4	1.1	1.4	1.4	7.3
0.50	1.3	1.0	2.1	2.3	3.2	9.9
0.51–0.99	1.0	1.2	2.0	7.5	7.9	19.7
1.00	2.5	1.1	2.5	6.5	32.3	44.9
All	17.8	6.3	9.2	18.6	48.0	100.0
Probability bequest ≥ $100,000 (N = 8,964)						
0.00	35.4	3.5	2.1	1.6	2.6	45.2
0.01–0.49	5.3	4.0	2.0	2.1	1.4	14.7
0.50	1.6	1.5	1.9	2.1	2.0	9.1
0.51–0.99	1.4	1.2	1.6	4.2	4.1	12.5
1.00	1.7	0.9	1.5	2.6	11.9	18.5
All	45.4	11.0	9.0	12.6	22.0	100.2

tion for a target of $10,000, there is a much greater percentage that report a probability of 0.0, reflecting the large difference between the target and the wealth of many households.

Table 11.7 has similar results for HRS waves 2 and 3. A noticeable difference when compared with AHEAD results is that the HRS distribution shifts toward higher subjective bequest probabilities between the waves. For example, in wave 1, 44.9 percent were certain to leave a bequest at the $10,000 target, but in wave 2, 48.0 percent were certain. At the $100,000 target these percentages changed from 18.5 to 22.0. There are several reasons for the differences between AHEAD and HRS results. The two-year mortality rate for AHEAD was about 0.11, whereas it was only 0.02 for HRS. Therefore, the increase in the chances of dying at advanced old age, and therefore, of dying with less wealth, were much greater in the AHEAD population than in the HRS population. Also, many in the HRS cohort are still working, and in the robust economic times between waves 2 and 3 (approximately 1994 to 1996) many likely had greater earnings than expected. Furthermore, the stock and bond markets had large capital gains, and the HRS cohort are more heavily invested in such assets than the AHEAD cohort.

11.5.3   Determinants of Change in Bequest Probabilities

We will study the determinants of changes in the subjective bequest probabilities by relating them to new information—specifically, changes in the subjective survival probabilities and in out-of-pocket medical expenditures; the onset of a new health condition; changes in household income and wealth; widowing; and retirement. Each of these may reflect new information and therefore cause a change in the subjective bequest probabilities. We will present results from several types of estimation and discuss them together, in that all the results pertain to the same underlying process.

Because tables 11.6 and 11.7 show substantial fractions of respondents to be at the extreme of 0.0, we will study the probability of reporting a positive probability in wave 2 conditional on reporting a probability of zero in wave 1. That is, we will estimate β in the probit function

$$P(p_2 > 0 \mid p_1 = 0) = f(X\beta),$$

where f is the normal distribution function, p_2 is the probability in wave 2 of a bequest at least as large as the target, and p_1 is the probability in wave 1. This probit is estimated over the 1,222 observations in AHEAD wave 1 that reported $p_1 = 0$ when the target was $10,000. Similar probits are estimated for the AHEAD target of $100,000 and for both targets in HRS. Table 11.8 lists these estimated probit coefficients.

Because tables 11.6 and 11.7 also show considerable bunching of responses at 1.0, we estimated probit functions for the probability of reducing bequest chances from 1.0 to chances less than 1. 0. That is, we estimated β in

$$P(p_2 < 1 \mid p_1 = 1) = f(X\beta)$$

over the 1,939 observations in AHEAD wave 1 that reported bequest chances of 1.0 for the target of $10,000. Similar probit coefficients were estimated for a target of $100,000, and among HRS respondents for both targets. The results are presented in table 11.9.

Our final type of estimation is regression in which the left-hand variable is the change in the subjective bequest probabilities and the right-hand variables are measures of new information. Because the left-hand variable is limited to the range of -100 to 100, both OLS estimates and tobit estimates are presented. Table 11.10 has the results for AHEAD and table 11.11 for HRS.

Several consistent patterns are revealed in these tables. First, it is rather remarkable that the overall pattern of coefficients in table 11.9 is the same as in table 11.8 but with reversed signs. For example, in table 11.8 an increase in the subjective survival probability is associated with an increase in bequest chances; in table 11.9 it is associated with a decrease in the probability of reducing bequest chances, or an increase in the chances of bequests. Because the estimations are based on different samples, the estimates are independent. Second, this positive relationship between survival chances and bequest chances is found both for the two target levels in AHEAD and HRS and for the several types of estimation. In tables

Table 11.8   Probits for Positive Probability of a Bequest Given Prior-Wave
Probability of Zero

| | Target Amounts | | | |
| | AHEAD | | HRS | |
	$10,000	$100,000	$10,000	$100,000
Change in subjective survival probability	0.002	0.003	0.002	0.002
	(1.82)	(3.11)	(1.69)	(2.40)
Change in subjective survival probability of spouse	−0.001	−0.001	0.003	0.002
	(0.32)	(0.75)	(1.78)	(1.37)
Out-of-pocket medical costs ($100)	0.027	0.004	0.006	−0.002
	(0.55)	(0.11)	(1.32)	(0.52)
New health condition	0.112	−0.038		
	(1.29)	(0.52)		
Minor			−0.164	−0.067
			(1.73)	(1.05)
Major			−0.001	−0.059
			(0.01)	(0.79)
Change in household income ($10,000)	0.016	0.028	0.004	0.016
	(0.52)	(1.40)	(0.38)	(2.28)
Change in household wealth ($10,000)	0.017	0.004	0.004	0.005
	(3.83)	(1.31)	(1.07)	(2.24)
Widowed	0.362	0.127	−0.214	−0.174
	(1.99)	(0.75)	(0.84)	(0.92)
Retired			−0.341	0.021
			(2.02)	(0.21)
N	1,222	1,591	1,310	3,379
Average conditional probability	0.296	0.153	0.401	0.217

Notes: Entries are estimated effects (probit coefficients) on the probability that a bequest will be positive given that the prior-wave probability was zero. Absolute t-statistics in parentheses. Includes controls for race, sex, ethnicity, education, region of residence, and birth cohort.

11.8–11.11, most of the coefficients on the change in the own subjective probability of survival are statistically significant.

To judge the magnitude of the effect of own survivor probability, consider the estimates in table 11.8 for the probability of moving from a zero response in wave 1 to a positive in wave 2, and consider an increase in survival chances from 0 to 100. Such a change would increase the probit index by 0. 2. Evaluated at the average probability of a transition from 0 to positive (0.296), the predicted change is about 0.06. That is, an increase in the subjective survival probability would increase the probability of reporting positive chances of a bequest from about 0.30 to 0.36. The effect at the target of $100,000 is somewhat larger, increasing the probability of reporting positive bequest chances from 0.15 to 0.22. The changes in probabilities for HRS would be approximately the same. These results are in accord with the effect of the subjective survival probability on bequest

Table 11.9   Probits That the Probability of a Bequest is Less Than 1.0 Given Prior-Wave Probability of 1.0

	Target Amounts			
	AHEAD		HRS	
	$10,000	$100,000	$10,000	$100,000
Change in subjective survival	−0.002	0.000	−0.003	−0.004
probability	(1.88)	(0.07)	(2.98)	(2.56)
Change in subjective survival	−0.002	−0.001	0.002	0.002
probability of spouse	(1.52)	(0.51)	(1.51)	(0.98)
Out-of-pocket medical costs	0.024	0.048	−0.001	−0.006
($100)	(0.71)	(1.04)	(0.16)	(1.22)
New health condition	0.048	−0.022		
	(0.72)	(0.22)		
Minor			0.029	−0.166
			(0.48)	(1.85)
Major			0.142	0.409
			(1.83)	(3.29)
Change in household income	0.024	0.023	0.001	0.001
($10,000)	(0.76)	(0.73)	(0.37)	(0.40)
Change in household wealth	−0.036	−0.035	−0.001	−0.002
($10,000)	(4.33)	(3.83)	(1.63)	(2.02)
Widowed	−0.059	−0.162	−0.279	−0.217
	(0.40)	(0.72)	(1.27)	(0.66)
Retired			0.017	−0.072
			(0.21)	(0.59)
N	1,939	827	3,528	1,468
Average conditional probability	0.368	0.432	0.281	0.360

Notes: Entries are estimated effects (probit coefficients) on the probability that a bequest will be less than 1.0 given that the prior-wave probability was 1.0. Absolute *t*-statistics in parentheses. Includes controls for race, sex, ethnicity, education, region of residence, and birth cohort.

probabilities among decedents (as shown later in table 11.15; in that table, those with higher subjective survival chances anticipated a smaller reduction in wealth before death).

As explained above, without any behavioral responses an increase in survival chances makes a large accidental bequest early in life less likely. However, individuals may react to their improved survival chances by reducing their current consumption so as to finance consumption over a longer lifetime, and the resulting larger wealth holdings would make bequests more likely. Our estimates indicate that the behavioral reactions dominate and that changes in bequests and survival probabilities are positively related.

Because the unit of observation is the individual, each spouse provides an observation on his or her subjective bequest probability and on his or her subjective survival probability. The estimates show that, especially in

Table 11.10   Change in the Probability (percent) of a Bequest: AHEAD

| | Target Amounts | | | |
| | OLS | | Tobit | |
	$10,000	$100,000	$10,000	$100,000
Change in subjective survival probability	0.085 (4.48)	0.065 (3.97)	0.090 (4.34)	0.097 (4.01)
Change in subjective survival probability of spouse	0.020 (0.66)	−0.051 (1.97)	0.021 (0.66)	−0.024 (0.69)
Out-of-pocket medical costs ($1,000)	−0.145 (1.98)	−0.105 (1.67)	−0.155 (1.95)	−0.083 (0.94)
New health condition	−0.246 (0.18)	−0.472 (0.39)	−0.287 (0.19)	−1.038 (0.62)
Change in household income ($10,000)	0.003 (0.03)	0.006 (0.08)	−0.028 (0.03)	0.018 (0.21)
Change in household wealth ($10,000)	0.038 (2.25)	0.030 (2.05)	0.040 (2.32)	0.023 (1.33)
Widowed	1.730 (0.55)	0.370 (0.37)	4.810 (1.42)	1.610 (0.42)
N	4,211	4,119	4,211	4,119

Notes: Entries are estimated effects on the change in the probability that a bequest will be at least as large as the target amount. Absolute *t*-statistics in parentheses. Subjective survival probability scaled 0–100. Includes controls for race, sex, ethnicity, education, region of residence, and birth cohort. OLS = ordinary least squares.

AHEAD, the effects of changes in the spouse's subjective probability of survival are small and often have no consistent pattern. This is to be expected. For example, a wife can give information about her own survival probabilities and how they affect her own bequest probabilities, yet not be aware of her husband's assessment of his own survival probabilities. Thus, were he to lower his subjective survival probabilities, the wife might not alter her bequest probabilities even though the subjective survivorship of the household would be lower. The estimates suggest this scenario.

There are two other health-related measures in these models: out-of-pocket medical expenses and the onset of new health conditions in the household. Out-of-pocket medical expenses had little effect on the transitions from 0.0 or from 1.0 (tables 11.8 and 11.9), but they reduced the average change in bequest probabilities (tables 11.10 and 11.11). In AHEAD, for example, out-of-pocket expenditures of $10,000 are estimated to reduce the probability of a bequest at the $10,000 target by about 1.5 percentage points. Of course, a considerable amount of the variation in health costs is likely to be anticipated because of their ongoing nature. If that were fully the case they would not be associated with any revision in bequest chances.

The onset of new health conditions has no consistent affect on revisions

Table 11.11   Change in the Probability (percent) of a Bequest: HRS

| | Target Amounts | | | |
| | OLS | | Tobit | |
	$10,000	$100,000	$10,000	$100,000
Change in subjective survival	0.085	0.065	0.088	0.067
probability	(5.95)	(4.72)	(5.83)	(4.71)
Change in subjective survival	0.024	0.037	0.027	0.039
probability of spouse	(1.16)	(1.82)	(1.22)	(1.84)
Out-of-pocket medical costs	−0.107	−0.105	−0.109	−0.107
($1,000)	(2.00)	(2.01)	(1.93)	(2.02)
New health condition				
Minor	−1.292	0.760	−1.308	0.763
	(1.23)	(0.75)	(1.19)	(0.73)
Major	0.797	−0.998	0.938	−1.114
	(0.61)	(0.79)	(0.62)	(0.85)
Change in household income	0.047	0.142	0.052	0.150
($10,000)	(0.97)	(3.04)	(1.02)	(3.10)
Change in household wealth	0.021	0.041	0.021	0.041
($10,000)	(1.72)	(3.38)	(1.68)	(3.35)
Widowed	11.980	8.710	12.500	9.230
	(3.50)	(2.64)	(3.46)	(2.69)
Retired	−2.990	−0.148	−3.090	−0.177
	(1.95)	(0.10)	(1.92)	(0.11)
N	7,735	7,645	7,735	7,645

Notes: Entries are estimated effects on the change in the probability that a bequest will be at least as large as the target amount. Absolute *t*-statistics in parentheses. Subjective survival probability scaled 0–100. Includes controls for race, sex, ethnicity, education, region of residence, and birth cohort. OLS = ordinary least squares.

in bequest probabilities, suggesting that survivor probabilities and out-of-pocket medical expenses may be the two principal mechanisms through which unexpected health events alter expected bequests.[7]

The effect of widowing is likely to increase bequest chances in AHEAD. The death of a spouse reduces needs for consumption relative to wealth, so that the death acts like an increase in wealth. Such an increase will increase bequests. At the same time, however, the death reduces life expectancy of the household. According to the theory, this reduction has an ambiguous effect on bequests, and according to our estimates it has a small effect. The sum of the two effects is likely to be to increase bequests.

In HRS these effects are dampened. Wealth is increased relative to needs, but the surviving spouse has many years in which to consume the

7. In HRS, new onsets are separated into severe and mild new onsets. Previous research has shown that there is not yet enough data to make this distinction in AHEAD, so that all new onsets are combined in that data. See Smith (1999b) for a discussion of these issues.

increase in wealth before mortality risk becomes substantial. Said differently, the surviving spouse can consume most of the increase rather than bequeathing it. Furthermore, in HRS most men are still working, so widowing is typically associated with an unanticipated loss of future earnings. The overall effect is likely to be a reduction in bequests.

Although no coefficients are significant, the pattern in AHEAD is consistent with this reasoning: Widowing is associated with an increase in bequest probabilities.[8] In the HRS, however, this reasoning is not supported. The only consistent pattern of significant coefficients is in table 11.11, which shows that widowing is also associated with an increase in the bequest probabilities. Apparently the reduction in need for consumption dominates the loss of human capital.

In the AHEAD population, changes in household income have little effect either on the transition probabilities or on the change in bequest probabilities. This is not surprising in view of the predictability of most AHEAD income sources, such as pension and Social Security income. A change in household income has an impact in the HRS sample at the $100,000 bequest target, possibly a reflection that some income changes were unexpected, due, for example, to better-than-anticipated salary increases.

Increases in household wealth are consistently associated with increases in the probability of bequests. This positive relationship is found both in the probits and in the expected changes in bequest probabilities. Yet the magnitude of this effect is not large. For example, an increase of $100,000 should increase substantially the chances of leaving a bequest of $10,000; yet the predicted effect in AHEAD would be an increase from 0.30 to 0.35. The effects on the other targets are even smaller. Of course, some of the observed wealth change in the panel may have been anticipated, which would explain the smaller effect.

As we have already discussed, only unanticipated wealth change should change anticipated bequests; yet in general we have no method for separating unanticipated from anticipated wealth change. However, HRS has a series of questions about new purchases and sales of stocks. We will say that the difference between the total change in the value of stock holdings and net new investments in stocks is unanticipated capital gains (Smith 2001). Total anticipated financial wealth change will then be total financial wealth change less unanticipated capital gains.

Table 11.12 summarizes the results of using these variables in estimation over the HRS sample.[9] Compared with previous tables and with the effects associated with anticipated wealth change, unanticipated capital gains

---

8. That is, the wave-to-wave subjective bequest probability of the surviving spouse increases.

9. The regressions include the other covariates listed in table 11.11.

Table 11.12   Change in the Probability of a Bequest: HRS

	Target Amounts			
	Tobit Estimates[a]		Probit Estimates[b]	
	$10,000	$100,000	$10,000	$100,000
Financial capital gains	0.007	0.003	−0.004	−0.008
	(0.32)	(1.46)	(2.62)	(5.24)
Other financial wealth change	0.045	0.082	0.002	−0.003
	(1.08)	(2.05)	(0.80)	(1.49)

Note: Capital gains and wealth change in $10,000.
[a]Expected value.
[b]$P(p_2 < 1 \mid p_1 = 1)$

have their greatest effect on the probit for the $100,000 target: Those with large gains have a high likelihood of continuing to state that their bequest probability is 1. 0. Compared with the target of $10,000, the differential effect is probably due to large capital gains being concentrated among the relatively well-to-do, who are certain to give a bequest of $10,000 regardless of capital gains.

In summary, we have shown in this section that at the individual level, subjective probabilities of bequests change with changes in covariates in a manner that is consistent with the predictions about actual bequests based on our model of consumption and saving. These results are consistent with the view that the subjective bequest probabilities are valid predictors of actual bequest probabilities.

11.6   Subjective Bequest Probabilities as an Index of Saving Intentions

Equation (4) in section 11.5 gives a relationship among the subjective bequest probabilities at wave 1, actual bequests by decedents between the waves, and subjective bequest probabilities by the survivors in wave 2. It can also be used, however, to show how the subjective bequest probabilities contain information about what the cohort anticipates bequeathing, and, when combined with actual wealth holdings, what the cohort anticipates saving or dissaving.

Suppose that in equation (4) t refers to the present time period and $t + 1$ to the greatest age possible. Everyone dies shortly after t, and the set d would be the entire baseline population and the set s would be empty. Then in equation (4) the second term on the right-hand side would be zero and the first term would be the fraction of the population that had actual bequests greater than b. Therefore, the average of the subjective bequest probabilities predicts the fraction of actual bequests greater than b. Equivalently, the average of the subjective bequest probabilities gives a point on the distribution of the bequests the cohort will actually make. We can compare this point with an appropriate point from the distribution of actual wealth holdings to learn about anticipated or intended saving or dissaving by the cohort. This result will be used to find whether the AHEAD population anticipates dissaving before death by comparing points on the distribution of wealth with subjective bequest probabilities.

There are a number of important reasons for wanting to establish whether the elderly are dissaving. If they do dissave, their control of economic resources will decline with age and, should they survive to advanced old age, they may be poor. Dissaving implies that they will bequeath less than their current wealth to the next generation. In that the elderly own substantial amounts of assets, dissaving by them will reduce the national household saving rate. Finally, anticipations of saving would be strong evidence for a bequest motive: A major implication of the pure life-cycle model (no bequest motive) is that wealth should decline with age among those of sufficient age.

Estimation of anticipated or desired saving behavior based on the subjective bequest probabilities has advantages over tests based on actual wealth change in panels that span just a few years. Unanticipated capital gains at the macro-level can cause observed wealth change to differ from anticipated wealth change over most households in a sample. The subjective probabilities of bequests take into account rates of return over long time periods, so that average rates of return would be closer to normal.

Table 11.13 shows, for the AHEAD baseline sample, the fraction of persons with wave 1 wealth at least as large as the target and the average of the subjective bequest probabilities. For example, in wave 1, 84.9 percent had wealth at least as large as $10,000, yet on average only 57.4 percent of households will die with bequests that large. That is, $10,000 is approximately the 15th percentile point in the distribution of wave 1 wealth but, under the assumption that the expectations about bequests are realized, it will be the 43rd percentile in the distribution of bequests. Similarly, $100,000 is approximately the 47th percentile in the wave 1 wealth distribution but the 72nd percentile of the bequest distribution. The implication is that the AHEAD population anticipates substantial dissaving before death.

These results are consistent with the average change in the subjective

Table 11.13   **Percentage with Wave 1 Wealth At Least As Large As Target Amounts and Subjective Bequest Probabilities: AHEAD**

	Target Amounts	
	$10,000	$100,000
Wave 1 wealth	84.9	52.6
Average subjective bequest probability	57.4	28.1
N	5,204	5,073

Table 11.14   **Percent of Decedents with Wealth or Estates At Least As Large As Target Amounts and Average Subjective Bequest Probability: AHEAD**

	Target Amounts	
	$10,000	$100,000
Wave 1 wealth	75.0	38.0
Actual estates	73.7	36.0
Average subjective bequest probability	47.8	19.6
N	456	450

bequest probabilities among survivors as reported in table 11.5. The average bequest probability at the $10,000 target declined by 1.97 percentage points with standard error of 0.58. At the $100,000 target the probability declined by 0.90 percentage points with standard error of 0.49 (p-value of 0.06). Declining subjective bequest probabilities are consistent with intended dissaving.

The decedents differed at baseline somewhat from the full sample, but they also planned to dissave before dying. Table 11.14 shows the percent of decedents that had wave 1 wealth at least as large as the target amounts, the percent with actual estates at least as large as the target amounts, and their average subjective bequest probabilities.[10] Their wealth was smaller than the average of the entire sample both because of their greater age and also because of differential mortality: The less well-to-do die sooner than the wealthy. At the $10,000 target the average of their subjective bequest probability was 47.8, which implies that had the decedents lived and consumed as they had anticipated when they responded in wave 1, about 48 percent of them would have died with estates at least as large as $10,000. Yet about 75 percent had wave 1 wealth at least as large as $10,000, and 74 percent had actual estates that reached $10,000. The implication is that the group planned or anticipated that they would decumulate wealth before dying. Because they died unexpectedly early, they were not able to decumulate.

As discussed in section 11.2, the life-cycle model makes no prediction about the response of bequests to a change in mortality risk: If there were no behavioral response to an increase in risk, bequests would increase because, under the assumption of wealth decumulation, people would die earlier when their wealth was higher. If there were a strong behavioral response, consumption could initially increase so much that actual bequests would fall due to lower wealth holdings. The net effect could be either an increase or a decrease in bequests, so the actual effect must be found from

10. The number of observations in the table differs from the number of decedents because of missing data on the subjective survival probabilities.

Table 11.15   **Percent of Decedents with Wealth or Estates At Least As Large As Target Amounts and Average Subjective Bequest Probability: AHEAD**

	Subjective Survival Probability			
	Target Amount $10,000		Target Amount $100,000	
	0–10	90–100	0–10	90–100
Wave 1 wealth	75.2	73.3	37.6	43.3
Average subjective probability	49.4	49.6	19.8	26.7
Difference	25.8	23.7	17.8	16.6

Note: N = 371.

data. Similar reasoning shows that variation across individuals in their perceived mortality risk does not produce a definite predication about the variation in bequests.

Table 11.15 shows the percentage of individuals whose wave 1 wealth reached the target amounts and their average subjective bequest probability classified by the subjective survival probability in wave 1.[11] Among respondents who reported a subjective survival probability of 0–10 percent in wave 1, 75 percent had wealth that reached $10,000. Their average subjective bequest probability was about 49 percent, and the difference was about 26 percent. Among those with subjective survival probabilities of 90 to 100, wave 1 wealth was slightly lower, the average subjective bequest probability was about the same, and the difference between them was about 24 percent. The difference is about the same for the $100,000 target.

These results show that greater subjective survival probabilities have small but positive effects on anticipated bequests. The results are in accord with the effect of a change in the subjective survival probability on bequest probabilities as shown in tables 11.6–11.9. In those tables, individuals who assessed that their survival chances had increased between the waves increased their probabilities of bequests.

In table 11.15, those with high subjective survival chances anticipated that their bequests would be somewhat larger than the bequests of those with low survival chances even though the wealth of the two groups was about the same. An implication is that the first group anticipated less dissaving than the second in order to reach their expected bequests despite their greater expected lifetimes. This implies a rather large behavioral response to mortality risk, which is in accord with estimates based on actual rates of dissaving in panel (Hurd 1993): Were the behavioral response min-

11. Because we have individual-level observations on the subjective bequest probabilities we compare wealth of the household in which the individual lives to bequest probabilities. Thus, both the husband and the wife appear as separate entries in table 11.13.

imal, the group with the higher survival rates would anticipate lower bequests.

11.7 Conclusions

We have presented results about the magnitude and distribution of bequests based on new methods of measuring actual and anticipated bequests. Actual bequests were measured in exit interviews given by proxy respondents for 774 AHEAD respondents who died between waves 1 and 2 of the AHEAD survey. Among other things, these exit interviews provide data about the medical and nonmedical costs associated with the illnesses of the deceased respondents and the value and distribution of their estates. Even though the deceased were quite ill before they died, medical expenses did not cause a substantial reduction in their estates. Because the exit interview obtained information about estates that is representative of the population, the distribution of these estate values is quite different than one would suppose from estate records, which are obtained for only a wealthy subset of the population.

Anticipated bequests were measured in two waves of HRS and AHEAD by the subjective probability of leaving bequests. We studied the reasons for between-wave revisions of the subjective bequest probabilities. We found that increases in the subjective probability of surviving, in increments in household wealth, and in widowing were all associated with increases in bequest probabilities, whereas out-of-pocket medical expenses reduced the likelihood of a bequest. By comparing bequest probabilities with baseline wealth we were able to test a main prediction of the life-cycle model, that individuals will dissave at advanced old age. The AHEAD respondents anticipate substantial dissaving before they die.

References

David, Martin, and Paul L. Menchik. 1985. The effect of Social Security on lifetime wealth accumulation and bequests. *Economica* 52:421–34.

Hurd, Michael D. 1987. Savings of the elderly and desired bequests. *American Economic Review* 77:298–311.

———. 1989. Mortality risk and bequests. *Econometrica* 57 (4): 779–813.

———. 1992. Population aging and the saving rate: The effect of mortality risk on saving by the elderly. Presented at the European Science Foundation Conference on the Economics of Aging, San Felieu de Guixols, Spain.

———. 1993. The effect of changes in Social Security on bequests. *Journal of Economics* (Suppl. 7): 157–76.

———. 1999. Mortality risk and consumption by couples. NBER Working Paper no. 7048. Cambridge, Mass.: National Bureau of Economic Research, March.

Juster, F. Thomas, and Richard Suzman. 1995. An overview of the health and retirement study. *The Journal of Human Resources* 30 (Suppl. 1995): S7–S56.

Mulligan, Casey B. 1995. Economic and biological approaches to inheritance: Some evidence. University of Chicago, Department of Economics. Working paper.

Smith, James P. 1999a. Inheritance and bequests. In *Wealth, work and health: Innovations in measurement in the social sciences,* ed. James P. Smith and Robert J. Willis, 121–49. Ann Arbor: University of Michigan Press.

———. 1999b. Healthy bodies and thick wallets. *Journal of Economic Perspectives* 13 (2): 145–66.

———. 2001. Why is wealth inequality rising? In *The causes and consequences of increasing inequality,* ed. Finis Welch, 83–116. Chicago: University of Chicago Press.

Soldo, Beth, Michael Hurd, Willard Rodgers, and Robert Wallace. 1997. Asset and health dynamics among the oldest old: An overview of the AHEAD study. *The Journals of Gerontology.* Series B, *Psychological Sciences and Social Sciences* 52B. Special Issue (May): 1–20.

Yaari, Menahem E. 1965. Uncertain lifetime, life insurance, and the theory of the consumer. *Review of Economic Studies* 32:137–50.

Comment   David Laibson

Hurd and Smith have made three very important contributions to the life-cycle literature. First, they have documented the usefulness and high quality of bequest data (anticipated and actual bequests) from the Asset and Health Dynamics among the Oldest Old (AHEAD) survey and Health and Retirement Survey (HRS) panels. Second, they have used this data to analyze the life-cycle hypothesis. Third, they have powerfully critiqued standard theories of bequest motives. I will discuss each of these contributions.

The Bequest Data: Anticipated and Actual Bequests

The author's analysis of the data on anticipated bequests suggests that these data are reliable. Four observations support this claim. First, anticipated bequests covary positively with income and wealth. Second, measurements of anticipated bequests are relatively stable between survey waves. Third, anticipated bequests are good predictors of actual bequests (as measured in exit interviews with the decedents' families). Finally, the anticipated bequest variable evolves over time in ways that are consistent with rational expectations. For example, predictable information, such as changes in income for retired adults, does not affect anticipated bequests.

David Laibson is the Paul Sack Associate Professor of Political Economy at Harvard University and a faculty research fellow of the National Bureau of Economic Research.

Moreover, unpredictable information, such as capital gains, does affect anticipated bequests. In addition, anticipated bequests appear to follow dynamics (from wave to wave) that are consistent with Bayes' rule.

The data on actual bequests is particularly useful because we have no close substitutes for this new data source. Most preexisting evidence on bequests comes from estate tax records and wills filed in probate courts; but these preexisting data sources are incomplete. Only a small fraction of estates are large enough (the threshold for the estate tax is $600,000) to appear in the tax files and few wills pass through probate court. Hurd and Smith's evidence suggests that only 2 percent of estates are valued at more than $600,000. Even on a dollar-weighted basis, only one-fourth of the bequests in the HRS and AHEAD samples are worth more than $600,000. Hence, the Hurd and Smith bequest data—which include all bequests— represents a very important step forward for the bequest literature.

A Test of the Lifecycle Hypothesis

Hurd and Smith's empirical analysis shows that anticipated bequests fall with age.[1] This finding sheds light on the ongoing debate about whether wealth falls with age (after retirement). An age-related fall in an anticipated bequest implies that wealth is probably also falling. Of course, falling wealth is a central prediction of the life-cycle hypothesis (LCH). Hence, Hurd and Smith interpret postretirement declines in anticipated bequests as evidence of the LCH.

I am uncomfortable with this conclusion. First, the authors have not shown that the fall in wealth has the same magnitude as predicted by the LCH. They have shown only that the sign is right. Second, they do not acknowledge that almost every sensible theory of life-cycle decision making—whether rational and optimal or not—implies that wealth and anticipated bequests will fall with age (after retirement). Consider, for example, the myopic mental accounting rule: Consume 90 percent of your current labor/pension/Social Security income and 20 percent of your financial wealth. Such nonoptimal consumption rules also generate declining wealth during retirement.

Evidence on the Bequest Motive

Hurd and Smith's analysis provides new evidence against the leading economic theory of the bequest motive. Specifically, they show that 79 percent of bequests are split evenly among the children, contradicting any theory that requires that the bequest be chosen to equate the marginal utility of consumption across children. In addition, Hurd and Smith show that bequests do not depend on the number of children, another result that seems to violate economists' intuitions about the underlying mecha-

---

1. The consumers in this population are all close to retirement or already retired.

nisms that drive bequest choices. These strong results may be mitigated by inter vivos wealth transfers, but the results nevertheless indicate important departures from the classical economic theory of bequests.

There are several sensible economic and psychological reasons that bequests may be equal across children. First, the bequest decision necessarily creates a moral hazard problem if parents try to use bequests to equate marginal utilities of their children at the time of the parent's death. Specifically, children with siblings have an incentive to raise and thereby distort their own consumptions while their parents are still alive. Children who overconsume early in life will have low consumption during midlife, raising their marginal utility at exactly the time that their parents are making the bequest decision. The relative poverty of overspending children will in turn lead their parents to transfer bequests to them, away from siblings who did not overspend. To avoid this incentive for competitive impoverishment, parents should rationally commit not to equate marginal utilities through bequests (Gatti 1998). Moreover, parents may want to commit to reward children who "do the right thing" (e.g., get a law degree). This motive along with parental concern about the moral hazard problem may partially or fully offset the motive to help children with relatively bad luck or low consumption.

Equal bequests are also predicted by prospect theory and loss aversion (Kahneman and Tversky 1979). An even split is a natural reference point, and deviations from this norm may help the winners less than the hurt experienced by the losers.

It is also important to note that parents are not the only economic actors who make transfers. Sometimes children make transfers to parents, generating a form of dynastic insurance. This may explain why increasing the number of children does not empirically raise the magnitude of bequests from parents to children. As a parent has more children, the parent may have a reduced incentive to save, since the children will serve as an important source of consumption insurance for the parent. Hence, it is not at all clear whether the relationship between bequest value and number of children should be positive or negative.

Hurd and Smith have provided a rich set of facts that dramatically improves our understanding of lifecycle consumption and savings decisions. Most importantly, their work highlights the counterfactual predictions of existing models of intergenerational wealth transfers. Hopefully, their analysis will spur the development of much-needed alternative models.

References

Gatti, Roberta. 1998. Harvard University dissertation.
Kahneman, Daniel, and Amos Tversky. 1979. Prospect theory: An analysis of decision under risk. *Econometrica* 47:263–91.

Contributors

Axel Börsch-Supan
Lehrstuhl für Makroökonomik und
  Wirtschaftspolitik
Seminargebäude A 5
Universität Mannheim
68131 Mannheim
Germany

Jeffrey R. Brown
John F. Kennedy School of
  Government
Harvard University
79 John F. Kennedy Street
Cambridge, MA 02138

Anne Case
345 Wallace Hall
Princeton University
Princeton, NJ 08544-1022

Courtney Coile
Department of Economics
Wellesley College
106 Central Street
Wellesley, MA 02481

David M. Cutler
Department of Economics
Harvard University
Cambridge, MA 02138

Angus Deaton
347 Wallace Hall
Princeton University
Princeton, NJ 08544-1022

Matthew Eichner
Columbia Business School
Uris Hall
3022 Broadway
New York, NY 10027

Jeffrey Geppert
National Bureau of Economic
  Research
30 Alta Road
Stanford, CA 94305

Jonathan Gruber
Department of Economics, E52-355
Massachusetts Institute of Technology
50 Memorial Drive
Cambridge, MA 02142-1347

Michael D. Hurd
RAND Corporation
1700 Main Street
Santa Monica, CA 90407

David Laibson
Department of Economics
Littauer M-14

Harvard University
Cambridge, MA 02138

Mark McClellan
Department of Economics
Economics Building, 224
Stanford University
Stanford, CA 94305-6072

Daniel McFadden
Department of Economics
549 Evans Hall #3880
University of California, Berkeley
Berkeley, CA 94707-3880

Ellen Meara
Department of Health Care Policy
Harvard Medical School
180 Longwood Avenue
Boston, MA 02115

Angela Merrill
Mathematica Policy Research, Inc.
50 Church Street, 4th Floor
Cambridge, MA 02138

Joseph P. Newhouse
Division of Health Policy Research
    and Education
Harvard University
180 Longwood Avenue
Boston, MA 02115–5899

Christina Paxson
347 Wallace Hall
Princeton University
Princeton, NJ 08544-1022

James M. Poterba
Department of Economics, E52-350
Massachusetts Institute of Technology
50 Memorial Drive
Cambridge, MA 02142-1347

Andrew A. Samwick
Department of Economics
Dartmouth College
6106 Rockefeller Hall
Hanover, NH 03755-3514

Sylvester J. Schieber
Watson Wyatt Worldwide
1717 H Street, NW, Suite 800
Washington, DC 20006

John B. Shoven
Department of Economics
Stanford University
Stanford, CA 94305

James P. Smith
RAND Corporation
1700 Main Street
Santa Monica, CA 90407

Steven F. Venti
Department of Economics
6106 Rockefeller Hall
Dartmouth College
Hanover, NH 03755

Finis Welch
Department of Economics
Texas A&M University
4228 TAMU
College Station, TX 77843-4228

David A. Wise
John F. Kennedy School of
    Government, Harvard University
and National Bureau of Economic
Research
1050 Massachusetts Avenue
Cambridge, MA 02138

Author Index

Subject Index

Retirement incentives: in German public
pension system, 16, 284–88; heterogeneity in Social Security, 323–28, 343–
45; peak value measure of Social Security, 331–33; in private pensions, 343,
345–48; Social Security decisions
about, 343
Retirement savings accounts: annuitization
in, 1; 401(k) assets rolled over into
IRAs, 2, 24; lump-sum distributions
from, 26–28; withdrawals from, 26–28.
See also 401(k) retirement plans
Retirement wealth. *See* Wealth

Social Security programs, proposed: tier
one defined benefit (DB), 62–66; tier-
two defined contribution (DC), 62–66
Social Security system, U.S.: actuarial estimate of PSA 2000 plan, 70; benefits to
dependents of covered workers, 317;
changes under proposed PSA 2000,
88–90; cost of shift to PSA 2000 plan,
74; earnings test under PSA 2000, 65;
literature on incentives for retirement
in, 317–20; OASDI trust fund under
proposed PSA plan, 70–76; PSA 2000
proposed reform plan, 59–77; recommended individual accounts under,
4–5; redistribution under, 89–90; retirement incentives, 17–19; subsidies associated with retirement decisions, 332;
trust fund accumulations under PSA
2000, 70–71; trust fund under current
OASDI, 70–71. *See also* Advisory
Council on Social Security; Benefits,
Social Security; Personal Security Account (PSA 2000)
Social Security wealth: after-tax patterns
of, 329–31, 344–45; formula for computation of, 338–40; peak value as, 331–
33; ratio of projected 401(k) assets to,
43–51; working toward peak year for,
331
Socioeconomic status (SES): relation between mortality and, 8, 129, 171–73,
196
Subjective survival probabilities. *See* Elderly people; Life expectancy; Mortality

Wealth: determinants of, 368–69; prediction in LCH, 390; tax-deferred accumulation in 401(k) plans, 2, 23–24. *See
also* Social Security wealth